The Presidency of
JOHN QUINCY
ADAMS

AMERICAN PRESIDENCY SERIES

Donald R. McCoy, Clifford S. Griffin, Homer E. Socolofsky
General Editors

George Washington, Forrest McDonald
John Adams, Ralph Adams Brown
Thomas Jefferson, Forrest McDonald
John Quincy Adams, Mary W. M. Hargreaves
Martin Van Buren, Major L. Wilson
James Buchanan, Elbert B. Smith
Andrew Johnson, Albert Castel
James A. Garfield & Chester A. Arthur, Justus D. Doenecke
William McKinley, Lewis L. Gould
William Howard Taft, Paolo E. Coletta
Warren G. Harding, Eugene P. Trani & David L. Wilson
Herbert C. Hoover, Martin L. Fausold
Harry S. Truman, Donald R. McCoy
Dwight D. Eisenhower, Elmo Richardson
Lyndon B. Johnson, Vaughn Davis Bornet

The Presidency of

JOHN QUINCY
ADAMS

Mary W. M. Hargreaves

UNIVERSITY PRESS OF KANSAS

© 1985 by the University Press of Kansas
All rights reserved
Second printing, 1988

Published by the University Press of Kansas (Lawrence, Kansas 66045),
which was organized by the Kansas Board of Regents
and is operated and funded by Emporia State University, Fort Hays State
University, Kansas State University, Pittsburg State
University, the University of Kansas, and Wichita State University

Library of Congress Cataloging in Publication Data

Hargreaves, Mary W. M., 1914–
The presidency of John Quincy Adams.

(American presidency series)
Bibliography: p
1. United States—Politics and government—1825–1829.
2. Adams, John Quincy, 1767–1848. I. Title.
II. Series.
E376.H24   1985   973.4'4'0927   85-11147
ISBN 0-7006-0272-0

Printed in the United States of America

To
Walter

CONTENTS

LIST OF TABLES

FOREWORD

The aim of the American Presidency Series is to present historians and the general reading public with interesting, scholarly assessments of the various presidential administrations. These interpretive surveys are intended to cover the broad ground between biographies, specialized monographs, and journalistic accounts. As such, each will be a comprehensive, synthetic work which will draw upon the best in pertinent secondary literature, yet leave room for the author's own analysis and interpretation.

Volumes in the series will present the data essential to understanding the administration under consideration. Particularly, each book will treat the then current problems facing the United States and its people and how the president and his associates felt about, thought about, and worked to cope with these problems. Attention will be given to how the office developed and operated during the president's tenure. Equally important will be consideration of the vital relationships between the president, his staff, the executive officers, Congress, foreign representatives, the judiciary, state officials, the public, political parties, the press, and influential private citizens. The series will also be concerned with how this unique American institution—the presidency—was viewed by the presidents, and with what results.

All this will be set, insofar as possible, in the context not only of contemporary politics but also of economics, international relations, law, morals, public administration, religion, and thought. Such a broad approach is necessary to understanding, for a presidential administration is more than the elected and appointed officers composing it, since its work so often reflects the major problems, anxieties, and glories of the nation. In short, the authors in the series will strive to recount and evaluate the record of each administration and to identify its distinctiveness and relationships to the past, its own time, and the future.

The General Editors

PREFACE

Historians have not been generous in assessment of the presidency of John Quincy Adams. Those who have most conspicuously upheld Adams's fame have, at the same time, virtually ignored his service in the White House. Critics, on the other hand, have described his administration as a failure, founded upon "bargain and corruption" and marked by exclusion of the United States from the British West Indian trade, the ineffectiveness of its efforts to promote strong Pan-American relationships, and the enactment of the "tariff of abominations." Some analysts have even argued that it generated the sectionalism which terminated the "Era of Good Feeling."

The present study contends, instead, that the basic effort of Adams and his associates was to harmonize divergent sectional interests. The focus upon national unity had brought Adams and Clay into political alliance, and they alone, of the contending candidates in 1824, were committed to promote such a program. That their measures failed in the areas noted was in large part the consequence of political obstructionism carried on by opponents who pursued concerns of regional, localized, and even merely personal advantage, without mutual agreement upon issues. The campaign of 1828 marked, in essence, the triumph of a masterful political organization that consolidated the fragments of narrow particularism to exploit the restraints required for advancement of the national interest.

In foreign affairs Adams, as president, displayed a flexibility that has been little recognized. The instructions that he and Secretary of

State Henry Clay drafted—in pursuit of expanded international trade and, in particular, as a basis for fuller inter-American cooperation—were Jeffersonian in their liberalism. Adams was, however, prepared to yield to colonial restrictions in West-Indian commerce, while Clay, on the issue of Cuban independence, retreated from the extremism of his ideological advocacy of world-wide republicanism.

On domestic policy the president strove to avoid sectional conflict but did not basically oppose the program of the American System that members of his cabinet promoted. Richard Rush emerges, in this account, as a more important spokesman of that policy than has been generally noted. Samuel L. Southard and James Barbour, likewise, assume significance as proponents of centralized executive authority. The Adams presidency can be fully evaluated only as a broad administrative effort, by a president and cabinet united in agreement upon the goal of integrated development for the nation as a whole.

Even before the president left office, the economic benefits of the program were apparent. They carried the nation to one of the highest rates of growth in its history. The principles of the American System, therefore, remained the issue base of partisan contention until the slavery controversy engulfed the debate in the mid 1840s, and the program reemerged in the nationalization of the Republican party in 1860. To ignore the Adams administration's record of commitment to nationalism is to overlook a fundamental segment of the struggle to establish the federal government's function of harmonizing diversity in the general interest.

My analysis evolved with tangential stimulus from a few scattered references. The first, published a quarter century ago, appeared as the conclusion to an article by Paul Nagel, "The Election of 1824: A Reconsideration Based on Newspaper Opinion," *Journal of Southern History* 26 (Aug. 1960): 328–29. Nagel's survey had shown intense sectional divisions ranging beyond the mere institution of slavery. Noting the "acrimony from the issues of the previous eight years," he commented that Adams had taken office "with the foundations for disunion in place." "A quarter century of compromise and cajolry" would intervene, he commented, before "the essential problems which clearly intruded in this campaign forced the sections to resolve their differences by violence." Some forty years earlier, Charles and Mary Beard, in their classic account of *The Rise of American Civilization* (new ed.; New York: Macmillan Co., 1934), had explained the Civil War on the same basis.

A second passage, noted after a first draft of this manuscript had been written, accorded so pointedly with the conceptualization of my analysis, albeit to a very different inference, that it served to sharpen my interpretive revisions. Concluding a chapter on "The Age of Mercantilism," in *The Contours of American History* (1961; reprint, Chicago: Quadrangle Paperbacks, 1966), William Appleman Williams observed that the mercantilists, including Adams and Clay, were concerned with goals beyond personal fortune, "with the *public* welfare and the spirit of a true corporate commonwealth"; but, he concluded, the mercantilists "never overcame their bias in favor of private property." "Unwilling in the final showdown to make a fuller commitment to social property in the name of a corporate commonwealth, they had no effective defense against the men who demanded that private property and interest be given full scope and unrestrained liberty in the name of individualism" (p. 223). Rush Welter, in *The Mind of America, 1820–1860* (New York: Columbia University Press, 1975), has identified the latter element in reference to Jacksonian Democrats as "atomism" (p. 152). For the sense of shared perceptions, however remotely related to the inferences that I have drawn, I am grateful.

I also have obligations for collegial support, more personally extended. James F. Hopkins, with whom I shared some thirty years of editorial labor on *The Papers of Henry Clay*, has directed a critical eye to most of this manuscript. George Herring has reviewed the chapters on foreign policy. Wayne Cutler, Robert Seager II, John Mayfield, and Michael Birkner have all provided insight out of their own research. That I have modified and sometimes rejected their suggestions does not lessen my gratitude for their assistance. I owe thanks to the staff of the Margaret I. King Library of the University of Kentucky for unfailing courtesy and to the History Department of that institution for the financial boons of a sabbatical leave and secretarial assistance. For the last, in particular, I am indebted to Miss Dorothy Leathers, who has typed and retyped with endless patience.

Finally, I am, as always, beholden to my husband, with whom I have shared the vagaries and excitements of engrossed scholarship throughout our adult lives. He has read most of my productions, tactfully pointed up their ambiguities, and yet encourages me to continue.

Mary W. M. Hargreaves

Lexington, Kentucky
October 1984

1

★ ★ ★ ★ ★

A TIME OF READJUSTMENT

"A People in Motion," "Everything's Changed," "Full Steam Ahead"—these are the phrases by which historians have characterized the years from 1815 to 1830. Robert Fogel saw a "more or less continuous increase" of manufacturing extending from 1820. Douglass C. North explicated his theory of American economic growth on the basis of the developing cotton-export staple with the settlement of the Gulf Plains. Richard Wade identified this as a time of approaching urban maturity. Vernon Parrington delineated it as "The Renaissance" in "The Mind of New England": "The old static agricultural order was broken in upon, and with the social disruption came naturally an intellectual disruption." John William Ward termed "transition" a "pallid word for what was happening to America," when "movement was not only westward geographically" but "upward socially," when "expansion was extensive, measured by land mass, and intensive, measured by economic development." And Frederick Jackson Turner, who recognized that our national life was perennially characterized by transition, characterized this period as "peculiarly one of readjustment."[1]

The administration of James Monroe, the last of the Virginia dynasty, had provided a canopy of nationalism, which for eight years enveloped the surging forces. His philosophy of office had emphasized consensus, compromise, a slow maturation of decision, which undertook to reconcile divergent views by thorough discussion within a cabinet that encompassed differing sectional interests. As Monroe's biographers have made evident, however, after 1822 his administration had sunk into an "Era of Bad Feelings" that "totally eclipsed the harmony evident during his first term."[2] Even the sectional identifications on which he had structured his alliance were breaking down.

New England merchants, cut off from normal investment opportunities during the War of 1812, had turned to textile manufacture. At a time when foreign competition was limited, when domestic supplies of raw materials were abundant, and when wartime inflation assured high prices, they had achieved significant progress. In 1805 only 4,500 spindles had been in use for cotton spinning; by 1810 the number had increased to 87,000; by 1815, to 130,000; by 1820, to 220,000; and by 1825, to 800,000.[3] With this development had come new concerns that began to shift the focus of political interest.

On issues of banking and internal improvements there was little disagreement within the region. New England manufacturers shared with merchants the desire for a stable and conservative banking system. Because capital for the new industrialization was plentiful within the local economy, they offered no great pressure for relaxation of credit controls. Good roads gave access to port facilities, which extended trade to world markets, and during the early 1820s a program to expand the system was initiated through construction of three relatively short canals to link upcountry areas to the tidewater. The development of transportation beyond such intraregional improvements attracted scant interest. To New England merchants the impractability of penetrating the mountain barrier to the west meant that larger schemes for a national network of roads and canals posed the threat of commercial advantage to New York, Philadelphia, and Baltimore at the expense of Boston. To New England manufacturers, these networks represented a facilitation of emigration, which would aggravate the problem of an already rapidly dwindling labor supply.

Such harmony of viewpoint disintegrated, however, as the demand for protection of infant industries took form in proposals for tariff legislation. Eager for arrangements that would foster foreign trade, merchants and shippers opposed the restrictions that manufacturers viewed as necessary for the survival of their enterprise. The divisions in the New England economy were reflected in the varying stances of regional politicians on the issue. Their vote in the House of Representatives was split into eighteen "ayes" and nine "nays," with fifteen abstentions, on the tariff of 1816, which offered very moderate and temporary protection of textiles. On a proposal in 1818 to continue that legislation until 1826, the response was an enthusiastic thirty "ayes" and one "nay," with nine abstentions; but upon a separate bill at that time to increase duties on iron, the New Englanders recorded eighteen "ayes" and fourteen "nays," with eight abstentions. They provided only fifteen "ayes" and twenty-three "nays" on the tariff bill of 1824, which raised all duties markedly.[4] Their interest in the protection of textiles was notably greater than that for other manufactures, but in coastal areas of Massachusetts, New Hampshire, and Maine even that concern could attract at most only an unreliable abstention from opposition.

Meanwhile, in the South, Thomas Jefferson and James Madison, whose opposition to Alexander Hamilton's "Report on Manufactures" had sparked the emergence of partisan differences during the early years of the nation, had themselves, under the responsibilities of national office and the pressure of wartime experience, espoused greatly modified views. Writing to a friend in January 1816, Jefferson commented:

> You tell me I am quoted by those who wish to continue our dependence on England for manufactures. there was a time when I might have been so quoted with more candor, but within the 30 years which have since elapsed, how are circumstances changed! . . . experience has taught me that manufactures are now as necessary to our independance [sic] as to our comfort. . . .[5]

Madison, in 1823, while warning fellow Republicans of dangers lurking in the trend toward "amalgamation of political sentiments & views," nevertheless recognized that his party had "been reconciled to certain measures & arrangements which . . . [might] be as proper now as they were premature and suspicious when urged by the Champions of federalism."[6]

Political loyalties, fired by the bitterness of Federalist attacks upon the Jeffersonian embargo and nonintercourse legislation, had generated a new Republican emphasis upon national self-sufficiency. The development of the southern back country, industrial as well as agricultural, had given impetus for a time to a regional demand for promotion of domestic industry, aid to internal improvements, and extension of credit facilities. At the national level, Jefferson, in his second Inaugural Address and again in his annual message to Congress in 1806, had endorsed a program calling for federal expenditures for internal improvements. While the necessity for wartime expenditures had compelled the suspension of such enterprise, it had reappeared as a theme in Madison's seventh annual message, in 1815, together with recommendations for chartering a second national bank and the enactment of a protective

3

tariff. On this last point, Madison's specific allusion to the need for support of "manufacturing establishments . . . of the more complicated kinds" clearly defined his contemplation of development at a stage beyond the level of household industries.[7] The leadership of William Lowndes and John C. Calhoun in pressing for adoption of Madison's program over the next two years expressed the new southern commitment to nationalist ideology.

Lingering concerns of an older regional focus remained to challenge this program, however. Southern congressmen were almost equally divided on a proposal, initiated by Calhoun in 1816, by which the "bonus" paid by the new bank for its charter and the net annual proceeds on the government's stock holdings in the institution should be set aside as a permanent fund for internal improvement. In the end, Madison, with Jefferson's enthusiastic approval, vetoed the legislation. Both leaders called for constitutional amendment as a necessary preliminary to such an extension of national authority, and Monroe was to urge a similar course in vetoing, in 1824, a bill for the collection of tolls on the Cumberland Road. Constitutional forms may, for Madison and Monroe, have represented only a technical qualification in pursuit of an accepted program. For Jefferson, however, at least as early as the summer of 1816, ideological opposition to the growing power of the national government had revived as rejection of the basic legislative agenda. He rejoined a factional wing of his party committed to a sectional, narrowly agrarian outlook that verged on paranoia.[8]

Southern particularism, accelerated by the bitterness of the Missouri controversy, rested also in the early 1820s upon widespread economic discontent. Despite the wartime efforts to promote industrialization, little such development had been achieved. High cotton prices from 1815 through 1818 had, instead, fostered agricultural expansion into the upland areas. Subsequent price declines had been counterbalanced for tidewater planters during the next four years by the fall in the general cost of living; but for those of the piedmont, whose newer ventures rested heavily upon credit, the pressures were severe. They were to grow worse as the decade advanced. Acre yields also declined when the shallow, sandy soils of the uplands deteriorated under heavy cropping. Increased cotton production, which accompanied the opening of the Gulf Plains to the west, drove prices ever lower, particularly for the marginal short-staple upland varieties. By 1831 the yearly average, which had reached a high of 30.8 cents a pound in 1818, had dropped to 8.3 cents.[9]

The trend toward economic nationalism that had characterized the outlook of South Carolina's political leaders into the early 1820s gave way to what a journalist of 1829 described as "a lurking suspicion that, in her attachment to the general government the State had perhaps, not been sufficiently vigilant in the maintenance of her own rights and in the protection of her peculiar interests."[10] Although Calhoun voiced only moderate reservations on the tariff of 1824, South Carolina's congressmen George McDuffie, Joel R. Poinsett, and James Hammond and Senator Robert Y. Hayne vigorously opposed the measure. Planters, selling the bulk of their staple abroad, anticipated little gain from the development of a home market, and they were convinced that foreign demand would be curtailed by tariff restrictions.

They had found, too, that the local branches of the Bank of the United States failed to support the demand for credit in the region. Because federal expenditures fell far below collections at Charleston, the bank merely facilitated drainage of specie from the state. Even the vigorous support for local internal improvements, to which South Carolina remained committed as a measure for sustaining competition with the newly opened lands of the West, was prosecuted without recourse to federal funds. The South Carolina Senate, in a resolution of 1824, asserted that it was unconstitutional for Congress to tax citizens of one state in order to finance the construction of roads and canals within another. Tidewater and upcountry interests, which were traditionally divergent, formulated in South Carolina, during the depression years, a shared opposition to the general package of nationalism.[11]

In Virginia, however, Shenandoah Valley and trans-Appalachian farmers—producers of wheat, livestock, hemp, and wool—retained an enthusiasm for a protective tariff and internal improvements which differentiated them from tidewater and piedmont planters. The development of manufacturing—salt, iron, and even some textiles—in the upper Ohio Valley gave added impetus to this divergence. Economic interest, superimposed on longstanding ethnic and cultural differences, contributed to mounting internal divisions which were to complicate the political history of the state until the separation that was effected in the outbreak of the Civil War. Western Virginia was increasingly to find its interests identified with those of neighboring districts to the north and west.[12]

The Middle States and the West provided the core of support for measures of economic nationalism. Here, as early as the Revolutionary period, an economy had evolved which rested upon interchange with other sections. Gunpowder, firearms, ironware, leather goods, furs, hats, jeans, fustians, woolens, and, especially, foodstuffs had been supplied to the war-disrupted areas of New England and the South. With expansion of commerce in the Caribbean during the Napoleonic Wars, the opening of the West after 1795, and the accelerated demand for domestic supplies during the War of 1812, the Middle States had developed a surplus in both manufactures and agricultural produce that depended upon extraregional markets.

In this area, internal improvements that could facilitate this traffic were a major concern. Ohio, under its Enabling Act, had been accorded 5 percent of the net proceeds from the sale of public lands for road construction, a precedent that was to be extended as the remaining public-land states joined the Union. For those of the Old Northwest, two-fifths of the 5 percent fund had been reserved for use by the federal government to promote interregional transportation. Construction of the Cumberland Road, which was completed to the Ohio at Wheeling by 1818, represented the eastern link of this development. On the eve of the Adams administration, western leaders won legislation for extension of the system to the Mississippi River. Despite Monroe's repeated vetoes of legislation to permit regular maintenance of the roadway, they had also obtained, in 1824, a federal appropriation for making limited repairs. Even more important, an act of 30 April 1824 fostered hopes for a vast expansion of federally sponsored projects, by establishing a board of internal improvement to conduct surveys, including route plans, assessment of technical feasibility, and cost estimates, for such roads and canals as the president deemed "of national importance in a commercial or military point of view, or necessary for the transportation of the public mail. . . ."[13]

Despite the predominance of regional support for this program, however, it did not command universal acclaim. New York, opened to the west by state funding of the Genessee Road, had won federal aid only for the limited project of the Plattsburg Military Road northward to Lake Champlain. New York's bid for assistance in opening water routes to the north or west, even after need for them for defensive purposes had been demonstrated during the War of 1812, had been rejected. New York—once it had financed its own development, via the Erie and Champlain canals, begun in 1816 and opened in the mid 1820s—had less interest in a federal program that would promote rival routes at its shared expense.[14] Here again a traditional stance of sectionalism was fragmenting.

The protariff arguments of nationalism also posed troublesome questions for the Middle States. What would be the effects upon seaboard areas, which were heavily committed to foreign trade? What would be the effects upon farmers? Could legislation designed to protect fabrication also benefit producers of hemp, raw wool, corn, and wheat? As early as 1820, proponents of tariffs were wrestling in the Middle States, as well as the South, with the problem of defining the degree of "home industry" to be protected.

Pennsylvania, which to all outward appearances solidly backed a high-tariff policy, reflected the disruption posed by the issue. The annual messages of Pennsylvania governors from 1815 through the succeeding decade regularly called for a protective tariff, and the state legislature repeatedly instructed Pennsylvania congressmen to lend support to the program. Even without such a directive, a large majority of the state's representatives and both of its senators had voted in January 1816 to continue the double duties of the war period. Henry Baldwin of Pittsburgh and John Tod of Bedford successively served as chairmen of the House Committee on Manufactures, which had introduced the protectionist proposals that culminated in the legislation of 1824. Of the entire Pennsylvania delegation, only Samuel Breck, a Philadelphia merchant, opposed that measure.[15]

This agreement, however, had been achieved out of major dissension. Although the editor of the *Village Record* (Westchester) voiced his own endorsement of protective legislation, he noted that letters poured across his desk both for and against such proposals. The instruction that Pennsylvania congressmen support tariff legislation in 1816, which had passed the state's house of representatives by a large majority, had failed in the state senate by a vote of sixteen to nine. Similar instructions in 1820 had passed the state senate by a margin of only one vote. During the next two years, such resolutions had been tabled even in the house, and strong opposition still remained in both branches of the assembly in 1824.[16]

Even at Washington, where Pennsylvanians had been leading the fight for protective legislation, all had not been harmony amidst the state delegation. In 1816 John Ross of Northampton County had reiterated the old Jeffersonian argument that "all manufactories were conducted with slaves, because the occupation had a tendency to degrade and debase the human mind," that it was "a vain attempt to carry manufactories to such an extent" in the United States, "where there were so many inducements to seek an independent support by agriculture and other beneficial pursuits." Senator Abner Lacock of Pennsylvania's western district had at the same time opposed duties that might become prohibitory. In 1821 Thomas Forrest of Philadelphia County, as chairman of the House Committee on Agriculture, had presented a scathing refutation of protectionist arguments. James Buchanan of Lancaster County, maintaining that the tariff was intended solely as a revenue measure, which offered aid to agriculture and industry only as a by-product, carefully advocated a middle course in 1823 and 1824.[17]

For the Middle and Western States, currency and credit policies had constituted yet another divisive issue. Officially, Pennsylvania, as the home site of both the first and second Banks of the United States, had been firmly committed to support of the national institution. When the bank, during the summer of 1818, had initiated strenuous efforts to curtail its discounts, the Pennsylvania legislature had reinforced the stand for banking conservatism by enacting legislation to annul the charter of any state bank that refused to pay its notes in specie. But in back-country communities—such as Meadville, Bedford, Bellefont, Huntington, Milton, Carlisle, Greencastle, Lewistown, Washington, and Pittsburgh—where this policy by 1822 had forced the disincorporation of local firms, resentment had arisen against the bank and its operations.[18]

To the west and south, even proponents of the national bank had been warning the parent institution of the disastrous effects of its actions. In October 1818 the Charleston, Fayetteville, Richmond, Pittsburgh, Chillicothe, Cincinnati, and Louisville branches had been called upon to provide, altogether, $700,000 in specie, while the Richmond and Baltimore offices had been required to reduce their discounts by $400,000 and $1,000,000, respectively. Branches had been forbidden to accept any notes but their own, except in payments to the United States, and even from drawing upon each other. Henry Clay, advising Langdon Cheves, the new president of the parent bank, in April 1819, had questioned that "the debtors to the Branches in this quarter [Kentucky] could pay their debts suddenly, without absolute ruin to many of them; nor that they could do it in two or three years without infinite distress." After elaborating upon the imbalance of payments between the West and the East, stemming in particular from an excess of governmental receipts over disbursements amounting annually to about $1.5 million in the western country, Clay had concluded: "This is a hopeless picture for us beyond the mountains. For it is not likely that that current will shortly so change its course."[19]

In the West and South, less sympathetic critics of the bank than Clay were moving to destroy the institution and the federal influence that sustained it. As early as 1816, Indiana had constitutionally barred the establishment of a branch of any bank that was not chartered by the state, and the Illinois Constitution of 1818 had carried a similar provision. Between 1817 and 1819, Maryland, Tennessee, Georgia, North Carolina, Kentucky, and Ohio had enacted legislation that heavily taxed branches of the bank; and proposals for such action had been considered in the legislatures of Virginia, South Carolina, New York, and even Pennsylvania. Meanwhile the states had created locally chartered institutions and enacted stay laws, which were designed to force acceptance of their notes in collection of debts. As state courts upheld these challenges to the power of the bank, the federal judiciary had become the arbiter that maintained its survival—in the famous decisions on *McCulloch* v. *Maryland* (1819) and *Osborn et al.* v. *The Bank of the United States* (1824), which denied the states authority to tax the bank, and *Wayman and Another* v. *Southard and Another* (1825), which upheld the power to enforce executions.[20]

While the challenge to the authority of the bank, as well as to the restraint in financial policy that it imposed, gathered momentum in the South and West, established commercial interests, even in those areas, protested the irresponsibility of the attack. Nowhere in the country were the divisions on this issue so strong and so deep as in Kentucky. When Hezekiah Niles expressed the shock of eastern financial circles that the Kentucky legislature had established a system of banks that were authorized to issue notes without the backing of specie, spokesmen from the Bluegrass Region echoed the alarm.[21] Their commercial ties, as the oldest mercantile center west of Pittsburgh, were dependent upon the preservation of their credit standing in Baltimore and Philadelphia. Henry Clay might interpret to the East the western concerns, but he was also the agent for eastern commercial and financial expansion into the West; and he represented a local constituency that shared his broad perspective. Profound divisions in economic alignments had been geographically and politically delineated in Kentucky since before the founding of the state. That disagreement, aggravated by financial crisis, extended during the 1820s into the arena of national politics, as one more manifestation of the intraregional disharmonies that complicated efforts to achieve the programs of nationalism.

Monroe's design for unity through cabinet representation of diverse sectional interests had rested upon shifting sands. Within every major sectional identification, significant segments of opposition challenged the predominant stands on issues. Superimposed upon these instabilities, in some cases generating them and always exacerbating them, was a generalized postwar economic depression. Peacetime adjustments were delayed for several years when, in 1816, bad weather curtailed harvests throughout Europe. American wheat and rye were abundant and of good quality that season, and harvests in 1817 were

9

even better, reportedly one-third to one-half greater than usual in all sections of the country. With flour prices phenomenally high, ranging to fifteen dollars a barrel at coastal markets during the spring of 1817, American exports to Liverpool increased from about 19,000 barrels in 1816 to over 538,000 barrels in 1817.[22]

During these years, agricultural production financed an enormous American importation of European manufactures, stimulated by a demand that had grown up under the prolonged wartime restraints. Whether or not British policy dictated a deliberate campaign to glut American markets with foreign manufactures before the domestic industry was securely established, as Henry Peter Brougham urged before Parliament in April 1816, American imports rose from a value of less than $13 million in 1814 to over $113 million in 1815, to $147 million in 1816, and to $121.17 million in 1818. But as European agriculture recovered toward the end of the decade, corn laws and the reimposition of mercantilistic restraints upon the West India trade sharply curtailed the market for American produce abroad. By 1822 the excess of imports over exports in the merchandise trade of the United States amounted to more than $18.5 million, and over $7.4 million in coin and bullion exchange was leaving the country.[23]

American manufacturers and a growing number of their unemployed were among the first to demand protective legislation. At Philadelphia a committee of the Society of Friends of Domestic Industry reported that the number of local industries engaged in manufacturing products that competed with large importations had declined from 9,672 in 1816 to about 2,137 by 1819. At Pittsburgh the number of workers in manufacturing had dropped from 1,960 to 672. Seven of the eight bagging factories in Lexington, Kentucky, where hemp manufacturing was the principal industry, had closed their doors. Hezekiah Niles estimated that 50,000 people were either unemployed or irregularly employed in the cities of New York, Philadelphia, and Baltimore in 1819; and James Flint reported that half a million were unemployed over the nation as a whole in 1820.[24]

Mercantile interests, which traditionally were opposed to trade restrictions, at this time joined in the cry for discriminatory legislation. Under the impact of the massive importation of foreign goods, the normal marketing system, by which such trade had been handled largely on consignment through wholesale importers, was disrupted. Supercargoes and ships' captains had placed surplus cargoes, which were introduced without prior orders, at public auction. Credit had been generously extended, and package sales from broken lots had been initiated. As a result, importers and wholesalers, in port cities from Boston south to Charleston, demanded relief.

Even shippers joined the outcry. Renewed barriers to American participation in the West Indies trade had curtailed both the direct commerce to the islands and the indirect triangular traffic with Europe. By the summer of 1816 newspapers were reporting that English merchants, who could afford to carry goods from Liverpool to New York at a loss by making up the difference on the runs to the West Indies and thence to Liverpool, were shipping beef and tallow, butter, hams, and potatoes from Ireland to the American market at prices that undersold domestic produce.[25] Shipping interests now persuasively argued the broad basis for retaliatory legislation.

Samuel Smith, a Baltimore merchant and congressman, had endorsed the tariff of 1816 and, after illness had forced Lowndes to relinquish his leadership for the measure, had conducted the debate for its passage. As with most spokesmen for commercial interests, Smith's support for protective legislation set moderate limits and had dissipated by 1824. But his concern for trade reciprocity was persistent. Between 1815 and 1822 he sponsored a series of measures which imposed discriminatory action against nations that denied access to their ports for United States vessels on terms equivalent to those of domestic shipping.

Sectional economic differences had, however, proved to be divisive among mercantile interests by 1823. Specialized concerns of New England's triangular shippers, as distinguished from those of the direct traders, who were more commonly identified with the Middle States, dominated the policy decisions of the then secretary of state, John Quincy Adams. Spokesman for the northeastern interests in Monroe's regional coalition, Adams had interjected into the reciprocity legislation of that year a demand for access to the European carrying trade, which merchants from Baltimore, Philadelphia, and New York were prepared to forego as long as they were admitted to the West Indies. The requirement that European states, and particularly Great Britain, permit Yankee merchantmen to compete with equal access to trade within colonial dominions, while the United States denied to foreigners participation in the domestic coasting trade, seemed excessive. How was "reciprocity" to be defined?[26]

Meanwhile, American farmers by 1818 had begun to know the depression that other segments of the economy had already experienced for the past two years. While the general price level declined from an index figure of 220 (1825 = 100) in 1813 to 145 by 1815 and to 100 by 1820, prices for farm products had risen from 175 in 1814 to 200 by 1817, a trend that had aggravated the plight of the urban poor. But with the recovery of foreign production and the closing of the West Indies markets, agricultural income had sagged. Flour prices at Baltimore dropped from a height of $15 a barrel in the spring of 1817 to about $8.60 the following autumn. Though the market improved somewhat through 1818, the price declined steadily from $9.60 a barrel in November 1818 to less than $6.00 in the autumn of 1819, then to a low of less than $4.00 through the winter of 1820/21. Much the same trend was reflected in prices at interior markets, but with an exaggeration at the lower level, as it became no longer profitable to transport produce eastward. At Pittsburgh, flour prices dropped from a general level of about $5.90 a barrel in the period 1818/19 to a low of $2.10 at harvest time in 1820 and, finally, to about $1.50 in the spring of 1821. The index of general farm prices fell below 100 in 1820 and remained low throughout the succeeding decade.[27]

In this situation, many farmers, for a time at least, looked to the "home market" development that was envisioned by tariff proponents. The indifference and negativism that in 1816 had characterized voting attitudes toward tariff legislation in most of the agricultural districts of Pennsylvania—the Delaware, the upper and lower Susquehanna, the Allegheny, the Monongahela, and the Youghiogheny valleys—were largely eliminated among their delegations in the state house of representatives and in Congress in 1820. But opposition from those areas was again evident toward proposals to extend tariff action in 1822; and it reappeared, primarily as abstention from voting, on the legislation of 1824.[28]

Farmers, it became apparent, were not content to await the indirect benefits of the increased demand for their products associated with growth of domestic manufactures. Some farmers sought immediate gains through protection of raw materials at the cost of that development. Some were prepared to relinquish the policy of retaliatory legislation if to do so would assure their foreign markets. Grain and livestock producers of the Middle States were particularly concerned about access to the West Indies trade. The instability of agrarian support for tariff and reciprocity measures was to prove critical to the development of that program over the next four years.

European travelers identified this as a period of strident nationalism throughout the land. Jackson's victory at New Orleans had not influenced the peace negotiations, but it had triggered a surge of public pride in the fact that United States forces had repulsed the might of Britain. Military heroes were accorded new veneration. As the nation approached the golden jubilee of its revolutionary conflict, the remaining veterans of that struggle achieved heroic stature. General pension legislation in 1818 had assured monthly compensation for life to all who had served nine months or longer in the "continental establishment." Efforts to raise the level of these allowances gained momentum over the next decade despite pressures for retrenchment in governmental spending.

Glorying in their achievements, Americans nevertheless looked to the future, not to the past, as their time of greatness. Even the years of depression had not stunted the optimism. Men who failed in one community pushed on to another. By the mid 1820s, construction of the Erie Canal was already luring thousands of New Englanders into western New York. South of the Ohio, hundreds of wagons were observed passing from Kentucky and Tennessee northward into central Indiana and Illinois and westward into Missouri and Arkansas. In the deep South a hydrant of settlement channeled the flow from Tennessee southward into the Huntsville Basin and on to the extension of the piedmont into Alabama. Americans were "on the move." Merchants and businessmen, as well as farmers, joined the rush to embrace new opportunity.[29]

No longer protected by British diplomatic and trading interests, the Indians north of the Ohio had surrendered the bulk of their holdings by 1821. Jackson's victories over the southeastern Indians had prepared the way for a "land mania," also, in the opening of Alabama and Mississippi between 1817 and 1820. As sales of public lands slackened with the coming of depression, Congress in 1820 had reduced the minimum price on future transactions from $2.00 to $1.75 an acre and had lowered the minimum units of tracts to 80 acres. Relief legislation, beginning in the following year, had extended credit to debtors under past contracts by four, six, or eight years, depending upon the size of the remaining deficit, with a discount of 37.5 percent to those who had completed their payment by the following September. On the basis of past relief measures, even those who had failed to extend their contracts could anticipate action for compensation on forfeited payments. The assurance of a government responsive to the needs of its people formed the ideology of which Americans were most boastful.

Even as they celebrated the benefits of their nationhood, however, they had become aware that their interests were not unified. The Hartford Convention of 1814 had capped a decade of disaffection in New England. The Missouri debates of 1820 and 1821 had pitted North against South in determining the development of the West. Cooler heads and a spirit of compromise had prevailed in those crises, but the instabilities of sectional stances on public policies had demonstrated hazards in the national path. Sharpened recognition of divergent

13

identities and suspicion of the motivations of those who held opposing views had revived in political debate. Newspaper comment on the approaching election of 1824 emphasized such cleavages.[30]

In the aftermath of the Missouri controversy, the southern commitment to slavery and the spreading northern opposition to that institution focused the struggle. Culturally, however, the differences were much broader. For the New Englander they were apparent in the pervasive ramifications of southern plantation organization—the sparsity of urban centers, the scale of individual land holdings, the distances that hampered growth of educational and religious institutions and fostered an exaggeration of social expression. For the southern planter, the differences stood out in perceptions of the Yankee's moralistic emphasis upon school and church, his work ethic, his "trader's mentality," his staid reserve. These characteristics derived from cultural patterns that were more basic than the labor system, from variant conceptions of life goals that had shaped the early settlement process.

Long before the Revolution, additional tensions had formed as Quakers and Catholics had founded separate colonies and as differing ethnic groups, notably the Germans and Scotch-Irish, had pushed into the hill country of New England and into the interior valleys. Blended later into the funnel of the Ohio River system, all these people sought the promise of new beginnings while yet clinging to much of the distinctiveness of their cultural heritage. In the brief quarter-century of mingled relationship, the divergences still ran deep. Pockets of Quaker settlement in Indiana and of New England Congregationalism in northern and eastern Ohio continued to reflect public-policy views that were distinct from those of their southern emigrant neighbors. South of the Ohio the internecine differences of the individualistic Scotch-Irish splintered their Presbyterian fellowship into myriad sectarian groupings, but a shared emotional pietism linked them in revivalistic fervor against eastern infusions of intellectual liberalism. Jeffersonian deism and Bostonian Unitarianism were, alike, anathema to them. In Kentucky, dispute over the leadership at Transylvania University had developed as early as 1816 and was to grow as the issue was politicized in the legislative control of trustee appointments and state financial relief. Elections, contemporaries noted, were won or lost on the basis of religious denominational affiliations.[31]

Within the West and between the East and the West, further conflict centered in divergence between the old and the new. Challenging the entrenched elitism of first comers, aspiring entrepreneurs and political climbers called for a "changing of the guard," whether or not rascality could be proved. Conceptions that were associated with such localized, even personalized, concerns fragmented popular attitudes. The nation, during this period of rapid development, suffered the growing pains of adolescence.

Political disorganization reflected the economic and social flux. Even the unity suggested by Monroe's decisive victory over the Federalist Rufus King, in the presidential election of 1816, was illusory. The Virginian had won the Republican nomination with difficulty over William H. Crawford. Philosophical divisions on the role of federal authority soon shattered the Republican party as its leaders, with varying enthusiasm, responded to the demands for extended governmental activity. Meanwhile, the disintegration of the Federalists cast fragments of uncertain commitment into local contests, where, alone, they could register political impact. Reviewing the situation in May 1820, Calhoun noted that there had been "an immense revolution of fortunes in every part of the Union; enormous numbers of persons utterly ruined; multitudes in deep distress; and a general mass of disaffection to the Government, not concentrated in any particular direction, but ready to seize upon any event and looking out anywhere for a leader."[32]

State governments were already reflecting popular dissatisfaction with the existing order. Legislation for the relief of debtors was debated at length in New England, as well as in the West and South, between 1819 and 1822. Stay laws, which provided moratoria on the collection of debts, were enacted in Vermont, Maryland, Pennsylvania, Ohio, Indiana, Illinois, Missouri, and Kentucky. In most of the West, such measures were linked with legislation providing for expansion of the currency through state-chartered banks or loan offices.[33]

Strong opposition marked the campaign for these enactments everywhere but in Ohio and Indiana. Similar proposals were defeated in Massachusetts, New York, New Jersey, Delaware, Virginia, and North Carolina. The arguments that they violated constitutional guarantees of contractual obligations and further limited the already restricted supply of credit were effective. By 1822 most of these laws had been terminated. Not, however, in Kentucky, where the agitation for relief provided the basis for party organization that controlled the gubernatorial elections of 1820 and 1824 and, in the latter year, the legislative poll as well.

The issue that climaxed the relief controversy in Kentucky was the authority of the courts. By two decisions announced in October 1823, the State Court of Appeals declared the replevy principle unconstitutional, as a violation of contract. Popular reaction by debtor interests against this ruling merged with more broadly based local criticism of the United States Supreme Court, which in February of that year had held that Kentucky's "occupying claimant" laws were in violation of the agreement on land division under which that state had been separated from Virginia. Kentucky legislators, in December 1823, adopted a preamble and resolutions denouncing both the state and the federal judicial actions. The General Assembly subsequently sent to Congress a remonstrance directed against the Supreme Court decision, and only the action of the state senate defeated a proposal to revise the Kentucky Constitution so as to limit the terms of judges.

The victory of the relief forces in the following election prepared the way for legislation, enacted in December 1824, that repealed all laws organizing the Court of Appeals and provided for the appointment of four new judges.[34] The judges of the Old Court, however, maintaining that their appointments for life rested upon constitutional, rather than legislative, mandate, refused to disband. Over the next two years, Kentucky presented, at least institutionally, two Courts of Appeals. Relief proponents were repudiated in the elections of 1825 and 1826, but the subsidence of political controversy centering on their unrest was temporary. It reemerged the following year, when a large majority of the New Court's adherents provided the cadre of support for the presidential candidacy of Andrew Jackson.

The egalitarian protest that was identifiable in the Kentucky political scene may not have been so predominant a force in the rise of the Jackson movement in other states, but the repercussions of economic and social conflict were evident as a disturbance to old political alignments in many areas by 1824. In Indiana, revulsion against the bankruptcy of the state bank at Vincennes, shortly after it had paid a 40 percent dividend to its stockholders, including many of the local federal officeholders and state political leaders, fueled a demand for "independence" from association with the existing political and economic order as the principal issue in the gubernatorial campaign of 1823 and the ensuing presidential election. In Ohio, Jacksonian support centered in Cincinnati and the southwestern counties, where the closing of the local office of the Bank of the United States in October 1820 had forced the liquidation of three state-chartered institutions, which caused widespread, radiating business failure. In Pennsylvania the antibank reaction forged the alliance of western rural areas with urban artisan discontent to challenge the leadership of the Philadelphia-based "Family Party" in its backing of John C. Calhoun.[35]

A growing demand for suffrage and electoral reforms to permit popular participation in government denoted the mounting dissatisfaction. Most of the new states had entered the Union with constitutions that provided for suffrage by nearly all adult white males, and about half the original states had early developed a similar democracy. But the change had not come to Massachusetts, Connecticut, and New York until 1821; and in the last two instances it had been bitterly contested. The payment of taxes, which remained as a slight restriction generally, still limited suffrage in Louisiana to only about 47 percent of the adult white males at mid decade. Property qualifications yet continued to disenfranchise almost as many in Rhode Island, Virginia, and North Carolina. Extended residency and registration requirements also limited voting in Kentucky, Pennsylvania, and South Carolina.[36]

The lagging readjustment of district representation in the state legislatures was a continuing problem for residents in western areas of Virginia, North Carolina, and Louisiana and for those in some cities, notably Providence, Baltimore, Richmond, and New Orleans. In Virginia, pressure for both suffrage and redistricting reform was stimulated by the mounting divergence of western economic interests from those of the ruling tidewater planters. By July 1825 a convention at Staunton, which was attended by representatives of only the western district, demanded constitutional revisions. Three years later a popular referendum, by the vote of 21,896 to 16,646, with seven-eighths of the tidewater voters and about half those of the piedmont in opposition, finally led to the call for a convention in 1829. After bitter controversy, compromises on suffrage and reapportionment shifted political power into the piedmont and central-valley areas but still failed to mollify the transmontane counties, where the size of election districts remained a barrier to the exercise of liberalized voting provisions.[37]

Generally the movement toward fuller participation in the electoral process advanced greatly during the 1820s. In many areas, election districts were being reduced in size, thus providing polls that were more accessible to voters. More offices were being made elective or, as in New York, were being transferred from the control of entrenched councils of appointment to the patronage of elected officials. In Pennsylvania, where the governor held appointive powers over a wide range of local offices and through them was able to control state and national elections, petitions poured into the assembly, urging a call for constitutional revision. When such a proposal was put to a vote in October 1825, it was defeated, 59,000 to 44,000; but the western counties, which were notable for their early support of the Jackson cause, endorsed the request overwhelmingly.[38] Massachusetts and Indiana shifted the selection of presidential electors to popular suffrage in 1824, and six other States—Vermont, New York, Kentucky, Illinois, Louisiana, and Georgia—made that change by 1828. In the election of the latter year, only Delaware and South Carolina still vested those appointments in the legislature.

With such changes, old leadership controls were disrupted. Increasing population and heavy emigration into new geographic areas increased the deterioration of old political associations that were founded on personal loyalties. Militia units, which in many states had long shaped such relationships, were disintegrating. As early as the campaign of 1824, partisan conventions were emerging as an alternative format for consolidating local political effort. The trend was to spread throughout much of the nation over the next four years. It was a grass-roots approach, as yet rudimentary in structure, that depended upon translation of the heterogeneous particularistic elements into associational aggregates. To identify such groupings and to elevate them beyond the level of local interest demanded a degree of political management that the nation's leaders had not exerted generally since the early years of the republic.

No other change in the broad spectrum of transformation that was then sweeping the nation was to have such far-reaching effects. In view of the expansion of suffrage opportunities, the development for a large proportion of the electorate entailed the generation, rather than merely the reconstruction, of partisan interest. Men who had never been pressed to consider matters beyond their personal concerns were now to be drawn into the electoral process. Whether they were to be attracted by personalities or issues and how broad was the cohesive force of either appeal were questions newly to be tested. Political confrontation became, during this period, the normal accompaniment of every public decision.

The situation would enormously complicate the efforts of any leader who personally lacked unquestioned popular support. Apathy, rather than satisfaction with President Monroe's administration, had permitted his reelection, virtually without contest, in 1820 by one of the lowest voter turnouts on record. The deteriorating organizational base over the next four years failed to develop even so limited a political accord. That no one candidate could legitimately claim majority endorsement was the crucial problem to emerge from the presidential election of 1824.

2

★ ★ ★ ★ ★

THE MINORITY ELECTION

Monroe's second administration had quickly disintegrated into a struggle for power among his cabinet members, Secretary of State Adams, Secretary of the Treasury Crawford, and Secretary of War Calhoun, together with the Speaker of the House, Clay, and the military hero Jackson. Since all were nominally members of the Republican party, the breakdown of political discipline was manifest. Only 68 of 261 members of Congress participated in the caucus of February 1824, which, with the remnant of the party's organizational backing, endorsed Crawford's candidacy as the heir of the Virginia dynasty. The emergence of Jackson, politically almost unknown, as a major contender for the presidency—evidenced in his victory over Calhoun for Pennsylvania's endorsement the following month—proved that the old leadership structure of the party had succumbed.

The count of the electors chosen the following autumn gave the general 99 votes; Adams, 84; Crawford, 41; Clay, 37. The electors of 11 states supported Jackson; 7, Adams; 3, Crawford; 3, Clay. In those states in which electors were selected by popular tally, Jackson received 152,901 votes; Adams, 114,023; Clay, 47,217; Crawford, 46,979; but in six states, including populous New York, the electors were designated by legislative rather than popular vote. Although the general's preeminence appeared decisive, he had not attained the requisite constitutional majority, and his claim to popular preference was at least controvertible. Popular interest, moreover, remained nearly as low as at Monroe's second election, with only a quarter of the eligible voters expressing a

19

choice. As the election was thrown before the House of Representatives, the basis for political consolidation remained in flux.

Limitations in public service, personality, or political organization—all relatively standard components of the politician's arsenal—handicapped, in some significant aspect, each of the candidates. Alone among them, Jackson had served briefly in the American Revolution, a patriotic connection that was magnified in popular view as the nation approached its golden jubilee. The general's subsequent feats as the hero of the Creek campaign and the Battle of New Orleans, in notable contrast to the generally disastrous record of army action during the second war with Britain, had greatly enhanced his aura of glory. However, Jackson had held federal office only intermittently—as a member of the United States House of Representatives from December 1796 to March 1797, as a member of the Senate from September 1797 until April 1798, as territorial governor of Florida for a brief three months during the winter of 1820/21, and again as United States senator from December 1823 to October 1824. With obvious disinterest he had relinquished all these posts. His career had so far been identified primarily with military, not civil, leadership.

Adams, Crawford, Clay, and Calhoun—all, in contrast—based their pretensions upon lengthy governmental service. Each had sat for at least five years in Congress, Clay as Speaker of the House of Representatives for nearly thrice that period. The first three had performed major foreign missions; and Adams, after eight years as emissary to the courts of St. Petersburg and London, had returned to establish a distinguished reputation as secretary of state. Crawford, as Treasury secretary, and Calhoun, in the War Department, had each, by administrative talents, contributed notably to the structural revisions of postwar governmental operations. Under the criteria of experience, their qualifications so far exceeded Jackson's that few politicians had considered his a serious candidacy until the closing months of the presidential campaign.

In personality, Jackson held the attributes of the successful military leader; he was vigorous, shrewd, decisive, and tough. To the civilian electorate, campaign propaganda presented the portrait of a rough-hewn hero, self-educated, one of nature's noblemen, triumphant over lowly origins as well as the nation's enemies, through individual prowess and divine favor. For some, however, like the lowly militiamen who had experienced his sharp censure and rigid discipline, these attributes did not evoke unalloyed adulation. Kentuckians had bitterly resented the general's allegations of cowardice when their meagerly armed, undermanned, and badly positioned forces had fallen back in his lines before New Orleans. Some two hundred Tennessee militiamen under Jackson's command at Mobile had been arrested for mutiny when they protested an arbitrary and confusingly mandated extension of their enlistment; six, by order of court-martial, had been shot, with Jackson's approval. Citizens of New Orleans had been outraged as the general had prolonged martial law and, moreover, had repudiated the findings of his own military court when it exonerated a Louisiana editor and legislator arrested for criticizing the Jackson regime. All but Adams of Monroe's cabinet had called for censure of the Tennessean's conduct in the Seminole campaign of 1818, when Jackson had not only invaded Spanish territory, seizing St. Marks and Pensacola, but also had ordered the execution of two British citizens. Adams had subsequently, again and again, found it necessary to defend the general from diplomatic protests against the latter's handling of the transfer of Florida. Jackson's departure from what Monroe described as "The *momentary* govt." of that territory had not been unwelcome to any of the concerned parties.[1] Political leaders, viewing Jackson's pretensions in 1824, looked upon his high-handed exercise of authority as more disqualifying than his inexperience in civil administration.

Among the other contenders, Clay and Calhoun—tall, magnetic, quick-witted, and socially at ease—also brought dazzling presence to the political scene. Neither, however, had developed the broad popular appeal or political organization to capture mass support in a day of expanding suffrage qualification. Theirs was the charisma of the legislative hall and the drawing room. Their extraregional ties rested upon youthful associations and congressional friendships. Clay had reminded Virginia legislators, as he argued Kentucky's land claims before them in 1822, that he was a son of the Old Dominion. Calhoun had attempted to extend his political breadth by emphasizing his Scotch-Irish family's early residence in Pennsylvania and his own education at Yale and the Litchfield law school in Connecticut. In both cases, their appeal was directed primarily to the established political leadership. In that framework, however, neither commanded electoral support comparable to that of the relatively colorless Crawford or Adams.

Crawford, a huge, ruggedly handsome man, who had an excellent mind, warm family ties, and a strong sense of honesty, was at the same time somewhat awkward, lacked social grace, and expressed himself with a bluntness that appeared ill-tempered and overbearing. As a senator from 1807 to 1813, he had opposed his party's stand on embargo legislation and the refusal to renew the charter of the Bank of the United States. He had served uncomfortably as minister to France during the next two years, a role that was difficult, at best, in that unsettled period, but one in which his brusque speech and distaste for social amenities

21

were serious handicaps. Since 1818 his administrative duties as secretary of the Treasury had brought him further discomfiture when the program of retrenchment, introduced in response to the depression, occasioned acrimonious criticism and political attack. His manipulation of the vast patronage of his department for personal advancement had contributed greatly to the disharmony of Monroe's second term. During the closing months of the administration a quarrel over the control of such favors had led the president and his Treasury secretary to the verge of blows.[2] This was not the background to support a personality claim to political preference, but Crawford had developed the only semblance to a national party organization then in operation. Despite illness and a paralysis that carried him close to death and incapacitated him for public activity throughout the election year, he had won the caucus nomination and third ranking in the vote of the electoral college.

Adams, who placed second in electoral and popular preference, was the least attractive as a political personality. Although the eldest son of the Federalist former president, John Adams, he was ill at ease in public appearances and was stiffly formal in social relationships. Short and somewhat plump, with a high-pitched voice and tearing eyes, he had little physical presence by which to command attention. He was coldly critical in his judgments, acerbic and outspoken in expressing them, and self-centeredly ambitious. By his carping suspicion of his colleagues, he, like Crawford, had at one point provoked the phlegmatic Monroe to open anger.

Psychologically, the New Englander was sensitive, shy, and insecure. Reared in early childhood by a strong-willed mother, proud of her husband's eminence in governmental affairs and ever conscious of her frequently solitary role in imparting the familial cultural values, young John Quincy had grown up under an oppressive mandate of duty. At the age of ten, charged with smothering admonitions and exhortations, he had accompanied his father to Europe. During the next seven years, at schools in France and Holland and by employment as an amanuensis and secretary in the diplomatic service, the youth had acquired, for an American of his generation, an unparalleled perspective on the mores of court and cosmopolitan society. He had nevertheless retained the strong sense of obligation to justify parental expectations, expectations that were now heightened by recognition of his peculiar advantages. Introspectively throughout his life, in soul-searching family correspondence and diary record, he committed himself to persistent struggle for the idealized standards of a heritage that combined Puritan moral values with the secular focus on scholarly inquiry and public-service responsibility of the eighteenth century Enlightenment. His compulsions, which he directed toward himself at least as rigidly as toward those around him, demanded persistent striving—for moral perfection, for intellectual development, and for conscientious civic leadership.

Admirable as were these aspirations—and Adams of all the presidential incumbents has come closest to attaining that combination—they set him apart from cultural identification with the mass of his contemporaries. Jacksonian publicists described the New Englander as "a closet man," who had acquired all his knowledge from books and knew "little of man as he is." The observation sprang only partly from the hostile perceptions of a regionalized, partisan opposition. Adams's wife, Louisa Johnson, the musically gifted and socially accomplished daughter of a Maryland merchant who had become the first United States consul at London, was awed by her husband's "superior talents" and his "unshaken purity and integrity beyond all praise" but confessed that she "often shrank from the severity of his opinions in passing judgment on others less gifted than himself." His son, Charles Francis, wrote that his father was the only man he had ever seen whose feelings he "could not penetrate," and Adams himself recognized that he was "a man of reserved, cold, austere and forbidding manners."[3]

Despite his lengthy career in public service, Adams had never, prior to the campaign of 1824, attempted to develop an organized political following. Returning to the United States to complete his education at Harvard in 1787, he had subsequently established a law practice in Boston but in 1794 had returned to Europe as minister, under appointments by President Washington to the Netherlands and by his father to Berlin. Following the elder Adams's defeat for reelection in 1800, John Quincy had resumed his career at law. Despite an interest in "political controversy," he had at first renounced it because of a disinclination to assume party identification. Within six months after his return to Boston, however, he had been elected to the state senate as one among four designated "the Federal ticket." Running for Congress independently the following autumn, he had been defeated. Shortly thereafter, he had been named to the United States Senate under a "caucus compact," after his legislative colleagues had reached a stalemate on two prior ballots for nomination of the High Federalist leader, Timothy Pickering. Family name and factional association, rather than personal following, had brought Adams to Washington.[4]

Already his intellectual independence had disconcerted party leaders. He was viewed as being "too unmanageable." The day of his entry into the Massachusetts Senate he had proposed that two or three of the nine Federalist caucus nominees for the Commonwealth Council be of the opposing party, "by way of conciliatory procedure." He had voted with the Republicans on the only question that divided parties during that legislative session and, prior to his removal to Washington the following autumn, had twice more cast votes in opposition to clearly defined Federalist positions. Five years later, after a history of instability on partisan stands, he had been dropped from the Federalist senatorial ranks because of his endorsement of resolutions drafted by a Republican-called state meeting to protest the British attack upon the *Chesapeake.* He had responded to his detractors by publishing a pamphlet in which he philosophically stated his political principles and refuted the arguments against the embargo legislation; but he had held remarkably aloof from the personalities of political opposition. Shortly thereafter, a year before the expiration of his senatorial term, the Massachusetts General Court had named a successor, and the repudiated incumbent had promptly resigned.[5]

Adams's subsequent career had blossomed under Jeffersonian patronage. He had been named envoy to Russia from 1809 to 1815, one of the commissioners to negotiate peace with Britain at Ghent in 1814, then minister to Great Britain until he became secretary of state in 1817. His claim to the presidency rested primarily upon his achievements in the last capacity—contemporaneously recognized as his defense of the country's international commercial interests and his support of continental territorial expansion.

By patient and persevering effort, Adams had resolved the difficulties barring Spanish cession of the Floridas and, in the negotiation, had achieved a boundary settlement that reinforced the national claims westward to the Pacific. Boldly enunciating the noncolonization principle as a barrier to Russian advance southward in the Northwest, he had won both a favorable boundary delimitation and concession of trading rights northward along that coast. Against Britain he had steadfastly maintained the national territorial pretensions south of the forty-ninth parallel and, by accepting an arrangement for joint occupation of the Oregon country, had testified to his vision of the expansive thrust of the American frontier. His strict definitions of the criteria of neutrality and recognition, which restrained popular support for the emerging republics of Latin America, had been less well received in public favor; but they, too, are acclaimed today as stands marking John Quincy Adams as one of the nation's greatest delineators of foreign policy.[6]

Such involvement had held him apart from public association with the divisions that were developing in regard to domestic programs. As an apostate, however, he was politically suspect to Federalists and Republicans alike. His role in the traditional position of cabinet preeminence had brought him under continual criticism from rival presidential candidates—from Clay and his supporters until mid 1822 and from the Crawfordites, with increasing virulence, during the next two years. Even the New Englander's early friendship with Calhoun had deteriorated. Adams accepted the South Carolinian as his vice-presidential choice only after the popular vote had been cast, when his supporters warned that Calhoun would carry the electors and that to reject him would be " 'shewing our teeth without being able to bite'. . . ."[7] Monroe, meanwhile, had steadfastly refrained from designating a preference in the contest for the succession.

The campaign of 1824 revived political ideology as yet another criterion of partisan differentiation. For thirty-two of the nation's thirty-six years, Virginians had held the presidency, and since the turn of the century, Jeffersonian leadership had shaped governmental actions. In the bitterness of the Missouri statehood debates of 1820 and 1821, this geographically identified dominance had acquired new significance. Northern Republicans, reminding their southern cohorts of their long-standing support, demanded a turn at power, which the latter were increasingly fearful to share. Monroe's conception of regional balance in the federal administration had not forestalled the discontents. Moreover, the instabilities of postwar readjustment had fragmented even sectional interests. Programmatic disagreements were being translated into controversies that were founded on the constitutional divisions of the nation's formative years. Concern for States' rights reemerged as a countering force to the agenda of nationalism. Crawford, Calhoun, and Jackson all began to identify their bid for public favor with this issue around 1824. None of them, however, could point to a record of consistency as exponents of narrowly limited authority in the federal government.

Crawford has been delineated as basically an economic nationalist in his cabinet roles under the Madison and Monroe administrations. He had favored a national bank, even in 1811. His views on protective tariffs and federal aid for internal improvements were pragmatic. He seems initially to have feared that tariffs would curtail revenue; but by 1821 he urged some raising of the rates and, particularly, protection for woolens. When the revenues increased beyond expectations during the following year, he argued that further increases in the tariff could support aid for internal improvements. While he deferred to President Monroe's sensitivity on the role of the federal government in promoting and maintaining such a program, Crawford himself, during this period, expressed no constitutional scruples. He dismissed Monroe's opposition to elaborating the national road system with the comment that the development was inevitable. Crawford's support among Virginia's "Old Republicans," guardians of strict adherence to limitations on federal authority, rested upon his commitment to "retrenchment" of national expenditures—a policy that was dictated, not by his philosophy of government, but by the need to offset declining revenues. The Richmond Junto were won to his cause only for want of a better choice. They had not initially espoused his candidacy in the nominating caucus of 1824.[8]

Calhoun's transition from nationalism to advocacy of States'-rights during this period is so generally recognized as not to require elaboration. Whether the change stemmed from his personal ideological conversion is more questionable. It emerged, at least, as the mantle of a pragmatic politician. Calhoun's upcountry backers, after seven years of agricultural depression, were devastated in 1825, when the price of upland cotton dropped from 32 cents to 13 cents a pound between June and October and continued downward to an average of less than 10 cents through 1832. To support a tariff, which in 1820 had provided levies of 20 percent ad valorem for protection of domestic industry, was less expedient among these constituents, when those rates were raised in 1824 to 33⅓ percent, and was impracticable in 1827/28, when they were being elevated to 50 percent. For the district that represented Calhoun's political power base, the issue of the tariff now focused a growing discontent.[9]

Calhoun's abandonment of nationalist positions evolved slowly, however. As secretary of war he had taken no active role in the debates on the tariff of 1824, notwithstanding the vigorous opposition to the legislation voiced by his South Carolina political allies. Four years later, Calhoun yet reiterated his belief in the constitutionality of tariff legislation and agreed that by "a prudent exercise of the power" Congress might achieve "much good." In 1825 he was an active proponent of the Chesapeake and Ohio Canal as a project to be executed by the "General Government." His opposition to such measures was to emerge primarily in reaction to their identification with the political associations of the Adams administration and, specifically, their packaging as Clay's "American System."[10]

Andrew Jackson's commitment to any stance on public measures was unknown to the national electorate of 1824. During his brief periods of civil service he had established no program commitment. He had generally supported the tariff of 1824, although on the final vote he had opposed the duty on cotton bagging. In his only public statement on the general issue, he had called for "a judicious examination and revision" of the legislation, not only to enable the nation to provide "within ourselves" the means of national defense and independence, but also to maintain "a home market." He had voted for the General Survey Act of 1824, to lay the groundwork for a program of national support for internal improvements, although he had not spoken publicly on the measure. While state governments of the South and West, including that of Tennessee, were turning to relief measures to counteract restrictions on currency, Jackson had urged the limiting of note circulation. The Overton faction of his Tennessee supporters was, in fact, actively promoting the establishment of a Nashville branch of the Bank of the United States as an institution to remedy the evils of state banking. Jackson's personal opposition to rechartering the bank was not generally known until after he had assumed the presidency.[11]

The general's political supporters during the presidential campaign of 1824 did, however, provide a major thrust to the emerging ideological challenge to nationalism. His friends, perhaps because of the very improbability of his political pretensions, exerted extraordinary efforts to set forth his qualifications. John H. Eaton's earlier military biography of Jackson was revised and reissued, together with several similar, shorter accounts of his career. Most notable, however, was the publication during June and July 1823 of a series of letters, signed "Wyoming" although written by Eaton, extolling as a political asset the elemental fact of Jackson's immunity from involvement in current governmental operations. His unfamiliarity with and his disassociation from the ways of the entrenched administrative bureaucracy were exploited to identify him with those among the general public whose fragmented discontents looked to some organ of change.[12]

Administrative historians have long contended that a common bond of noblesse oblige extended through both the Federalist and the Jeffersonian civil service, that a sense of public responsibility, drawing upon eighteenth-century ideals of commitment to virtue, justice, and liberty, remained central to the conception of government.[13] Whether such ethical standards in fact survived the pressures of expanding wartime activity and the postwar resurgence of national programs may be doubted. Nevertheless, the continuing strength of the moral imperative established a critical standard that was seldom absent from the rhetoric of political campaigning.

Hezekiah Niles had noted in 1818 that rumors of corruption among clerks in governmental offices had been familiar "for nearly twenty years past, and almost every body seems to believe that it exists extensively there." Congressional investigation at that time had revealed no overt corruption but had established a need for administrative safeguards, which were subsequently adopted in four of the governmental departments. Four years later the ethics of public officers had again come under review, centering then upon possible conflict of interest through the private employments of civil servants. Once more the investigators found little to condemn. Meanwhile, under pressure for retrenchment in governmental expenditures, Congress had required that arrears on wartime contracts and military accounts be settled by 1821. Thousands of relatively minor functionaries, as well as some major defaulters in governmental business, were brought before the courts. Implications of corruption and the haunting fear of such harassment beset public officials on every side.[14]

Charges and countercharges during the presidential campaign of 1824 reflected the theme. Calhoun's War Department became an early focus for such attack, and not only because of the defective records of such hapless army paymasters as the Kentucky portrait painter Matthew Jouett, who worked himself into an early grave in the effort to clear his record. The Johnson family of Kentucky, then active in Calhoun's political promotion, had received contract advances of nearly $200,000, supplemented by nearly half a million dollars in loans from the Bank of the United States, to finance an unsuccessful project for supplying the government's Missouri River forts via steamboat. Congressional investigation of that arrangement and of the involvement of Calhoun's chief clerk, Christopher Van Deventer, in assisting his brother-in-law to obtain a contract for construction of Fortress Monroe, raised such questions that a requisition system was introduced, requiring Treasury clearance of all contracts. Thomas L. McKenney, formerly superintendent of the Office of Indian Trade and now editor of the *Republican and Congressional Examiner* (Washington), which supported Calhoun, was also subjected to embarrassing review of "inexplicable" shortages.[15]

The *National Intelligencer* (Washington), a Crawford organ, had led in the criticism. In retaliation, the Calhounite Ninian Edwards, senator from Illinois, published in 1823, over the initials A.B., a charge that the editors, as official printers for the government, had withheld documents damaging to the Treasury secretary. The ensuing inquiry exonerated the journalists but made clear that Crawford had dispensed political favors through transactions with public funds. As Edwards continued the attack into the spring of 1824, he admitted his authorship of the allegation and, during subsequent investigation by the House of Representatives, lost much of his credibility when it was shown that he had previously denied having played that role.[16]

Such revelations, in the view of Jackson's proponents, established the fact that corruption flourished in Washington, condoned and practiced by its "leading men." The argument set a framework in which the governmental experience of the general's rivals became ipso facto grounds for suspicion. He alone of the candidates lacked identification as a participant in the halls of iniquity. "Wyoming" noted that Jackson had never been "in *Europe*" and "never the HEAD OF A DEPART-MENT": "look to the city of Washington, and let the virtuous patriots of the country weep at the spectacle." The morality of the Revolutionary era was fast disappearing! Jackson "was of the Revolution!" He would restore the government to the virtue of a simpler age. "Wyoming" saw "but little reason to infer that the mind is on the march, or the nation pressing to that proud advancement, which her sanguine friends have anticipated." Jackson, the "private citizen," stood "committed to no party, pledged to no system, allied to no intrigue, free of all prejudice, but coming directly from the people, and bearing with him an intimate acquaintance with their feelings, and wants. . . ."[17] The Tennesseans had not yet developed ties with the remnant of old Virginia's strict-constructionist interpreters of the Constitution, but they had laid the foundation for an ideological counterthrust against entrenched federal administrators and the program of nationalism that extended their operations.

Although John Quincy Adams's long involvement in foreign affairs had kept him relatively removed from identification with the range of domestic measures that since 1816 had set the course toward federal promotion of the nation's economic development, he had not, in renouncing his Federalist antecedents, rejected that party's governmental philosophies. During his Senate service in 1807 he had introduced a resolution asserting the power of the general government to engage in internal improvements. That he still held such views in the early 1820s was evidenced in his diary comments disagreeing with Monroe's constitutional scruples on the issue. In a letter written in 1822 to his Massachusetts friend James Lloyd, he had spoken of "the first *duty* of a nation, [as] that of bettering its own condition by internal improvement." During the campaign of 1824, in letters calculated to circulate where interest in such benefits was strong, Adams brought forward a copy of his 1807 resolution and reiterated his views on the constitutionality of federal action.[18]

On the tariff issue he was more circumspect. Aware of the changes in sectional sentiments on the protective policy, he at that time endorsed a "cautious" approach, maintaining "tender and sincere regard to the agricultural interest of the South and the commercial interest of the

North." Expressing these views to his editorial backer Robert Walsh, Jr., of the *National Gazette* (Philadelphia), Adams added: "These are my opinions and I hope you will think I have been sufficiently explicit in avowing them. I am not desirous of obtruding them here or elsewhere." Some months later the editor of the *Delaware Gazette* (Wilmington) complained that Adams was identified with widely varying opinions, according to the locale of the pronouncements: in the South he was represented as opposed to the tariff, while in the North his views were seen as the opposite.[19]

In foreign affairs he was outspoken in his nationalism. Defending Jackson's invasion of Florida in 1818, Adams had rejected diplomatic protests on the ground that Spain had failed to uphold the responsibilities of sovereignty. A state, he had argued, must maintain force "adequate at once to the protection of her territory, and to the fulfilment of her engagements, or cede . . . a province of which she retains nothing but the nominal possession. . . ."[20] He had pressed that argument as a basis upon which to negotiate the Florida purchase. His persistent demand that Great Britain concede the United States a right to participation in imperial trade had led him to urge retention of discriminatory duties even in the face of concessions which, in the spring of 1822, had opened West Indies ports to a direct exchange of certain enumerated commodities. With similar aggressiveness he had insisted upon the unilateral form of American response to George Canning's overtures for a joint British-American pronouncement of the principles that were to become known as the Monroe Doctrine.

In the bitterness of partisan dissension the nationalism of Adams's diplomatic record had not, however, gone unquestioned. In foreign affairs, as on domestic program, pragmatism governed his analysis. His goals were measurable in realistic terms—fishing privileges, commercial advantages, territorial accessions. These were benefits that served the economic interests of his seafaring constituents, and his critics so identified them. But the gains were not bounded by those limits. Moreover, Adams had urged the application of strict neutrality and recognition standards in relation to Spain's rebellious colonies, although a developing South American commerce was thereby temporarily restricted. As early as 1811 he had envisioned a time when the whole North American Continent would constitute "one nation, speaking one language, professing one general system of religious and political principles, and accustomed to one general tenor of social usages and customs"; yet for four years he had resisted efforts to expand this association. His immediate purpose was to preserve the harmony requisite for Spanish ratification of the Florida purchase. In his view, neither sectional nor ideological concerns warranted jeopardizing that end. "America," he had proclaimed in a celebrated Fourth-of-July address in 1821, ". . . goes not abroad in search of monsters to destroy. She is the well-wisher to the freedom and independence of all. She is the champion and vindicator only of her own."[21]

When two years later he enunciated the concept of the two spheres, he conceived an extension of United States hegemony that was limited hemispherically. The operational force that he might have applied to that projection was never to be fully tested, but even amidst the afterglow of the initial pronouncement, he had rejected as hypothetical Colombia's query in August 1824 whether the United States would enter into an alliance "to save America in general" from interference by the Holy Alliance "for the purpose of subjugating the new Republics or interfering in their political forms." That his view of the nation's role remained pragmatically and geographically bounded was evident in the cabinet debates, when Monroe proposed recognition of Greek independence and censure of France for military action to put down constitutional government in Spain. "The ground that I wish to take," Adams had argued—urging, instead, the renunciatory clauses of the Monroe message—"is that of earnest remonstrance against the interference of the European powers by force with South America, but to disclaim all interference on our part with Europe; to make an American cause, and adhere inflexibly to that."[22]

While not unsympathetic to ideological distinctions between the Old World and the New, Adams was skeptical that the newly liberated Spanish colonists had yet developed the will to found political freedom upon economic independence. In January 1819 he had advocated that the United States take the lead in recognizing the sovereignty of the Latin-American states and persuade Britain "to move in concert" in that action, but he had no desire that the initiative should be identified with the latter power. He was determined that the terms of the arrangement should be American and, specifically, that they should center upon American principles of open and competitive trade.[23]

Rival candidates portrayed the New Englander's views as being not only antithetic to the republican ideology of the Jeffersonians but so anti-British as to inhibit effective negotiation. Perhaps out of the Revolutionary background of his Braintree boyhood, more certainly out of his concern for New England commercial interests, Adams regarded the rivalry of Britain as the predominant threat to the security of the United States. As early as 1795 he had identified Britain's war with France as a struggle for maritime supremacy. After the defeat of Napoleon, Adams's fears centered, not upon the reactionary political philosophy of the Holy Alliance, but upon the menace of British dominance in international relations. His commitment to the protection of neutral rights, to the countering of colonial exclusivity, even to the guaranteeing of Spanish sovereignty over Cuba—all represented efforts to restrict the extension of British influence.

In his Fourth-of-July statement of policy, Adams had seized the patriotic occasion to emphasize a stand that the Russian minister reported to his government as ''d'un bout à l'autre qu'une diatribe virulente contre l'Angleterre. . . .'' The offensiveness of the secretary of state's language then, and repeatedly in preliminary drafts of notes to the British, may, as has been argued, have represented mere political posturing, which was counteracted by caution in his diplomatic actions. If so, it engendered a public perception that was more damaging than helpful when his negotiations proved to be unsuccessful.[24]

Critics questioned whether Adams's fundamental concerns in fact rose above the commercial interests of his New England constituency. Clay partisans in 1822 had publicized the disagreements at Ghent, when Adams's willingness to barter the interests of the West for a guarantee of fishing privileges off Newfoundland had polarized the United States delegation. Throughout Adams's tenure in the State Department, Clay had assailed the delay in support of Latin-American independence. The Florida settlement, with its tender regard for compensating the claims of shipping and mercantile houses, claims that had long since passed onto the books of insurance companies, seemed less important to the spokesman for the Ohio Valley West than did the opening of new regional markets in the former Spanish colonies. That the Florida accord relinquished territorial pretensions along the Texas border heightened western criticism.

To an Illinois supporter, Adams argued his concern for the national interest in effecting the Florida treaty—''as a servant of the whole Union, the interests of every part of the Union were equally dear to me.'' Nevertheless, he confessed his disinclination, ''as an Eastern man,'' that either Florida or Texas should be annexed without a restriction excluding slavery from them.[25] Southerners, following the Missouri statehood debates, shared western concern about the sectional identification of the New Englander.

Adams had with reluctance supported the Missouri Compromise of 1820, but he was already privately questioning whether division of the Union might not be a necessary prelude to eradication of slavery. Indeed, as the second stage of the Missouri debates raised the question of the state's right to restrict immigration of free persons of color, Adams had advised the congressman from his home district to move that admittance to the Union be conditioned upon recognition of the constitutional requirement relating to the rights of the citizens of each state in the several states. He had reiterated this view in a conversation with Henry Baldwin, a House member from Pennsylvania, and added: "If the dissolution of the Union must come, let it come from no other cause but this." Conceding that such an event must involve both servile and civil war, the New Englander had been prepared to contemplate so "calamitous and desolating" a course to achieve the end of extirpating slavery from the continent.[26]

Adams had not pressed the issue beyond the compromise arrangement, but his views had contributed to highly politicized opposition to his proposed treaty for Anglo-American suppression of the slave trade. In spite of his general dislike of the British and his longstanding commitment to defense of American views on the rights of neutrals, Adams had yielded to growing pressure during the early 1820s for such an accord. As a stratagem to justify concession of the right of search to British patrols, the secretary of state had proposed that the slave trade be defined as piracy, a state of belligerency and, therefore, exempt from the protections of neutrals. The resulting treaty, submitted to the Senate in May 1824, was, however, ratified only with qualifying amendments, one of which excluded the coast of America from the right of search. The British rejected this limitation, and so the treaty died. Both Calhoun and Crawford, in cabinet discussions, had opposed Adams's efforts to effect such an agreement, and their supporters provided the principal hostility to it in the Senate.[27] Sectionalism, masked in pretensions to national interest and already a powerful force in American politics, was thus focused upon Adams's conduct of foreign affairs.

Like the other candidates, the Kentuckian Clay also voiced a nationalism that was colored by particularistic interests; but with Adams, alone among the candidates, he shared a dependence upon nationalism as a vehicle for the fulfillment of those interests. The New Englander recognized that only through American strength could New England's far-flung trading concerns be projected. Spokesman for the Ohio Valley back country, Clay represented a borderland blending of North and South, East and West, that found its inherent particularity as an intersectional amalgam for composite unity. In personality and cultural tradition, as well as on a variety of localized problems, the New Englander and the Kentuckian differed significantly; but they agreed on a conception of governmental purpose that differentiated them from their rivals.

Clay had embraced the programmatic package of the home-market argument—an agricultural hinterland, to be tied through expanded internal improvements to developing industrial centers, which, in turn, were to be promoted by tariffs for encouragement of manufactures, with a national banking system to stabilize currency and credit arrangements in the exchange. His endorsement of internal improvements and tariff proposals dated from one of his earliest pronouncements on the national scene, in the United States Senate in March 1810. He had returned to those themes in an outline of his public-policy positions upon returning to Congress from Ghent, in January 1816. Several months later, citing the general suspension of specie payments, he had recanted his earlier opposition to a national bank. Thereafter he had again and again argued for "the great *home system*" as the basis for building "the strength and prosperity of the Union." Jabez Hammond of New York, in the summer of 1824, lauding Clay's "*Domestic policy,*" saw him as "the *only* Candidate for the Presidency . . . committed to that policy—." A Kentucky supporter, considering Clay's role in the formation of the Adams administration, placed the issue squarely as one "involving the interests of the American System and of the States of the Interior."[28]

Clay's perception of the American System extended beyond domestic policy. Despite his recognition of the need to develop home markets, he was not prepared to relinquish hope for expanded foreign trade. And his concern for American interests abroad embraced a nationalism that was even more sweeping than that of the prickly Adams. In 1809, Clay had fought a duel with the Federalist Humphrey Marshall in upholding the merits of homespun garments over foreign importations. The stand then marked Clay's support for Jeffersonian nonintercourse legislation as a program to compel international recognition of United States rights in neutral commerce. A War Hawk in opposing Britain's continuing violations, the Kentuckian had been the most unyielding of the commissioners at Ghent. Upon at least two occasions he had been prepared to break off the talks altogether, rather than yield to British interests.

In both instances, Clay's stand had rested predominantly upon western sectional concerns, but he had pursued the argument as an aggressive nationalist. In response to British demand for a negotiated Indian boundary, the Kentuckian had drafted the note by which the Americans had agreed to continue the meetings only upon the basis that their opponents no longer seek to include the Indians, "as parties, in the peace." He had split the delegation in rejecting a proposal, suggested by Albert Gallatin and backed by Adams, that the British right to navigate the Mississippi River be continued in exchange for reaffirmation of the United States liberty to fish and dry the catch within areas of British control. Instead, Clay had won the adherence of his colleagues to a statement that the fishing rights were derived together with United

States independence and were not negotiable. When the British had finally proposed to omit reference to both the navigation and the fisheries issues, Clay had sought to win the New Englander's agreement to terminate the negotiations unless both matters were satisfactorily clarified.[29]

Clay's agitation for United States recognition of the Latin-American republics has been generally interpreted as a move dictated by personal pique that he had not been chosen, rather than Adams, to direct the foreign affairs of the Monroe administration. The vehemence of Clay's argument may have been fired by such considerations, but his commitment to the cause had been expressed as early as January 1813, when he had asserted in Congress that, except for their possible bearing on the United states, European affairs did not interest him half as much as did "the movements in South America." Three years later, when Congress was considering a motion to reduce the army, Clay had warned of the contingency that "it might be proper to aid the people of South-America in regard to the establishment of their Independence." In January 1817, still before Monroe had assumed office and some nine months before Adams had taken over the duties of secretary of state, Clay had protested against American neutrality policy, which he saw as discountenancing aid to the rebellious South American colonies.[30]

While the commercial interests of Clay's Ohio Valley constituents encouraged support for ties to the emerging states, the Kentuckian founded his rationale much more broadly, upon the political ideology of his Jeffersonian background. In a major address in March 1818, calling for extension of diplomatic recognition to the Argentine provinces, he had defensively pointed to the "valuable acquisition" of such a neighbor "in a commercial point of view"; but his emphasis had centered upon patriotic linkage of the revolt to the United States experience. Voicing the conception that Jefferson had earlier expressed and that Monroe was later to incorporate in his Doctrine, Clay had argued that the governments of the independent Spanish-American states "would obey the laws of the system of the New World . . . in contradistinction to that of Europe." They, like the United States, had challenged the European "principle of legitimacy"; they had a common stake in winning recognition of the right to self government. By May 1821 Speaker Clay was urging "that a sort of counterpoise to the Holy Alliance should be formed in the two Americas . . . to operate by the force of example and by moral influence, that here a rallying point and an assylum [sic] should exist for freemen and for freedom."[31]

The geographical nationalism that Secretary of State Adams had delimited in his Fourth-of-July address but a few weeks later marked a fundamental difference in their outlooks; the pronouncement had been intended to illuminate that distinction. The Kentuckian had subsequently spoken out in sympathy for the constitutional movements in Spain and Italy and for the Greeks in revolt against Turkey, as well as in warning should the European powers forcibly intervene to restore to Spain her former American colonies. He set no hemispheric boundary to his projection of American interest in republican government:

> It was evident, after the overthrow of Bonaparte, that the alliance by which that event was unexpectedly brought about, would push the principle of *legitimacy,* a softer and covered name for despotism, to the utmost extent. . . . And if we, the greatest offender of all against the principle of legitimacy, had not been brought under their jurisdiction . . . , we owed the exemption to our distance from Europe, and to the known bravery of our countrymen. But who can say . . . , how long this exemption will continue?[32]

For Clay, national defense held an ideologic dimension that conceded nothing to the New Englander's isolationism in pragmatic relevance to the safety of the republic.

As the fourth candidate with a cohesive following, Clay confronted a difficult choice when the election was thrown before the House of Representatives in February 1825. Should he support the nominee of the party caucus, Crawford, who had been stricken with paralysis in the autumn of 1823 and was still seriously disabled? Clay had regarded the Georgian as a confidante and adviser during the Ghent negotiations. The Kentuckian had seriously considered Crawford's pretensions over those of Monroe for the presidency in 1816. During the intervening years, however, their paths had parted. Clay's ultimate endorsement of Monroe's candidacy, his personal ties with members of Crawford's local political opposition, and his efforts to expand internal improvements, in conflict with the Georgian's retrenchment program, had marked the separation. Although by the summer of 1824 uncertain of his own success in the presidential election and convinced that Crawford could not long survive, Clay had spurned second place on the latter's ticket.

As a westerner, should he then support Jackson, who had divided with him the regional vote? For Clay and his partisans, personal rivalry was heightened by realization that a sectional claimant might not succeed to the presidency in 1828 if a westerner had already achieved that recognition. But Clay's opposition to Jackson had deeper roots, dating at least from 1819, when as Speaker of the House of Representatives, the Kentuckian had led congressional criticism of the general's violent assertion of military over civil considerations during the Seminole campaign. Jackson's subsequent manifestations of distaste for civic duties had not lessened Clay's conviction that the Tennessean lacked serious regard for responsible government. Arguments, which Clay was to voice until the end of his life, concerning the damage that military predilections threatened to republican institutions explained his rejection of the western candidate.

Reviewing the alternatives upon reaching Washington in December 1824, Clay found the decision "painful," "only a choice of evils." He considered the state of Crawford's health a decisive bar to the latter's election. Toward either of the viable candidates, Jackson or Adams, Clay held "strong personal objections."[33] Although he had repudiated the effort by his Ghent colleague and political friend Jonathan Russell to revive in 1822 the bitterness of the Ghent differences with Adams, Clay had then appeared in print with a statement that he would publish his own version of those transactions "at some future period," when his motives could not be misinterpreted. Because no further elaboration of Clay's stand had appeared, western opponents of Adams still magnified the dispute. Adams's belated recognition of Latin-American independence and his espousal, in the Monroe Doctrine, of views that Clay had long promulgated had not silenced western criticism of the boundary settlement in the Florida-purchase treaty. The years of bitter personal attack by Speaker Clay upon Secretary of State Adams had contributed to a sectional basis of opposition to the New Englander, which the Kentuckian must now reevaluate and perhaps confront.

Clay had, in fact, made his decision months earlier. William Plumer, Jr., recorded in his diary in June 1824 that Clay expressed unwillingness to support Jackson because of the threat to democracy posed by the general's military role. While the wish may have fathered the thought as reported by Plumer, a Federalist supporter of Adams, the Jacksonite Thomas Hart Benton also testified that, given the alternatives of Jackson or Adams, Clay had voiced his preference for the latter in October, weeks before the results of the state election were known. Clay's criticism of Adams had subsided over the past two years, since the Monroe pronouncement and the extension of diplomatic recognition to the Latin-American states. Robert P. Letcher, Clay's Kentucky confidante and political friend, discussed with the secretary of state in mid December the Russell publication concerning the differences at Ghent. While Adams still believed that Clay had inspired the attack, the New Englander responded that he had repelled the charges successfully and that he harbored no resentment.[34]

On January 1, Clay requested an interview for clarification of their views. Adams described their meeting eight days later:

> Mr. Clay . . . spent the evening with me in a long conversation explanatory of the past and prospective of the future. . . . He wished me, as far as I might think proper, to satisfy him with regard to some principles of great public importance, but without any personal considerations for himself. In the question to come before the House between General Jackson, Mr. Crawford, and myself, he had no hesitation in saying that his preference would be for me.[35]

This terse diary entry, the only available record of the Adams-Clay "arrangement," makes evident that it rested upon issue, not patronage, agreement. Over the next four years, both men clearly compromised their previous conceptual outlooks. In regard to domestic policy, Adams was not yet ready to stand decisively in favor of extended protection for home manufactures. As late as December 22 he had assured the Virginian James Barbour that he, Adams, was "satisfied with the tariff as now established" and, indeed, should "incline rather to reduce than to increase it."[36] In regard to foreign policy, Adams also held a far-more-restricted view than did Clay of the boundaries of national self-interest. Yet these two, more than any of the other candidates, shared commitment to a harmonizing programmatic base. For Crawford, Calhoun, or Jackson the public weal that had emerged from the postwar experience was becoming increasingly localized. For Adams and Clay, on the other hand, it was expanding beyond the traditional partialities of personal and regional outlook to a broader framework of nationalism—a nationalism that was to be fostered in foreign relations by exploiting the initiatives of the Monroe Doctrine and in domestic policy by developing the linkages of home-market expansion. Lacking Monroe's sense of constitutional restriction, the New Englander and the Kentuckian embraced these programs as more than a mere compromise of disparate sectional concerns. Adams and Clay sought an integration of the heterogeneity so as to promote a general welfare transcending particularity. They looked to an American System, abroad and at home, to provide a positive thrust to the course of change.

Whether such intentions could be translated into effective action depended, however, upon more than a harmony of conceptualization. Success required that the leadership goals be translated to a coalition of followers at local levels, where perspectives were more limited. There, instabilities that had entered into the support of either leader would be magnified. While attacks focused upon either must be shared, the dangers of fragmentation were enhanced. And even before the election in the House of Representatives, the assaults had begun, with charges of "bargain and corruption" challenging formulation of the alliance.

Moreover, Clay's endorsement could not alone resolve the issue of the election. In the electoral college, Jackson had won the vote of eleven states to Adams's seven. With Clay's support, Adams might gain the votes of Kentucky, Missouri, and Ohio and perhaps that of Louisiana, where he already held two of the five electors; but he would remain two delegations short of the thirteen requisite for a majority. As the House members recorded their choice on February 9, considerations that bore little relevance to personality or to governmental program carried Illinois and Maryland from Jackson to Adams and held for the New Englander the wavering vote of New York. Clay's influence was strong in all these states, but Adams himself weighted the balance.

Illinois' lame-duck congressman, Daniel Pope Cook, son-in-law of the Calhounite Ninian Edwards, was no friend of Clay's. He believed that the Speaker had appointed a hostile congressional committee to investigate Edwards's involvement in the "A.B. Controversy." Adams, however, had publicly aligned himself in protest against the political ostracism of the Illinoisans. As Calhoun's supporters generally threw their support to Jackson in the presidential canvassing, Cook reacted against their heavy-handed pressure. He gave the New Englander the vote of Illinois.

The crucial tests centered among the representatives of New York and Maryland. In the former delegation Adams's electoral preponderance—twenty-six of the thirty-six votes—was threatened by a division that assured him of support by only seventeen of the thirty-four representatives, leaving the possibility that consolidation of the remainder could produce a tie. Among Maryland's congressmen, where Adams commanded only three of nine votes, four of the outstanding ones were equivocal. George E. Mitchell, a Jacksonite, had pledged to follow the choice of his district, which had narrowly supported Adams in the electoral count. Peter Little, a friend of both Adams and Clay, on the other hand, found himself bound to follow the heavy mandate of his district in support of Jackson. Henry Warfield, a Clay supporter, and John Lee, a Jacksonite, were both Federalists, strongly concerned about the prospects for their fellow party men. In this complex situation, Adams's renunciation of the pattern of Federalist proscription that had prevailed for the past quarter-century proved to be decisive.

Daniel Webster, a Massachusetts Federalist and former Calhounite, performed a major role in effecting this commitment and thus emerged as a central figure in the political operation of the Adams presidency. During a lengthy discussion on January 29, Clay had mentioned to Adams that Webster held "some jealousy" of those upon whom the New England candidate appeared to rely. When Adams thereupon stressed his "high opinion" of Webster's abilities and voiced an "earnest desire to conciliate him," a meeting was arranged. There Webster obtained approval of a draft letter to Warfield, containing a statement of "full confidence, that Mr. Adams administration . . . [would] be just and liberal, towards Federalists as towards others. . . ." Adams hastened to explain that the statement must not be interpreted as a pledge to appoint a Federalist in his cabinet but agreed that he approved "altogether the general spirit" of Webster's note and "should consider it as one of the objects nearest to . . . [his] heart to bring the whole people of the Union to harmonize together." Subsequently expressing similar views directly to Warfield and to Stephen Van Rensselaer, a New York Crawfordite of Federalist antecedents, Adams won the votes of both.[37]

Cautiously as they were phrased, such assurances nevertheless posed complications for the organization of Adams's administration. The straight-laced New Englander found them an embarrassment, as were also the circumstances of his election. Discussing his situation at the end of the year, he viewed it as "the summit of laudable, or at least blameless, worldly ambition" but noted that he had not been elevated "in a manner satisfactory to pride or to just desire; not by the unequivocal suffrages of a majority of the people; with perhaps two-thirds of the whole people adverse to the actual result."[38] From the outset he was inextricably enmeshed in the partisan pressures of a minority presidency.

3

ORGANIZING
THE ADMINISTRATION

After two successive sleepless nights, Adams entered upon the presidency. He was aware from the outset that his administration must confront a determined opposition. Beginning and ending his Inaugural Address by devoutly committing his efforts to divine guidance, he begged also for human tolerance and support:

> Less possessed of your confidence in advance than any of my predecessors, I am deeply conscious of the prospect that I shall stand more and oftener in need of your indulgence. Intentions upright and pure, a heart devoted to the welfare of our country, and the unceasing application of all the faculties allotted to me to her service are all the pledges that I can give for the faithful performance of the arduous duties I am to undertake.[1]

The address promised additionally a continuation of the programs of his predecessor—peace with preparedness for defensive war, justice to other nations while preserving the rights of his own, support for freedom and equal rights wherever proclaimed, promotion of the work of civilizing the Indians, "equal protection to all the great interests of the nation," action on internal improvements "within the limits of the constitutional power of the Union," and, withal, payment of the national debt as quickly as possible. He acknowledged that some differences persisted concerning the congressional power to legislate on internal improvements, but he reminded his audience that Monroe had "emphatically urged" the topic in his inaugural remarks. The new president hoped that by "friendly, patient, and persevering deliberation all constitutional objections . . . [would] ultimately be removed."[2]

Adams had pegged his pronouncements to a program of continuity, not change. He proposed to build on the established foundation of neonationalism. It was not Monroe or Monroe's program that occasioned the New Englander's uneasiness. In mid January, prior to the House's vote deciding the election, Adams had sought and obtained Monroe's pledge of "friendly counsel after the event. . . ."[3] The two men had spent together most of Monroe's last day in office; the retiring president had participated fully in the inauguration ceremony; and the two leaders had extended mutual felicitations during the postinaugural festivities.

The threat to the administration, a menace that was already well developed by Inauguration Day, came from the disappointed proponents of Calhoun, Crawford, and Jackson. Adams's suspicions of Calhoun's motives and machinations were deep-seated. They dated at least from the Missouri debates and had grown bitter during the last two years of the presidential canvass. The New Englander's preference for the vice-presidency had been Jackson, not Calhoun. Adams's supporters had endorsed the South Carolinian only after the general's growing popularity had made clear that he would not be satisfied with the second place, and they had explained their distasteful endorsement penitently.

A letter attributed to William Wirt and forwarded by Henry Wheaton, both Calhoun supporters, had proved decisive in winning for the South Carolinian the New England endorsement but also had pointed up the alternative sources of opposition to Adams. The writer argued that if Calhoun were to become vice-president, the North would be able to resist a southern candidate for the presidency. On the other hand, a New England division on the issue of the second place could not forestall the South Carolinian's election but, by splitting the friends of Adams and Calhoun, would surrender political dominance to Crawfordites: "This is their game. The defeat of Mr. Adams is their principal concern. . . . It must of course, force them into the ranks of Jackson whom they hate next to Mr. Adams & the Devil."[4]

By refusing to split their electoral ticket during the complicated maneuvering of the New York campaign in November, the Adams forces had defeated the Crawfordite–Van Buren coalition. The "caucus party" was not "prostrate," Joseph Blunt informed Adams, but the repercussions of that bitterly fought campaign ran deep. The *"national,"* or caucus, candidate had "not been able to obtain *one* vote, out of his native & adopted states, except by management or bargain," Blunt continued. "But through organization & good understanding," and by supporting Jackson, Crawford's supporters had brought about Adams's loss of the New Jersey and Maryland electoral vote and had threatened to transfer to Jackson their strength in New York. Clinton and Calhoun backers had also at that time joined in the coalition for Jackson, Blunt reported—not to elect the general, but to reduce the vote for Adams.[5]

The coalescence of political rivals was under way. Adams had seen it in January, in the developing coolness of Samuel L. Southard of New Jersey, Monroe's secretary of the navy; in the varying reports on the role of Ambrose Spencer of New York; in the equivocal stance of Richard M. Johnson of Kentucky—all of whom were former Calhoun backers professing friendship for Adams. Repeated rumors had told of the growing support for Jackson among Adams's old political allies, the Clintonians. The public announcement on January 24 that Clay and the majority of the Kentucky and Ohio delegations would support the New Englander had brought the confusion to a focus. As Adams recognized: "This immediately produced an approximation of the Calhoun, Crawford, and Jackson partisans, and will effectually knit the coalition of the South with Pennsylvania."[6]

Intrigue, charges and countercharges of corruption, this formed the political climate out of which Adams had attained the presidency. He knew the weakness of his position—almost to the last he had anticipated defeat. His inaugural bid for unity and support, his pleas and those of his followers that the administration be given a chance to develop a program committed to the national good, masked an awareness that the vultures were gathering.

Adams's dependence on the alliance with Clay brought with it an opposition that had already effected defeat for the Kentuckian and now served as the rallying point for coordinated assault. Calhoun's backers viewed Clay as the only other candidate whose age would render him available for the succession eight years hence. Western Jacksonites saw the Kentuckian as the personification of their regionalized rivalries. New York Crawfordites, smarting from the failure of Clay's supporters to carry the Regency nominees over Adams, a defeat that once again had marked Clinton's triumph over Van Buren, translated their localized concerns into the framework of the only established national party structure. Hostility to Clay was the basis on which all could unite.

That Clay became Adams's secretary of state hastened the solidification of opposition but probably did not alter its course of development. Crawford subsequently professed to have "approved" Clay's vote in the House election but to have "disapproved" his acceptance of the cabinet post; and the Old Republicans generally appear to have remained divided on the Adams election at least until the news of Clay's appointment. By December of 1825, however, Adams's program and Federalist appointments had completed the rupture.[7]

Calhoun's friends, on the other hand, had reacted vigorously to the mere suspicion that an Adams-Clay alliance had been formed. Three days before the public announcement of support for Adams by Clay and the latter's friends in Kentucky and Ohio, Daniel Pope Cook had reported to Adams that there was heavy pressure from Calhoun's backers—Samuel Ingham, Jacob C. Isacks, and George McDuffie—to bring the Illinoisan into Jackson's camp. According to Cook, McDuffie had asserted that "there was no doubt that an arrangement had been made between Mr. Clay and & Mr. Adams for the former to transfer his influence to the latter and that for doing so he was to be made Secretary of State. . . ." McDuffie had further warned that "a tremendous storm" would be "raised in the West if Jackson were defeated by the Western votes in Congress," that Adams "could not sustain his administration" and "would go out, to a certainty, at the end of four years—." Ingham had repeated the threat and predicted that Adams's election "would produce two parties in this country," with a unified opposition to the administration, born of consolidated Southern hostility to Adams on the slavery issue, Western indignation in behalf of Jackson, and the backing of "Clinton in New York & the state of Pennsylvania"—an opposition "so powerful that it must break him [Adams] down."[8]

Jacksonians had laid the groundwork for opposition to anyone other than the "Hero" a year and a half before the election. Eaton's "Wyoming" Letters had set the tune. On 14 October 1824, Duff Green's St. Louis Enquirer had reiterated the themes—hailing Jackson's republican purity and inflexibility of character, lauding the Tennessean as the candidate "of the people," and projecting his election by their voice as the method to forestall the machinations by bargain and intrigue of the "leading men" in Congress. Two separate letters to Adams from Pennsylvanians on January 27 had conveyed warnings: "Clay is deeply very deeply hated," wrote an anonymous "Sincere Friend" from Philadelphia, "and if you succeed by his coming to you I fear it will go so far as to lead to nothing else than a civil war." Edward Patchell, of Pittsburgh, spoke of the dishonor of "crawling into the Presidential chair through the base intrigue of corrupt polatitions [sic], to gratify the revenge of their disappointed ambition (I mean the friends of Henry Clay, & Wm. H. Crawford) for it is generally believed that a secret combination of this kind is now a carrying on in Washington City." Both correspondents, with singular harmony from such widely separated points on a given date, had called upon Adams to withdraw from the House contest in favor of Jackson.[9]

The capstone of this preelection maneuvering to counter Clay's endorsement of Adams was the publication in the *Columbian Observer* (Philadelphia) on January 28 of a letter, dated three days earlier, by a member of Pennsylvania's congressional delegation, accusing Clay of giving his support in return for the cabinet post as secretary of state. In a discussion on the following evening, Adams and Clay apparently agreed that this "blustering" must be met. Accordingly, on January 30 the Kentuckian requested the publication, in the *National Intelligencer* (Washington), of a "Card" denouncing the author of the letter as "a base and infamous calumniator, a dastard and a liar," who, if identified, would be called upon to respond "to all the laws which govern and regulate the conduct of men of honor."[10]

When George Kremer, a political unknown serving his first term as representative of a central Pennsylvania farming constituency, professed to be the author of the letter, Clay realized that a duel would appear ridiculous. He was convinced that Eaton had drafted the document, and in an address to his constituents and an exchange of correspondence with Eaton some weeks later, the Kentuckian attempted unsuccessfully to elicit such an admission. Kremer himself, on February 4, explained that he had "never intended to charge Mr. Clay with corruption or dishonor in his intended vote for Mr. Adams as President, or that he had transfered, or could transfer, the votes or interest of his friends," that the "letter was never intended to convey the idea given to it."[11]

He nevertheless backed away from testifying before a congressional investigating committee, which was established at Clay's urging on February 3. That body, selected by ballot and, at Clay's request, excluding his supporters, reported six days later that without such testimony it had no reason to pursue the matter. William Henry Harrison, charged by the absent Clay to safeguard his interests, subsequently explained that while he, Harrison, had not heard the proceedings, he had been assured that Clay had been exonerated. On motion of the committee chairman, the Crawfordite Philip Pendleton Barbour, the report was tabled, with provision for publication of the papers, including a statement by Kremer challenging the constitutionality of the investigation and consigning judgment of the issue to "the American people, or the ordinary tribunals of the country. . . ."[12] The presidential canvass of 1828 was under way.

Adams did not formally offer the cabinet post to Clay until February 11, but both men had been considering such a nomination for weeks. As early as December 5, Joseph E. Sprague had commented to Adams on "the secret intrigues of Mr. Calhouns friends" and had suggested that Clay's aid might be sought: "If Clay makes proper concessions for his letter his appointment to an important department by you would secure him Northern influence" for the future. Sprague anticipated, further, that Clay's selection "would secure to the administration strong western support & conciliate the friends of Mr. Crawford in a degree—."[13]

How closely Clay was identified with the efforts toward a rapprochement with Adams as promoted by his fellow Kentuckian and Washington messmate Robert P. Letcher has never been ascertained. Adams's diary records that he met with Letcher repeatedly between December 10 and January 1, that they discussed past disagreements between Clay and the New Englander, and that Letcher made clear on December 17 the willingness of both Clay and his friends to support Adams "if he [Clay] could thereby serve himself" and if his friends "could *know* that he would have a prominent share in the Administration. . . ." "But," Adams concluded, "Letcher did not profess to have any authority from Clay for what he said, and he made no definite propositions."[14]

Adams's sardonic reporting of these meetings does not belie the ample evidence that Clay had, months earlier, determined to support Adams, given the alternatives confronted in the House of Representatives. More serious criticism has been fixed upon the assumption that the Kentucky congressional delegation, acting in defiance of instructions by the state legislature that their votes be given to Jackson, were pressured into endorsing Adams under the assurance that Clay would receive the cabinet office. Since news of the Kentucky resolutions of instruction did not reach Washington until mid January, Clay's commitment to Adams and Letcher's negotiations, however related to it, had already transpired at least a week earlier. Francis Johnson subsequently testified that, at the caucus of the Kentucky delegation which discussed the predicament posed by the late-arriving instructions, Clay confined his statement to an announcement of his own intentions.[15] As a representative of a congressional district, not of the state legislature, he believed that he was free to express the will of his constituents, who never, then or later, repudiated his leadership.

The choice was manifestly the decision of individual members as they saw their interests and commitments. Francis Preston Blair, even after aligning with the Jacksonites, conceded that he had never seen "criminality in the members of Ky. ascertaining who were to be Adams' counsellors before they voted for him. . . . The public . . . would never have considered Such a care of the western interests by the Western members a corrupt bargain but for the mystery that was [hung] around it—.''[16] That "mystery" was the carefully developed ploy of defeated politicians.

The situation warned the incoming president of the difficulties that he would confront in organizing the cabinet. In a lengthy conversation with his friend George Sullivan on February 11, before the secretaryship of the State Department was offered to Clay, Adams was informed that the Calhounites recommended Joel R. Poinsett for the post and that if Clay were named, ''a determined opposition to the Administration would be organized from the outset; that the opposition would use the name of General Jackson as its head; that the Administration would be supported only by the New England States—New York being doubtful, the West much divided, and strongly favoring Jackson, as a Western man, Virginia already in opposition, and all the South decidedly adverse.'' Later the same day, still before he had proffered the appointment, Adams consulted President Monroe on the proposal. The chief executive, expressing willingness to give his opinions as desired, apparently voiced no objection in this instance, although he could not have been unaware of Clay's role in the election. Subsequently, when the Kentuckian had already accepted the position, Monroe did warn of the dangers of public criticism.[17]

For a week, Clay pondered his decision. On February 17 Adams's friend Robert Walsh, Jr., commented to Alexander H. Everett that he did not think Clay could ''accept, *now*, of any appointment after all the noise made about bargains.'' Walsh had apparently also written to Clay about his dissatisfaction with the latter's response to the Kremer attack. On February 18 Clay announced to Walsh and to his own Virginia friend Francis Taliferro Brooke that he had ''just communicated'' his decision to Adams. ''They will abuse me for it,'' Clay observed. ''They would have abused me more if I had declined it.'' The decisive considerations, as he elaborated them, were that for him to decline the position would have accomplished ''the very object of propagating the calumny''; that, conscious of his pure intentions, he should not magnify the force of the assault; that he could not, having contributed to Adams's election, refuse to enter the administration; that he was needed there to provide administration ''balance''; and that his ''own section could not be dissatisfied'' by his placement where his ''services might have a more extended usefulness.''[18]

Clay's allusion to the regional ''balance'' of the administration pointed up one of the president's organizational goals. In his Inaugural

Address, Adams dismissed as "transitory" the old "collisions of party spirit," originating "in speculative opinions or in different views of administrative policy." The "candid and the just," he asserted, must now admit that both the great political parties had "contributed splendid talents, spotless integrity, ardent patriotism, and disinterested sacrifices to the formation and administration of this Government, and that both . . . required a liberal indulgence for a portion of human infirmity and error." Ten years of peace, however, had now "assuaged" the old political animosities. More permanent and more dangerous, in his view, were the new disagreements "founded on geographical divisions, adverse interests of soil, climate, and modes of domestic life." To counteract such diversities he looked to the operations of the "General Government."[19]

Adams hoped to continue the focus upon national unity which had been promoted by the Monroe administration, not only in program but also in personnel. He invited the members of Monroe's cabinet to remain at their posts—Crawford as secretary of the Treasury, Samuel L. Southard as secretary of the navy, and William Wirt as attorney general. The postmaster general, John McLean, not yet a cabinet officer, was also asked to stay on. Adams's old role as secretary of state would be filled by Clay; and Vice-President Calhoun's position as secretary of war would, Adams proposed, pass to Jackson. Politically the Titans would all have a role—Crawford, Jackson, and Clay directly; and Calhoun through Southard and McLean. Geographically, New England would be linked by Adams with the West through Jackson and Clay; with the South through Crawford and Wirt; and with the Middle States through Southard and McLean.

Adams's design was broken at two key points, however. Crawford, who was offered the Treasury post on February 10, declined it on the following day. On February 16, Adams, before he had invited Jackson to take over the War Department, was advised that the general "would take in ill part the offer. . . ." Meanwhile the Calhounites, besides objecting to the appointment of Clay, urged that McLean be shifted to the War Department. James Gallatin, who sought for his father, Albert, the nomination to the State Department, proposed that Clay be placed in War, where, in view of Gallatin's foreign birth and Crawford's ill health, Clay might yet, through promotion of internal improvements, garner support for succession to the presidency. As the personal animosities and rivalries took shape, Adams concluded: "I am at least forewarned. It is not in man that walketh to direct his steps."[20]

On February 21 he offered the War Department post to James Barbour of Virginia, a Crawfordite who, since 1820, had been identified as an opponent of protective tariffs and federal aid to internal improvements. During the period of electioneering in December and January, Adams on two occasions had discussed with Barbour "confidentially" the probable Virginia vote and had been informed that, while the state's first choice would be Crawford, Adams was "their next preference," the "determination at all events [would be] to vote for another than a mere military leader." On the basis of Adams's assurances that his goal would be to seek *"conciliation,* and not *collision,"* within the country, Barbour accepted the cabinet nomination with alacrity.[21]

Crawford's rejection of the Treasury Department position also occasioned difficulty. Gallatin, too, declined the nomination, although he renounced any intention, by his action, of expressing opposition to the administration. Calhounite pressure in behalf of Langdon Cheves for the position was countered by James W. McCullok, a Baltimore merchant and banker, who warned that the South Carolinian was "incompetent, unworthy, impracticable [*sic*], unjust and *grossly* ambitious." Adams's friend Walsh thought that Cheves "would do well for the Treasury; but he [had] deserted the cause of Adams for that of Clay, & then allowed himself to speak disparagingly & acrimoniously of Adams."[22]

The president resolved the dilemma of the Treasury appointment by recalling from London Richard Rush of Philadelphia, a generally well-liked Republican, whose absence from the country as minister to Britain since 1817 had kept him apart from the bitter campaigning of the election period. Rush was a capable lawyer who had had experience from 1811 to 1814 as comptroller of the Treasury and had worked with Adams effectively as a diplomat. He shared the New Englander's understanding of the self-interest of British policy and his commitment to a nationalistic outlook on American concerns. Friendship with Mathew Carey, a Philadelphia publicist, and with Friedrich List, a German economist—both strong proponents of protective tariffs—stimulated the secretary's attachment to the conceptualization of the American System. Rush was to prove as ardent as Clay in its promulgation.

Southard, Wirt, and McLean remained in their former positions. Adams knew them to be capable administrators. Barring proof of incompetence, he saw no cause for change. Born in New Jersey and educated at Princeton, Southard had begun his legal career in Virginia, where he had studied under Clay's good friend Judge Francis Taliferro Brooke, and had retained strong ties with the Taliferro family, to which James Monroe was related. After five years on the New Jersey bench, Southard had entered the United States Senate in 1821 and had been named secretary of the navy in 1823. He had preferred Calhoun as a presidential candidate, had expressed appreciation of Jackson's "many high qualities," and had been critical of the pretensions of Adams, Clay, and Crawford. Indeed, Southard held strong predispositions against Clay, for he believed that the Kentuckian had appropriated, without acknowledgment, his draft of resolutions for settlement of the second Missouri crisis in 1821 and that Clay had opposed the Southard reappointment. Yet despite these possible grounds for friction and Adams's personal awareness of the navy secretary's support for Calhoun, the president held to his assurances, expressed prior to the House vote on the election, that Southard should continue in the Navy Department and should remain an influential counsellor.[23]

Southard, on his part, maintained that he entered the administration "with a perfect understanding that it was to be a continuation of Mr. Monroe's; founded on the same principles, governed by the same policy." At the end of the first year he asserted that he had "seen nothing" to raise doubt about its being so and pledged continued support. Even the relationship with Clay appears to have been cordial, both socially and officially. By January 1828, Southard commented on the Kentuckian: "I have been taught by my intercourse with him, to place a high estimate on his talents and worth."[24]

Wirt, born in Maryland, had served before the Virginia bar for more than thirty years and from 1808 to 1810 had been a member of the Virginia House of Delegates. He had entered Monroe's cabinet with an understanding that he would be permitted to remain in private practice, and he continued such activity at Baltimore and Annapolis throughout the Adams administration. Although hard-working and punctilious in the performance of his cabinet responsibilities, he was not an active participant in either the program development or the political course of the administration. Wirt professed "a total exemption from that canker, political ambition!" Nearing the conclusion of his service, he noted that he had "always been too fond of ease and quiet to have any taste for political contention." That in which he had engaged had "been rather forced" upon him than sought. "And as for what are called political honours, I would as soon put on the poisoned shirt of Hercules."[25]

McLean, on the other hand, was a politician; he was generally viewed as an active Calhoun-Jacksonsite partisan in the midst of the administration. Adams's reactions to that difficult situation reveal much concerning his handling of the political aspects of the presidency. Despite his longstanding personal suspicions of Calhoun's activities, the president was slow to recognize the role that McLean filled in supporting an opposition under the patronage dispensation within his charge. Even when convinced of such operations, the chief executive retained in office the enemy whom he regarded as an able administrator.

As early as March 23, probably on the basis of information supplied by Clay's editorial henchman, Charles Hammond of Cincinnati, the president questioned McLean about reports that Maj. Henry Lee, whom the postmaster general had brought into his office, was writing editorial pieces for the *Washington Gazette*, which were highly critical of Clay, Adams, and their alliance. After McLean had relayed the inquiry to Lee, the latter denied any affiliation with the journal, although he conceded that during the closing weeks of the election he had preferred Jackson. In September, Wilson Allen of Virginia advised Clay that the editors of the *Enquirer* (Richmond, Va.) condemned the Lee appointment. Allen himself argued that it constituted the most serious grounds for attack on the administration and also warned that Lee was supplying opprobrious editorial comment to the *Gazette*. Again Adams relayed the reports to McLean but took no further action.[26] Two years later, Lee finally resigned his post and moved to the "Hermitage," where he devoted his talents exclusively to Jackson's campaign.

Meanwhile, protest mounted concerning McLean's patronage appointments and other political activities centering in the postal service. In November 1825 a young friend of Clay's sought the vacant postmastership at Jackson, Tennessee, but found that it went, instead, to Robert Johnson Chester, a staunch Jacksonian. Joseph Ficklin, insolvent as proprietor of the *Kentucky Gazette* (Lexington), had transferred the journal in 1824 to John M. McCalla, a leader of the Relief party and a Jacksonian, and had then received the appointment as postmaster, a coincidence that was locally attributed to "bargain & management." One Clay supporter reported that Ficklin forbade "the Post riders from takeing any bundles or papers or handbills suspected to be in favor of the administration." Apparently in response to Clay's inquiry on this matter, Thomas Smith, editor of the *Kentucky Reporter* (Lexington), conceded that charges against Ficklin's administration of his office "might be explained, perhaps refuted," but contended that the postmaster served as "the grand pivot" in disseminating intelligence for the Jacksonians throughout Kentucky. Jefferson would not have permitted such an opponent "to remain in office a single day," Smith argued. If the president did not himself see the need for Ficklin's dismissal, "a representation . . . must be made."[27]

Adams's friends, too, protested McLean's appointments. Josiah Bunce, the deputy postmaster of Litchfield, Connecticut, complained bitterly in November 1825 that although he and the state's congressional delegation had been informed the previous spring that he would replace the incumbent, who was about to be removed for intemperance, the office had been given, instead, to the incumbent's son. McLean explained that Federalist charges of malfeasance against Bunce, which the postmaster admitted he had not investigated, had determined him to seek an alternative who was independent of either faction. Expostulating to the president, Bunce claimed that he carried the backing of Governor Oliver Wolcott, an Adams elector, and three hundred of his fellow townsmen. If such support did not influence McLean, the president should intervene, Bunce insisted.[28]

At Philadelphia a more serious concern developed during the spring of 1826, when John Binns, the administration's editorial voice in that critical center, lamented that he had been denied the printing of the post office, under the Calhounite-Jacksonian Richard Bache. A year later, Adams, taking note of repeated criticism against Bache, questioned McLean on the matter but accepted the explanation that "there was nothing proved against him [Bache] upon which the removal of him could be justified." As Binns assailed the postmaster editorially, Bache responded with physical assault, and the incident came before the courts. Adams then suggested that Bache's conduct "might deserve further consideration" but again deferred to McLean's explanation. The postmaster general finally removed Bache in 1828 for continued delinquency in his accounts; in his place, however, McLean appointed Thomas Sergeant, Bache's brother-in-law and publishing partner. The latter arrangement, which kept the printing patronage with the opposition press, produced, as Adams recognized, "an instantaneous and most violent fermentation among the friends of the Administration. . . ." The president's relationship with his postmaster general had reached a point of "great trouble."[29]

Somewhat smugly, Adams had at first dismissed complaints against McLean as the consequence of the postmaster general's partiality for Calhoun and dislike of Clay. Since McLean was "an able and efficient officer," the president was prepared to make "every allowance for the peculiarity of his situation. . . ." The appointment of Sergeant, however, occasioned a lengthy confrontation. Adams accused the postmaster general of acting "disingenuously" and demanded a "candid exposition of facts. . . ." The interview terminated, nevertheless, with assurances from Adams that he "still confided" in McLean, although the latter "might in this affair have been misled. . . ." The president yet hoped that the episode "would ultimately be satisfactorily explained."[30]

Meanwhile, the Jacksonians were chortling. Sam Houston, who was urging that there be an investigation of the activities of the Nashville postmaster, John P. Erwin, a brother of Clay's son-in-law, advised the general in February 1827: "The Postmaster General has pursued a manly course, and will do it, at the hazard of his place." John Wilson Campbell, an Ohio congressman, had previously assured McLean: "Should Mr. C. be quiet you have nothing to fear."[31]

But Clay was not quiet. In May 1828 he "very earnestly" urged that McLean be removed. Adams now viewed the situation with less equanimity: "The evidences of McLean's double-dealing, and the treachery to the cause of the Administration, have multiplied upon me till it would require the credulity of January in the tale to believe him honest or faithful." Learning that Bache's defalcation would amount to more than $25,000; that Ingham, as his surety, had been released from responsibility on the bond; that the postmaster general had awarded the highly profitable contract for transporting the mail between Philadelphia and New York to the Jacksonian James Reeside; and that Reeside, contrary to law, had been given an advance payment on his service, the president was convinced of McLean's "deep and treacherous duplicity." Despite protestations of loyalty to the administration, McLean had for three years been "using the extensive patronage of his office in undermining it. . . ." He was a "double-dealer," Adams exclaimed: " 'His words are smoother than butter, but war is in his heart.' "[32]

Yet with the election now at hand, the president believed it "impolitic" to remove the postmaster general. He could "fix upon no positive act that would justify" that course. Adams's preelection assurances to Webster had pledged that he "should exclude no person for political opinions, or for personal opposition," and that his "great object would be to break up the remnant of old party distinctions, and bring the whole people together in sentiment as much as possible."[33] This maxim was not confined, under Adams's interpretation, to the old problem of Federalist proscription; it stood as a general rule against partisan removals unless there was demonstrated failure in work performance. The postmaster general retained his post until Jackson assumed the presidency and named him to the Supreme Court.

Adams's strictures against political considerations in appointment policy extended through the wide range of administrative staffing. Critics have pointed to his preelection assurance to William C. Bradley that Richard Law would not be removed from the collectorship at New London, Connecticut, as evidence of a willingness to bargain for votes; but the candidate's responsive pledge that he would "turn out no person for his conduct or opinions in relation to the election" was a statement of policy to which as president, he adhered with remarkable persistence.[34] Crawford's vast organization of customs collectors and inspectors, land office registers and receivers, and local bankers holding deposits of public funds retained appointment.

Continuity as a consideration for patronage had brought Monroe into conflict with the Senate during the closing weeks of his administration. Already, state governments, notably those of New York and Pennsylvania, had introduced a "spoils system" of distributing offices. Enactment of the Tenure of Office Act of 1820, which limited the terms of most middle- and upper-level federal officeholders, had laid the groundwork for such a practice nationally. Accordingly, the Senate had declined to consider renominations by Monroe for a large number of subordinate appointments when the commissions of incumbents would not expire before the end of his term. Adams, however, on the day after his inauguration, submitted four nominating messages, for the most part reappointing incumbents whom Monroe had previously recommended. The new president contended that the "principle of change or rotation in office at the expiration of these commissions . . . would make the Government a perpetual and unintermitting scramble for office." He had "determined to renominate every person against whom there was no complaint which would have warranted his removal. . . ."[35]

On this basis, as well as because of his own familiarity with their performance, Adams retained a large proportion of the diplomatic service. James Brown, Clay's brother-in-law, remained at Paris, more because of his experience and popularity in France than in recognition of the family connection or of Louisiana's support for Adams's candidacy. Henry Middleton, a former South Carolina governor and congressman and later a leader of the forces in that state who opposed Calhoun, continued as minister at St. Petersburg, where, since 1820, he had demonstrated abilities that, in Adams's regard, outweighed any political considerations. Richard C. Anderson of Kentucky, minister to Colombia, and his successor, Beaufort T. Watts, a South Carolina Calhounite, were also carry-over Monroe appointees, as were Condy Raguet, who was raised from consul as chargé to Rio de Janeiro; William Tudor, consul at Lima, later transferred to chargé at Rio; Samuel Larned, secretary of legation, later named chargé at Valparaiso; Thomas Ludlow Lee Brent, consul and chargé ad interim at Lisbon, subsequently appointed by Adams to the latter office; and John J. Appleton, secretary of legation at Madrid, sent first as commercial agent to Naples and subsequently as chargé to Stockholm.

Where personal favor was evident as a factor in Adams's appointments, they could usually be justified also on the basis of experience. Christopher Hughes, Jr., of Baltimore, who as a secretary to the Ghent Mission had been the friend of both Adams and Clay, was shifted from chargé at Stockholm to the slightly more prestigious post at The Hague, with some consideration for the wishes of his politically influential father-in-law, Senator Samuel Smith. Three other personal friends of the president's received appointments—Appleton, as noted; John M. Forbes, as chargé to the Provinces of the River Plate; and Alexander Hill Everett, as minister to Spain. All three were experienced in diplomatic service; only Everett, whose brother, Edward, was a Massachusetts congressman long identified as a Federalist, held strong political ties.

In the attempt to win multifactional support, Calhoun's friend Joel R. Poinsett, who had voted for Jackson in the House election for the presidency, was named minister to Mexico City. De Witt Clinton, governor of New York, was invited to assume the mission at London. When the latter declined the post, the president nominated Rufus King, the aged Hamiltonian Federalist, opponent of the War of 1812, and presidential candidate in 1816, who was now retiring from the United States Senate. That King was a bitter opponent of Clinton aggravated the already tense factional divisions in New York, a situation that Adams merely intensified when, as a countering move, he named the Clintonian and former Federalist Alfred Conkling to a district judgeship. The effort to deflect and ignore partisanship as a consideration in appointments not only left few plums for the president's adherents but, amidst the complex political instabilities of the period, frequently alienated sectors that he was seeking to woo. At midterm, however, Adams was still holding to his contention that in the matter of political appointments, "justice must sometimes make resistance and policy must often yield."[36]

Familial connections, as a patronage consideration, had a long history among governmental officeholders; and in relation to those who were already established, the president made no move to break the pattern. Joseph Nourse, register of the Treasury since 1789, had been joined in that office by his sons Michael, as chief clerk, and John, as a clerk, while another son, Charles J., was chief clerk in the War Department. Daniel Brent, who had become a clerk in the State Department under President Washington and continued in the post as chief clerk, was a cousin of George Graham, chief clerk in the War Department from 1813 to 1823 and since then commissioner of the General Land Office. Succession to office among kinsmen, which was common in consular appointments and was perhaps justified in that service on the basis of continuity of experience in a foreign locale, was not infrequent in domestic appointments as well.

Nepotism was, however, in Adams's view, a factor that precluded new appointments. On at least two occasions while serving in Monroe's cabinet, Adams had rejected nominations on this ground. During his own administration, he ignored recommendations for the appointment of James G. Forbes, brother of John M., as commercial agent at Havana and of John Clay, brother of Henry, as naval agent at New Orleans. William DuVal's request that his son, John P., be named navy agent at Pensacola was also unavailing. As Clay explained to a mutual friend, "His [DuVal's] wishes in behalf of his son will be considered; but the fact that he has one son a Governor under the General Government and another holding a Captains Commission (this latter now applying for another appointment) will operate against his success." Adams responded similarly to Judge John B. Thruston's request that one of his sons be commissioned in the Marine Corps. Noting that the judge himself held a lifetime office, that one son was already a clerk in the State Department, and that another son was an army officer, the president explained that he "sometimes heard complaints that too many places were accumulated in families."[37]

There were exceptions to the rule, however. In 1827, Adams appointed as judge of the Middle District of Florida Thomas Randall, brother-in-law of third auditor Peter Hagner and son-in-law of William Wirt. Clay sent his son Theodore as a bearer of dispatches to Mexico. The secretary of state also hired, to do special copying, William P. Elliot, son of a Patent Office clerk, William Elliot, and William Cranch, Jr., son of the president's cousin William Cranch, chief justice of the Circuit Court in the District of Columbia. A State Department clerkship went to George Watkins, a son of fourth auditor Tobias Watkins, who served as one of the principal political organizers of the administration. Adams appointed his friend Alexander Hill Everett minister to Spain, notwithstanding the fact that the latter's brother Edward was a member of Congress. When Senator James Noble's brother Lazarus, receiver of public moneys at Brookville, Indiana, died, another brother, Noah, was named Lazarus's successor. Rufus King's announcement that he was taking his son John A. King as secretary of legation to London occasioned another deviation from the announced policy, a deviation that the administration, for perhaps obvious reasons, punctiliously sustained.

Relationship to a prominent and valued friend was, even in this administration, a customary channel for preference. The death in May 1825 of John Warner, commercial agent at Havana, provided one of the earliest evidences of the scramble for place and of the range of criteria that were urged for selection. De Witt Clinton was among those who wrote on behalf of Andrew Garr, a Havana merchant. Vincent Gray, another Havana trader, promised that he would send recommendations to Clay from their "mutual friend T.B. Robertson Esqr. late Governor of Louisiana," from James Brown, and from "Brother John" Clay. William H. DeCoursey Wright mentioned that his father, Robert, a former congressman and United States Senator, governor of Maryland, and, at this time, a federal district judge, was Clay's "old friend." Edward Lloyd, Republican governor of Maryland; Robert H. Goldsborough, formerly a Federalist senator from that state; Sam Smith, one of the current Senators; and William Wirt, of the president's cabinet, also endorsed young Wright's candidacy. Senator Smith, who likewise wrote on behalf of the Baltimoreans J. W. Symington and Samuel Purviance, noted particularly that the latter was a brother of John Purviance, a well-known lawyer, "son of the late collector [Robert Purviance]," and nephew of Samuel Purviance, who "was an important Character in Maryland during the War of the Revolution." Hezekiah Niles, after first endorsing Symington, yielded his preference finally to Thomas McKean Rodney, son of the deceased Republican leader Caesar A. Rodney, on the ground that the young man was the only source of support for eight sisters and his mother.[38]

The last argument appears to have been most persuasive. Rodney was commissioned, but he resided in Havana for only about a year before deputizing his duties to Gray, who continued to perform them during the regular appointee's intermittent and extended absences. Wright, in September 1825, was named consul to Rio de Janeiro, despite his father's employment in federal service.

A tie to mercantile concerns was a major consideration in consular appointments. That men of commercial training should have been selected for such posts satisfied the requisite of competence, but it also accorded with the administration's attachment to trading interests. While consular remuneration, dependent upon fees rather than salary, was generally meager, the prestige and business opportunities for the associated commercial houses rendered the appointments much in demand. Rivals contended that the benefits also encompassed access to special trade information and preferential tariff evaluation.

Residence in the locale of the office was another customary requisite, although some leeway was permitted in filling territorial positions. When Clay's friend Francis T. Brooke sought a place for his son, the secretary of state replied that none was then available but explained that settlement must precede appointment to any office that might develop in one of the new states: "As it regards appointments in any State it is extremely difficult, if not altogether wrong and impracticable to Send a person from one into another State." While previous settlement was not deemed indispensable for territorial appointments, even there it was "advisable."[39]

The practice in relation to Florida indicates, however, the measure of flexibility in the latter consideration. William P. DuVal, who was recommissioned as governor of the territory in 1825, still considered his home to be Bardstown, Kentucky, where he spent some six months that spring and summer, although he promised to hasten his return to Tallahassee. Samuel R. Overton of Tennessee, a member of a family that was prominently identified with Jackson, had been named one of the Florida land commissioners in 1822 and register of the Tallahassee land office in February 1825. Such residence qualified him for appointment as navy agent at Pensacola the following summer. Benjamin D. Wright and Adam Gordon of Pensacola, consecutive prosecuting attorneys of Middle Florida, both resigned after brief tenure because their duties were inconvenient so far from home. Petitions were filed in 1825 and 1826 against Marshal John M. Hanson, also of Middle Florida, on the ground that he had "been but once within his said district since his appointment [in 1824] and then only for a few days." When Hanson subsequently resigned, however, he was replaced by an appointee from Alabama. Thomas Randall, who was named in 1827 as judge for the Middle District, had earlier served as a commissioner under the Florida Treaty, but his residence when he was proposed for judicial appointment was at Washington, where he practiced law. The territorial delegate, Joseph M. White, finally complained: "Most of the appointments lately made, have been out of the Territory, & although of Competent and well qualified persons, it would be more satisfactory to the people there to have some, from among themselves."[40]

Jacksonians were particularly critical of appointments to military and naval services, on the ground that they concentrated patronage among the elite. Such charges appear in large part to have been predicated upon Calhoun's practice during the previous administration. Barbour noted that when he assumed office, 123 of the cadets for the West Point class of 1825, 34 of those for 1826, and 1 for 1827 had already been designated "by anticipation." These commitments he honored as a courtesy to families who had planned careers accordingly. In 1828, however, he formally enunciated the generally prevalent policy under which nominations to the United States Military Academy were allotted among the states on the basis of congressional districts, with two additional candidates named by the senators. Southard also initiated at that time an attempt to distribute commissions for navy midshipmen according to similar standards. Marine Corps appointments, limited to entering rank as second lieutenants, were made from among the graduating army cadets.[41]

Despite the president's idealistic views on appointment policy, office holding under his administration was vulnerable to partisan criticism. The adherence to the principle of continuity fostered superannuation and inefficiency, if not corruption. Richard Rush complained that he served as "head overseer, and journeyman too, of the octogenarian department." The physical incapacity of John Steele, collector of the port of Philadelphia, largely contributed to the scandalous episode relating to several hundred "Chests of Tea," which were removed from the government warehouse without payment of taxes. Theodorus Bailey, who had been postmaster of New York since 1804, was paralyzed from a stroke at the beginning of Adams's administration, but despite "much dissatisfaction" arising from his "age infirmities & mental imbecility," he was permitted to remain in office until his death four years later. Deputization of duties was widespread and led to charges of sale of office, as well as complaints of inconvenience when officers were not available to perform functions for which they alone were duly commissioned. Continuity in office during good behavior degenerated into a policy in which few officials were dismissed for any cause. Adams's removals, as reflected at the level that required the Senate's confirmation of replacements, totaled only twelve in four years. He had not initiated the practice of lenience toward incumbents, but his personal predilections carried it to a level that embarrassed his friends and legitimized opposition.[42]

Moreover, political interest was not eliminated in the administration's appointments, and at times, concerns of the president's personal adherents governed the choice. Charges of corruption against Mark L. Hill, collector of customs at Bath, Maine, rested upon his violations of the embargo legislation of 1808/9 and were motivated in large part by rivalries stemming from Hill's accession in 1820 to the office long controlled by members of the Dearborn family. He was removed in 1825 after formal investigation, but the bitter conflict over naming his successor made clear the powerful political undercurrents. Strong representations of the ties between Hill and Governor Albion K. Parris and their mutual Crawfordite connection determined that the governor's application for the post was rejected in favor of that of the relatively unknown deputy collector, John B. Swanton. Support for Parris by Secretary of War Barbour and Maine's Congressman John Holmes was offset by the partisan arguments of Adams's friends Benjamin Ames, Timothy Fuller, and Henry Dearborn of Boston, Joseph E. Sprague of Salem, and John Bailey of Dorchester.[43]

Political considerations also dictated the naming of John Williams and John P. Erwin of Tennessee, respectively as chargé to Central

America and postmaster at Nashville; John G. A. Williamson of North Carolina as consul at La Guaira; Daniel Pope Cook of Illinois as special agent to Cuba; Robert Trimble of Kentucky as federal district judge; and Adam Gordon of Florida as federal attorney, to name only a few obvious instances. Victor Du Pont, who was influential in Delaware politics, was flattered by Adams's "kind personal attentions" in appointing him as director of the Bank of the United States and in promoting his son as a midshipman. Thomas Yeatman and John P. Erwin, known as Jackson's opponents in Tennessee, enjoyed marked success in their recommendations for office, as did Daniel Webster and Clay's friends John J. Crittenden of Kentucky, Joseph Vance and Charles Hammond of Ohio, and James Noble of Indiana. Clay's political connection was particularly discernible in the nominations of William B. Rochester of New York as secretary of legation at the Panama Congress and to the Federation of Central America; William Henry Harrison, as minister to Colombia; Peter B. Porter, Barbour's replacement in 1828 as secretary of war; Philip S. Markley, as naval officer at Philadelphia; and Crittenden, as Supreme Court justice. "Nobody can say that *I* neglect *my* friends," Clay was quoted to have boasted in 1827.[44]

The appointment of John Binns as public printer in Philadelphia illustrates one stratagem by which the rigidity of Adams's policies was effectively circumvented. Long identified with the Clay faction of Pennsylvania Republicans, the editor was opposed by both Calhoun's supporters, personified in Postmaster Richard Bache, and Adams's personal friends, including editor Robert Walsh, Jr. Clay, as secretary of state, awarded the contracts for publication of the laws, a much sought patronage, which was limited to three presses in each state. Although he announced and generally followed the Adams policy—"an established rule of the Department, never to dismiss a public printer without a good cause"—Clay shifted the printing at Philadelphia from John Norvell's *Franklin Gazette* to Binns's *Democratic Press* before the First Session of the Nineteenth Congress, in December 1825.[45]

Binns, however, wanted more. He found that his press had been denied the printing of the post office and the customs house. When he attempted to bring pressure upon Bache by appealing to Postmaster General McLean, the latter replied: *"I hold it as a principle, I make it a rule, never to assume to influence a Post Master for, or agst. patronising the Printer he may choose to select."*[46] Binns's complaints, underscored by politicians' reports of imminent disaster to the administration if his services were lost in Pennsylvania, prompted one of Clay's unsuccessful protests to the president in regard to McLean's hostile attitude.

Shortly after William Jones had replaced John Steele as customs collector, in January 1827, the secretary of state advised the appointee "candidly" of the anticipation that he would provide "a direction of the office which would render· it less inimical to the Administration. . . ." Jones replied that he had been on duty only two days but that he had been "indecorously pressed by Mr. Binns" from the time the appointment had been announced. Explaining that no printing would be wanted during the first quarter of the year, Jones protested that he had not yet observed any of the reported "virulent and clamorous opposition" to the administration within that office: "I am sure it is not intended (and if it was I am not a fit instrument) to proscribe any officer for the decent expression of his opinions and exercise of his regrets." He nevertheless promised to consult Richard Rush about the printing. The Treasury secretary's ensuing directive to the recalcitrant officer afforded Binns the necessary support.[47]

While cordial interdepartmental relationships thus occasionally eased confining policies, the secretaries did not have many opportunities to satisfy their personal predilections. Apart from the president's strictness, patronage was closely watched by a congressional opposition that fixed searching eyes upon new appointments. Comparative lists of the former and current publishers of the laws were demanded and released to public view. Urgent requests for authorization to hire additional personnel were repeatedly rejected. Even the demands of the rapidly growing West for extension of the judicial system failed to surmount the impasse of the potential expansion of patronage. Although he found a backlog of mandated record keeping that had been neglected since the founding of the nation, Clay regretfully rejected one applicant for a clerkship in November 1826, with the explanation that since his entry into the department, there had "not been a solitary appointment to any office attached to it, of any description, from the first Clerk to a Messenger." Rush, pointing to similar restriction of necessary clerical aid "at the desks of my superannuated beauraus [sic]," lamented, in December 1827, that he was "so galled, so whipped up, so ground down, morning noon and night, and night noon and morning," that he had resolved to withdraw from social activities so long as Congress sat, "if it lasts 'till doomsday. . . ."[48]

Hard work was general in the Adams administration. The president's strong sense of personal discipline set a pattern that extended to all members of the cabinet. Describing his days at the end of April 1825, Adams recorded that he rose about five; read his Bible, newspaper, and public papers from the departments until breakfast, which he had from nine to ten; met with cabinet members and "a succession of visitors, upon business, in search of place, solicitors for donations, or for mere curiosity, from eleven till between four and five o'clock''; walked three or four miles before dinner; dined "from about half-past five till seven''; signed documents and worked on his diary evenings, which were "not so free from interruption as . . . hoped and expected''; and retired about eleven. To his friend George Sullivan he commented at mid May that the "Presidential Chair" was no "bed of roses." Clay assured an elderly correspondent a year or so later that "day break scarcely ever . . . [found Adams] in bed" and added that he himself rose early, "but not so early as" the president. Rush, in commenting upon the demands of Congress, only half-facetiously alluded also to the president as " 'our worthy little master' over the way.''[49]

Less completely involved in the daily grind than were other cabinet members, Wirt described himself in 1828 as "frequently . . . in the Condition of Issachar.—'Issachar is a strong ass bowed down between two burthens.'—The Supreme Court being in one pannier and the President and Heads of Department in the other." But, he noted, since his health was good, he was "generally ready 'to cut and come again.' ''[50] His colleagues, on the other hand, complained of heavy fatigue.

Cabinet members met as a group about once a week and, as individuals, consulted with the president almost daily, depending upon the problems of office. Through such contacts Adams kept informed on the detail of departmental activities with considerable specificity, but he left the working out of policies very largely to the secretaries. He viewed his presidential role very much as that of the chairman of a modern corporate board, available for consultation, but delegating operational responsibility. Even matters of policy were thoroughly aired and disagreements were resolved by discussion within the cabinet. Adams's public messages, his most pridefully formulated statements, passed through such collaborative and rigorous review.

Despite his long involvement in foreign relations and his personal satisfaction in literary composition, the president relinquished the preparation of even the most sensitive diplomatic notes and instructions to the secretary of state and rarely drafted revisions. Accordingly, during his first six weeks in office, Clay, besides familiarizing himself with the routine of his department, prepared instructions for six major diplomatic assignments; responded to important proposals that were submitted on behalf of the governments of Great Britain, Central America, and Brazil; published a pamphlet, "Address to the People of the Congressional District," in defense of his vote for Adams; and engaged in a running public correspondence with John H. Eaton concerning the Kremer charges. By early April, Clay, like Adams, was lamenting to friends that his office was "no bed of roses"; "With spirits never more buoyant, 12 hours work per day are almost too much for my physical powers."[51]

Ill health became a general complaint for most members of the cabinet. Clay's debility became so great during the spring of 1826 that friends, warning him of Crawford's collapse, urged him to make greater use of clerks and to employ an amanuensis. Extended summer leaves for the president and the secretaries were viewed as a necessary measure for physical restoration. Even then, however, the mails conveyed continued demands for decisions on programs, and partisan pressures for political fence mending required numerous public appearances. Family woes added to the personal stress. The financial difficulties and waywardness of Adams's eldest son, George Washington, and the alcoholism of Clay's second son, Thomas Hart, brought grief to the concerned parents throughout the administration. Such sorrows were heightened during the summer and fall of 1826 by the death of Adams's father, two daughters of the Clays, and a son of the Rushes.

By the autumn of 1827 Clay's stamina had declined so far that he was forced to take additional leave, for a two-week tour of the Pennsylvania and Virginia springs, and finally, in the spring of 1828, an excursion to Philadelphia for professional consultation with the distinguished physicians Philip Syng Physick and Nathaniel Chapman. Both advised "relaxation from public cares and duties," and the former urged "retirement from public service altogether." Toward the end of April, Clay submitted his resignation, and Southard then doubted that the Kentuckian would live another month. Lamenting this "disastrous occurrence," Adams was himself greatly depressed and complained of lassitude and loss of weight.[52]

Cheered somewhat by the physicians' assurance that no specific malady had been found and stung by Jacksonian comment that he suffered only from a "guilty conscience," the secretary of state remained at his post; but news of the political reverses during the autumn again threw him into a prolonged period of physical decline. Meanwhile, Rush, in the summer of 1827, sought unsuccessfully to obtain appointment to the legation at Mexico City. Barbour, a year later, "save[d] himself from the wreck," as the president described the move, by resigning from the War Department to accept appointment to the mission at London. Southard, too, suffered failing health. When he left office the following spring, his friends, also, questioned whether he could long survive. He was described as "very much broken, stoops like a man of seventy, and seems melancholy."[53]

Despite hard work, the bitterness of political opposition, and the attendant physical and emotional strains, Adams and the members of his cabinet, except for the vice-president and the postmaster general, who were not officially identified with that body, discountenanced predictions of disharmony and enjoyed a remarkably compatible relationship. None of the suspicion and carping criticism with which Adams had viewed his colleagues in the Monroe cabinet appears in his contemporary record of his own administration. He assumed that, having chosen department heads for their representational role in relation to broader goals, they would not have joined him had they not been prepared to offer loyalty to the cause with which they thus became identified.

That such accord persisted was attributable in part to the equanimity of Adams's approach to administration; but it evolved at least equally from Clay's personal affability. The Kentuckian's attitude was the more remarkable in view of his arrogance toward political opponents, including Adams, during the Monroe administration, his vital role in the 1825 election, and the president's strong assertion of restraints on patronage. The requirement, under the Tenure of Office Act, that a large number of officials, even at the intermediate level of bureaucracy, must be nominated for confirmation by the Senate placed the responsibility for selection of candidates clearly with the chief executive. In assuming his own role as secretary of state, Adams had recognized that his place was *"subordinate,"* that his duty was "to *support,* and not to counteract or oppose, the President's administration. . . ." He had not thereby renounced the obligation to advise the chief executive; but as he defined the relationship: ". . . when a head of Department is consulted upon a nomination which he disapproves, his duty of resistance ceases when the President has decided."[54] Adams's pursuance and Clay's acceptance of such a cabinet relationship early became apparent.

Only after he had already submitted the nominations to the Senate did the president inform Clay that he had proposed to renew Monroe's suspended recommendations, to send Poinsett to Mexico and King to England, and to offer diplomatic posts to his personal friends Everett and Forbes. Clay was reportedly "well satisfied" with the appointment of King but expressed a wish that William H. Harrison might go to Mexico. Privately, Clay voiced great regret that two other of his friends, Gorham A. Worth and Peter B. Porter, both of New York, were not accommodated in the administration. Yet Adams noted that Clay offered "no particular objection to Mr. Poinsett," and the issue rested. Nearly three years later, Adams commented of Clay that the latter had never pressed any appointment "with importunity."[55]

The question of political removal of James Sterret, naval officer at New Orleans, "as a noisy and clamorous reviler of the Administration," severely tested the compatability of the president and his secretary of state during the opening weeks of the administration. Clay argued that in respect to offices that were held at the will of the president, "the course of the Administration should be to avoid, on the one hand, political persecution, and, on the other, an appearance of pusillanimity; that so long as the election was pending, every man was free to indulge his preference for any of the candidates; but after it was decided, no officer . . . should be permitted to hold a conduct in open and continual disparagement of the Administration and its head." Adams retorted that removal by "mere Executive fiat" or at "the pleasure of the President" would be "inconsistent with the principle . . . of removing no person from office but for cause. . . ." He insisted that removals "must be upon some fixed principle" that could be generalized. If political proscription were to be applied in one instance, he would "be called upon . . . to do the same in many." Under such practice, he contended, "an invidious and inquisitorial scrutiny into the personal dispositions of public officers will creep through the whole Union, and the most selfish and sordid passions will be kindled into activity to distort the conduct and misrepresent the feelings of men whose places may become the prize of slander upon them."[56]

Again Clay did not pursue the issue further. His notation in conjunction with a letter of resignation from an Alabama judge the following year, requiring the State Department clerk "to have all the recommendatory letters . . . collected to be laid with this before the President," indicates that Adams continued to exercise decisive control in such matters.[57]

Possibilities for conflict were numerous within such a political coalition. Yet Clay's comments to friends on the rigors of his work were coupled with observations on the "entire harmony as to public measures" that existed between himself and the president. To Ohio Congressman John Sloane, he wrote in early April 1825: "Things are going on well here. There is entire coincidence between Mr. Adams and me on public affairs." Dismissing the events that had accidentally cost him the vote of Louisiana, the Kentuckian commented at the end of April: "I have long since ceased to regard them even with any regret. The House could not have done better. . . ."[58]

He refused to countenance divisions among factional adherents, which at local levels, most evidently in New York and Pennsylvania, complicated working relationships. To one of his personal followers, no friend of Adams, Clay early sent the message by announcing his determination to take no part in "regard to the local parties and politics. . . ." He reiterated this stand with reference to Kentucky controversies as they shifted from local to national concerns the following year. When Jacksonian pressures forced the administration to a more active political involvement in 1827, Clay, Barbour, and Southard consolidated their efforts actively with Webster and Edward Everett in behalf of the president.[59]

Adams himself strove to remain aloof from partisan embroilment. After leaving office, he explained that from the first he had realized that no other course could succeed: ". . . I had concluded that the supporters of three of the . . . candidates, Jackson, Crawford, and Calhoun, however inveterate against each other then, would in the main combine against the Administration, and *they* would have constituted a majority." Whether motivated by stratagem or sense of propriety, Adams assumed a nonpartisan stance which required that he base his appeal for popular support upon a unifying program. His Inaugural Address, pedantic, stiff, and defensive in its argument, set forth this aspiration. With more optimism than the chief executive, Clay rallied his supporters to that course: "Mr. Adams, I am persuaded, will strive, by the wisdom and prudence of his measures, to deprive opposition of all just cause of complaint. A fair trial and an impartial decision are all that is asked."[60]

4

A FOREIGN POLICY
FOR COMMERCE

Responding in 1836 to a request for a summary of public affairs during his administration, Adams pointed to his Inaugural Address and the four annual messages to Congress as encompassing the "principles and political system" and also the public measures and events of those years. Beyond that, he recalled only his address at the departure of the marquis de Lafayette, who was terminating a visit to the United States in September 1825, and his remarks on 4 July 1828, commemorating the breaking of ground for the Chesapeake and Ohio Canal, as expressions of views warranting greater than transient interest.[1] These papers make clear that President Adams regarded foreign affairs as the focus of his administration and, under that category, the interests of United States commerce as paramount.

As secretary of state, he had already initiated negotiations that denoted the issues as claims, chiefly for depredations on American shipping, and access to foreign markets under terms favorable to American carriers. While his concerns had thus been very largely those of the coastal commercial community and particularly those of his New England constituency, he had forcefully upheld the Jeffersonian goal of competitive world trade, rather than the Hamiltonian program of concession to British preferential arrangements. By congressional decision in 1815, the United States had translated the Republican policy into an invitation for commercial agreements based upon reciprocal repeal of discriminating duties. A treaty that Clay and Gallatin, with Adams's agreement, had signed with Great Britain in July 1815 had constituted the first expression of the positive aspects of that program. The discriminatory provisions regulating the West Indies trade after 1818 had, on the other hand, evidenced the retaliatory restraints of the system. In advocating those restraints, Adams and Clay had again acted in consonance, and they had been joined by other congressional leaders who were more concerned for agricultural than for shipping interests.[2]

As Adams assumed the presidency, however, regional economic differences, growing out of the retaliatory program, threatened as of old to politicize commercial policy. Divisions between farmers and shippers and even within the mercantile community itself delineated strong partialities on the focus of that effort. In that context, Adams's geographic and political associations manifestly shaped a concern for extended carrying trade. Many, friends and foes alike, identified this response as a commitment to localism.

Adams's administration, however, embraced broader objectives. The president and his secretary of state sought generalized trade expansion. Shipping was to be increased, but so, too, were cargoes. Markets were to be developed as well as freights. When, indeed, the issue in the West Indies controversy took shape specifically as a choice between those ends, the president yielded to the market interest. "Commerce," so defined, encompassed a wide format of economic nationalism in foreign relations. The constraining voice of particularism belonged instead to the opposition.

One exception, both to the general emphasis upon commerce and to the partiality to northern interests, was the concluding of a convention with Great Britain, signed on 13 November 1826, that provided for settlement of a longstanding controversy over indemnity pledged by the British under the first article of the Treaty of Ghent. At issue were claims that Americans estimated at well above $2.5 million for slaves and property seized during military operations in Virginia, Maryland, Georgia, and Louisiana, with accumulated interest over the succeeding decade. Under the terms of a convention signed at St. Petersburg in 1822, through the mediation of Czar Alexander I, a mixed commission had been attempting to evaluate the claims but had been unable to agree on several basic principles, including the United States demand for interest. For more than six months, Rufus King pressed upon the British Ministry a request that their commissioner be instructed to refer the controverted issue to arbitration. Albert Gallatin, who succeeded Rufus King as minister to London in June 1826, finally accepted an arrangement under which the United States would assume the obligation of indemnifying its citizens upon payment by the British of $1,204,960, "as a full and final liquidation of all Claims. . . ." It was scarcely a diplomatic triumph; but recognizing that documentation on many of the claims was deficient, the administration had authorized acceptance of as little as $1,151,800.[3]

Indemnity claims arising from depredations to United States shipping proved to be far more difficult to adjust; they entailed major diplomatic effort. Recognition of their validity was, however, vital to Adams's basic concern to establish recognition of American freedom to trade. That the claims had, to a considerable extent, passed into the hands of insurance companies in New York, Boston, and Philadelphia did not lessen the importance of establishing the principle upon which they rested. They underscored the national commitment to neutral rights.

A major group of such claims stemmed from violations of those rights under French decrees issued during that country's conflicts between 1793 and 1815. One segment of them had been assumed by the United States Government in payment for the Louisiana Purchase; another, in compensation to Spain for Florida. Yet, negotiations for vast sums were still pending with Sweden, Denmark, Naples, Holland, and France for seizures under Napoleonic edict. The administration undertook to press these obligations not only through direct negotiations but also by assistance to private agents representing the claimants.

In 1825 John Connell of Philadelphia, such an agent, with aid from Christopher Hughes, the American chargé at Stockholm, effected a compromise on the Stralsund claims, arising out of enforcement of the restrictive decrees in Swedish Pomerania in 1810/11. Connell accepted $60,000, "about one half the Sum the Swedish Government acknowledge to have received for the goods sold at Stralsund," Hughes reported; but he considered it "a miracle" that the agent got so much. Beyond "formal presentation of Mr. Connell's Memorial," the diplomat noted, he had had "*no official* connection whatever with the Minister, on this subject, so far as any projects or principles of *compromise* were suggested, or acted on"; but he had discussed the claims with the Swedish foreign minister, who had agreed either to submit the issue to the Diet or to proffer "a round sum." Hughes subsequently listed the arrangement as one of his major diplomatic achievements.[4]

The administration assumed a more active role on the claims against Naples and Denmark. John J. Appleton and Hughes were sent to those states, respectively, under special instructions in 1825. In both cases the United States was reviving pressure that had not been exerted in nearly a decade, since 1816 upon Naples and since 1818 upon Denmark. The administration, Clay explained, thus served notice of American "determination not to abandon those claims, but to continue to assert them until satisfaction" was rendered. With the assistance of Henry Wheaton, who was appointed chargé to Denmark in 1827, Connell was able to arrange settlements amounting to about $76,000, covering a half to three-quarters of the damages claimed for detention of three vessels at Kiel in 1812 under somewhat special circumstances. On the main body of such claims, however, European states that had acted under Napoleon's decrees persisted in the contention that the liability lay with France, into whose treasury had been garnered the proceeds from the confiscated American shipping.[5]

Negotiations with France had thus far proved fruitless. As United States minister in Paris, Albert Gallatin had urged the American claims steadily for seven years before his resignation in 1823. Reviewing that record, Clay found that the duke of Richelieu, France's foreign minister, had orally conceded in 1817 that his government recognized the claim to "indemnity for vessels burnt at sea and for those, the proceeds of which had been . . . sequestered and deposited in the Caisse d'Amortissement" but, because of contemporaneous heavy demands by the victorious European entente, had then declined to enter a written contract and had postponed the subject until the French financial situation improved.[6] That time appeared to have come with French prosperity in the mid 1820s. Meanwhile, however, in 1822, Count Villèle, as minister of finance and president of the Council, had introduced counterclaims demanding, first, United States payment of a debt to the heirs of Caron de Beaumarchais for supplies furnished to the Continental Congress and, second, indemnity arising out of United States denial of most-favored-nation status to France, as stipulated under the terms of article 8 of the Louisiana Purchase treaty. Refusing to link unrelated issues, Gallatin had returned from his mission convinced that only a manifestation of strong national support for the claims would effect a satisfactory French response.

President Adams alluded to the problem in his first annual message. As he presented the first draft of that statement for cabinet review, he proved to be considerably less rigorous in behalf of commercial interests than were most of his colleagues. While commenting that a resort to force "would be fully justified" in seeking the long-deferred reparation, he explicitly rejected this recourse. Clay protested that "this would be equivalent to a total abandonment of the claims" and recommended issuance of letters of marque and reprisal or, at least, the threat of such action. Secretary of War James Barbour was "quite averse" to the latter proposal. He considered the claims of little interest,

.

"excepting among the claimants," and he "deeply deprecated war." Secretary of the Treasury Richard Rush, however, openly supported Clay's views; and Secretary of the Navy Samuel L. Southard, while silent at the meeting, privately advised against the renunciation of force.[7]

Adams tried a second draft. The substitute, in turn, "was thought to savor too much of a recommendation of reprisals." The passage finally conveyed a wordy pledge that the claims would not be abandoned while hope could "be indulged of obtaining justice by the means within the constitutional power of the Executive, and without resorting to those means of self-redress . . . within the exclusive competency of the Legislature."

The latter body, as Barbour had argued, was not greatly interested in the problem. In May 1826 it requested from the State Department a schedule of the demands against the European states "for illegal captures, spoliations, confiscations, or any other illegal acts, since the year 1805. . . ." Correspondence to develop that record weighed heavily upon the overworked staff of the State Department during the remainder of the year. The 169-page document, filed on 30 January 1827, listed claims totaling over $14.5 million. Other entries, which the government regarded as equally valid, were filed subsequently. Committees of both houses of Congress urged that negotiations for settlement be continued.[8]

Clay's instructions to Brown, as finally transmitted in May 1827, were considerably milder than the secretary had originally recommended. In consultation with Adams on the form that they should take, Clay then expressed doubt of success unless some concession were made to the French demand for "indemnity upon their Louisiana Convention claim." When the president refused to link the issues, Clay duly advised the United States minister to stress the incongruity of the topics—the one arising out of a contract on which the parties might sincerely differ in interpretation; the other, out of a breach in "public law," on which there could be "no difference of opinion." While Brown was authorized to submit to arbitration the dispute on interpretation of the treaty and to allow any amount thus awarded as a credit against the American claims, he was not "to refer the question, upon the condition of submitting to the same arbitration the American claims, and those of France." Regardless of the reception accorded this overture on the treaty question, he was to press for satisfaction of the claims.[9]

Informed of the new United States proposal, the French foreign minister abruptly commented that he did not believe it acceptable. Brown persisted in seeking a formal response; but as Villèle's ministry fell in January 1828, Brown found that the whole ground must be gone over again. So the matter stood when the Adams administration ended. That administration had kept the issue alive; with some stiffness it had attempted to conciliate the principal French counterargument. The only satisfaction had been that a formal rejection was suspended.

Negotiations with Russia were more successful. Two disputes, involving relatively small claims, were resolved. One grew out of measures taken against United States shipping in 1807, in counteraction against the Napoleonic decrees. Israel Thorndike, a prominent Boston merchant and politician, sought compensation for seizure of his brig *Hector* by a Russian frigate in the Gulf of Smyrna. Additionally, Eliphalet Loud and Samuel Bailey, also of Massachusetts, partners in the Weymouth Importing Company, had lost the *Commerce,* seized en route to Lisbon when she had put into Corfu for repairs. In 1828, under a settlement arranged through the efforts of the United States minister, Henry Middleton, the Russian authorities agreed to pay 255,731 rubles, 28 kopecks, as adjustment for both incidents.[10]

The other controversy resulted from seizure of the *Pearl*, owned by the Boston firm of Bryant and Sturgis, under a Russian ukase of 1821 which forbade foreign vessels to approach within one hundred Italian miles of the northwest coast of North America as far south as 51 degrees, north latitude. Middleton and Sir Charles Bagot, the British minister at St. Petersburg, had protested the Russian action in 1822. The United States treaty with Russia in 1824, followed by a similar Russo-British accord, restricting the czar's territorial pretensions, had provided the basis for a settlement. Indemnity for the *Pearl* was readily arranged in April 1825, through discussions initiated informally by Clay and the Russian minister, Baron de Tuyll, at Washington. Owners of the vessel, who had agreed to accept as little as $10,999, or whatever they could get, received the capital investment, without interest, $16,994.69.[11]

Another category of claims to which the administration devoted careful attention grew out of a variety of problems associated with the developing trade with the new Latin-American republics. Privateering seizures in connection with their struggle for independence continued occasionally into the Adams administration and were duly protested. A claims convention signed with Colombia in March 1825, under negotiations initiated prior to Adams's accession to the presidency, covered losses in four such incidents involving vessels sailing from Philadelphia and Salem.[12] Violations of neutral rights by both Brazil and Buenos Aires, during a conflict between them that began in 1825, led to more serious controversy. At issue were both the American definition of blockade and the rights of United States seamen to remain unmolested under their flag when sailing the high seas.

Both John M. Forbes, chargé at Buenos Aires, and Condy Raguet, his counterpart at Rio de Janeiro, protested vehemently Brazilian Admiral Lobo's proclamation of a blockade at the mouth of the Rio de la Plata. Capt. Jesse D. Elliott of the United States Navy also issued a "spirited" declaration of the United States position—namely, that a blockade could be legal only for the river above the position of the Brazilian squadron. Lobo, on the other hand, in January 1826, required bond of vessels leaving Brazil with goods of foreign production, as assurance that they would not enter enemy ports. Over the next year and a half, more than a dozen United States vessels were seized, and their crews, in several cases, were brutally mistreated, removed from their vessels, and imprisoned.

In September 1826 Raguet recommended instructions urging that he be recalled if such practices were not stopped and satisfaction rendered. *"Now* is the moment to make *our* nation respectd by *this,"* he urged. *"Now* is the moment, to make this Governmt *feel* the influence which we are destined to maintain in the Hemisphere of Liberty. . . ." Raguet was concerned, moreover, that in circumstances when British traders and naval vessels were also experiencing the "humiliating" consequences to violation of neutral rights, they should perceive the wisdom and firmness of the United States stand, which their own government had long contested. He bellicosely gave notice to the Brazilian authorities that if one of "the publick ships of the United States . . . had occasion to go" to Buenos Aires, no permission would be asked and that "if she was stopped, it must be by the force of balls."[13]

Notice of this action was received in the State Department during the president's annual visit to his home in Quincy, but upon Adams's return, Clay, on October 22, responded with praise for Raguet's "zealous exertions." Relying upon such encouragement and a comment by the president in his annual message of December 5, citing the "very great irregularities" of Brazilian naval officers in relation to neutral navigation, Raguet pressed demands for restitution and damages. Clay's warning, addressed to the chargé on January 20, that the manner of his "remonstrances and reclamations" had led him into "a state of relation" with the Brazilian government that might prove harmful to his public functions, arrived too late to forestall a break. On March 12 Raguet informed the State Department that he had demanded his passports.[14]

United States trade with Brazil was, however, important to both parties. Vessels from the United States regularly stopped at South American ports en route around the Horn. The Brazilian representative in Washington, José Silvestre Rebello—emphasizing that Brazilian products, notably coffee, were complementary, while those of Argentina and Chile were competitive—had for some time been urging that the diplomatic exchange be elevated to ministerial rank. Following Raguet's withdrawal from his mission, Rebello called upon the administration to discountenance the action but pledged that if a successor were named, he would find in Brazil "the most pacific dispositions" to resolve the pending differences.

The incident was quickly settled. While refusing to disapprove Raguet's stand, Clay explained that it had been taken "without orders." Privately he and Adams agreed that Raguet had acted "precipitately."[15] William Tudor, a Boston intellectual and political leader who had been named consul at Lima in 1823, was transferred as chargé to Rio, with instructions to pursue the promised arrangement. A claims agreement was signed by Tudor, in Brazil, during the spring of 1829.

Raguet was bitterly offended by his government's reaction. Returning to the United States in the spring of 1827, he anticipated that he would be given another diplomatic assignment. When none was forthcoming, he addressed a memorial to Congress, calling for repudiation of the "calumnious charges" published in the official *Gazette* of Brazil, which had announced that he would be reprimanded and denied further employment. Responding to his pleas for release of the documents, the administration supplied only the Clay-Rebello correspondence dealing with the proposed resumption of diplomatic intercourse, without reference to Raguet's notes protesting the blockade, capture of United States vessels, and maltreatment of United States seamen. With Jacksonian support, the retired chargé finally, at the end of April 1828, won passage of a resolution calling upon the president for the correspondence concerning violations of neutrality. As Adams's compliance with this request then came too late in the session for congressional investigation, Raguet carried his case to the public in a lengthy communication published in the *Philadelphia Gazette* and reprinted in other Jacksonian organs. It became a feature of the ensuing presidential campaign, charging that the administration had failed to defend United States rights.[16]

Meanwhile, during the summer of 1827, the government of Buenos Aires issued secret instructions, proclaiming the entire coast of Brazil under blockade and authorizing privateers to seize any vessels that violated it. The Philadelphia brig *Ruth*, which had only recently been released from seizure by the Brazilian navy, now fell prey to a Buenos Aires privateer. After vigorous protest by Forbes, a decree repealing the instructions was announced the following October. A court decision, calling for release of the *Ruth*'s cargo and for payment of damages, was finally won in November 1828. Shortly thereafter the Brazilian government also agreed to pay damages for its earlier seizure of the vessel.[17] While the administration's success in diplomatically accomplishing these goals commanded little public attention in the afterglow of Jackson's election, precedents had been upheld for protection not only of the specific interests of shippers but also of the broader national concern for neutral rights as a basic principle of trade in the New World.

Prosecution of a wide range of grievances against Mexico further defined international responsibility in commercial dealings within the hemisphere. The Mexican government was unstable, its control over local officials loose, and its protection for travelers almost nonexistent. Foreign merchants complained about shipping seizures related to violations of neutral rights during the revolutionary upheaval, irregularities and corruption in the collection of port fees, brigandage on the highways, and uncontrolled Indian raiding. Clay, on the other hand, made a point of the compensation that had been extended by the United States to the Mexican trader Manuel de Escudéro, for losses sustained in crossing United States territory. The secretary of state demanded, in return, protection for United States citizens trafficking to Sante Fé.[18]

Upon entering the State Department, the Kentuckian was particularly pressed to support the interests of these traders. Almost as soon as he assumed office, he received a petition from Auguste Pierre Chouteau and Jules de Mun of St. Louis, who were seeking indemnification for a claim dating from 1817, when Spanish authorities had imprisoned them and confiscated their property while on United States soil. The traders had looked for compensation under the Florida purchase treaty without success. Thomas Hart Benton, writing now in their support, noted the protracted dissatisfaction of French inhabitants of the West with their treatment under the federal government. He emphasized their anticipation that Clay's appointment would open "new prospects" for them and their expectations that "in a question of indemnity to *western* citizens . . . the President would be decidedly influenced" by the Kentuckian's advice.[19]

Clay urged the Missourians' case strongly. A settlement now, however, depended upon Mexican acceptance of the boundary limits of the Florida purchase agreement, as well as recognition of the specific claim. Neither problem was resolved before the administration ended. The indemnity struggle was to drag on for another quarter-century, until the conclusion of the war with Mexico. While an administrator for Chouteau and de Mun was ultimately compensated to the full extent of their loss, with interest, Clay's western supporters derived no immediate satisfaction. He could assure them only that he had upheld their claim for later resolution.

Claims settlements, at most, merely remedied commercial undertakings that had gone awry; the president and his secretary of state hoped to broaden the scope of mercantile activity and to ground it on formal agreements that would forestall similar controversy. Prior to assuming the presidency, Adams had already initiated negotiations looking to the regulation of trade between the United States and Colombia. The exchange of ratifications on a general convention of peace, amity, navigation, and commerce, concluded at Bogotá on 3 October 1824, was one of the first diplomatic acts of the new administration.

That treaty, written under instructions of 27 May 1823, incorporated only the concept of most-favored-nation treatment. By legislation of 7 January 1824, however, Congress had reemphasized the United States policy's focus upon reciprocity.[20] In his initial instructions to Joel R. Poinsett as minister to Mexico, Clay stressed the distinction between these arrangements.

He noted that the principle of "most-favored-nation" seldom operated equally upon two contracting nations. Such a result could come about only "if the measure of voluntary concession by each of them to the most favoured third Power were precisely the same. . . ." Citing the difficulty of assessing "the actual state of the Commercial relations between the Nation on which the claim of equal favour is preferred, and all the rest of the Commercial world," he alluded specifically to the special considerations under which France and Spain had been given privileges for limited periods in the major ports of Louisiana and Florida after their transfer to the United States. Such concessions, he contended, rested upon "a received equivalent" which was not generally applicable. "Reciprocity" provided "a plain and familiar rule for the two parties themselves," free of considerations involving relationships "between either and third parties." It would reduce misunderstandings.[21]

For the Adams administration, however, the principle of reciprocity represented more than a means to obviate confusion. The policy conveyed political overtones by which Republicans had sought to delineate their break with Federalist concessions in pursuit of access to British trade. Jefferson and Madison had looked to open a broad world market for American produce. They had been willing to retaliate in countering British preferential restrictions. The controversy, joined in 1789 when Madison had proposed legislation to impose restraints upon European commerce according to the terms of its access to United States traders, had been at least partially resolved as, under Republican administrations, the British commercial convention of 1815 and generalized legislation of 7 January 1824, had set forth the policy of reciprocity in direct trade. President Adams hoped to define it even more broadly.

For him the principle had still deeper roots. In 1776, for a committee of the Continental Congress, his father had drafted negotiating instructions that sought reciprocal liberties for American ships and citizens in foreign ports and territories on the basis of full equality with nationals. The commercial convention with France in 1778 had departed from so sweeping an arrangement; it limited reciprocity to direct trade between ports of the United States and France and proportioned it to that extended to the most-favored nation, contingent upon allowance of equivalent concessions "if the Concession was Conditional." The elder Adams had continued, however, to urge reciprocity, as opposed to most-favored-nation treatment, in negotiating commercial arrangements after the Revolution. When the British resisted the American overtures, he had urged the retaliatory features of the policy—an American navigation act—to compel concessions.[22] In the view of John Quincy Adams, the long struggles to win access to foreign colonial trade and to counteract French claims to privileges under most-favored-nation clauses of the treaty for the purchase of Louisiana had demonstrated the soundness of his father's recommendations.

The concern to establish equality in trade relationships with the Latin-American states, whose independence from colonial ties was not yet fully recognized, enhanced the importance of arrangements that would avoid the vagary of "conditional concessions." In his first annual message, Adams asserted that the day was past when those states "might in their anxious desire to obtain a nominal recognition, have accepted of a nominal independence, clogged with burdensome conditions, and exclusive commercial privileges granted to the nation from which they have separated to the disadvantage of all others."[23] But in respect to Haiti and Brazil, such demands for special concessions persisted as barriers to the administration's trading interests.

In 1826 the Haitian government accepted the heavy indemnity claims of the French ordonnance that acknowledged the island's independence. While Haiti rejected the mother country's further demand for a reduction of export and import duties to 50 percent of those required of "most favored nations," controversy over the mode of indemnification forestalled settlement of a basic commercial accord between the separated governments until 1838.[24] Without such an agreement, the argument of American southerners that the "Black Republic" was not, in fact, independent blocked even the formal act of governmental recognition by the United States. Trade negotiations could not be opened.

Brazil, which ratified its treaty of independence in 1827, preserved, in its commercial agreement with the United States in the following year, an exception from the most-favored-nation concession for any conventions, current or future, with Portugal. The United States, by accrediting Rebello as chargé on 8 May 1824, claimed priority in recognizing Brazilian independence, "disregarding all the risks incident to the fact, and to the nature of its recent establishment"; and Clay's instructions in March 1825 to Raguet, as chargé at Rio, insisted "upon equal justice to their commerce and Navigation." The president, Clay added, was "altogether unprepared to see any European State, which has come tardily and warily to the acknowledgment of Brazil, running off with commercial advantages which shall be denied to an earlier and more uncalculating friend." Pending a formal commercial convention, Brazil was to be invited to trade under the reciprocity act of 7 January 1824.[25]

The dual personal role of Pedro I as emperor of Brazil and heir to the throne of Portugal, as effected in the subsequent political settlement between those two nations, was disappointing to the United States. It not only rejected the republican governmental model projected under the Monroe Doctrine; it also posed the danger that Brazil, upon the death of John VI of Portugal, might return to colonial status. The activity of the British agent Sir Charles Stuart, in mediating the adjustment between Portugal and Brazil, was also disturbing. Raguet conjectured that it would lead to exclusive trading advantages for the British in Brazil.[26] Such undercurrents complicated the general tenor of Raguet's diplomatic activities and exacerbated his negotations on commercial relations as well as neutral rights. His proposal for a reciprocal abandonment of discriminating duties was declined in November 1825. When he withdrew from his mission a year later, prospects for an accord appeared slim.

While Raguet's belief that strong pressure was necessary in order to bring about more favorable consideration may have been justified, his action increased the tensions. Brazilian authorities, dissatisfied with the secondary level accorded their diplomatic mission, also resented the partiality for the Buenos Aires cause expressed in American journals reporting the conflict between the South American states. Rebello's complaints against public sympathy for the republican, as opposed to the monarchical, government became so strident in mid November 1827 that Clay refused to accept the correspondence and demanded that it be rephrased. Throughout the following year the Brazilian chargé, with considerable justification, protested the practice of recruitment and shipfitting for Buenos Aires privateers in American ports. By May his correspondence with Clay had again become so heated that the secretary of state warned of United States competence to protect its commerce from any threatened "hostile attack." At the same time, however, he reiterated hope for "friendly intercourse," to be established "at no distant day, upon a just and equal footing."[27]

Only the prompt appointment of Tudor to replace Raguet forestalled a complete rupture of relations. Tudor's instructions, written in October 1827, required that he first pursue the promised claims settlement and then negotiate a commercial accord to remove the inequalities suffered by United States shipping and products in Brazil. The disadvantages stressed were those in comparison with the trade of Great Britain and France, which paid ad valorem duties of 15 percent, while that of the United States was taxed at 24 percent. In the resulting convention the United States achieved parity with its commercial rivals; at the same time, however, in pressing for equal treatment, it conceded, as had Britain and France, exclusion of Portugal from the most-favored-nation standard. The administration's original directives against persistent colonialism were abandoned, as were those for prior settlement of claims. Adams left to his successor the choice of accepting or rejecting a trade convention signed on such terms in December 1828.[28]

Possibilities for achieving trade equality under arrangements with the former Spanish colonies appeared initially to be more promising. By 1826, Mexico, Central America, Colombia, Peru, Chile, and the Provinces of Rio de la Plata were all free of Ferdinand's authority. In Poinsett's instructions as minister to Mexico, in March 1825, Clay expressed Adams's confidence that "the priority of movement on our part, which has disconcerted plans which the European Allies were contemplating against the independent Governments, and which has, no doubt, tended to accelerate similar acts of recognition by the European Powers, and especially that of Great Britain, will form a powerful motive with our southern neighbours, and particularly with Mexico, for denying to the Commerce and Navigation of those European States, any favours or privileges which shall not be equally extended to us." Although preferring reciprocity, the president authorized the drafting of a Mexican convention based upon most-favored-nation status.[29]

The anticipation was not fulfilled. The deterioration in Mexican-American relations that marked the years of Poinsett's ministry resulted from a complex of events for which he was not entirely responsible. Counteractive foreign policies of the two nations, centering on Cuba, generated a broiling backdrop. British rivalry for commercial favor interjected goading diplomatic maneuvers. The multiplication of claims disputes, developing tension over the activities of Americans in Texas, and instructions that called for boundary revision as well as a commercial accord—all placed Poinsett in a demanding role. One of his first official duties was to protest high levies on a cargo of cotton shirtings produced in the United States, as the Mexican Congress, called to extraordinary session in the summer of 1825, pondered upward revision of the tariff. His recourse to meddling in Mexico's internal politics quickly brought him into disfavor with the ruling junta and, in 1830, finally led to his recall.

When Poinsett arrived in Mexico City, the British chargé, Henry George Ward, had already been at work for two and a half months promoting a commercial accord. The American emissary reported that Mexico's president, Guadalupe Victoria, and his cabinet officers had been won to the British interest but that "a very respectable party in both houses of Congress and a vast majority of the people" favored "the strictest union with the United States."[30] To solidify that support, Poinsett set about organizing a group of friends under the framework of a York-rite branch of the fraternal order of Masons, for which he was instrumental in obtaining a charter, in contradistinction to the already established Scottish-rite branch of the order. Members of the rival rituals quickly assumed political identity on respective sides of the issue of federalism, as opposed to centralism, in Mexican governmental organization; and Poinsett became enmeshed in the domestic conflict. During the spring of 1827, as revolts occurred in several Mexican provinces, a manifesto was issued by the legislature of Veracruz, one of the major centers of unrest, calling for his dismissal.

Poinsett defended his actions in a public address to his Mexican critics. In notes to President Adams and to Clay, he offered to relinquish his mission. Because Adams, Barbour, and Southard were out of Washington, Clay, Wirt, and Rush conferred. Rush, who had previously expressed interest in being assigned to Mexico, said little at the conference but joined in the conclusion advising that Adams replace Poinsett. Clay reported the recommendation to the president and expressed his own satisfaction "that an opportunity" now permitted Poinsett's replacement "by some more suitable person. . . ."[31]

But Adams demurred. He contended that since Poinsett had not asked to be replaced, the United States should await Mexico's reaction to the incident. When the latter government did not present a formal demand for recall, Clay, at Adams's direction, expressed "satisfaction" that Poinsett had withdrawn from the York-rite body in Mexico after it "took a political direction." He was given the option of continuing at his post, with the decision left to his personal "feelings and discretion." He was not to lodge a formal complaint against "the extraordinary course which the Legislature of Vera Cruz . . . thought proper to adopt," but it was not to pass "altogether unnoticed." He was to express informally, to Mexico's president, "the surprise and regret" with which the manifesto had been viewed by the United States, "to remonstrate against such a practice in future," to say that his government had seen nothing to disapprove in his conduct of the mission, but to offer assurances that any complaints "through the regular and established organs of communication" would be given "the fullest investigation, and the most friendly consideration."[32]

With some difficulty the British had successfully completed a commercial treaty with Mexico in 1826. The negotiations of the United States lagged until 1831. The difference did not arise solely from Poinsett's ineptitude or Adams's tolerance of it, but those circumstances did seriously handicap the American effort.

A British convention, signed in Mexico as early as April 1825, before Poinsett's arrival, had been ratified by the Mexican legislature only after heated debate, centering upon its provisions for freedom of worship and reciprocal most-favored-nation treatment. The agreement had also reserved special trading privileges for American states that had formerly been Spanish colonies. On the basis of that exclusion, as well as because the treaty acknowledged that the flag of a vessel protected its cargo in time of war, the British government rejected the arrangement. The Mexicans yielded on both the latter points in the subsequent negotiations, completed at London on 26 December 1826. Ratifications were exchanged the following July.[33]

The same effort to preserve a privileged relationship among the Latin-American republics was introduced by the Mexicans and rejected by Poinsett in discussions for the proposed United States treaty. The American negotiator signed an agreement in July 1826, which called for most-favored-nation status but relinquished exemption from conditional concessions as well as the principle of reciprocity. Because of the pending British demands, he had encountered strong opposition to the United States position on neutral rights; but in the end the Mexicans had accepted narrowly restricted definitions of blockade and contraband as well as the principle that in time of war "everything shall be deemed free and exempt which shall be found on board the vessels belonging to the citizens of either of the contracting parties, although the whole lading, or any part thereof, should appertain to the enemies of either," contraband excepted. Deference to the flag of the vessel was to be extended to the persons aboard, unless they were soldiers actually in the service of the enemy.[34]

The Mexican negotiators, Poinsett reported, had agreed to seek revision of their constitutional bar to religious toleration but, because of the delicacy of the issue, had refused to incorporate the pledge in the protocols. The treaty, nevertheless, assured United States citizens residing in Mexico that they should "not be disturbed nor molested in any manner on account of their religion, provided they respect that of the country where they reside, and its constitution, laws, usages, and customs. . . ." United States requests for restraint of Indian incursions and for return of fugitive slaves had also been accepted.

But Poinsett had yielded, in an "additional article," a provision renouncing opposition to "any measure of precaution" that the Mexican government might adopt, during the continuance of its war against Spain, on the treatment of visitors born in Spain and subsequently established in the United States, even though they might have been naturalized under United States laws. This concession drew particular opposition from the United States Senate. That body proposed, instead, a compromise restricting the protections of the treaty to United States "Citizens," rather than "Inhabitants."[35] During a prolonged stalemate occasioned by growing Mexican alarm at United States border incursions as well as opposition to Poinsett's role in their internal politics, the eight months allotted for exchange of ratifications expired without a response.

A second treaty, signed in February 1828, effected the desired rewording but expressed further Mexican dissatisfaction with the reciprocity concept by authorizing a ten-year suspension of such arrangements as they applied to shipping. Although the United States Senate ratified this agreement, mounting hostility within the Mexican Senate against Poinsett's continued relationship with the York-rite movement again provoked reaction. The Mexican body now rejected the treaty because of the clauses relating to return of fugitive slaves and liability for Indian border depredations. While these provisions had not been delineated as *sine qua non* under Poinsett's instructions, they met demands of Jacksonian constituencies which, in December 1828, could not be counteracted. Adams was forced to report to Congress that "from various successive obstacles" the negotiation was "not yet brought to a final conclusion." He left its continuance to his successor.[36]

A treaty signed by Clay at Washington on 5 December 1825, with Antonio José Cañaz, minister plenipotentiary of the Federation of Central America, served both as the showpiece of the administration's goals in international commercial relationships and as a model for its negotiators in drawing up subsequent arrangements.[37] It provided for both reciprocity and most-favored-nation treatment, with a stipulation that particular favors granted to other nations should become common "if the concession was freely made, or on allowing the same compensation, if the concession was conditional." In its definition of reciprocal navigation privileges, it stipulated, in the broadest terms, that "whatever kind of produce, manufacture or merchandize of *any* foreign country" could be imported into one of the signatory states, in its own vessels, might be imported in vessels of the other, and that "no higher or other duties, upon the tonnage of the vessel, or her cargo, . . . [should] be levied and collected, whether the importation be made in vessels of the one country or of the other." Similarly, whatever could "be lawfully exported or re-exported from the one country, in its own vessels, to *any* foreign country, . . . [might], in like manner, be exported or re-exported in the vessels of the other country," and with the same bounties, duties, and drawbacks to be allowed and collected on such exportation or reexportation.

The treaty also bound the parties to the views on neutral rights for which the United States had been long contending against Britain and the European imperial powers. Blockade and contraband were narrowly restricted, and the policy was enunciated that "free ships shall also give freedom to goods," excepting the property of enemies who failed to acknowledge this principle. Vessels might be searched on the high seas for contraband, but only such cargo might be removed; if it was too bulky for removal, the vessel was to be sent to the nearest safe port for adjudication. Seamen of the neutral state were in no case to be required to board an examining vessel.

The two nations extended to the citizens of each, when under jurisdiction of the other, freedom of conscience, freedom of access to courts, freedom of asylum, freedom for disposition of personal goods and withdrawal of the proceeds without molestation. In the event of war between the contracting parties, citizens of one who were residing within the other were to be allowed from six months to a year to close their businesses; neither their funds nor the sums due to them were to be sequestered. Diplomatic and consular establishments were to be held inviolable and were to be accorded the privileges of the most favored nation.

The code of commercial conduct thus defined, for peace or war, the goals of a New World trading system. It was a program by which the upstart new nations of the West might hope to operate independently amidst an international setting of colonial and contractual alliances. Like republicanism itself, it set forth the promise of freedom, an open door to competitive trade.

The development of the concept of reciprocity was particularly significant, for it encompassed not only a direct traffic, between the states party to the agreement, but also indirect shipping, in which they might serve merely as entrepôts. For the Central American Federation, which lacked a merchant marine, such a concession permitted the development of its ports as international trading terminals. For the United States the arrangement assured access to the freights of an extended traffic. Clay, who had long boasted of his role in negotiating the first reciprocity agreement, in 1815, later cited this extension of the principle as one of his most important achievements in the State Department.[38]

Such arrangements with the new Latin-American republics were tenuous. The Central-American agreement was to remain in force twelve years, insofar as it related to commerce and navigation, and permanently as it dealt with peace and friendship; but in 1826 the Central American Federation began to disintegrate and by 1828 no longer existed as a national government. Elsewhere to the southward, apart from Brazil, similar instability complicated the effort to formalize trade relations. The struggles of Peru and Chile to maintain independence from the encroachments of Bolívar and the unwillingness of the interior Rio Plata provinces to accept the hegemony of Buenos Aires discouraged moves toward international commitments. Even Colombia began, in 1826, the process of division that, over the next five years, led to the separate organization of Venezuela, Bolivia, and Ecuador. Uruguay was to be founded in 1830 out of the disputed territory claimed by Brazil and Buenos Aires.

Meanwhile, varying commercial regulations—which at times differentiated the arrangements at the port of Maracaibo from those at Cartagena, those at Montevideo from those at Rio de Janeiro or Buenos Aires, those at Callao from those at Lima, and those at Guayaquil from those at Lima or Cartagena—led to continuing seizures, persistent requests for governmental intercession, and additional claims for reparations. Though compensation was usually long deferred, the administration punctiliously recorded and pressed these demands. In the process, it fostered an identification with the mercantile community generally which was to constitute one of its major bases of support.

For Europe, as for the United States, this period was marked by revived efforts to expand commercial relationships. The Adams administration attempted to bring the United States into this trans-Atlantic development. The general reciprocity act of 1824 had suspended United States discriminating duties on direct trade with the Netherlands; Prussia; the Hanseatic cities of Hamburg, Lübeck, and Bremen; Oldenburg; Norway; Sardinia; and Russia. The Papal States and Hanover applied for the terms of this legislation and were admitted by presidential proclamation in 1827 and 1828. Gallatin, as United States minister at London, signed in 1827 an agreement that indefinitely extended the commercial convention of 1815 with Great Britain, thus continuing the reciprocity in direct trade.[39]

In his annual message of December 1825, Adams referred to "the serious consideration of Congress" a proposal that the existing policy might be extended "to all articles of merchandise not prohibited, of what country soever they may be the produce of manufacture," thus inviting reciprocity in indirect shipping. A bill introduced by Senator Lloyd of Massachusetts in the following month sought such an amendment of the general legislation of 1824, but disagreement on whether the measure would apply to trade with the colonies of European powers led the administration's supporters to halt action on it, pending current negotiations on the West Indies trade. The change was finally adopted in 1828, when, after Britain had rejected the latter discussions, a bill for expanded reciprocity, under Jacksonian auspices, carried enthusiastic, but somewhat embarrassed, administration endorsement.[40]

Meanwhile, this broader reciprocity principle, as well as most-favored-nation status, was incorporated in treaties signed by Clay at Washington, with Denmark on 26 April 1826, the Hanseatic cities on 20 December 1827, and Prussia on 1 May 1828. After the expiration of the earlier treaty with Sweden and Norway, John J. Appleton obtained, on 4 July 1827, an accord on similar terms, excepting only access to the trade between the two Scandinavian countries and with Finland and that involving importation of tallow and candles from Russia, "founded upon equivalent advantages. . . ." A treaty with Austria under the principles of the revised legislation had also been prepared in November 1828 but was delayed when the Austrian minister referred the document to his government for approval prior to signature. The formalities were concluded during the following summer.[41]

Where reciprocity was impracticable, the administration sought arrangements to assure access to trade and port facilities on terms at least equal to those of other powers. Thomas ap Catesby Jones, commander of the United States Pacific Squadron, signed articles of agreement on the latter basis in 1826 and 1827 with the islanders of Tahiti and Hawaii. Commodore John Rodgers, of the Mediterranean Squadron, carried secret instructions, drafted by Clay in September 1825, for a similar accord with the Ottoman Empire.[42]

Disturbances in the Middle East doomed this last undertaking under the Adams administration. As early as 1820 Secretary of State Adams had sent Luther Bradish, of Cambridge, Massachusetts, as a secret emissary to seek the admittance of United States vessels into the Black Sea. Although Bradish had found the Ottoman government fearful of jeopardizing its relationship with the European states by yielding to the American overture, he had persisted until he was convinced, by the outbreak of the Greek revolution in 1821, that nothing could then be gained. In 1823 George Bethune English, another Cambridge native who had been junketing for several years in Egypt and the eastern Mediterranean region, persuaded Adams that an accord might be achieved through the intervention of a sympathetic Turkish official, Capt. Pasha Khosref Mehemet, grand admiral of the fleet. The instructions to Rodgers were issued in pursuance of this effort.

The United States naval officer met Mehemet off Asia Minor in the summer of 1826, at a time when the Sublime Porte was being hardpressed by the Greek conflict. United States sympathy for the struggling Greeks now counteracted the commodore's efforts; his proposals brought no response. In the spring of 1828, however, some months after the Ottomans were defeated by the European powers at Navarino, David Offley, a United States merchant and consul at Smyrna, reported that he had received encouraging overtures from Turkish officials and that a United States vessel had been admitted to Constantinople. He urged that a further attempt be made to arrange a treaty. Instructions for this undertaking were issued in July to Offley and to Rodgers's successor, Commodore William Montgomery Crane.

By then war had erupted between Turkey and Russia. Because the latter state had been strongly supporting the American efforts, circumstances were again unpropitious. Offley opened discussions at Constantinople; but upon his demand for most-favored-nation treatment, specifically in relation to tariff concessions accorded to France, he was rebuffed. No report on his mission had been filed before Adams left office. Again the groundwork of a negotiation that had been pressed by the administration with great persistence passed to the Jacksonians as unfinished business.[43]

Even where trading ties had been consummated, all did not run smoothly. France, which in 1822 had signed a temporary agreement providing for reciprocal abandonment of discriminating duties over the next four years, repeatedly expressed dissatisfaction with the United States tariff on spirits and silk and threatened to terminate the accord. Tension was increased by the claims dispute and by the conflicting interpretations of the most-favored-nation clauses of the Louisiana Purchase treaty. In the latter arrangement no conditional limitation had been stipulated; but Secretary of State Adams, rejecting in 1817 a French demand for concessions such as had been granted to England, had argued that the benefits were not extended gratuitously. He offered, instead, to afford "every advantage enjoyed by the vessels of Great Britain, upon the fair and just equivalent of reciprocity."[44] Unresolved in the commercial accord of 1822, the dispute continued throughout his presidency.

French irritation took form in a rigid enforcement, during 1826 and 1827, of regulations levying the high duties of indirect traffic upon United States vessels that "merely touched on the other side of Channel for orders to have the advantage of the best market," the "Cargo remaining intact." In March of 1827 Adams yielded to a complaint by the French ambassador, Baron Mareuil, concerning United States levies of discriminating duties on several French vessels arriving by way of Martinique and, at the same time, expressed regret that "a different interpretation" was applied to the commercial convention in France. Noting that the Franco-American agreement was "equally silent both as to Colonies and Foreign Countries," Adams concluded that it applied whether or not, during the course of a voyage, a vessel of either power happened "to touch at the Colonial port, or the port of a third power, provided the vessel, on her arrival at her destination, imports only the produce of the Country to which she belongs." While the arrangement under this intepretation encompassed only a limited indirect commerce, it was thus extended to permit a circuitous traffic.[45]

Upon instruction, Brown pressed the argument in Paris. In August 1827 Baron Damas, the foreign minister, conceded that collection of discriminating duties upon vessels that merely touched a foreign shore for orders was a mistake, but he maintained that the vessels under consideration had lacked proper certificates of origin. Investigation revealed that the documents had not been obtained because the French government had forbidden its consuls to issue them to masters who had first called at ports outside of France—as Brown noted, this "had rendered the obtaining of that document impossible." Count de la Ferronays, who in 1828 succeeded Damas in office, proved to be no more conciliatory. He agreed to admit vessels that somehow had obtained the required certificates in the United States and "duplicate certificates" from French consular officials at the intermediate port, verifying that "no commercial operation" had been carried on during the stopover. But Brown's request for restitution of some fifty thousand francs paid as discriminating duties on five United States vessels and their cargoes of cotton and tobacco was ignored. Yet another body of claims had thus been accumulated for later settlement.[46]

By the autumn of 1827 Brown, depressed and frustrated, questioned whether the administration might not wish to recall him. He had not been able to resolve the dispute on Napoleonic seizures; his protest over the duties that had been levied on United States vessels had been ignored; and he had been warned that the commercial convention "could not continue" unless the French received "some commercial advantages." Contending that the United States had "every advantage in the navigation and . . . [would] under the convention continue to possess it," he urged that there be some reduction in United States duties on brandy.[47]

In tariff legislation during the following spring, Congress sharply reduced the levies on wines, particularly the red wines of France and Spain and —further to assuage the French—imposed a higher rate on silks imported from the Orient. The action preserved the convention. Southern proponents of these measures recognized that they were, in effect, barter arrangements, because imports from France offset exchanges of American cotton, tobacco, potash, and rice. The concept of reciprocity had taken on a new dimension. The scope of "commerce" was being redefined.[48]

Existing commercial arrangements with the Netherlands were also in jeopardy. Under United States legislation of 1818 and 1824, all discriminating duties against the vessels and produce of that nation had been abolished upon assurances of reciprocal action. The Dutch, however, in 1822 had instituted a bounty of 10 percent in return of duties to domestic vessels and goods, a benefit from which United States commerce was excluded. Arguing that a favor to their own interests, effective against all other nations "without exception," was not discriminatory, the Netherlands government rejected United States protests.

Christopher Hughes, whose assumption of the mission was delayed until the summer of 1826, then warned the foreign minister, Baron J. G. Verstolk Van Soelen, that by congressional mandate, reciprocal treatment was "the fundamental basis" of United States "intercourse with all nations, and would be departed from in no case. . . ." On the requirement for retaliatory action, "the President's duty was very plain, & though the necessity to perform it might be regretted, yet it would be done. . . ." A year later, however, Hughes advised his government that reciprocal discriminatory action would prove far more damaging to the United States than to the Netherlands. Few Dutch vessels frequented American ports, while American shipping to Holland was already extensive and was increasing rapidly.[49]

Adams evaded counteraction by referring the matter to Congress, with the explanation that the statute had not expressly provided the executive with the authority to determine what constituted "revival of discriminating duties by a foreign government to the disadvantage of the United States. . . ."[50] At the same time he warned that retaliation might foster similar action rather than promote the desired expansion of trade. There the issue rested. Neither the president nor Congress called for retaliatory measures under the law.

Adams had set as his priority in foreign relations the advancement of the nation's commercial interests. His policies in that effort were not new. He sought to provide for reciprocal equality of access to the world's markets in time of peace and to preserve the neutral's rights to that freedom of trade in time of foreign war. Even in the most novel emphasis—the focus upon reciprocity—he continued themes in the Jeffersonian tradition, sanctioned by congressional determination in the instructions for the British commercial accord of 1815 and the generalized trade invitation of 1824.

What was significant was the scope of the effort. The administration developed the groundwork for ultimate indemnification of a vast number of individual claims, some of which had been virtually forgotten over the decades since the violations. During these four years, Adams and Clay also concluded nine general commercial treaties, more than in any comparable period prior to the Civil War. They preserved, against strong foreign dissatisfaction, the earlier arrangements with Britain, France, and the Netherlands; and they initiated the successful negotiations with Austria, Turkey, and Mexico completed early in the Jackson era.

The progress had not been without major disappointments. The treaty with Mexico was stalemated. The accords with Central America and Colombia were of declining significance. None could be negotiated with the Argentine provinces, Chile, or Peru. The dream of New World commitment to an American trading system was fragmented.

The goal of reciprocal commercial equality had sometimes required concessions. The French accord was sustained by proffering unilateral adjustments. The Netherlands traffic was continued by overlooking that state's preferential domestic bounty. The Swedish treaty incorporated a form of Baltic exclusivity. The old colonial preferential ties persisted between Portugal and Brazil. Above all, the renewal of the British treaty continued the exclusion of the West Indies.

The flexibility by which Adams had pragmatically accepted these arrangements is remarkable. He had yielded to the necessity for concession to attain preferred ends. On the issue of reciprocity, however, his commitment had been strong. He had been critical of the West Indies exclusion under the British commercial treaty of 1815, which had been virtually completed by Clay and Gallatin before Adams had arrived in London. Through the intervening years he had sought to extend its reciprocity over indirect trade through the islands. He had won such terms covering the traffic through the Swedish West Indian island of St. Barthélémy. He had achieved the acceptance of indirect trade under the Central American treaty, under several other commercial accords negotiated upon that model, and under the extension to the general reciprocity legislation in 1828. Yet the instructions that he approved for reopening the British–United States negotiations in 1826 withdrew the demand.

The subsequent failure, marked not only by British insistence upon colonial preference but also by complete closure of the island traffic, was a staggering disaster. Regional critics, as they lamented the outcome, ignored the extent of the overall commercial gains and even the concessions that had been made to attain their particularized interests. Viewed by some scholars as "preparing the way for Adams' downfall in 1828," the controversy over colonial trade warrants separate, more extended analysis.[51]

5

★ ★ ★ ★ ★

THE COLONIAL
TRADE CONTROVERSY

In attempting to penetrate the mercantilistic barriers of European trade relationships with American colonies the Adams administration suffered its most serious diplomatic reverse. Domestic divisions, rather than diplomacy, played a major role in that failure. Whether the divisions on that issue translated into political disaster for President Adams in 1828 may be questioned; but farmers, viewing a sharp decline in commodity prices between 1825 and 1829, were at least responsive to criticism of a foreign policy that had culminated in the closing of an important market.

The diplomatic effort was not, however, entirely unsuccessful. While neither Spain nor the Netherlands would stipulate by treaty that Americans might trade with their West Indian possessions, in practice Cuba and Puerto Rico as well as St. Eustatius and Curaçao were open to United States vessels without restriction other than high import duties. Surinam (Dutch Guiana), which technically was closed to foreign commerce, also admitted American traders, although under strict regulation as well as high duties. By the Danish treaty of 1826, citizens of the United States were excluded from trade with Iceland, Greenland, and the Faeroe Islands and from direct commerce between Denmark and her West Indies islands; but that between the Danish West Indies and the United States, both directly and in goods ''from or to the ports of any other foreign country,'' was opened reciprocally. The treaty with Sweden and Norway in 1827 specifically identified the island of St. Barthélémy as being reciprocally opened to both direct and indirect trade with the United States and permitted Americans, on such terms, to enter Swedish and Norwegian ports "from whatever place they may come."[1]

Under these arrangements, American trade in the West Indies, generally, increased somewhat during the Adams administration. That with the Danish and Swedish islands expanded notably. Unfortunately, in large part, the latter development represented a reaction to deterioration in the much more significant United States trade with the British West Indies.

Declining American commerce with the West Indies, and particularly with the British colonies there, had been a serious national concern since the onset of the postwar depression of 1819. American domestic exports, which during the halcyon days of the early Napoleonic conflict, in 1801, had totaled nearly $9.7 million to the British West Indies, over $1 million to the Danish, $7.1 million to the French, and nearly $9 million to the Spanish, had declined by 1811 to $4.6 million to the British, $40,216 to the Danish, $55,571 to the French, and $3.6 million to the Spanish.[2]

After a general collapse during the war, they had reached in 1817 a total of but $3.8 million to the British West Indies, somewhat over a million dollars to the Danish, nearly $2.5 million to the French, and $3.6 million to the Spanish; and by 1821 they had sagged to less than $265,000 to the British and about $847,000 to the French. Only the trade with Danish and Swedish islands had increased, and the gain to neither amounted to as much as $200,000. The pattern demonstrated the effects of regulatory restraints imposed by the colonial powers and called forth, with particular reference to the British trade, an American retaliatory response.

Since the British-American commercial convention of 1815 specifically excepted England's New World possessions, trade by the United States with Canada and the British West Indies was regulated under domestic legislation, which had fluctuated over the years through chesslike moves of action and counteraction. Acting on President Madison's message in 1816 that new British regulations had closed the trade of her West Indies colonies to United States vessels, Congress had imposed an additional tonnage duty of two dollars on foreign ships arriving from ports of those islands. Foreign importations were also restricted to goods carried by American vessels or by vessels belonging to subjects of the country in which those goods had been grown, produced, or manufactured. The latter provision was apparently intended to restrict triangular traffic; but when a Treasury Department ruling established that British nationality was not divisible among the parts of the empire, it became evident that the measure had imposed no bar to a British indirect commerce involving the United States and the islands.[3] Adopted in preference to a proposal for nonintercourse, the law served American farmers, particularly those of the Middle States and the West, by permitting a continuance of their exports. Shipping interests, however, complained that it lacked sufficient retaliatory force to effect relaxation of the British restrictions on navigation.

After President Monroe, a year later, noted the continuing problem, Congress had introduced countervailing legislation, which not only specifically closed American ports to British vessels arriving from ports closed to American vessels "by the ordinary laws of navigation and trade" but also required that British vessels sailing with cargoes from American ports post bond, assuring that the goods would not be landed in a colony closed to American shipping. The Federalist Rufus King and the Republican Crawfordite James Barbour had been the principal advocates of the bill in the Senate; and Clay, in the House, had spoken "decidedly in favor" of it. With nonpartisan agreement, these leaders had emphasized that the action was but the beginning of a struggle "knowingly" undertaken, "with an unalterable determination to adhere to it until it . . . produced the effect it was designed to accomplish." Further legislation, in 1820, had tightened the pressure by limiting all intercourse of British vessels with the United States to direct trade in products of the colony where laden and whence imported, thus excluding the use of free ports in British North American colonies as entrepôts.[4]

Such retaliatory measures were effective. They had been designed to force a modification of the British policies through placing restrictions upon the trade in provisions—flour, bacon, and lumber—for which West Indian planters were almost wholly dependent upon American producers. The goods continued to reach the island markets, but they bore the additional costs of longer routes and broken voyages, occasioned in transshipment by way of the West Indian colonies of other powers. Protests of British West Indian planters and merchants induced their government in 1822 to revise the West Indian regulations so that for the first time a direct commerce with the islands was authorized on a regular basis under navigation rates that were equal for British and foreign vessels insofar as the action was reciprocal in ports of the foreign shippers. Since Great Britain had not yet entered into reciprocity arrangements with other European powers nor yet recognized the Latin-American republics, the benefits of the legislation were in effect restricted to commerce of the United States.[5]

Americans generally, and even the leaders of the British cabinet, viewed this action as a triumph attributable to the counteractive measures of the United States. American self-congratulation overlooked, however, Britain's retention of protective duties which, even in direct trade, afforded advantages to the commerce of her North American colonies in the West Indies. It also ignored the fact that the trade was limited to specifically enumerated colonial ports and to specifically enumerated articles, which notably excluded fish and salted provisions, products of New England. Moreover, the United States had yet failed to gain access to the indirect traffic through the islands, which would afford its shipping interests the advantages of circuitous voyages. The legislation appeased the demands of the islanders while protecting British shippers. At the same time, it heightened the divisions between the productive and navigational concerns of the American Northeast and the agricultural interests of the Middle States, the Ohio Valley, and the South.

Adams had taken the lead in drafting congressional legislation of 1823 in response to the British requirements. It authorized the opening of United States ports to British vessels coming directly from enumerated British colonial ports and the importation of articles produced in those colonies, provided that they could be exported to the United States on equal terms, whether carried in British or American vessels— and provided also that American ships or goods were admitted to the colonial ports without payment of any higher duties or charges than were levied on British vessels or "upon the like goods" entering those ports "from elsewhere." Until these restrictions were met, the measure authorized a discriminatory duty of 10 percent on goods imported in British vessels and the standard tonnage and light money fees of a dollar a ton on foreign vessels entering American ports, as distinguished from fees of but six cents a ton on American vessels.[6] By this measure the United States continued pressure for access to the British islands on the same terms as those applied to British vessels from North America or from the mother country. It challenged the British policy of imperial preference, and it tied the opening of the direct trade to restraints contingent upon admittance of the United States to the circuitous indirect traffic.

Adams maintained that the meaning of his proposed text had been explained to the Monroe cabinet and to Congress. Stratford Canning, the British minister in Washington, had certainly requested and received clarification before the law was enacted. Consequently, the Jacksonian Thomas Hart Benton's later assertion that the significance of the word "elsewhere," attached to the second proviso of the law, had been generally overlooked by Congress in 1823 seems scarcely conceivable. In any event, a British order in Council of 17 July 1823, raising tonnage and cargo duties on American shipping in British American and West Indian ports equivalent to the American rates, had quickly brought the differences to attention. Richard Rush, sent to London in the summer of 1823, was authorized to negotiate a treaty establishing the West Indian trade in accordance with the existing legislation but with removal of the discriminating duties levied by both nations, and particularly those which protected British intercolonial cargoes. It appeared "from long experience," Monroe had informed Congress the following December, "that no satisfactory arrangement could be formed of the commercial intercourse between the United States and the British colonies in this hemisphere by legislative acts while each party pursued its own course without agreement or concert with the other. . . ."[7]

The United States, under both the Monroe and the Adams administrations, from that point consigned the issue to diplomatic rather than legislative action. When Rush was recalled to assume his Treasury post in the spring of 1825, the disagreement had still not been resolved. He left London, however, with an understanding that negotiations, which had been "suspended" on 28 July 1824 "by the necessity of referring to Washington . . . some of the subjects which had been presented for discussion," were to be resumed.[8]

Renewal of the talks was delayed—delayed longer than the president had wished, Clay subsequently wrote. In explanation, the Americans pointed to the change in administration and Clay's unfamiliarity with his office; Rufus King's prolonged illness after assuming his London mission; the indisposition of Foreign Minister George Canning and the dispersal of the British cabinet until late in the autumn of 1825; King's involvement, first, with discussions on other issues; and of greatest importance, Britain's enactment of new trade legislation about which Washington had not been informed. Canning's suggestion, transmitted to Clay in March 1826, that someone else be joined with King in the negotiations and the latter's resulting resignation occasioned further delay, until Albert Gallatin could be sent to take over the mission.[9]

Meanwhile, the circumstances of the trade disagreement were changing drastically. Clay's assumption of the State Department introduced a new fluidity. Discussing with Adams the instructions for King upon the colonial-trade question, the Kentuckian argued that there was "more than plausibility in the British claims, and that we ought to concede something on this point." Accordingly, in early May 1825, Clay addressed inquiries seeking the views of several congressional leaders— Samuel Smith of Baltimore, Daniel Webster and James Lloyd of Boston, and John Holmes of Alfred, Maine: "Do we not contend for too much in insisting upon the introduction into the W. Indies of our produce on the same terms with that of Canada? In the mean time, are we not now suffering more than the British from the existing alien duties of the two Countries?" In developing his thought, he pointed to the fact that the United States employed much the larger tonnage in the West Indian trade, queried whether that tonnage would not improve in competitive position against the British by a mutual abolition of discriminating duties, and questioned whether the Americans could logically adhere to their protest against British regulations that maintained colonial prefer- ence while themselves barring foreign nations from the coasting trade. Was not the New Orleans sugar and molasses traffic benefiting over British West Indies shipments of such products under the existing discriminatory legislation?[10]

All the correspondents represented port interests, but Smith dif- fered from the New Englanders. Emphasizing the trading concerns of Middle State farmers, he argued that the freights of the West Indies traffic were meager and stressed the issue as one of commerce rather than navigation. As he reviewed the policy of discriminating duties, he concluded, although with some mixture of concerns, that the British legislation of 1822 was about all that the United States could demand. He recognized that the West Indies colonies were British territory and argued that the Americans might, with equal propriety, ask that their produce be admitted to Britain and Ireland free of protective duties. While he conceded that the British distinguished among their posses- sions in trade regulation, he warned that the principle of the exclusive- ness of intercolonial traffic "might be made to operate powerfully" in relation to American reservation of the coasting trade. He centered his hopes upon the potentiality for an expanded market under the limited direct trade. He saw no serious danger of "a competition in the article of flour, or in *any other article*" that Americans were permitted to send to the islands under the proposed British terms. If the alien duties were reciprocally repealed, "our *enterprize,* our *proximity* and our *articles* essential to the Islands will do the rest . . . ," he argued.[11]

The New Englanders agreed that Americans could not reasonably anticipate reciprocity without an equivalent in the colonial trade, yet they all urged that the discriminating duties be continued. Lloyd maintained that the United States regulations, in comparison with the British "limited permission" as to ports and merchandise, yielded "to this principle of reciprocity an equivalent many times over. . . ." Holmes commented that he had been "among the last" to adhere to the retaliatory principle, that he had, indeed, opposed the American legislation of 1820; but noting the "great unanimity" of the congressional support upon which it had been passed, he contended that such restrictions, once adopted, should not be hastily abandoned. He "would be the last to *retract*."[12] Under the current legislation, Holmes continued, seven-eighths of the value and nine-tenths of the tonnage of American exports and imports in trade with the British-American and West Indian colonies during the past year had been carried in American vessels. With full reciprocity, United States shippers could "successfully compete with any nation on earth." Without such equality, they would succumb to "a vain and fruitless competition, with no prospects of success." Once dependent upon British carriers, American traders, too, would feel the consequences, he warned: "Freights would assume their former prices, and the articles of export and import settle to their ordinary standard."

Webster conceded that abolition of discriminating duties might increase the sale of agricultural products to the West Indies, but he questioned the long-run importance of that trade, since the British restricted it to serve their colonial necessities. He foretold its ultimate exclusion and pointed to the recent introduction of the British warehousing system applicable to Latin-American imports as "a master stroke of commercial policy" that would foster trading rivals. For Webster the critical problem was the issue of indirect shipping, the privilege of continuity in voyages. He opposed "any measures of an injurious, or of a doubtful tendency, as to our general commerce, or our means of sustaining a general competition with England in the carrying trade."[13]

The British initiative to which Webster accorded laudatory recognition had, by the early summer of 1825, rendered impracticable the retention of the existing system of discriminating duties as advocated by the New Englanders. In a note of March 26, received in the State Department on May 19, Rush reported that William Huskisson, president of the British Board of Trade, had urged upon the House of Commons a program designed to raise the British American colonies "as rivals to the United States, making them more powerful by widening their range of free action, and conciliating them by boons, so as to render for the future their union with the mother country more cordial and more efficient."[14] This proposal, in fact, called for a fundamental reshaping of British laws on trade and navigation.

Huskisson's remarks had encompassed much broader recommendations than those related to the United States–West Indian trade. He spoke of the domestic "benefits to be derived from the removal of vexatious restraints, and meddling interference, in the concerns of internal industry or foreign commerce." Noting that a relaxation of trade restraints had been under way gradually since the end of the war with France and that the policy had been successful, he now called for abolition or, at least, radical reduction of duties on cotton manufactures, woolens, linens, iron, and raw materials entering home ports. He also urged a variety of general measures to relax restraints upon colonial commerce: repeal of quarantine duties and fees on shipping and trade in the colonies; reduction of duties on drawbacks or bonds when goods were to be transshipped; payment of consular officials through the civil list, rather than by local fees; and opening the colonial trade—except for that in firearms, munitions, sugar, and rum—to ships of all friendly states.

On this last point he advised that the intercourse be free between the colonies and other countries, in either British or foreign ships, to permit export of all articles of colonial growth, production, or manufacture, either to the country of the vessel's origin or to any other part of the world, except for the United Kingdom and its dependencies. Trade with Latin America was to be particularly fostered by extending to the colonies the British warehousing system, whereby goods could be bonded and deposited without duty, pending subsequent sale or reexport. Arguing that American traders from New Orleans lacked the capital or credit for handling such large wholesale shipments, he offered the last recommendation as one of particular force in defeating their competition. And while he was thus proposing to open the colonial trade to general traffic, he urged retention of the system of retaliatory discriminating duties upon United States vessels entering British colonial ports.[15]

The legislative formulation of this package was complicated. A measure covering specific features was enacted separately on 27 June 1825; but a week later, on July 5, it was incorporated, with some modifications, into a series of eleven measures, which constituted a revised code of British trade regulation. Among these latter actions was a blanket repealing law that canceled more than four hundred specifically named acts on the subject, including that of 24 June 1822 but not those of 18 July 1823 (authorizing the procedure for the order in Council of the previous day) and 27 June 1825.[16]

Of particular importance was the fact that the July 5 reenactment of the June 27 statute included a preamble to the section restricting the privilege of trade with the West Indies:

And Whereas by the Law of Navigation Foreign Ships are permitted to import into any of the *British* Possessions abroad, from the Countries to which they belong, Goods the Produce of those Countries, and to export Goods from such Possessions to be carried to any Foreign Country whatever: And Whereas it is expedient that such Permission should be subject to certain Conditions; Be it therefore enacted, That the Privileges thereby granted to Foreign Ships shall be limited to the Ships of those Countries which, having Colonial Possessions, shall grant the like Privileges of trading with those Possessions to *British* Ships, or which, not having Colonial Possessions, shall place the Commerce and Navigation of this Country, and of its Possessions abroad, upon the Footing of the most favoured Nation, unless His Majesty by His Order in Council shall in any Case deem it expedient to grant the Whole or any of such Privileges to the Ships of any Foreign Country, although the Conditions aforesaid shall not in all respects be fulfilled by such Foreign Country.[17]

Since the section of the act of June 27 that authorized indirect trade through the British colonies had been limited to the vessels of countries in Europe, Africa, or Asia "within the Mediterranean Sea," no statute had yet extended such an offer to the United States. The British foreign minister, George Canning, subsequently argued that the proposal rested in the preamble of article 4, as above quoted. William Scott, Baron Stowell, sitting on the British High Court of Admiralty in 1826, ruled instead according to the text of the June 27 measure.[18]

Even under the broader view, Americans found themselves asked to accord most-favored-nation privileges while acceding to West Indian duties on goods that, if imported through British North America, would be given a drawback of 10 percent. They saw nothing advantageous to either American shipping or trading interests but, on the contrary, a competition opened in the West Indies through the extension of new privileges to Latin-American and European commerce. Viewing the system as but a continuation of the old program of discriminating duties, the administration still relied upon pending diplomatic negotiations to resolve the problems.

What they did not perceive was that the repeal of the old legislation had foreclosed the continuance of the trade, even under the unsatisfactory regulations of 1823, beyond the first week in January 1826, when the new program would go into force. No notification, let alone explanation, of the new law was afforded by the British government. Moreover, the Americans' normal channels of information and response were disrupted.

On 2 May 1825 Rush had entrusted the affairs of the mission to the secretary of legation, John Adams Smith, the president's nephew, and had returned to assume his new duties in the cabinet. King did not arrive in London until late in August, after a stay of nearly six weeks at Cheltenham, recovering from seasickness. In the interim, young Smith, on August 13, transmitted copies of the new British trade regulations, without comment on their implications.[19]

The dispatch arrived in the State Department on September 22, during the absence of the president, who did not return for another five weeks from his annual vacation at Quincy. Clay, who had himself been out of Washington from mid May to mid August, selling the furnishings of his Lexington estate and transferring his family to the capital, was still mourning his daughter's death en route. By the end of September he was to learn of the death of another daughter. Meanwhile, he struggled to catch up on a summer's workload—instructions to John Rodgers, as secret emissary to treat with the Turks; to William C. Somerville, under similar secrecy to talk with the Greeks; to Richard C. Anderson, Jr., seeking modifications in the recent treaty arrangements and clarification of the aims of a proposed Pan-American conference; and to Poinsett, in response to his first sixteen dispatches.

The circumstances readily explain the administration's decision to defer, pending further clarification, any response to the British trade regulations. Clay had informed King, who left for London before the secretary's consultations on the subject were completed, that "the matured form" of Huskisson's proposals had not yet been received and that, consequently, instructions on the matter would be delayed until September. They were not sent before King resigned his mission the following March.

Meanwhile, a few American newspapers, including the principal Washington and New York journals, alluded to the new British legislation with recognition that direct trade with the islands was to be opened to foreign powers generally. In some accounts—perhaps most, initially— the move was viewed as hostile to American interests. The *New York Albion*, however, in September 1825, applauded the new policy as a liberalizing trend. Emphasizing that a wide range of goods was to be accepted and that maximum duties were not to exceed 15 percent, the journalist contended that Americans, sailing shorter voyages than their competitors, would easily dominate the West Indies markets. "The port charges in the West India islands have long and deservedly been complained of," he concluded, "but, as far as relates to the exacting of the foreign tonnage duty, it now rests entirely with the United States to abolish it, and to establish that reciprocity of trade with the colonies which the United States so long sought for."[20]

In this context, Adams's suggestion, in his annual message the following December, that the American reciprocity act be amended to encompass indirect as well as direct trade appeared to be a tangential and inadequate response. In introducing the proposal for amendment of the general legislation, Senator Lloyd specifically referred to the recent liberalization of British policy as encouragement for the view that reciprocity in indirect trade might be effected. Congressman Churchill C. Cambreleng, of New York, a critic of the administration, argued, however, that United States trade with the British West Indies was regulated under special act, containing "some provisions of a peculiar character, and unless some modification of that act should be adopted," the necessary relaxation of restrictions would be doubtful. With his demand for such amendment, Lloyd's bill was sent to committee, where it died, while debate continued on the implications of the British legislation.[21]

Continuing uncertainty—on the part of the United States and British officials, alike—was evidenced when port authorities at Halifax announced that after 5 January 1826 American vessels would be barred. Responding on December 25 to a letter from Congressman Cambreleng, who brought the Halifax ruling to attention, Clay cited a number of considerations to argue that the British government had no such view: it would be inconsistent with the pending negotiations; no notification of the contemplated action had been given to United States representatives, either at London or Washington; and the British minister to the United States had not been advised "of any intention to close the Colonial Ports against our Vessels. . . ."[22]

On February 18 the British minister, Charles R. Vaughan, transmitted a copy of an order by the lieutenant governor and Council of Nova Scotia, specifically announcing that United States vessels would be admitted to the port of Halifax and would "be allowed to carry on Trade as they have hitherto done." Governor Kempt, Vaughan noted, expressed regret at the brief interruption of American trade. The British minister commented, with satisfaction, that the order removed "the difficulties . . . apprehended . . . from the construction put, by the Comptroller of the Customs at Halifax, upon the late Acts of the British Parliament regulating the intercourse with British Colonies." The countermanding action, which had already been presaged in newspaper reports of the movements of British official couriers, had been taken on direct advice from the London authorities. A month later, Vaughan informed Clay that the British government was now prepared to proceed with the pending negotiations; and his announcement that Huskisson was to be associated in the discussions made clear that they were to embrace the trade issue.[23]

At mid March, then, the British government was inviting a resumption of the talks. The one point upon which they had been broken off in 1823 was the dispute centering upon American access, under equal terms, to trade within the structure of the British colonial system. That the British were still not prepared to yield on that matter was manifest amidst the confusion of the parliamentary actions of 1825. In drafting instructions for Gallatin as negotiator, the Adams administration, on June 19, authorized concession to the whole extent of the disagreement:

1st. That there shall be a reciprocal and entire abolition of all alien or discriminating duties upon the vessel or cargo, by whatever authority imposed, so as to place the vessels of the United States and those of Great Britain, whether colonial or British, concerned in the trade, upon a footing of perfect equality and reciprocity.

21y. That the United States consent to wave [sic] the demand which they have heretofore made, of the admission of their productions into British Colonies at the same, and no higher, rate of duty, as similar productions are chargeable with, when imported from one into another British Colony, with the exception of our produce descending the St. Lawrence and the Sorrel [sic]. . . . And

31y. That the Government of the United States will not insist upon a participation in the direct trade between the United Kingdom of Great Britain and Ireland, and the British American Colonies. But they do expect and require that their vessels shall be allowed to trade between those Colonies and any foreign country with which British vessels are allowed to trade.[24]

Gallatin had no opportunity to communicate these terms. He arrived in Liverpool on July 31 and in London on August 11, whereupon he learned that on July 27 a British order in Council had suspended trade between the United States and the British West Indies, the Bahamas, Bermuda, the British possessions in South America, and Newfoundland. Commerce with British North America was permitted to continue, as the basis for a profitable traffic for British shipping. While Canning at mid August still promised to resume negotiations on the West Indies trade "after the beginning of September," on September 11 he specifically rejected any discussions on the issue.[25]

When Gallatin protested that this stand was "entirely unexpected and avowed a change of policy," Huskisson conceded that this was so. He explained that the British Colonies "were now opened on certain conditions to all nations, and Great Britain could not enter into arrangements on that subject with the United States without exposing herself to much inconvenience with respect to other Nations." The policy decision had undoubtedly been fixed a year and a half earlier, and perhaps in Huskisson's view the procedural approach had also been determined then. But as late as March 1826 Canning had intended to resume the negotiations; he had, indeed, invited their renewal; and he had done so with a request for a change in American negotiating personnel, which must inevitably have occasioned further delay. Now he waspishly complained that "the Government of the United States seemed to have considered the intercourse with the British Colonies as being of the same nature with that with Great Britain itself, and which ought therefore to be adjusted by mutual arrangement," whereas Great Britain regarded it as "only permissive, and accordingly to be regulated by her own laws."[26]

To attribute this reaction merely to Canning's longstanding antipathy toward Adams, to view it as a direct consequence of Adams's pretensions in drafting the American legislation of 1823, even to explain it as the result of the administration's delay in responding to the British ultimatum fails to account for the situation that confronted Gallatin. A new component had been interjected between March and July 1826—the domestic political and sectional divisions, which complicated the administration's formulation of policy, had been brought into focus. Canning identified the British order of July 27 as a direct response to Congress's refusal to place British colonial trade "on the Footing of the Most Favored Nation and in consequence the United States within the provisions" of the parliamentary legislation of 1825. That action, the British maintained, had been at issue in congressional debate during April and May on a series of petitions from Baltimore merchants, shipowners, and manufacturers, seeking removal of the discriminating duties.[27]

The Baltimore petitioners, more concerned to maintain the trading market than to gain access to shipping privileges, had based their appeal upon the perceived threat, under the July 5 revisions of the British legislation, to terminate the existing American intercourse with the colonies. They ignored the evidence of an ameliorating will in the Halifax ruling and the invitation to resumption of negotiations. They were determined to set the terms under which Gallatin must operate. Senator Sam Smith urged action to meet "the very liberal offers of Great Britain, made by her act of Parliament of the 27th June, and her two acts of 5th July, 1825."[28]

The administration, on the other hand, had no assurance of such liberality. Until Gallatin reported Canning's interpretation from London, there was no knowledge that the July 5 legislation extended to Americans the privilege of indirect transit through the West Indies to Europe. As late as 20 October 1826 Vaughan was unable to respond to Clay's request for verification on the matter.[29]

Under such uncertainties the administration had discouraged congressional action specifically related to the West India trade. On 31 March 1826 the Senate Committee of Commerce, reporting on one of the Baltimore petitions, responded unanimously that in view of negotiations that were under way, it was "not expedient at this time, to legislate on the subject. . . ." The report pointed to the shipping disadvantages for Americans under the British proposal—yielding "a full freight, and beyond it, to the like articles when imported into the West Indies from elsewhere"—and the total exclusion of such produce as fish, salted meat, "and other minor articles." Lloyd, as committee chairman, maintained that the president and the secretary of state were "decidedly of opinion" that since the subject was currently under "diplomatic discussion between the Governments," it would be better to attempt to adjust the differences "by convention, than to surrender at once the whole game: give to the British a carte blanche; take away all the offsets we have to offer, and admit them into our ports precisely on the same terms as our own vessels, or those of the most favored nation. . . ."[30]

In accordance with this expression of the concerns of New England leadership and a Yankee president, the Committee on Commerce was discharged from further consideration of the matter. The petition was then referred, on motion of Littleton W. Tazewell of Virginia, to Senator Smith's Committee on Finance. That body, on April 19, proposed repeal of the discriminating duties, provided that the action was reciprocal on American vessels entering British colonial ports. By the narrow vote of 16 to 14, this bill was tabled on May 13. Meanwhile, Cambreleng's similar proposal was stalled in House committee. The first session of the Nineteenth Congress adjourned on May 22 without taking further action on the issue.

In subsequent instructions to Gallatin, Clay correctly pointed out that the Congress had not rejected the terms of the British legislation; that its discussions had been suspended, not terminated; and that this action had been dictated primarily by "the belief, generally entertained, that the Colonial subject was in a course of negotiation, and would be satisfactorily arranged by treaty."[31] The Danish treaty, signed at Washington on 26 April 1826 and ratified by the United States Senate on May 4, had, in fact, clearly indicated, as did the Gallatin instructions of May

10, the administration's willingness to yield the contested point on participation for United States vessels in the direct traffic between mother country and colony. Deliberately or inadvertently, the British government misread the United States legislative process and displayed as great a misunderstanding as the Americans concerning the intentions of its adversary.

Canning later informed Gallatin that Vaughan, during the congressional deliberations, had been instructed, upon receiving assurance of the withdrawal of "the restrictions and charges on British shipping and colonial produce," to inform the United States government that the discriminating duties on American ships and cargoes in the West Indies would "immediately cease." Emphasizing the misleading "effect of the double & opposite instructions" under which Vaughan had, instead, proceeded to invite renewal of negotiations, Clay concluded: "We think it now quite apparent that the B. Govt. had altered its views with respect to the Col: intercourse and . . . availed itself of a mere pretext to occasion a rupture in the negotiation."[32]

The secretary of state found the explanation in the mounting difficulties of the British shipping industry. The following November he received a copy of an address that Huskisson had delivered to Parliament the previous May, stressing the efforts of the British government, through its navigation laws, to relieve the plight of these interests. Gallatin subsequently transmitted a copy of a British *Sessional Paper* showing that the ratio of British tonnage employed in trade with foreign countries, excepting that with Spain, Portugal, Russia, and Turkey, which had almost no merchant marine, was "about two to three" during the months ending in October 1826. In this connection, Americans observed that Russian vessels were permitted entry into the West Indies, despite the failure of that nation to conform to the stipulations of the parliamentary enactment of July 5.[33]

Americans found, too, that when Gallatin, under renewed instructions of 11 April 1827, proposed a settlement, by which the President should request congressional action to extend the blanket concessions that Gallatin had been authorized to offer through negotiations the previous spring, the British Ministry declined. Huskisson bluntly declared it "the intention of the British Government to consider . . . any relaxation from the colonial system as an indulgence, to be granted on such terms as might suit the policy of Great Britain at the time, when it might be granted. . . ." More tactfully, Lord Dudley, who was then foreign minister, explained the decision as "the result of considerations general in nature, and conclusive against a prospective pledge of any description respecting the colonial policy of Great Britain, whether of relaxation or restriction."[34]

In the face of the British refusal to negotiate, Adams had no choice but to bring the issue back to Congress, in his annual message of 1826, with, for the first time, a full record of the diplomatic correspondence. He was particularly anxious that the terms of his instructions to Gallatin should be included; and while he now personally believed that the United States response should "totally" interdict the trade with British colonies in both the West Indies and North America, he made known his willingness to accept any concessions that Congress might adopt, "to yield whatever the trade would bear."[35] Proposals brought before the Senate and the House of Representatives by administration forces called for nonintercourse "from and after September 30, 1827," unless the president, prior to that date, received notification that the colonies were opened to American vessels on the same terms as British vessels from the United States and that American vessels were permitted to export on the same terms as the British from the colonies to anywhere but Britain or her dominions. If the president were so informed, the United States retaliatory acts of 1823, 1820, and 1818 were to be repealed. In the event that Americans were admitted only to direct trade with the British possessions, then only the nonintercourse sections of the current system were to be suspended.

In the Senate, opposition leaders, again led by Smith, won passage, by a vote of 32 to 10, of a substitute bill, which provided that after 31 December 1827 no other or higher duties should be levied on British than on American vessels coming from British colonial ports. It deferred until the later date the enforcement of the United States acts of 1823, 1820, and 1818, except as they imposed discriminating duties on foreign vessels; and it authorized an earlier suspension or repeal of the punitive legislation if the president were to receive satisfactory evidence of the changes in British policy as required in the administration's proposal. The substitute bill was notable chiefly for delaying application of the United States law of 1823 and for withholding any explicit statement of policy in the event that the British did not respond satisfactorily.

On the latter point the House required, by vote of 80 to 56, an amendment so that under such circumstances the legislation of 1818 and 1820 would be reactivated and the section of the statute of 1823 that opened American ports to direct trade with the British colonies would be repealed. From the standpoint of the administration, this amendment "was necessary to give effect to . . . [Smith's] bill, and called for by the honor and character of this Country. . . ." The opposition feared that it would be offensive to the British. Neither house would recede from its stand, and so the legislation died when Congress adjourned.[36]

Adams was, therefore, compelled to carry out the mandate of the act of 1823, reactivating the interdictions of 1818 and 1820, which declared that American ports were closed to trade with the British colonies in retroaction to the British prohibition. The British closure had become effective on 1 December 1826. Adams's proclamation was dated 17 March 1827. There the issue rested throughout the remainder of the administration.

Political reaction from the Jacksonian press was intense during the fall of 1826, when word was received of the British order in Council; it was still stronger through the spring and fall of 1827, following Adams's counterproclamation. During the latter period the *Enquirer* (Richmond, Va.) carried a series of twenty articles by Littleton W. Tazewell, critical of the administration's role on the "Colonial Trade." Editor Thomas Ritchie lamented that the British order in Council would rest "very hardly upon the Southern States." Adams had made his stand, it was argued, "to promote the interest of the owners of the *lumber* and *live stock of the Northern States*." The trade of the Atlantic States and the Western States had been sacrificed, while that of western New York and New England might continue through the British North American ports. Opposition editors assailed Adams for his emphasis upon diplomatic, rather than legislative, process: "If a law had been passed, no treaty would have been necessary. Our diplomatic administration set their faces against the first; and now they cannot accomplish the last." Adams's erstwhile friend Robert Walsh, Jr., editor of the *National Gazette* (Philadelphia), recoiling in Federalist disillusionment during 1827, professed to see the issue as a serious threat to harmonious relations between the United States and Britain: *"The question of peace or war hangs upon it."* Picking up the theme, William Coleman, of the *Evening Post* (New York), contended that Adams's "strong and unconquerable prejudices against the English nation, imbibed in his youth, and wilfully cherished through life, . . . disqualified him for conducting the affairs of his own country whenever they related to her, with that amicable spirit and good temper which a regard for our interests and honor imperiously demanded."[37]

Since the criticism bridged the period of mid-term congressional elections, the administration was wary in defense of its position. Lloyd, in a visit with Adams early in October 1826, was "profoundly alarmed for the Administration, at the probable consequences. . . ." Concerned to defend his own role in the Senate leadership, he requested removal of the secrecy under which the proceedings of the Rush negotiations had been withheld from the public in deference to the continuance of the negotiating process. He subsequently published a pamphlet defending the March 1826 report of the Committee on Commerce. Webster, discussing the reaction in Massachusetts and New York; Robert H. Goldsborough, discussing that in Maryland; and John H. Pleasants, that in Virginia, similarly warned of the importance of the issue in those areas.[38]

Clay's elaborate defense of the United States position in instructions to Gallatin on November 11 was designed with clear recognition of its utility in domestic politics, and Adams's release of the documentation on the negotiations in his annual message of 1826 was in large part an effort to put the administration's case before the public. On at least three occasions during the spring of 1827, Clay prepared editorials for Washington journals in defense of the administration's position. Adams himself wrote a lengthy anonymous article for the *American Quarterly Review*, published in September 1827, which was designed "to illustrate the uniform policy and spirit of Great Britain and the United States respectively, and to teach our countrymen how they ought to feel, as well as reason, in this controversy. . . ."[39]

One expression of the political agitation connected with the issue occurred in Congress's passing, on 9 May 1828, of a measure that specifically provided for the abolition, on a reciprocal basis, of discriminating duties on vessels from the French islands of Guadaloupe and Martinique. Responding to Britain's legislation that opened trade with its West Indian colonies to European states granting like privileges in their possessions, France, by royal ordonnance in 1826, had extended a general offer of freedom to trade in the French West Indies to vessels of nations that extended reciprocal freedom from discriminating duties. In March 1828, Levi Woodbury, a New Hampshire Jacksonian, alleged in the Senate, with great alarm, that the American traffic was in serious danger of being closed, for want of specific legislative response. A year earlier, in notifying the American authorities of his nation's action, the French minister in Washington had commented that he found "in this disposition, a motive on which to ground . . . claim to a reciprocity in favor of French vessels coming from the colonies." Yet the matter had not been brought before Congress.[40]

Alluding to the loss of the British West Indian trade and the enhanced importance consequently attached to that through the French islands, Tazewell warned: ". . . should we now be deprived of this, too, by the same means, those who are interested in the trade (and all are so interested) will not, and ought not, to be satisfied with the authors of such mischiefs." John Branch of North Carolina assailed the administration as acting "in a manner which merits the severe reprehension of the People of this country." Robert Y. Hayne noted rumor "that, in consequence of the delay on the part of the American Government, in reciprocating the French ordinance, it had actually been repealed." His constitutents, the rice growers of South Carolina, had lost heavily over the past year, he contended, by the failure to win for them a market in the French islands. In open session, Samuel Smith explained how unfavorably the Bordeaux merchants fared under the French commercial treaty and how eagerly they would avail themselves of an opportunity to damage their American competitors.[41]

Administration supporters again protested that legislative interference was damaging pending negotiations. The French commercial treaty was under review, a discussion that had been delayed by French ministerial change. Mareuil had been satisfied by Clay's explanations, and there was no threat to the continuance of trade with the islands. "The interference was unnecessary and uncalled for," contended Josiah Stoddard Johnston of Louisiana. "The bill ought now to pass, but I regret the discussion."[42]

A letter from Clay to Woodbury on March 4 had pointed to the current controversy with France over the taxing of American vessels that touched at intermediate ports, "although only for information, and without breaking bulk," as contrasted with the American policy of permitting French cargoes to pass through the islands to the United States. He conceded, however, that direct trade to and from the West Indies was not encompased in the reciprocity provisions of the French commercial treaty. If Congress wanted to open the traffic free of alien duties, it should enact the appropriate legislation. The bill was accordingly passed, without recorded vote in the Senate and without even reported debate in the House.[43]

The administration had manifestly been dilatory in reacting to foreign legislation that might have an impact upon the direct trade with the West Indies. Having early adopted the practice of retaliatory domestic regulation, the United States had opened the door to such a mode of diplomatic counteraction. The reliance now upon pursuit of negotiations rendered Adams and his secretary of state vulnerable at least to charges of naïveté. Farmers of the increasingly depressed agricultural hinterland were prepared to believe that the New Englander had sacrificed their interests to the possibility of extracting more favorable concessions for his seaboard constituents. Sectional as well as political divisions blended in criticism of the administration's handling of the issue.

The effect of the controversy during the succeeding presidential campaign is not, however, clear. Notwithstanding congressional agitation about the French island traffic in the spring of 1828, the topic had virtually dropped from the press by the previous winter. Release of the diplomatic correspondence had made evident that the British action was not dictated by the administration's negotiating terms. Whether formulated in response to Clay's concerns or under pressure to conform to the British navigation acts, the goals that were stipulated in Gallatin's instructions represented a retreat from Adams's earlier effort to penetrate the barriers of European colonialism. Reciprocity, as projected in the president's first annual message, in Clay's commercial treaties, and by act of Congress in 1828, was extended to indirect traffic; but in the Danish treaty of 1826 and in negotiations with France, as well as in the proposed arrangement with Britain, the administration had been willing to exclude from that principle the access to the carrying trade between mother country and colony. Adams's supporters had not failed to emphasize the rigidity of the British position and to point up its unpatriotic acceptance by their domestic critics: "We are amazed," wrote the editor of the *American* (New York), "at the arguments adduced, and at the quarter whence they come to justify Great Britain at the expense of America. . . ."[44]

The losses fairly to be attributed to the closing of the British island traffic were moderate. The value of United States exports to the West Indies generally, including Cuba and Haiti, declined some 4 percent in the two years ending 30 September 1828, compared with the similar period ending 30 September 1826; but it remained slightly greater than when Adams had assumed the presidency. Increased shipments to other islands in the area largely compensated for the decrease in those to the British. The difference may also have been offset for northern producers by increased sale for transshipment through Canadian ports.[45] Agricultural regions of the Middle States, the West, and the South tended to oppose the administration in the election of 1828, but they found in the campaign literature then other concerns that were being argued far more pressingly than the West Indies controversy.

Shipping interests generally appear to have remained loyal to the administration. Although Jacksonians attempted to evoke criticism that the administration had been lax in the defense of neutral rights, shipowners and ship and cargo insurers recognized that the primary thrust of Adams's foreign policy had been shaped to their demands. The American tonnage engaged in foreign trade increased by 7 percent during the period between September 1826 and September 1828, as compared with that of the earlier years of the administration; earnings

TABLE 1

Domestic Exports of the United States (in thousands of dollars)

	To British West Indies	To Swedish West Indies	To Danish West Indies	To Dutch West Indies	To French West Indies	To Spanish West Indies	To Cuba[a]	To Haiti	To British North America
1806	$5,092	$ 214	$1,421	$ 571	$2,770	$2,391	$	$	$ 938
1807	5,322	417	1,615	496	2,902	2,470			1,130
1808	1,428	68	192	98	803	631			273
1809	1,512	2,758	31	33	15	3,352			647
1810	2,323	1,619	33	40	59	3,182			1,293
1811	4,626	884	40		56	3,607			1,612
1812	1,775	1,061	21		204	2,641			643
1813		1,698			132	2,810			2
1814		1,246			165	1,972			10
1815	1,684	722	496	97	1,520	2,833			1,396
1816	3,074	262	682	194	1,484	2,732			3,323
1817	3,802	315	1,053	747	2,470	3,607			3,691
1818	3,489	279	984	637	1,895	2,532		94	2,356
1819	843	346	1,121	491	1,461	3,519		384	3,039
1820	877	450	1,590	432	1,266	3,439		526	2,886
1821	265	507	1,316	533	847	683	2,950	1,740	2,009
1822	450	570	1,611	921	919	1,743	3,201	1,746	1,881
1823	1,618	242	1,231	656	804	256	3,271	1,670	1,818
1824	1,751	205	1,150	590	771	307	3,612	1,902	1,773
1825	1,636	194	1,281	497	137	216	3,277		2,538
1826	2,079	121	1,391	434	904	211	3,750		2,564
1827	683	417	1,464	388	980	218	4,161		2,797
1828	26	612	2,202	415	1,009	222	3,913		1,618
1829	1	685	1,942	380	1,057	210	3,719		2,724
1830		553	1,688	319	792	246	3,439		3,650
1831	1,417	252	1,421	371	705	262	3,634		4,026
1832	1,655	141	1,393	358	606	323	3,681		3,569
1833	1,754	100	1,280	288	614	394	3,966		4,390
1834	1,532	81	1,084	285	561	432	3,693		3,478
1835	1,755	73	1,256	319	549	586	3,917		3,901

SOURCE: Charles H. Evans, comp., "Exports, Domestic, from the United States to All Countries, from 1789 to 1883, Inclusive," U.S. Congress, *House Misc. Docs.*, 48th Cong., 1st sess., vol. 24, no. 49, pt. 2, table 5, pp. 78–89.
[a] Recorded separately from the Spanish West Indies, beginning in 1821.

for shipping also increased slightly. A 21 percent increase in tonnage of the coastal marine during Adams's presidency also greatly counter-balanced the decline in Caribbean traffic.[46] As an alternative, moreover, the administration offered hope that the vigorous prosecution of world-wide trading arrangements would bring further expansion, a trend that was already evidenced in growing commerce with the Scandinavian countries, the Netherlands, the German States, the Mediterranean area, and Brazil and Chile in South America. Adams, who was frequently assailed by Jacksonians for his pursuit of Federalist and Hamiltonian policies, had in fact attempted to withhold concessions to the British while pursuing the Jeffersonian goal of opening generalized commerce.

The most serious problems of decline in foreign trade during the period did not arise from administration policy. The value, as distinct from the volume, of United States exports decreased by 10 percent during the last two years; and the value of overall merchandise imports fell by 9 percent. Losses were marked particularly in trade with Haiti, Britain—as well as its possessions—and the Latin-American republics of Mexico, Colombia, Buenos Aires, and Peru.[47] In the first instance, the decline resulted from the island's renewed ties with France, a preferential arrangement against which southern racial prejudices forestalled American protest. Falling prices on sales of cotton in Britain, a development that was bitterly lamented by southern leaders, reflected a production surplus, not falling demand; the volume of cotton exports increased steadily throughout the decade.[48] The indefinite extension of the British commercial treaty and the pressure for tariff concessions that would mollify French interests, in fact, marked efforts by the administration to safeguard markets for southern products.

The collapsing commerce with so large a segment of Latin America resulted, in part, from the instabilities of New World development. It derived, too, from the inability of the United States, as a young nation with pressing internal demands for capital, to compete effectively on a basis of international investment. But the Adams administration entered this contest with the advantages of precedence in hemispheric leadership and identification with the conception of an American System as a continuing concern of its foreign relations. That policy was challenged and largely nullified in partisan conflict over the next four years. Economic, as well as ideologic, goals were lost in the struggle.

6

★ ★ ★ ★ ★

DIPLOMACY OF MISSION

While trade considerations entered into most concerns of the administration's foreign policy, interests that have come to be identified as the traditional American sense of democratic mission were correlative and complicating. Despite their commitments to regional demands, both Adams and Clay were dedicated nationalists—proud of the American form of government, eager to extend its influence, and wary to protect its opportunities for territorial expansion. Yet their past relationship in dealing with such concerns had been sharply antagonistic. Clay—enthusiastic, warmly responsive, and romantic in his first reactions—translated ebullient patriotism as love of liberty and defense of democracy *to be projected internationally,* because only then could the American Revolution be legitimized. Adams, on the other hand, cautious and introspective in his outlook but with no less regard for this nation as the embodiment of freedom and independence, saw its welfare as *insular,* an insularity that he had only recently extended to hemispheric bounds.

These differing approaches to the preservation of a shared attachment must surely have stood high on the agenda that was discussed in the formation of the Adams-Clay alliance. How far Adams would be prepared to extend the ideologic association and how narrowly Clay would consent to define it were fundamental issues in the harmony of their arrangement. Their alliance introduced the potentiality of a new dimension in the national diplomacy.

The marquis de Lafayette's year-long visit, running through the first six months of the administration, also exerted a powerful liberalizing influence. During the summer of 1825 the president spent many hours with the Frenchman, who was a guest at the presidential mansion as arrangements were completed for the latter's return to his homeland. Adams's farewell remarks, delivered in a public departure ceremony, a highly emotional tribute to the general's service in the American cause, reflected the strong impact of the association.[1] Throughout the succeeding years of the administration a warm personal correspondence with the president and the secretary of state, as well as with other public leaders, gave continuing emphasis to Lafayette's ardent sympathy for the Greek revolution, his persistent concern for civil rights in France and Spain, and his enthusiasm for the development of representative government in Latin America.

The president's religious interests, and his desire that his administration should be so identified, was another force in the expansion of his diplomatic outlook. Throughout his life he read the Bible daily and regularly attended Sunday worship. In October 1826 he formally joined the Quincy Church. Patriotism and religion marched in tandem during the mid 1820s, correlating the cause of developing freedom in Latin America with the opening of Catholic lands to Protestantism and translating republican leadership as a mighty force to hasten world-wide spiritual regeneration in accordance with God's will. In 1823 the American Bible Society contracted for printing an edition of the Bible in Spanish. In that year, too, the American Board of Commissioners for Foreign Missions sent a team to survey opportunities for opening work in South America. Presbyterians, Methodists, Episcopalians, and, to a lesser degree, Dutch Reformed congregations were active in the effort through the end of the decade. Reporting upon the project in 1826, John C. Brigham emphasized the identity of political and religious concerns. The people of the United States, as "patriots and christians," should seek to enlighten their southern neighbors: "If one part of this new national family should fall back under a monarchical system, the event must threaten, if not bring down evils on, the part remaining." The viewpoint was to form one of the arguments on which the administration urged United States participation in the first Pan-American Congress. Adams's friend George Sullivan, applauding that diplomatic initiative, highlighted this rationale: "I think the moral effect of your administration will mark a new era in the history of our constitutional developement. . . ."[2]

History and the unfolding of seemingly providential events added to the association of nationalism with the operation of divine will in 1826.

As Americans marked the jubilee of their independence on July 4, the coincident deaths of John Adams and Thomas Jefferson, who had been politically opposed during the nation's early years, seemed to be symbolic in projecting unity for the great cause of expanding liberty. Throughout the land there was amazement at the extraordinary circumstance. The son who now held the presidency echoed but a general reaction when he wrote: "The time, the manner, the coincidence . . . are visible and palpable marks of Divine favor. . . ."[3]

Sentimental patriotism flourished under such omens. Even the intellectually disciplined Adams responded to their influence. During his presidency he projected foreign-policy initiatives that were far more expansive in their involvement beyond the domestic concerns of national self-interest than he had been willing to embrace as secretary of state. Although George Canning exaggerated the institutional framework of the design, he recognized the current of change when he warned the British agent at the Panama Congress that ". . . any project for putting the United States of North America at the head of An American Confederacy against Europe would be highly displeasing to your Government."[4]

In the outcome, however, the administration's efforts were to fall far short of the international outreach in behalf of struggling democracy which Speaker Clay had urged. Constraints were still dictated by the pragmatic focus of the president's nationalism: he rarely jeopardized his commercial priorities, and he remained cautious of international commitments. Limits were also set by the instabilities of the revolutionary governments, as Secretary of State Adams had anticipated. But in the final analysis, it was political opposition which, as in the prosecution of the administration's trade policies, proved decisive in countervailing the program. Measures that were intended to project United States leadership, ideologically as well as economically, at least to hemispheric bounds were in large part nullified. Even the "political system" that Adams had designed and that Monroe had proclaimed as a statement defining Old and New World relationships was virtually repudiated.

That the administration, in boundary disputes along Texas, Maine, the Great Lakes, and Oregon, undertook to protect, and even to extend, the nation's territorial claims is not remarkable. Significantly, however, the president and the secretary of state attempted to resolve the problems by patient negotiation rather than confrontation, despite strong local pressures for more forceful action. As their critics snidely observed, this was a "diplomatic administration."

Clay's old concern that legitimate pretensions had been surrendered in the Adams-Onís Treaty clearly dictated the instruction to Poinsett that he seek revision of the Texas boundary. Suggesting the Brazos, the Colorado (of Texas), or the Rio Grande as alternatives, Clay explained that the Sabine approached too closely "our great western Mart." Perhaps Mexico might welcome a boundary that would place its capital more nearly in the center of its territories, he ingenuously argued. Such a line would also, he noted, free Mexico of responsibility for curbing the warlike Comanches.[5]

The Fredonia uprising, initiated by Americans protesting Mexican land administration in northeastern Texas during the winter of 1826/27, was discountenanced by the administration. The president promptly expressed regret for the disturbance and directed that federal officers along the border act to thwart any American intervention. At the same time, Clay seized the occasion to urge again that Poinsett should press for revision of the boundary. Warning that such "collisions" might be "anticipated with confidence" and might "lead to misunderstandings," he reiterated his view that the Sabine brought Mexico too near to New Orleans. Since the ease with which United States citizens obtained large tracts in Texas fostered "belief that but little value . . . [was] placed upon the possession of the Province by that Government," he proposed that "a reasonable pecuniary consideration" might promote a boundary revision—$1 million for a line to run from the mouth of the Rio Grande to "the mouth of the Rio Puerco [Pecos?], thence, ascending this river to its source, and from its source, by a line due north to strike the Arkansas; thence, following the course of the southern bank of the Arkansas to its source, in Latitude 42° north; and thence by that parallel of latitude to the South Sea"; or if that be unattainable, $500,000 for a line ascending the Colorado to its source and thence due north to the Arkansas and continuing as in the alternative.[6]

On the northeast border of the nation, where the boundary under the Treaty of Paris, which ended the American War for Independence, had yet to be delineated, the states of Maine and Massachusetts were vigorously asserting claims to the lands of the Aroostook and Madawaska country along the St. John River. The arrest by New Brunswick authorities of an American settler, John Baker, who held title derived from the states, forced the federal government to intervene. Gallatin, in London, was directed to propose an arbitration of the dispute, preferably on the basis of briefs summarizing the respective territorial claims, but, as an alternative, if necessary, by submitting all the maps and documents to analysis by the arbitrator. Meanwhile, the impatient state officials were being urged to refrain from taking any measures that "would change the state of the question. . . ."[7]

Settlement of the northern, or Great Lakes, boundary, which was thought to be virtually resolved upon Adams's accession to the presidency, collapsed in 1827, when Britain demanded access to the channel south, rather than north, of St. George's, or Sugar, Island, in the Neebish Straits of the St. Mary's River. Peter B. Porter, the American commissioner, questioned the bargain that the British, in this situation, attempted to found upon their earlier concession of Barnhart's Island in the Long Saut of the upper St. Lawrence River. Although he believed that the falls of the St. Lawrence were unnavigable, he suggested that the administration might concede the point in return for a confirmation of the "right to the free navigation of the St. Lawrence from the St. Regis to its mouth." Clay went a step further, arguing that because "the best and, for descending navigation, the only channel of the St. Lawrence, between Barnhart's Island and the American shore," was already within defined limits of the United States, the trade of the upper St. Lawrence belonged to this nation and could therefore be regulated by it to force British concessions in the navigation of the lower river.[8]

Access to St. Lawrence navigation was a major goal in Gallatin's instructions; but the American negotiator, recognizing the futility of the demand, never seriously pressed it. The relevance of the objective was, however, a factor in the maintenance of United States boundary claims in Oregon. Gallatin, who contended that the land north and west of the Columbia River was "extremely worthless," urged "that the 49° line, after having crossed the waters of the Columbia, deviate so far southwardly as to leave within the British claim the whole watershed of the Gulf of Georgia." He was convinced that the British would never concede United States control of the rivers emptying into the Gulf or the Straits of Fuca. Adams and Clay, however, sharply curtailed their negotiator's authority to offer any territorial concessions south of the forty-ninth parallel. Instead, Clay proposed the offer of navigation on the lower Columbia, conditioned upon British control of its headwaters, and argued for reciprocity of this concession in reference to American access to navigation of the St. Lawrence: "The British Government has not been committed by a positive rejection of a line on the parallel of 49; but, if it had been, its pride may take refuge in the offer which for the first time, you are to propose of a right in common with us to the navigation of the Columbia River."[9]

None of the administration's boundary proposals was successful. A Mexican settlement was signed by Poinsett in January 1828, but it provided merely for the continuation of the Sabine River line. So restricted, the treaty had not been ratified by either nation when the administration left office. An arrangement had been completed by

Gallatin in September 1827, calling for arbitration of the Maine boundary dispute, but it was to be conducted under the United States' *"pis-aller"* choice for arbitrator, the king of the Netherlands, recognized as, next to the Portuguese sovereign, the one most "likely to be influenced" by Britain. Already the governor of Maine, Enoch Lincoln, had registered a bitter protest that the federal government was subjecting the state's "strength, security and wealth . . . to the mercy of a foreign individual," operating under a process that Gallatin had described as biased, "to try, if possible to split the difference." Maine would never, Lincoln warned, "assent to the results of an arbitration unfavorable to her interests" in this matter. To the west, the boundary relating to St. George's Island and the water communication from Lake Superior to Rainy Lake was undefined when the commissioners broke off their meetings *sine die*, in October 1827. The Oregon question was also relegated to indefinite suspension, under a renewal of the arrangement for joint occupation without a termination date.[10]

The extent of the president's expanded outlook on the American role in foreign affairs was most notable in his altered stand on the proposal for a mission to Greece. Secretary of State Adams had objected when President Monroe had proposed to incorporate into his annual message recommendations that the Greeks be recognized as an independent state and that an appropriation be made for a ministerial appointment. He had feared United States involvement in European turmoil, and he had been unwilling to jeopardize the growing Smyrna trade of Boston merchants.

But Daniel Webster, with Clay's strong endorsement, during the succeeding weeks had urged congressional authorization for "appointment of an agent or commissioner to GREECE, whenever the President . . . [should] deem it expedient. . . ." Arguing for this "encouragement . . . to a nation of oppressed and struggling patriots in arms," Clay had then derided opponents who found in such action a threat of war: ". . . he who follows the dictates of a heart warmed with humanity, and with the love of freedom, has a better guide than that cold, unfeeling, pence-calculating policy, which shrinks before it is menaced, and will never do a noble deed, for fear of some remote, possible consequences, of conceivable danger." In a major speech on the subject, on 23 January 1824, Clay had dismissed any worry that "the watchful jealousy of the Turks" would react hostilely. To those who voiced alarm for American commerce, he expressed contempt that "a miserable invoice of figs and opium" was "presented to us to repress our sensibilities, and to eradicate our humanity."[11]

The Webster resolution had died, on a unanimous vote for tabling it, in January 1824. The Calhounite Joel R. Poinsett had led strong southern opposition to the measure on the ground that it threatened to provoke European hostility at a time when United States support for Latin-American independence was already endangering the nation. Followers of Crawford had blended that argument with their own view of the limited powers of the federal government. Alexander Smyth of Virginia had been one of several who had contended that Americans could best uphold the cause of freedom by preserving their own security. John J. Wood, of New York, had argued that the treaty-making authority was to be restricted to the interests of the nation's industry and commerce. The army and navy existed only to redress injury, not to support ideologic venturism: "We have no authority under the Constitution to embark in wars of ambition, or to propagate the principles of religion or liberty by the sword." John Randolph had protested that arguments in behalf of the resolution implied "a total and fundamental change of the policy pursued by this Government, *ab urbe condita.*" The debate had provided a warning to those who would espouse democratic mission.[12]

Yet in September 1825 the Adams administration set in motion a project which, in the context of the steps that had been taken preliminary to United States recognition of Latin-American independence, presaged similar action in support of Greece. William C. Somerville, a Marylander who had fought in the South-American struggle and had traveled extensively in Europe, was sent as a secret emissary to investigate the progress of the Greek revolt. He was instructed to aid American commerce and seamen in the ports of Greece; to discourage American transport of military personnel or equipment in support of the Turks as conduct "unworthy of American Citizens, and . . . contrary to their duty, as well as their honour"; and, as the principal object of his mission, to collect information about the Greeks' capacity "to prosecute the war, and to sustain an independent Government." To Greek authorities he was to present assurances "that the people of the United States and their Government, throughout the whole of the . . . struggle of Greece, have constantly felt an anxious desire that it might terminate in the reestablishment of the liberty and independence of that Country. . . ."[13]

Whether congressional leaders then or subsequently during the Adams administration knew of this project is doubtful. When it was initiated is also uncertain. Somerville's appointment as chargé to Sweden and Norway had been approved before Congress had adjourned in March. At mid April, formal instructions for that mission had been written. Later that month the president had agreed to permit Somerville "to postpone his departure for Sweden till July or August, to accomplish his matrimonial project" with a New Orleans belle. In June, Christopher Hughes, at Stockholm, had anticipated the envoy's arrival in August, and at mid August, after being delayed by illness, Somerville had reported his readiness to depart for that destination. Clay, who had left the capital at mid May, had also prolonged his return; because of his daughter's illness while they were en route, he did not reach Washington until August 21. Two days later, Adams noted discussions with Clay concerning "Somerville; Sweden and Greece." On August 28 the president told Lafayette of his intentions concerning the mission to Greece.[14]

Under new instructions, dated September 6, Somerville's salary was to continue as that of a regular diplomat, but his commission to Sweden was to terminate on his arrival in Europe. Adams's concern that Somerville should travel with Lafayette aboard the *Brandywine* further indicates the serious purpose associated with the mission. Had the president, in accompanying Lafayette to Monroe's estate during early August, been swayed finally to initiate the investigation? Whatever the precipitating impulses, the president and Clay, by interim appointment, were undertaking to project a role in Continental Europe that the Congress, in accordance with the views of Secretary of State Adams, had rejected only a year and a half earlier.

Nothing in the scant evidence suggests, however, that Adams had yet determined to move so far as an extension of full diplomatic recognition. A qualifying caveat in the new instructions evidenced his continued restraint. Somerville was to maintain the policy of neutrality that the United States "have hitherto prescribed, and probably will continue to prescribe, to themselves." "It is better for both the United States and Greece that it should not be departed from in the present instance," the emissary was advised.[15]

Ill when he sailed, Somerville died en route, at Auxerre, France, in January 1826. He was buried on Lafayette's estate. The Frenchman's enthusiasm for the mission was evident in his expressed regret that the tombstone could not record Somerville's appointment until the administration should "find No inconvenience in it."[16] That time did not come during Adams's presidency. The plight of the Greeks grew worse; their prolonged defense of Missolonghi collapsed in April 1826. The administration abandoned the projected mission—perhaps because the principal concern of inquiry had been answered.

Americans did not, however, hesitate to express publicly the sympathies and hopes that Somerville had been directed to transmit. Their support, privately channeled, contributed nearly a quarter of a million dollars and the personal services of some fourteen young adventurers to the Greek cause. When American cupidity was also manifest, the administration openly intervened.

Leroy, Bayard and Company and G. G. and S. Howland, New York shipping firms, had arranged for the construction of two frigates on order for the Greeks. Since William Bayard was chairman of the New York Greek Committee, financial payments had been left flexible. No definite contract had been drawn; Greek deputies were to pay for materials at intervals as required. Expecting that the vessels would be completed in November 1825, the deputies found in October that payments had run to $750,000, $200,000 beyond their estimates, that another $300,000 would be required to finish the work, and that it would not be completed for another four months. With administration support, Congress, in May 1826, amended earlier legislation for naval construction by the United States, so as to permit the president to suspend the building of one of several projected ships and to authorize an alternative purchase. The government accordingly paid the Greeks $221,487 and took over one of the uncompleted vessels, thus, as Clay explained, enabling them "to Sail the other."[17]

Adams's encouragement for the Greek effort continued throughout his presidency. In his annual message of December 1827 he publicly avowed hope that the "suffering Greeks" would "obtain relief from that most unequal of conflicts," that they would "enjoy the blessing of self-government," and that their independence would be "secured by . . . liberal institutions. . . ." A year later, reporting the outbreak of war between Russia and Turkey, he anticipated that it would afford "collateral agency" in securing to the Greeks "ultimately the triumph of humanity and of freedom."[18]

Coupling this last remark with an expression of regret for a war involving the Ottoman Porte, Adams cited the absence of commercial ties as a factor that was holding Americans apart from that nation, "in a state, perhaps too much prolonged, of coldness and alienation." The argument that Clay had scorned in 1824—that "the watchful jealousy of the Turks" would react against partiality for the Greeks—was no idle concern when the administration was seeking an accord for trading access to Constantinople. In the autumn of 1825 George Bethune English explained that difficulties which Commodore Rodgers had experienced in meeting with Khosref Mehemet could be attributed to an indifference "influenced by the fabulous statements contained in the American newspapers relative to the affairs of the Greeks. . . ." Offley reported a year later that the pasha had inquired about "the arrival of a

Frigate in Greece under the American flag which was then transfered to the Greeks."[19]

In the absence of treaty relations with the Turks, formal adherence to United States neutrality legislation may not have been mandatory, but practical consequences were a consideration. In March 1827, when Mathew Carey requested "protection from the pirates" for a vessel that was carrying supplies to the Greeks, Southard rejected any special provision for naval convoy. Instead, he advised that "they fall in with any of our Ships of War." Although the United States Mediterranean Squadron was expanded in the following year, its operations were directed against depredations by either belligerent. In the later stages of the conflict, when the Turkish fleet was in disarray, Greek, more often than Turkish, "pirates" came under American naval fire. United States negotiators reminded their Turkish counterparts, after the Ottoman defeat at Navarino, that the American fleet had not joined the European allies in that attack. United States support for the Greeks, it was evident, still operated under some constraints.[20]

While the president, in projecting the Somerville mission and in his general expressions of support for the Greeks, had moved considerably closer to the ideological stance of the secretary of state, Clay's direct involvement in the development of this position is unclear. Intervening circumstances had, moreover, forestalled a policy decision that challenged the fundamental premises of either leader. On Latin-American interests the two men had already established a superficial community of viewpoint. The diplomatic undertakings in that area, despite external interferences which here, too, thwarted the accomplishment of their goals, clarified much more sharply the measure of their agreement.

The friendship that was accorded by the Central-American Federation and the disintegration that marked the end of the state's brief role in history epitomized the height and the depth of the administration's hemispheric relations. In instructions to William Miller, who had been appointed chargé at Guatemala in 1825, Clay cited "circumstances in its origin and subsequent conduct" which entitled that nation "to the interest and regard of the United States, perhaps even superior to that which they have ever felt in any of the other Southern Republics."[21] The six provinces of Guatemala, Chiapas, Honduras, San Salvador, Leon (Nicaragua), and Costa Rica, which had loosely been joined under Spanish rule as the captaincy-general of Guatemala, had remained so disorganized that sporadic revolts had been easily suppressed while independence movements were spreading elsewhere in Latin America.

Severance of the tie to Spain had finally come in 1821. Chiapas, in February of that year, had elected to join Mexico, under the imperial rule of Augustín de Itúrbide. Nicaragua, Honduras, and Guatemala, strongly divided between adherents to such a union and proponents of independence, had declared for the latter course when in September, Guatemala, with the capital city still under Spanish jurisdiction, made the choice. Upon learning of this action, Itúrbide had sent a Mexican army southward; and in order to avoid warfare, a Guatemalan junta, in January 1822, had declared that the Central American provinces were "incorporated" in the Mexican empire.

Costa Rica and San Salvador, however, had remained apart from the Guatemalan union. When the Mexican government sought to assert authority over San Salvador, in February 1822, that province formally proposed annexation as one of the United States. Over the next year, Salvadorean resistance to Mexican rule had continued, with hope and even expectation that a United States force would be sent to provide assistance. In May 1823, commissioners from the Salvadorean Congress had been sent to Washington with full powers to arrange for union.

But with Itúrbide's fall from power and with the establishment of Mexico as a federal republic in March 1823, circumstances had changed for the Central American provinces. San Salvador had joined with Guatemala in organizing an independent state, which was formally proclaimed on 1 July 1823 as the United Provinces of the Center of America. Honduras, Nicaragua, and Costa Rica entered the federation during the next few months. The Salvadorean commissioners to the United States, one of whom, Manuel José de Arce, became the first president of the new republic, returned home without having seen either President Monroe or his secretary of state.

These events, antecedent to the pronouncement of the Monroe Doctrine, provided a basis on which the Adams administration enjoyed a particularly cordial diplomatic relationship with the new state. The Central American treaty of commerce, signed at Washington in December 1825, was, as previously noted, the model representative of the goals that Adams and Clay sought to achieve. The secretary of state's instructions to Miller, as United States chargé in Guatemala, pointed to another interest on which the Central American government proved to be similarly cooperative. On 8 February 1825 Antonio José Cañaz, its minister in Washington, had proposed a joint treaty "perpetually to secure the advantages . . . to the two Nations" of a canal "uniting the Atlantic and Pacific Oceans" through Nicaragua. The administration requested that Miller ascertain whether route surveys had been made, what provision the country and its population could afford for constructing the canal, and what were the estimates of its cost. He was not to "inspire the Government of the Republic of Guatimala [sic] with any confident expectation that the United States . . . [would] contribute, by pecuniary or other means, to the execution of the work," but he was to gather the requisite information on which the latter government might determine its course. To Cañaz, Clay expressed the president's "very great sensibility" of the "sentiments of consideration and friendship" under which the proposal had been made. Clay emphasized, however, the importance of caution in proceeding upon the venture and the necessity for consultation with Congress about any cooperation in the effort.[22]

Miller died of yellow fever en route to his mission, but his instructions on the subject of a canal were redated and assigned to his successor, John Williams, on 10 February 1826. An account published in the *National Intelligencer* (Washington) and *Niles' Weekly Register* during the spring of 1825, reporting British interest in such a canal and the practicability of the Central American route, may have been inspired by these discussions. In July, Adams's friend Joseph Blunt wrote to him at length on the subject, pointing to the utility of a canal in relation to an increasingly valuable trade and to the "importance of having the property of this canal in American citizens in preference to British subjects."[23] In December 1825 a group of Rochester, New York, businessmen also addressed the president on the matter and urged that it be brought to the attention of a proposed inter-American Congress at Panama, as a project to be developed under the common ownership of all the parties of the confederation, "with the right in common for all the Americans to use it. . . ." Clay's instructions, as dispatched in May 1826 to United States commissioners to the Panama assembly, cited the possibility of a canal "somewhere through the Isthmus that connects the two Americas" as "a proper subject of consideration. . . ." Noting that it would be a matter of interest "to all parts of the world" and of particular benefit to the states ranged between Peru and the United States, he concluded that its advantages to all America required that it "be effected by common means and united exertions, and . . . not be left to the separate and unassisted efforts of any one Power."[24]

The Rochester group was particularly fearful that the proposed canal might become "the property & stock of speculating Individuals, or charter Incorporations." Such an approach had been encouraged by the Central American government under a decree of 16 June 1825. In response to petitions by various commercial houses advocating a canal, the congress of that state directed that a canal, adequate to handle the largest vessels, should be opened through Nicaragua and pledged to indemnify those who should undertake such a project for their costs. At the same time, the congress reserved the right to set the rates for use of the canal and stipulated that its navigation should be common to all friendly and neutral nations.[25]

The Central American authorities received proposals from European, particularly English, as well as American groups. Still the friendship for the United States prevailed—a "prejudice" so marked, one observer reported, that English traders attempted to assume American identity as an advantage to their intercourse. On 14 June 1826 a contract was awarded to a group of New York and Philadelphia mechants, acting under the name of Aaron H. Palmer and Company, shortly thereafter reorganized as the Central American and United States Atlantic and Pacific Canal Company. John Williams, as chargé, boasted to Adams that his arrival had contributed greatly to the success of the United States promoters: "The private suggestion you made to me respecting the British possession at Belize on the bay of Honduras & their predilection for commanding positions in all parts of the world were used with effect in wresting this contract from them."[26]

Under the arrangement the firm, within six months, was to deposit $200,000 in the city of Granada for preliminary expenses. Williams himself subscribed $20,000 to the project; and his successor, William Phillips, a Philadelphia merchant, also invested heavily in what he later delineated "that infamous *canal bubble.*" Others interested in the project, headed by the New Yorker Palmer, were Governor De Witt Clinton; Congressman Stephen Van Rensselaer; Morris Robinson, cashier of the New York branch of the Bank of the United States; Edward Livingston, a congressman from Louisiana; and Charles J. Catlett of the District of Columbia, who together constituted the board of directors. The company was to receive two-thirds of the tolls until it had been reimbursed for the full cost plus 10 percent interest and, thereafter, half the tolls for seven additional years. The Central American government agreed to provide the available surveys and maps, labor at specified wages, native timber, and release from customs duties on importations of machinery necessary for the construction. Work was to commence within one year.[27]

The contractors were unable to raise the requisite deposit. While the Central American authorities were disposed to extend further time to Palmer and his associates, their efforts to raise funds in England during the winter of 1826/27 were also unsuccessful. Meanwhile, the collapse of the Panama Congress ended the hope of inter-American action under governmental auspices. In 1828 a group of Dutch capitalists, under royal patronage, became interested in such a venture and in 1830 obtained a contract similar to the one that had formerly been extended to the Americans. The outcome of the Palmer enterprise, as Phillips reported to Clay, had "had an unfavorable influence" in United States relations at Guatemala.[28]

Want of the anticipated United States investment contributed to virtual collapse of the Central American regime. In January 1827 the central government was forced to put down a rebellion in the state of Guatemala. By mid April, open warfare had broken out between Guatemala and San Salvador, and during the course of the ensuing year the forces of the latter assumed control of most of the country outside the cities of Omoa and Guatemala. Guatemala City itself fell in April 1829. After another decade of conflict the federation was dissolved in 1839. The Adams administration's concern for the special relationship with the republic had ended in May 1828, when William B. Rochester, who had been named chargé over a year earlier, finally arrived off the port of Omoa, learned of the governmental disruption, and sailed on without landing.

While the bonds of sympathy were never so warm between the United States and other Latin American republics, the president and the secretary of state viewed the hemispheric relationship as the core of their foreign policy. Both Adams and Clay undoubtedly looked upon Latin American independence as a development of potential economic benefit to their constituents, but both rested their espousal of the cause upon ideologic grounds. Clay's argument had moved to economic considerations only secondarily. While congressional opponents in 1818 argued that the new states would, in fact, increase competition in products that the United States exported, he had protested that "it was too selfish, to mean a principle, for this body to act on, to refuse its sympathy for the Patriots of the South, because some little advantage of a Commercial nature might be retained to us from their remaining in the present condition. . . ." Disclaiming any intention "to force upon other nations our principles and our liberty, if they did not want them," he nevertheless acclaimed the Latin-American struggle as one "for liberty and independence; for precisely what we fought for." To a pro-Jackson pamphlet, which in the spring of 1824 identified the principles of Monroe's message as being essentially Clay's policy and reiterated the objection that it promoted the development of agricultural competition, Clay's supporters rejoined that his stand was the cause of liberty.[29]

As early as 1793 Adams, too, had orated upon the difference in governmental philosophy between the Old World and the New. That this was not merely the Fourth-of-July hyperbole of youth was evident when, in cabinet discussions preliminary to the formulation of Monroe's statement, Adams had urged that it include a declaration of "our expectation and hope that the European powers . . . abstain from the attempt to spread their principles in the American hemisphere. . . ." He then included "Continental Spanish America" with the United States as "a distinct *American* portion of the human race . . . differing from Europe in the fundamental principles upon which their respective Governments are founded." Americans, he contended, vested their liberties in "the natural rights of mankind, and the sovereignty of the people"; Europeans, on the other hand, sought them "in the will of kings." He interpreted the role of the United States, in its relations with Latin America, as that of a leader providing guidance to "those very fundamental maxims which we from our cradle at first proclaimed and partially succeeded to introduce into the code of national law."[30]

Throughout Latin America, United States diplomats under Adams's administration operated under this conception. When Colombia, under the rule of Simón Bolívar's subordinates, threatened to reject his constitution, Beaufort T. Watts, acting as chargé, addressed a personal letter to the Liberator, urging him to return and to reassume authority. Watts's action was criticized by Adams and was reprimanded by Clay, but their opposition stemmed less from Watts's intervention in Colombian domestic affairs than from the administration's growing suspicion that Bolívar cherished imperial dreams. In November 1827 Clay received coldly a letter from Bolívar, which was apparently designed to vindicate Watts's performance but incidentally expressed admiration for the Kentuckian's "affectionate love of liberty" and gratitude for his service to the cause of Latin-American independence. Responding only after the elapse of a year, Clay stiffly voiced concern at reports of Bolívar's personal ambitions and hope that "preferring the true glory of our immortal Washington, to the ignoble fame of the destroyers of liberty," the South American had "formed the patriotic resolution of ultimately placing the freedom of Colombia upon a firm and sure foundation."[31]

The administration conveyed no censure to William Tudor, its chargé at Lima, whose strong criticism of Bolívar led the diplomat actively to support the movement rejecting the Liberator's constitutional proposals. When junior officers of the Colombian army in Peru overthrew their superiors because, as Tudor reported, "they would not be made the instruments of enslaving" that people, the United States chargé transmitted letters inviting the return from exile of the liberal Francisco Luna Pizarro. Tudor also called upon Bolívar's general, Andrés de Santa Cruz, and "wishing to have him act fully with the patriot party," advised him that "to maintain the public tranquillity," he must follow "the wishes of the nation."[32]

Bolívar's governmental aspirations were not the only disturbing element as United States diplomats sought to project "the American way." Condy Raguet, the chargé to Brazil, viewed the personal immorality of Emperor Pedro I and the pretensions of his newly created court nobility as evidence of the corruption that monarchy brought to the New World. Fear that the European powers might act to erect a Bourbon throne in Mexico underscored Poinsett's political meddling. Samuel Larned, secretary of legation and later chargé in Chile, responded in 1825 to journalistic attacks upon the religious and political institutions of the United States by publishing his own "Observations" in a spirited reply. He readily complied when he was subsequently invited to advise the Chilean Committee on the Constitution concerning the nature of the federal form of government. John M. Forbes, deploring what he viewed as Argentinean servility to the British, republished Larned's essays as a pamphlet for circulation in Buenos Aires and regularly translated public papers by Adams and Clay for similar distribution. "It has ever been an object of earnest desire and constant effort on my part to impress this ungrateful People with a due sense of the friendship of the U.S. towards them . . . ," he reported.[33]

The priority of United States recognition of Latin-American independence and the annunciation of Monroe's famous message provided the basis on which the Adams administration undertook to assert hemispheric leadership. "Noncolonization," "noninterference," "no transfer"—the protective concepts of the so-called Monroe Doctrine—had not yet been systematically set forth. Only the first two had been enunciated by Monroe, and then they had been separated, interjected as appendages to diverse topics of major comment. The "no transfer" policy, operational since the founding of the republic, had reappeared in Adams's instructions to Hugh Nelson, as Minister to Spain, in April 1823. That Adams envisioned these ideas as formulating a unified program had been evident the following November, in the secretary of state's projected response to correspondence from the baron de Tuyll concerning recognition of the new Spanish American states:

It was meant . . . to be eventually an exposition of the principles of this Government, and a brief development of its political system as henceforth to be maintained: essentially republican—maintaining its own independence, and respecting that of others; essentially pacific—studiously avoiding all involvement in the combinations of European politics, cultivating peace and friendship with the most absolute monarchies, highly appreciating and anxiously desirous of retaining that of the Emperor Alexander, but declaring that, having recognized the independence of the South American States, we could not see with indifference any attempt by European powers by forcible interposition either to restore the Spanish dominion on the American Continents or to introduce monarchical principles into those countries, or to transfer any portion of the ancient or present American possessions of Spain to any other European power.

Subjected to cabinet and presidential revisions, Adams's response to Tuyll, delivered orally on 27 November 1823, still followed the indicated outline, coupling the "noninterference" and "no transfer" principles but omitting reference to more general "noncolonization." State Department files indicate that, in written form, Adams merely referred the Russian to Monroe's message, without elaboration. The policy statements remained fragmented.[34]

Under the Adams administration they were promptly and formally consolidated. In instructions to Poinsett in March 1825, Clay stated the concepts of "noncolonization" and "noninterference" jointly, identifying them as the basic principles of Monroe's message. Again to Poinsett, in the following November, he also cited "no transfer" instructions, as recently addressed to James Brown at Paris, in evidence of the administration's commitment to "the memorable pledge of the President . . . in his Message to Congress of December 1823."[35] The handwritten drafts of these documents and the relatively minor emendations in the course of their development—in particular, the meagerness of the interpolations in Adams's hand—indicate that the secretary's views were essentially those of the president. Poinsett cited them, as had been intended, to oppose Mexican proposals for preferential trading arrangements among the Latin-American states. Adams's "political system as henceforth to be maintained" thus emerged as a unified body of operational doctrine.

The inference to be drawn concerning the enforcement action remained, however, undefined. How "protective" the commitment, how meaningful its "pledge"—this was a question to which Colombia, Brazil, Mexico, and Buenos Aires, each, sought an answer before Adams left office. Responding to the first of these inquiries in August 1824, Secretary of State Adams had asserted that there was not at the time likelihood that foreign intervention would endanger the independence of the republics. If such an occasion should arise, the president would then call upon the United States Congress to take the appropriate action. Under the Constitution, he had explained, that body must give "the ultimate decision of this question." A similarly evasive answer was given by Clay to Brazil in April 1825: the administration adhered to the principles of Monroe's message but saw no current danger that Portugal would be able to draw other powers to her aid in "resubjugating the Brazils." While the war was "confined to the parent country and its former Colony," Clay added, the United States could not, without inconsistency, depart from its policy of neutrality.[36]

When, in the summer of 1825, movements of the French fleet in the Caribbean aroused fears that Spain's entente ally was about to take over Cuba and Puerto Rico, Mexico called upon the United States for a response. Poinsett gave assurance that his government "would not view with indifference" such a development. At the same time, Clay directed Brown, in Paris, to reiterate an earlier pronouncement of that position and to add, "with the hope of guarding, beforehand, against any possible difficulties on that subject . . . that we could not consent to the occupation of those Islands by any other European Power than Spain, under any contingency whatever." But the minister was informed that in communicating this view, "it should be done in the most conciliatory and friendly manner."[37] French authorities promptly explained that the activity was related to negotiations for resolving their own dispute with Haiti, and the whole episode became, in effect, a request for better information on projected naval operations in the area. The United States policy had been reaffirmed diplomatically, but still without evidence of prospective sanctions.

By January 1828 the evasion verged on retreat. In a long-delayed answer to the Buenos Aires government, which in August 1826 had inquired concerning the applicability of Monroe's pronouncement to the war that was being waged upon that South American state by Brazil, yet nominally a colony of Portugal, Clay still emphasized the administration's belief that the Monroe message and their own subsequent efforts had "had great, if not decisive, influence in preventing all interference, on the part of the Allied Powers of Europe to the prejudice of the new Republics of America," but he saw "no longer any danger whatever of the contingency happening, which is supposed by Mr. Monroe's message." That declaration, he reiterated, had been an executive action, to which, under the Constitution, Congress alone could give effect, should a specific case arise. While there was "every reason to believe that the policy which it announced was in conformity with the opinion both of the nation and of Congress," Clay continued, "the declaration must be regarded as having been voluntarily made, and not as conveying any pledge or obligation, the performance of which foreign nations have a right to demand." As for the specific issue of the war between

Brazil and Buenos Aires, that was "strictly American in its origin and its object"; the European allies had taken no part in it; and the United States, although viewing it "with great regret," did not regard it as a case warranting deviation from the "general policy . . . of strict and impartial neutrality in reference to all wars of other Powers."[38]

The administration had been eager to establish the formula of an American System, but they had been wary to avoid stipulated commitments. Operational determinants of the policy were to be set pragmatically and nationalistically. However greatly the president and the secretary of state might have been inclined to extend the ideological boundaries of democratic mission, they were aware that actions required congressional sanction. Developing partisan opposition by 1828 had compelled Clay even to qualify his allusion to the "pledge" of Monroe's pronouncement. Moreover, the concern for the national interest, which underlay the missionary impulse of both Adams and Clay, pointed up dangers that required diplomatic flexibility. Out of the lingering conflict between Spain and her former colonies, problems had developed that radically altered the hemispheric relationship predicated upon United States influence.

Perhaps to alleviate the pressure for a defensive alliance, certainly to reassert the leadership role of the United States in the Americas, the administration, within two months of assuming office, had initiated a generalized diplomatic effort to bring about Spanish recognition of the independence of the severed colonies. British recognition of the new states of Buenos Aires, Mexico, and Colombia had been communicated to the foreign ministers of the European powers on 31 December 1824 and had been publicly announced in Parliament on 7 February 1825.[39] Knowledge of this action, which was reported by Richard Rush to Secretary of State Adams on January 18, in a dispatch received on March 8, emphasized the need to reassert the priority of United States action, while it also implied at least tacit British support for the peace movement. Although Canning might, as in his reaction to Monroe's unilateral pronouncement, find the United States stand an embarrassment, a diplomatic maneuver to be denigrated, he would not oppose it.

Nevertheless, the venture was initiated under discouraging portents. On May 6 Clay received from Hugh Nelson, then closing his ambassadorial duties at Madrid, a report that Spain was urging a rupture of relations between the Continental powers and Britain and that "something . . . [was] in preparation between France and Spain." Despite this warning, the secretary of state four days later dispatched instructions to

Henry Middleton directing him "to endeavour to engage the Russian Government to contribute its best exertions towards terminating the existing contest between Spain and her Colonies." On the next day, instructions for Rufus King, who was about to assume his mission in England, emphasized the "coincidence in the policy of the United States and Great Britain" on the matter, noted that Poinsett, at Mexico, and Alexander H. Everett, en route to Spain, carried instructions urging "a disposition to peace," advised that United States emissaries to the other American states and to Brown in France would carry a similar message, and transmitted a copy of the official note to Middleton.[40]

The Middleton instructions began with a reference to the seventeen years of protracted conflict, "marked by the most shocking excesses" and "an almost incalculable waste of blood and treasure." Conclusion of the warfare would be important to both Europe and America; and Russia, although not directly involved in the situation, could "have a controlling influence on its useless protraction or its happy termination." In addressing the appeal to Czar Alexander, the administration was attempting to build upon the good will that had been evinced over the past three years by the czar's role in the drafting of the St. Petersburg convention on Anglo-American claims, the settlement of the territorial controversy on the Northwest Coast, and, most recently, the adjustment of the *Pearl* indemnity. The power of the czar, "and the profoundest respect for the wisdom and the justice of the august Personage who wields it," were to be lauded and invoked. Surely, this was a strange mandate from a president who cherished American independence of European power politics and a secretary of state who challenged Old World commitment to the concept of legitimacy!

The instructions, nevertheless, pointed to the rupture of the colonial relationship as an inevitable development in the tradition of the United States movement for independence. The victory had now been won over Spain—"from the western limits of the United States to Cape Horn. . . ." There was no prospect that Spain could recover her possessions—"The re-conquest of the United States by Great Britain would not be a more mad and hopeless enterprize. . . ." Whatever the "intestine divisions" that might arise within the new states, the "political changes" that must arise, they had known independence and had tasted its fruits. The colonial cord to the parent country, "being once broken, is never repaired."

Linked, however, to this paean on the triumph that had been achieved was a threat that the conflict might be extended if Spain were "obstinately" to persevere. Without acknowledgment of their victory, the new states dared not disband their armies. They would direct "their combined and unemployed forces" against the enemy wherever he could be reached. Lured by the wealth of the prize and by its service as a base of counterattack, they would move against Spain's "remaining insular possessions," Clay warned. And, he continued, their success in the effort was "by no means, improbable," indeed, it was "almost certain." Apart from their proximity to the islands and the acclimatization of their forces, the new states would hold great advantage in that "a large portion" of the inhabitants of the islands sought separation from Spain "and would therefore form a powerful auxiliary to the Republican arms. . . ." "Cuba," Clay concluded, "is in the mouth of a sack, which is held by Colombia and the United Mexican States."

Cuba! To Adams the island represented a dagger held at the throat of United States commerce, controlling the traffic of the Caribbean and American sea routes to South America. Concern for its status had underlain his focus in promulgating the Monroe Doctrine. Cuba in the hands of a weakened Spain could be tolerated; Cuba as the colony of France or Britain could not. But no more readily could the island be permitted to pass into the possession of American states that were too weak to defend it against European encroachment. To forestall such lamentable eventualities, Adams was prepared to go beyond hemispheric isolationism, to seek Russian mediation in the resolution of this New World problem.

For Clay the possibility of Cuban independence remained as late as October 1825, yet another alternative, one that accorded particularly with his ideological convictions. To assure the stability of such an arrangement the secretary of state was at that time even willing to consider a tripartite guarantee in association with France and Britain. That President Adams, who was then at Quincy, endorsed such a solution may well be questioned. How far he might have moved in support of Greek revolutionaries was never revealed, but his identification with the Monroe pronouncement, as well as his delayed recognition of the new Spanish American republics, had connoted specific acknowledgment of the legitimacy of existing colonial political ties. Over the ensuing months, Clay was to abandon this proposal, yet there is no evidence that the president and his secretary of state were in disagreement as they turned aside from the option of an independent Cuba. The limits of the concern for democratic mission were manifest for both leaders in the problem of Cuba's relationship to the New World system. In pointing to that dilemma, the American leaders raised a specter that was as disturbing to their own policy objectives as it was to the colonial pretensions of Spain.

7

THE CUBAN PROBLEM
AND THE PANAMA CONGRESS
IN THE NEW WORLD SYSTEM

Cuba had long represented a pawn of international concern. Tension had heightened when France in 1823, in behalf of the Holy Alliance, intervened to put down republican government in Spain. George Canning had made clear Britain's warning, as, disavowing any British intention to "trespass" on Cuba, he had expressed an understanding that France shared similar views. The Polignac Memorandum of 9 October 1823 had provided the desired French response—"that she abjured, in any case, any design of acting against the colonies by force of arms." The power of the British navy appeared to discourage such adventurism, but the danger could not be discounted. Mexico's alarm over the movements of the French fleet in August 1825 and the United States' request for explanation of them reflected the unease of Cuba's western neighbors. As a consequence, Brown was directed to inform the French government that the president conceived "it due to the friendly relations . . . between the two Nations . . . that the purpose of any similar movement, hereafter, made in a season of peace, should be communicated. . . ."[1]

Adams's views on the status of Spain's island possessions had been fully discussed in the instructions under which Middleton had been directed to seek Russian intervention for resolution of the colonial conflict. The United States minister was authorized to disclose them "without reserve," and France and Britain, together with the Latin-American states, had been informed of their content. On June 15, upon taking leave from his mission, Hugh Nelson had stated them in similar terms to the Spanish government. The United States was satisfied with the existing situation, under which the islands were open to its commerce. It questioned that Cuba could maintain independence and feared that "a premature declaration" of such a state "might bring about a renewal of those shocking scenes" that had afflicted Haiti. In that situation, only a guarantee and an occupying force of foreign powers could forestall disaster, but the arrangements for international action "would create very perplexing questions of very difficult adjustment, to say nothing of the continual jealousies which would be in operation." This government, therefore, desired "no political change" for Cuba or Puerto Rico.[2]

Canning, describing as "desperate" the American hope for Russian intervention to effect the desired peace, responded that Britain would herself attempt to prevail upon Spain to declare an armistice. To that end he proposed that an accord be signed by Britain, France, and the United States, assuring that Cuba and Puerto Rico should remain under the mother country.[3] Again, however, as in the pronouncement of the Monroe Doctrine, the Americans drew back from international commitment.

Clay instructed Rufus King, in England, to inform Canning of the United States note to France renouncing interest in any change in Spanish possession of the islands and warning that this government would oppose transfer of the islands "to any other European Power." If Britain were to direct a similar protest to France, Clay suggested, the latter state must surely abandon any designs that it might entertain toward intervention, and "the substantial object of the British Government" would be attained "by means but little varied from those which it had devised." On the other hand, he continued, an international guarantee to Spain would withdraw "a powerful motive of peace." Spain, "tranquilized in all her apprehensions about further Colonial losses," would find strengthened hope of recovering her former power "on some part of this Continent. . . ."

> If, instead of approaching Spain, with a diplomatic instrument, lulling her most serious apprehensions about Cuba, she were left to speculate upon all the possible dangers, from every quarter, which may assail her most important Colonial possession; and if, moreover, she were told by the three Powers, or by Great Britain and the United States, that, in the event of the people of Cuba declaring their independence, those Powers would guarantee it, she would be much more effectually awakened to a true sense of the perils to which perseverance in her present misguided policy might expose her.[4]

Cuban and Puerto Rican revolutionaries had long been seeking United States support—some for annexation to their northern neighbor; others for independence. Presidents Jefferson and Madison had both considered the possibility of annexation. The first had been rebuffed in a direct approach to the island authorities. Madison had been unwilling, and unable, to afford the guarantee of military aid which Creole planters demanded against the possibilities of a British blockade or internal anarchy from slave revolt. William Shaler, the United States consul at Havana under Madison, had, however, conferred with the disaffected planters, had himself strongly supported their movement, and, in consequence, had been forced, at Spain's request in 1811, to leave the island.[5]

Annexationist sentiment had been revived during the early 1820s. Cuban planters, fearful of the weakness of Spain, as evidenced in the Latin-American independence movement, were increasingly alarmed at the possibility of slave revolt. Growing abolitionist sentiment in Britain and opposition to slavery in the Latin-American republics made a juncture under such alternatives unattractive, but a tie with the United States promised many advantages. The growing importance of slavery as an institution in the American South and the possibility of access, domestically, to a slave trade that was legally barred as foreign commerce won adherents for annexation in the United States as well as Cuba. Coastal shipping and mercantile interests, as well as the farmers of the Middle States and the Ohio Valley, weary of the vicissitudes of colonial restrictions in the West India trade, might be expected to welcome the attachment, notwithstanding the accompanying expansion of an American slaveholding interest.

But only if the arrangement could be effected peacefully. When an agent for Cuban planters had presented an annexation proposal to Washington authorities in the fall of 1822, Monroe's cabinet had discussed the matter at some length. Although Secretary of War Calhoun had vigorously urged the importance of the tie, he had finally concluded, with Adams and the president, that the offer should be officially rejected. Concern that annexation might provoke war with Britain and the Continental powers and uncertainty about the extent of Cuban support were decisive considerations. More information on the strength of the island movement was, however, requested.[6]

A year later, when the French were marching to restore Ferdinand to the Spanish throne, Monroe's cabinet had again considered the Cuban situation, amidst fears that a transfer of the island might represent compensation, to France for reinstitution of absolutism or to Britain for the defense of constitutionalism. Calhoun had then advised "war with England, *if* she means to take Cuba." Secretary of the Navy Smith Thompson had suggested that the Cubans be encouraged "to declare themselves independent, *if* they . . . [could] maintain their independence." Adams had concluded that the islanders could not stand alone and that the United States would "not, and could not, prevent by war the British from obtaining possession of Cuba, if they attempt[ed] to take it." In that context the British proposals during the summer of 1823 for a joint declaration renouncing intent to take possession of the Spanish colonies that had achieved independence raised an important question, phrased in the following terms by Madison: "Does it exclude future views of acquiring Porto Rico etc. as well as Cuba?" The unilateral pronouncement of the Monroe Doctrine the following December had pledged noninterference "with the existing colonies or dependencies of any European power," but it had conspicuously failed to renounce a possible transfer of Spain's possessions to the United States by mutual agreement.[7]

Hope of such an arrangement lingered into the Adams administration. Everett's instructions as minister to Spain, like those of Hugh Nelson, whom he had succeeded in the summer of 1825, reiterated the assurance that the United States was "satisfied with the present condition of those Islands, in the hands of Spain, and with their Ports open to our commerce. . . ." "This Government," Clay advised, "desires no political change of that condition."[8] But in a coded letter, addressed to Adams on 30 November 1825, Everett argued a very different view.

The United States minister noted that he "and many others" thought of Cuba "as an appendage of the Floridas" and that in the hands of "a powerful and active nation" it could completely control United States commerce in the Gulf of Mexico and the mouth of the Mississippi River. So long as Spain continued the war on her former colonies, the situation of the island was "in the highest degree precarious," he warned. It could not continue in its present state more than two or three years. Since the white inhabitants were too few to constitute an independent state, it must either become a principality of blacks or fall into the hands of some power other than Spain, probably Mexico or Colombia. Neither alternative would be admissible to the United States. On these premises, Everett advised that an effort be made immediately to acquire the island by peaceful means. He suggested, because of Ferdinand's financial embarrassments, the offer of a loan, perhaps $20 million, on condition of a "temporary cession" of the island as security for repayment. Interest on the debt might be recovered out of island revenues; and if the principal were unpaid over "a pretty long time," complete sovereignty should be vested in the United States. Spain, Everett observed, might prefer the arrangement to loss of the island for nothing. Britain and France, he concluded, would probably find this arrangement less repugnant than a United States seizure by force.[9]

Everett assured the president that he, Everett, would not present such a proposition without instructions but admitted that he had already mentioned it informally in a conversation with Spain's foreign minister, Francisco de Zea Bermudez. Although that official had protested that the king would not alienate the island for a moment, he had invited a written proposal. With Zea's fall from power shortly thereafter, a memorandum on the discussion had passed into the hands of his successor, the duke del Infantado. The latter official was thought to be more responsive to the wishes of the Continental powers; but Everett, still hoping for acceptance of his scheme, requested instructions.

That a United States diplomat should have voiced this proposal under critical circumstances, uninstructed, but in full knowledge of the opposing stance that his government had assumed, is startling. Had Adams encouraged such views in private discussions with his friend from Massachusetts? Neither Adams's diary nor his correspondence provides an answer. Officially, Clay's instructions of 13 April 1826 communicated, in response, a reiteration of the established policy. Britain and France had been made "fully aware" that the United States could not consent to occupation of Spain's island possessions by either foreign state, "under any contingencies whatever"; and "the forbearance" of the United States could "be fully relied on" from this nation's "moderation heretofore exhibited" and its "established pacific policy." The "frankness" with which its views had been disclosed to those powers forbade "absolutely, any movement whatever, at this time," for its acquisition of Cuba. "The condition of the great maritime powers (the United States, Great Britain, and France) is almost equivalent to an actual guaranty of the Islands to Spain," the secretary concluded.[10]

During the succeeding months the administration in Washington apparently placed far greater reliance upon the effectiveness of the tripartite understanding than was shared by its representatives in Europe. Gallatin, during the winter of 1826/27, reported strong popular support in Britain for an attack upon Cuba, lamented that Canning's proposal for a formal agreement had been rejected, and urged that the Spanish governor of the island, Francisco Dionisio Vives, be advised "to be on his guard." Britain's decision at this time to send an expeditionary force to uphold the constitutional regime in Portugal against absolutist dissidents, who were based across the Spanish border, raised alarm that the extension of warfare against Spain would occasion seizure of her islands. Brown, at Paris, in February warned that a "trial of strength" between the forces of representative government and absolutism was "not far distant," although he believed the depressed economy of the European nations might for a time forestall the disaster that for the United States must center upon "the precarious situation of the important island of Cuba." Tension had eased considerably by the summer of 1827, as Britain joined France and Russia in aiding the Greeks and negotiations were begun for a mutual withdrawal of British and French occupying forces from Spain and Portugal. Yet, in August, Everett sent the first of a series of confidential dispatches, which extended over the next year, reporting rumors of a British plan to bring about revolutions in the Canary Islands and in Cuba.[11]

Cuban revolt! Whether British inspired, indigenous, or stimulated by the independence movements of Colombia and Mexico—that was the other horn of the dilemma for the administration's diplomacy. Clay's warning that Spain might lose its islands if it continued to reject reconciliation with its lost mainland colonies was no idle threat. Independence movements had developed later in Cuba than in Spain's other American possessions. Divisions centering upon attitudes toward slavery separated the large planter and mercantile interests, which had initiated the early approach toward annexation with the United States, from an emerging insurgence among small planters, intellectuals, free blacks, and slaves. On this disagreement the early independence movement had foundered. Some of its leaders had joined the ranks of revolutionaries in Colombia and Mexico and had sought assistance there for their own struggle. Others had pled their cause in the United States.

In the winter of 1811/12, one José Alvarez de Toledo y Dubois, a Cuban by birth who had become a refugee to the United States after earlier plotting rebellion on Santo Domingo, had been in contact with Secretary of the Treasury Alexander Dallas and Secretary of State Monroe. Toledo had apparently received encouragement from them in regard to a project contemplating revolt of the islands and their annexation to the United States. Outbreak of war between the United States and Great Britain and warnings to Toledo that the Spanish had learned of his plans had interrupted this venture. Instead, the Cuban had diverted his efforts to the movement for Mexican independence and, in that connection, had met William Shaler, the recently rejected United States consul from Havana, who, thoughout the spring and summer of 1812, was channeling American aid to the Gutiérrez-Magee filibustering expedition. Over the next fourteen months, Toledo and Shaler had worked together along the Louisiana border. When Shaler was sent as confidential agent to act with the United States commissioners at Ghent in 1814, his background and his associations must have become known to both Adams and Clay.[12]

In August 1822 another project against the Spanish islands had been initiated, with some backing from American merchants and led by an American publicist, Baptis Irvine, in collaboration with H. Lafayette Ducoudray-Holstein, a German who had served under Napoleon and Bolívar. The force had sailed from the ports of New York and Philadelphia in an effort to free Puerto Rico. Driven into Dutch Curaçao by a mishap at sea, the leaders had been imprisoned. Clay, who had had some previous acquaintance with Irvine, had appealed to President Monroe in June 1824 for intercession on the American's behalf. While Clay professed to know nothing of the undertaking beyond newspaper reports and Irvine's correspondence, which he submitted to the president, his interest in the developing movement was evident. With less sympathy, Adams, too, had taken cognizance of the activity. The Monroe administration had referred Irvine's correspondence, together with documents that were also supplied by Ducoudray-Holstein, to the Federal attorney at New York as grounds for prosecution under the United States neutrality law.[13]

On the island of Cuba, secret societies for the organization of rebellion had made rapid headway during the early 1820s. Masonic lodges, with ties to their fraternal brethren in Mexico, Colombia, and the United States, comprised an important segment of this activity—a link that Spain, in reference to the Philadelphia lodge, attributed to governmental countenance. Again, Clay, as a prominent Mason, must have learned of the mounting unrest. With the restoration of Ferdinand VII in the spring of 1823, Spanish authorities initiated drastic measures to quash support for independence on the island. Agents of Captain-General Vives infiltrated the underground organization. Many of its leaders were seized; others fled—to the United States, Colombia, and elsewhere in the independent states of Latin America. Masonic lodges were prohibited under a royal decree of 1824. The following year, Vives was accorded unlimited dictatorial powers and instituted a system of martial law that was to prevail for over half a century.[14]

The undercurrents of this situation, uncertainty concerning the strength of annexation sentiment, and fears of intervention by other foreign powers induced the United States to commission a series of secret inquiries concerning developments on the island. Such investigations had been initiated by President Monroe as early as the spring of 1823, when Thomas Randall, a Washington lawyer who served as commissioner of claims under the Florida Purchase Treaty, had been named also as commercial agent for the United States in Cuba, with instructions to report on the "political condition of the Island, the views of its Government and the Sentiments of its inhabitants." Under cover of his duties as treaty commissioner, Randall had continued his observations for nearly two years. President Adams authorized resumption of this activity in the fall of 1825, on the basis of reports to Clay that the political situation in Cuba was "extremely critical," "fast hastening to a crisis," and must shortly produce "an explosion."[15]

Thomas B. Robertson, a former congressman, governor, and, from 1824 to 1827, federal judge for Louisiana, spent six weeks in the vicinity of Matanzas during the spring of 1825 in an effort to recover his health. He wrote to the new secretary of state in April of the "mutual hatred" between the Spanish and Creole populations, a hostility so deep "that an attempt to establish either . . . [would] be attended with dreadful consequences . . . ," in that "the unsuccessful party might call in the aid of the free people of colour—indeed of the slaves themselves." Robertson reported that the Spanish in Cuba feared, alike, independence or union with Colombia or Mexico; they would accept interference by England or the United States "only under the most desperate circumstances"; and they had petitioned Ferdinand to recognize the independence of his former colonies so that peace might "be established & their commerce set free from its trammels." The Creoles, on the other hand, Robertson continued, wished for freedom "and would join with alacrity, any standard under which they might hope to establish and Enjoy these blessings." He was highly critical of the Spanish rule—its discouragement of education, its neglect of public improvements, and the continuance of the slave trade, in which "our own countrymen have a full share of interest. . . ."

When Joseph Hill Clark, an American with mercantile ties on the island, warned Clay similarly the following October, the secretary advised Adams that someone more experienced than young Rodney, the consul, be sent to provide accurate information. Robertson, known for "liberal opinions and feelings [which] would secure for him the confidence of the party in favor of Revolution," was Clay's nominee for the assignment. The state of the Louisianan's health would serve to "cover the object of his visit."[16]

Robertson was offered the mission, like Somerville at a salary equivalent to that of a minister plenipotentiary. Under his instructions, he was to supply information tending "to the formation of a correct estimate of the value of the Island, its resources, natural and artificial, its capacity to maintain its independence, or to resist any foreign attack . . . , and the dispositions and wishes of its inhabitants in respect to the continuance of its Colonial condition, to independence, or to a connexion with any, and which, of the new Republics." At the same time, he was warned that it was not the policy of the United States "to give any Stimulus or countenance to insurrectionary movements . . . by any portion of the inhabitants."[17]

Resenting the "secret nature of the employment," Robertson declined the appointment, but a year later the mission was accepted by Daniel Pope Cook of Illinois, who had recently been defeated for reelection to Congress. Now ill, Cook, like Robertson, was to travel for the announced purpose of recovering his health. He carried the same instructions, with two significant additions: he was to inquire particularly about the state of Cuban defenses, should war break out between Spain and Britain, and to inquire about the sentiments of the inhabitants towards a colonial tie with the latter nation. Moreover, the Spanish captain-general was specifically informed of the mission and advised that Cook sought information concerning "the capability of the island to resist . . . attack," whether "by an European power or by the new States of America." The Spaniard was, at the same time, reminded "of the explicit & repeated declarations of the Executive of the U. States that the actual posture of things in regard to Cuba should not be disturbed." The secrecy of the project was thus clearly directed against the possibility of foreign intervention.[18]

Cook's stay in Cuba was brief. Acquiring dysentery, as a complication of his original illness, he returned to his home within a month and, in October, died en route to Washington to file his report. His promised statement was an unintelligible mass of statistical and other memoranda; but it did transmit a reassuring letter from Vives, who professed to have "considerable sea and land forces," expectation of reinforcements that would be strong enough to repel any attack, and the support of a great majority of the island's inhabitants.[19]

Rumors of the episode provoked Jacksonian inquiry in 1828 regarding the expenditures from Clay's contingency fund. Partisan attack pointed to Cook's support of the Adams-Clay coalition in 1825 and to his rejection for reelection as explanations for his having been rewarded with a Caribbean junket. Rodney, perhaps resentful of the imputation against his own capabilities, emerged as a strident critic of the administration. He alleged that Cook had been sent out "for no other purpose than in order to enrich him with the spoils of the public Treasury under pretence of performing secret services for Government[,] That there was nothing of the kind to perform & that Mr. C. was totally incapable of performing such & did nothing but spend his time there as on a jaunt of pleasure. . . ."[20] The charges could not well be refuted. How could the background of secret agencies be revealed? How could the pattern of diplomatic uneasiness be openly discussed? How could the gamble of policy strategy be publicly explained? The political embarrassment centering upon the Cook appointment may have been merited, but the decision to send the mission was neither a personalized nor an isolated concern.

While Gallatin and Everett noted a continuing menace from Britain, the reports of Poinsett, Watts, and Anderson indicated a more serious threat in the New World. By the summer of 1825 Adams and his secretary of state were contemplating the serious possibility that Colombia and Mexico, jointly or severally, would act where the United States hesitated to move, either to annex the Spanish islands or to aid their struggle for independence. Such efforts must inevitably generate a civil war, a bitter racially divided conflict, reminiscent of the violence that had driven the French from Haiti. That savage affray was very much in the thoughts of Americans during the early 1820s, a memory that was revived and emotionalized by fears growing out of contemporaneous slave revolts in the southern states and by French legislation, enacted in 1826, to compensate the colonial refugees, many of whom were scattered over the United States. The thought that Bolívar might lead a Cuban uprising with "the aid of the coloured casts [sic]" caused the New Englander Alexander Hill Everett to question even the wisdom of urging that Colombia's independence be recognized: "A military despot of talent and experience at the head of a black army is certainly not the sort of neighbour whom we should naturally wish, if we had the choice, to place upon our Southern frontier."[21]

The Adams administration's concern for democratic mission was manifestly subordinate to other considerations in reference to Cuba. Clay's suggestion, in the King instructions of October 1825, that Britain, France, and the United States might jointly guarantee a movement by the Cuban people for independence was never developed. Instead the president and the secretary of state pursued the course that Clay himself delineated as a virtual assurance of continued Spanish dominance.

Yet they also refused to move so far as a treaty commitment for maintenance of the existing status. Much has been written depicting Adams's motivating interest as a "ripe-fruit" conception, under which he, like Jefferson and Madison before him, anticipated that the Spanish islands would ultimately fall under United States control. In the winter of 1825/26, however, the burgeoning conflict that threatened to involve this country in confrontation between the Old World and the New, a conflict that would test the basic hemispheric distinctions of the Monroe Doctrine, presented at least equal grounds for restraint.

In the face of mounting pressures on both sides of the Atlantic, Adams and Clay sought to develop the intercessionary role that they had initiated during the spring of 1825. At that time, neither Colombia nor Mexico was yet prepared to support the Cuban cause. In December 1824 Bolívar had, in fact, proposed to exploit the mere threat of a move upon Cuba in the same way that Adams and Clay were to adopt. Writing to Gen. Francisco de Paula Santander, the Liberator had proposed to advise Spain that if Colombia were not recognized and if peace were not established within a specified period, Cuba and Puerto Rico would be attacked. But he added: "It is more important to have peace than to liberate these two islands— I have my own policy— An independent Havana would give us much work to do while the menace would be worth more than the insurrection. This business, well conducted[,] could produce a great effect."[22]

During the summer of 1825 President Guadalupe Victoria of Mexico organized the Junta Promotora de la Libertad de Cuba, composed of Cuban emigrés and Mexican volunteers, as the basis for an assault upon the island. Cherishing what Poinsett described as "ambitious views," these leaders in June of that year spurned a proposal by Bolívar for joint intervention; they preferred "undertaking the expedition without the aid of Colombia." But the junta's petition to the Mexican Congress, with a recommendation of the Mexican cabinet in support of its project, was rejected by Mexico's Chamber of Deputies the following December. A resolution of Mexico's Senate, calling for action, was similarly defeated in the popular assembly in February 1826. The record, after a year of rumor and speculation, was not one to encourage confidence that hemispheric allies would cooperate effectively in a confrontation that must challenge the powers of Europe.[23]

The danger to Spain's island possessions was, however, apparent. As early as May 1825 Adams had assured Russia's minister in Washington that the United States would attempt to dissuade Mexico and Colombia from attacking Cuba, but warned that so long as the Spanish islands were being used as bases for expeditions against the American states, this nation could "neither demand nor expect that they should abstain from hostile enterprises . . . in their turn." On December 20, in identical notes to the ministers of Mexico and Colombia, Clay interceded, in an attempt to delay precipitate action. Reminding the diplomats of the efforts that were under way to effect peace through Russian intervention, he reported that "late advices just received" indicated support not only from the czar but also from the other great powers. Since time was "necessary for the operation of these exertions to terminate the war, and to ascertain their effect upon the Spanish Government," he urged "suspension for a limited time, of the sailing of the Expedition against Cuba or Porto Rico . . . understood to be fitting out at Carthagena, or of any other expedition . . . contemplated against either of those islands." Phrased as the request of the president, the correspondence was written on Clay's initiative upon learning of the fall of the last Spanish stronghold in Mexico. The evidence indicates that it was, as he stated, intended as a holding course. Still hoping that the threat to Spain's Caribbean islands might induce the mother country to accept conciliation, the secretary of state did not, until four months later, communicate a report of his intervention to Everett.[24]

Clay misjudged the Spanish reaction to the warning conveyed in the Middleton instructions. The movement of the French fleet into the Caribbean during the summer of 1825, a reinforcement of the Spanish garrison on Cuba in October, and the massing of a Spanish expeditionary force at Cádiz over the following winter marked the response. When on January 1 Everett reported the probability of an attack upon Cuba, the Spanish foreign minister queried what security the Americans could offer for the island if the desired recognition were to be granted.[25] The question made clear that, although Czar Alexander had, indeed, interceded, the threat which he had communicated raised a demand for guarantees that the United States was unwilling and unable to provide—in particular, a treaty commitment requiring that it control the actions of its southern neighbors.

By the spring of 1826 neither Colombia nor Mexico was greatly concerned about "recognition." In March the Colombian minister, José María Salazar, invited United States mediation to end the war or at least to suspend hostilities for ten or twenty years, but under the condition that during the period, Spain should not send reenforcements to Cuba, Puerto Rico, or the Marianas. At the same time, Poinsett commented upon the "great coolness" in President Victoria's response to the December note—Mexico had no fear of Spain, was indifferent whether the latter recognized the new American states, and, indeed, was most apprehensive that the interference of the Holy Alliance might induce Spain to accord such recognition in return for a guarantee of its island possessions. Mexican officials, suspicious that Colombia might independently intervene in Cuba, looked to a pending assembly at Panama as an opportunity for arranging joint operations.[26]

The plan for consolidation of the former Spanish colonies in the New World as a confederation of states sharing the same language, customs, and religion had been developing in the mind of Bolívar for at least a decade. In a circular letter of 7 December 1824 he had finally issued the call for an "Assembly of Plenipotentiaries" to gather at Panama. Over the years the purposes and the exclusivity of the design had been somewhat modified. Arrangements for preservation of peace and security as a counterweight to the activities of the Holy Alliance now shaped the broad format of the agenda. The stand of Britain, the Netherlands, and the United States in opposition to the reactionary ideals of the European powers led to extension of invitations to these non-Latin nations.

Shortly after Clay had assumed office, he reported to the president that overtures had been made by the ministers of Colombia and Mexico, inviting representation by the United States. It "was not expected that they would take any part in its deliberations, or measures of concert, in respect to the existing war with Spain," he noted, but rather that "other great interests affecting the Continent of America, and the friendly intercourse between the Independent Nations which are established on it might be considered and regulated. . . ." This approach had been carefully designed by Colombia's foreign minister, Pedro Gual, to attract Adams's interest in a possible "agreement upon certain principles of international law applicable to times of war." With Clay's urging, the president presented the issue of United States participation to the cabinet for discussion.[27]

At the cabinet meeting on May 7 Clay enthusiastically endorsed acceptance of the invitation. James Barbour, who had at first opposed such action, now "decidedly" favored it. Samuel L. Southard, perhaps reflecting views expressed by William Wirt, who was not in attendance, voiced some reservations, but acquiesced. Adams accordingly authorized the secretary of state to respond that while the United States could not become a party to the war with Spain or to deliberations on its prosecution, the government believed that such a congress as was proposed "might be highly useful in settling several important disputed questions of public Law, and in arranging other matters of deep interest to the American Continent, and to the friendly intercourse between the American Powers. . . ." Whether this nation would participate was still to depend upon "several preliminary points, such as, the subjects to which the attention of the Congress was to be directed; the nature, and the form, of the Powers to be given to the Ministers, and the mode of organizing the Congress."[28]

The aims and organizational structure of the proposed assembly had already engendered journalistic controversy in the United States. Bolívar had envisioned the gathering as an "Amphictyonic body or assembly," to be based upon treaties such as Colombia had signed in the early twenties with Peru, Mexico, and the Federation of Central America, respectively, containing mutual guarantees of political independence and territorial integrity; reciprocal rights of citizenship; and, as separate sovereignties, pledges of perpetual union, league, and confederation. Embracing the general conception, a correspondent in the *Democratic Press* (Philadelphia), on 18 March 1825, had called for the United States to send an ambassador to the deliberations, as an expression of "fraternal feelings towards the other inhabitants of the continent." He warned that if this nation were not represented, it would "most probably, and very deservedly, find those feelings that ought to unite all America, transferred to other governments. . . ." The organization of "so magnificent a work" as a "Confederation" of all the American nations would be difficult, he conceded. Its

> leading principle should be the establishment of a constitution something like our own, by which an Areopagus or Congress should watch over the mutual relations of the confederated states, without interfering with their several, or internal regulations or governments—which should govern to a limited extent, the relations with foreign powers, of the whole, and of the several confederated states—and which should wield the whole force of the confederated states in defence of any member that may be attacked.[29]

This article, reprinted on April 26 in the *Daily National Intelligencer* (Washington), had been vigorously criticized in an accompanying editorial comment. If such a confederation were to be merely consultive, the journalist commented, it would occasion no objection other than that it would produce "nothing beneficial." He even conceded that "voluntary co-operation with other nations for definite objects" might be acceptable. But an alliance requiring compulsory adherence to group decisions would destroy "the independence which is our boast." Independence would be "but a name," he railed, "if the question of peace or war, and other questions equally important," were to be determined "by a stupendous Confederacy, in which the United States have but a single vote." Protesting that he did not know how the president would respond to such an invitation, he voiced hope that this government would "never send a Representative to any Congress of Nations whose decisions are to be *law* for this Nation."

The dispute was to be cited by Samuel Ingham of Pennsylvania, in congressional debate the following year, as evidence of disagreement on the projected mission between "the two statesmen at the head of the executive department of the government at that time." The identification of either writer as Adams or Clay is, however, highly questionable. Adams, in diary notes on April 23 and 27, mentioned the secretary of state's enthusiasm for the meeting and, in both entries, indicated his own interest in the assembly. He specifically alluded to an article in the *Daily National Journal* (Washington) of April 23, a translation of a piece from the *Gaceta de Colombia* of February 27, outlining a planned agenda which differentiated the discussion on concerns of states that were still at war with Spain and those concerns that were shared jointly by belligerents and neutrals. In reference to the latter category, the president commented: "Besides the objects there noticed as fit subjects for the deliberations of this Congress, that of endeavoring to establish American principles of maritime, belligerent, and neutral law is an additional interest of infinite magnitude."[30]

Whatever Clay's anticipations, when formal invitations were received in November 1825, the proposed topics for discussion followed very closely the outlines of the *Gaceta* statement. The Colombian minister provided assurance that the deliberations would "have no tendency to violate the neutrality adopted by the U.S." Some of the matters to be considered would concern only the belligerent states; a second class of issues would be of general interest. Since the United States was not "to interfere in the former," he listed items only under the latter heading: "some principles of international law, the confusion of which have [*sic*] occasioned great evils to humanity," "the best way of resistance to any future colonisation of the European powers on the American continent, and to prevent their interference in the present wars between Spain and her ancient colonies," means for abolition of the African slave trade, and relations with Haiti and "other countries of our hemisphere that in future may find themselves in the same circumstances."[31] While a radical alteration of Bolívar's conception was evident in this response, the agenda yet posed serious problems for the administration—in particular, specific delineation of the meaning of the Monroe Doctrine, with reference to both European incursions and potential New World revolts; a stand upon recognition of the "black republic," Haiti; more rigorous enforcement of the legislation against the slave traffic; and perhaps, also, treaty commitments on that subject, which Adams had already found embarrassing insofar as they involved acceptance of the principle of search on the high seas. Beyond such topical focuses of controversy lay the broader issue of participation in multinational consultations, whatever the subject matter.

In his first annual message, however, the president informed Congress that the invitation had been accepted. On December 26 he nominated Richard C. Anderson, Jr., of Kentucky and John Sergeant of Pennsylvania as ministers and William B. Rochester of New York as secretary to the mission. All were identified as Clay adherents. Since in general aspect the project so clearly merged the interests of the president and his secretary of state, the issues of the agenda were scarcely relevant to the emergence of controversy. Adams's announcement provoked immediate, violent, and partisan attack. The Panama debate brought into the open the development of a consolidated opposition to the administration.

In submitting his nominations the president, after gratuitously asserting his right to accept the invitation without consulting the Senate, proceeded to explain his motives for sending the delegates. He gave assurance that the United States would not take part in belligerent deliberations and that this government would not contract alliances or depart from traditional neutrality. He contended that the meetings would afford opportunity to oppose Latin-American commercial exclusivity and to urge commitments to the views of the United States on maritime neutrality and religious liberty. He suggested that a general agreement might be reached under which each of the parties at the congress would undertake to "guard by its own means against the establishment of any future European colony within its borders"—a proposal that would broaden the authority of the Monroe Doctrine and at the same time free the United States of the police role. He argued that the meetings might enhance the "indirect influence" of this nation upon "any projects or purposes originating in the war" between the new republics and Spain "which might seriously affect the interests of this Union"—an obvious allusion to the attempt to deter action against Cuba and Puerto Rico. And as a "decisive" consideration, he cited participation in the assembly as a "token of respect to the southern Republics."[32]

By mid January the Senate Committee on Foreign Relations, appointed by Vice-President Calhoun and composed of a majority of his own and Crawford's supporters, had determined to oppose the mission. Littleton W. Tazewell of Virginia, a member of the Richmond Junto, wrote the report, although it was presented by Nathaniel Macon of North Carolina, another "Old Republican," as committee chairman. It criticized the acceptance of the invitation without prior consultation with Congress, questioned the objectives of the assembly, noted that the president had failed to mention Haiti and the slave trade as proposed topics for consideration, and deplored the abandonment of the principle, already historically apotheosized through identification with Washington and Jefferson, to refrain from "entangling alliances." A masterful statement of narrowly perceived national interest, the report advised that efforts to pursue the goals of commercial equality and maritime rights be pursued through bilateral treaty arrangements, that religious matters be left to the domestic politics of individual states, and that concern for the future condition of other Spanish colonies in America be deferred until the problematic danger should arise. Finally, pointing to the development of arrangements before the invitation had been extended, the report questioned whether the participation of the United States was greatly desired. Since the primary purpose of the meeting, for the states that had been engaged in revolt against Spain, was "to adjust between themselves the most effectual means of conducting this war to the most speedy and happy conclusion, . . . the presence of no neutral State could, therefore, be anticipated."[33]

The ensuing debate, under an organized program of opposition conducted by the Crawfordites Martin Van Buren of New York, John Holmes of Maine, and John M. Berrien of Georgia; the Jacksonian Thomas Hart Benton of Missouri; and Calhoun's henchman Robert Y. Hayne of South Carolina, elaborated the committee's views at great length. The Senate, it was argued, held a vital role to check the involvement of the nation under presidential authority in a "confederation" for the defense of the Latin-American republics against the powers of Europe. Van Buren introduced resolutions declaring that the power of forming "new political associations, or confederacies," was "reserved to the States, or People"; that it was "not within the Constitutional power of the Federal Government to appoint Deputies" to the Congress; and "waiving the question of Constitutional power," that "conditional acceptance" of the invitation would depart "from that wise and settled policy by which the intercourse of the United States with foreign nations . . . [had] hitherto been regulated." For this country to send delegates would, he contended, jeopardize friendly relations with the new states, "by creating expectations that engagements . . . [would] be entered into . . . at that Congress, which the Senate could not ratify, and of which the People of the United States would not approve."[34]

Other members of the opposition showed less heed for maintenance of good will on the part of the United States' southern neighbors. Rational discourse on the constitutional and foreign-policy issues gave way to bitter sectional diatribe by Hayne and Berrien and by Hugh L. White of Tennessee, who cited the potential threat to slavery as an institution and the encouragement to slave rebellion inherent in the projected attack upon Cuba and Puerto Rico. These opponents were also sharply critical of the proposal to recognize Haiti *"and others,* in the like condition."

On March 14 the Senate finally sustained the administration by defeating, 24 to 19, both the Van Buren resolutions and that of the committee, which had declared that participation in the conference was inexpedient. Still the attack was continued. In a rambling discussion on March 30, on a resolution contesting the competence of the president to appoint ministers without the advice and consent of the Senate, John Randolph centered upon Clay's relationship in the administration as the nub of the controversy. The mission, he asserted, was "a Kentucky cuckoo's egg, laid in a Spanish-American nest." The president's questioning of the propriety of a Senate request for public disclosure of the diplomatic documents had outraged Randolph. He had been "defeated, horse, foot, and dragoons—cut up—and clean broke down," he lamented, "by the coalition of Blifil and Black George—by the combination, unheard of until then, of the Puritan with the blackleg."

Clay promptly challenged the Virginian to a duel, and on April 8 the two met. After an exchange of shots, in which neither was hurt, the encounter was amicably terminated. The episode, nevertheless, shocked many of Adams's adherents and dismayed even some of Clay's. It counteracted the moral thrust of the administration's appeal among its own supporters.

With greater control in the House of Representatives, the administration, on April 22, won that body's approval of the requisite appropriations, by a vote of 132 to 60. Yet there, too, the issue was debated at length under an opposition headed by the Calhounites Samuel Ingham of Pennsylvania and George McDuffie and James Hamilton, Jr., of South Carolina; the Crawfordites Louis McLane of Delaware, John Forsyth of Georgia, and John Floyd and William Cabell Rives of Virginia; and the Jacksonians Charles A. Wickliffe of Kentucky and James C. Mitchell and James K. Polk, of Tennessee. Clay's allusion, in the Poinsett instructions of November 9, citing "the memorable pledge" of Monroe's message, became a focus of attack when it was realized that the minister's dispatch reporting his response to Mexico at the time of the movement of the French fleet had not been supplied in the State Department's file of relevant papers. The debate led to a general repudiation of any commitment to substantive action under Monroe's pronouncement, as it was learned that Poinsett, in the negotiations concerning Mexico's advocacy of Spanish-American customs preference, had in fact made such a statement in argument against less-favorable treatment for the United States than was being accorded to other American Republics. The policy was unjust, Poinsett had asserted, since the new states had demonstrated that they did not require assistance against Spain "and the United States had pledged themselves not to permit any other Powers of Empire to interfere either with their form of government or with their independence; and as, in the event of such an attempt being made by them, the United States would be compelled to take the most active and efficient part in the contest. . . ."[35] Even congressional adherents of the administration hastened to deny that so strong a diplomatic representation was intended.

The appropriation bill was not accepted in the Senate until early May. Then, again, it was approved on the rigidly defined lines by which that body had endorsed the mission. Reports of the controversy so alienated Latin-American leaders that any hope which the administration had entertained of developing at Panama a United States role of hemispheric leadership was effectively thwarted.[36]

On May 8 the secretary of state finally transmitted instructions to Anderson and Sergeant. With allowance for the differing functions to be served, they followed closely policy positions that the president had expressed to the House of Representatives in his message requesting the appropriation. The Panama assembly was to be viewed as diplomatic, not legislative; it was to be considered "as merely *consultative*. . . ," Adams had stipulated. The United States plenipotentiaries might refer propositions for the consideration of their government, but they were authorized "to conclude nothing unless subject to the definitive sanction of this Government in all its constitutional forms." Clay euphorically hailed the assembling of the Panama body as "a new epoch in human affairs," which would afford opportunity "for free and friendly conferences, for mutual and necessary explanations, and for discussing, and establishing, some general principles, applicable to peace and war, to commerce and navigation, with the sanction of all America." But he agreed that this was to be no "Amphyctionic [sic] Council" with legislative powers "binding a minority, to agreements and acts contrary to its will."[37]

Adams had directed the largest part of his message to emphasis upon the opportunity that the meeting afforded for expounding United States views on international relations. In this country's intercourse with the Latin-American states, he noted, the only controversies had sprung from "discriminations of commercial favor to other nations, licentious privateers, and paper blockades." He defined, as first steps in "the perpetual abolition of private war upon the ocean," the "establishment of the principle that the friendly flag shall cover the cargo, the curtailment of contraband of war, and the proscription of fictitious paper blockades. . . ." Clay, reasserting these criteria, urged particular efforts to resolve the violations of neutral rights in the conflict between Brazil and the Provinces of the River Plate and again pointed to the commercial treaties with Colombia and Central America as definitional models on the principles involved. Privateering was to be foresworn; "free ships" were to signify "free goods"; blockades must be "legitimate" according to some "clear definition." Reciprocity was to be pursued and was to encompass both direct and indirect traffic, if possible; the negotiators were to be careful to embrace insular arrangements. Mexico's proposal for preferential concessions among Spain's former colonies was to be countered. Special privileges, if condoned, were to be applied hemispherically.

Adams's absorption with trade considerations had dictated his discussion of the Monroe Doctrine in connection with the proposed Congress:

> With the exception of the existing European colonies, which it was in nowise intended to disturb, the two continents consisted of several sovereign and independent nations, whose territories covered their whole surface. By this their independent condition the United States enjoyed the right of commercial intercourse with every part of their possessions. To attempt the establishment of a colony in those possessions would be to usurp to the exclusion of others a commercial intercourse which was the common possession of all. It could not be done without encroaching upon existing rights of the United States.

For the president, the opportunity for consultation upon the means of resisting foreign interference "with the domestic concerns of the American Governments" was secondary in emphasis.

For Clay, however, the latter consideration was clearly dominant. Under his instructions the Monroe Doctrine was to be strongly upheld should the Holy Alliance intervene either "to reduce the new American Republics to their ancient Colonial state, or to compel them to adopt political systems more conformable to the policy and views of that alliance." Indeed, he argued, if the European powers were to engage in war "for either of the purposes just indicated," opposition by the United States, "with their whole force," would merit no praise for "generous sympathy with infant, oppressed, and struggling nations."

> The United States, in the contingencies which have been stated, would have been compelled to fight their own proper battles, not less so because the storm of war happened to rage

on another part of this Continent, at a distance from their borders. For it cannot be doubted that the presumptuous spirit which would have impelled Europe upon the other American Republics, in aid of Spain, or on account of the forms of their political Institutions, would not have been appeased if her arms, in such an unrighteous contest, should have been successful, until they were extended here, and every vestige of human freedom had been obliterated within these States.[38]

Clay concluded, however, that the danger of such a confrontation was no longer threatening. He alluded to the administration's peace initiative, cited Russia's support of the effort, and anticipated that, whether or not Spain conceded outright recognition of the independence of the new republics, there would be no resumption of warfare. An alliance, offensive or defensive, was consequently not necessary at this time. Participation of the United States in such an accord would violate traditional policy and was to be considered only upon reference to the government, should specific occasion warrant action.

The president had considered the situation of Cuba and Puerto Rico of great importance and "immediate bearing upon the present interests and future prospects of our Union." Alluding to the proposed invasion of those islands by Mexico and Colombia, "avowedly among the objects to be matured by the belligerent States of Panama," he observed that "the convulsions to which, from the peculiar composition of their population, they would be liable in the event . . . and the danger therefrom resulting of their falling ultimately into the hands of some European power other than Spain," forbade United States indifference. This nation's alternatives in that situation were left for Clay to elaborate in the instructions for the ministers at Panama.

Reiterating the views which Nelson had earlier sketched under Adams's instructions, the secretary of state emphasized that the United States desired "no change in the possession or political condition" of Cuba. This nation "could not, with indifference, see it transferred from Spain to any other European Power" and was "unwilling to see its transfer or annexation to either of the new American States." If the war between Spain and its former colonies were to continue, three alternatives must be considered in reference to the island—an indigenous movement for independence; independence "with the guarantee of other Powers, either of Europe, or of America or both"; or "conquest and attachment" to Colombia or Mexico. If Cuba could maintain independent self-government, that would be the preference; but on the basis of "the limited extent, moral condition, and discordant character of its population," it could not at this time "sustain self government, unaided by other Powers." If "at this premature period" independence were attempted, "one portion of the inhabitants of the Island, as well as their neighbours in the United States, and in some other directions, would live in continual dread of those tragic scenes which were formerly exhibited in a neighbouring island. . . ," that is, Haiti.

A guarantee of Cuban independence by external forces might afford relief from such dangers, but it would also pose "almost insuperable" problems in defining authority, Clay continued. Moreover, if Colombia or Mexico should attempt to conquer the island, "the whole character of the present war" would be changed from a struggle for independence and self-government, in which they had held "the good wishes and friendly sympathies of a large portion of the world," to a war of aggrandizement under which "the interests of other Powers, now neutral, must be seriously affected, and they may be called upon to perform important duties which they may not be at liberty to neglect." Under such a threat, European nations might "interpose forcibly"; and the United States, "far from being under any pledge, at present, to oppose them, might find themselves, contrary to their inclination, reluctantly drawn by a current of events, to their side." The ministers were to state "explicitly" and "without reserve" that "the United States have too much at stake in the fortunes of Cuba, to allow them to see with indifference, a war of invasion prosecuted in a desolating manner, or to see employed, in the purposes of such a war, one race of the inhabitants combatting against another, upon principles, and with motives that must inevitably lead, if not to the extermination of one party or the other, to the most shocking excesses."

For the fourth time, in identical words from the president, the secretary of state, and the minister to Spain, the fear of violent racial war recurred as a major consideration in the administration's statements on policy with regard to Cuba. Adams had suggested that the Panama meeting might develop agreement upon measures for "the more effectual abolition of the African slave trade," but the successful opposition to his efforts to incorporate such provisions in his treaties of 1824 with Great Britain and Colombia and the bitterness of the congressional debates on the Panama mission discouraged him from further challenging the peculiar sensitivities of his southern opponents. He took no action as president to uphold the antislavery views of his New England and Pennsylvania Quaker constituents.

Although Clay had been prepared to recognize Haitian independence, the president had demurred. The Panama instructions, instead, as had Adams's message to the House of Representatives, pointed to the commercial control that was being asserted by France and questioned the Haitian government's freedom of action. The issue, in any event, was not deemed of sufficient importance to warrant a joint declaration.

The ministers were urged to propose a joint resolution assuring religious toleration and to seek liberty of religious worship in any negotiations. While the president had expressed this concern, he had viewed it pragmatically as an issue that was relevant to the interests of United States citizens whose occupations might require occasional residence abroad. Clay interpreted the matter as an element in the fostering of democratic government. The United States, he conceded, could make no formal complaint should any of the other American states introduce a system of religious establishment, "unless it should be exclusive"; but this nation would regret such a decision. Although it would be "rash to assert that civil liberty and an established church cannot exist together in the same State," Clay argued, "it may be safely affirmed that history affords no example of their union when the religion of the State has not only been established, but exclusive."

Finally, the secretary outlined the role of the ministers as expositors of free institutions. Notwithstanding his own obvious interest in developing commercial regulations that would be favorable to the United States, the president had stipulated *"disinterestedness"* as the "first and paramount principle upon which it was deemed wise and just to lay the corner stone of all our future relations" with the new republics. Clay accordingly directed the ministers scrupulously to refrain "from all interference in the original structure, or subsequent interior movement, of the Governments of other independent Nations." Yet they were to attempt to dissuade the new states from succumbing to the influence of foreign powers, who were believed to have "been active in both Colombia and Mexico, if not elsewhere, with a view to subvert, if possible, the existing forms of free Government there established, to substitute the monarchical in place of them, and to plant, on the newly erected thrones, European Princes." The United States representatives were to seize "every fit opportunity" to emphasize "the solemn duty of every Nation to reject all foreign dictation in its domestic concerns." They were, at the same time, readily to respond to inquiries about the operation of state and federal governments in the United States "and to illustrate and explain the manifold blessings which the people . . . enjoyed . . . under them."

The United States spokesmen were never in a position to act under the directives of this briefing. The long congressional debate had delayed their departure until so late in the spring that Sergeant submitted his resignation rather than encounter the "risk of sickness" during the pestilential season. He was consequently permitted to postpone travel until the fall. Anderson, who attempted to make his way from Bogotá to Panama, died of tropical fever, en route, at Cartagena, on July 24. Meanwhile, the delegates at Panama opened discussions on June 22 without the United States representatives. The Latin-American plenipotentiaries concluded four accords—a treaty of confederation, conventions providing for future sessions of the congress and for organization of a permanent army and navy, and a secret arrangement on the operations of those forces. On July 15 they adjourned, to meet again at Tacabaya, Mexico, after, as was hoped, the treaties had been ratified by their governments. Although Sergeant, with Poinsett as a replacement for Anderson, announced the arrival of the United States delegation in January 1827, the Tacabaya assembly never convened. Only Colombia ratified the Panama agreements, and Bolívar himself opposed that action. Suspicion and discord among the partners had brought the effort to an end.

Bright hopes, shared by many American proponents of the assembly, collapsed along with those of their hemispheric neighbors. Administration supporters from New England through the Middle States into Ohio and Kentucky had reported a sympathetic public opinion, surprised and bewildered at the "shameful and indeed factious opposition" to the mission. Even Jacksonians conceded privately the popularity of the administration's action. Benton noted that the invitation "captivated all young and ardent imaginations." The legislatures of Maryland and Pennsylvania adopted resolutions endorsing the proposal to send delegates, the latter relating it to the Monroe declaration "in defence of the Cause of Liberty in this Western Hemisphere. . . ." Others projected the ideologic viewpoint still more broadly. William Ladd of New Hampshire, a pioneer advocate of peace through international organization, informed the president that the Panama meeting absorbed "all other political interests" and became "an object of the most intense anxiety." "On it," Ladd concluded, "must depend the peace & happiness of the American nations & the world in general."[39]

Such anticipations ignored the constraints of the Cuban problem. Even Clay had recognized that independence with stability for Cuba would require an international guarantee. But what would have been the role for the United States in such an overt arrangement? As the partner of France and Britain, the United States would have been pitted against its hemispheric neighbors; as the partner of the latter, it would have borne the residual burden of their domestic divisions. When Mexico and Colombia threatened intervention, they challenged the established neutrality policy of the United States and forced the administration into a reassertion of the renunciatory principle of the Monroe pronouncement, recognition of the existing European colonial possessions. Congressional criticism of the Panama mission not only reinforced the inhibitions against a broader national commitment but, in repudiating Poinsett's "pledge," negated even the vague assurances that had already been extended. Clay's instructions to the Panama commissioners, written in this context, defiantly reasserted adherence to the principle of defending the new American republics and their choice of political system, but preserved national freedom of judgment in evaluating the circumstances for intervention. While he called for encouragement of self-government and religious freedom in already independent states, he relinquished all serious consideration of support for extending the struggle beyond those bounds.

Exploiting the absence of the American delegates and the revelation of the limited perspectives under which they must eventually operate, the British agent, Dawkins, found little difficulty in counteracting the administration's bid for hemispheric leadership. He assured Secretary Canning that the influence of the United States was not to be feared. Inasmuch as Mexico and Peru were "suspicious of the North Americans upon all commercial points," Dawkins anticipated that the proposed commercial treaty would be reduced "to some regulations for the internal commerce of Spanish America." Even with Colombia, the United States' principal supporter, the relationship had been "very much weakened . . . by their protests against an attack on Cuba, and by the indiscretions they have committed at Madrid."[40]

The primacy of trade considerations as an inhibiting influence to the administration's missionary goals was very evident in the outcome of the efforts, contemporary with the Panama meeting, to win Spanish recognition of Latin-American independence. Dawkins's report of that assembly noted that "an accommodation with Spain . . . [was] the first object of all the Deputies, and the purchase of her Recognition . . . [was] not objected to." He believed that but for the opposition of the Mexican delegate, a proposal on that subject would have been adopted at Panama, and he emphasized that it was to be a matter for full discussion when the congress reassembled. Discounting the American appeal for Russian intercession, he proposed British mediation. To that end he suggested a package of property and trade concessions by which the Latin Americans might win Spanish favor, somewhat as Haiti had negotiated the settlement with France. To his great surprise, he learned that Spanish agents had already "mentioned it to the Peruvian Minister . . . [at London] as a measure which would be favorably considered at Madrid."[41]

For a variety of reasons—the American notes may well have exerted more influence than has been generally recognized—European powers had been pressing Spain over the past year to settle the differences with her former colonies. From Paris, Brown informed Clay that French eagerness to open Latin-American trade was restricted only by sensitivity to Spain's concerns; the French minister had been urging negotiations. From Madrid, Everett reported that as early as May 1825 Austria, like the United States, had warned of the danger to Cuba and had offered mediation. In January 1826 Everett had undertaken to supplement the United States government's appeal for Russian intercession by himself addressing to the Spanish foreign minister a forty-seven-page memorandum calling for recognition of the new republics. In the course of his argument, stressing the hardship to Spain in the continuing conflict, both from the costs of military action and from the loss of trade, Everett had suggested that "the American States would doubtless consent to furnish in return of the acknowledgement of their independence, such pecuniary supplies as would be sufficient to remove all financial embarrassments and to reestablish the public credit on a solid basis."[42]

Responding to this note in the following June, the duke del Infantado acknowledged that "several of the Powers had offered their advice . . . and had interested themselves one way or other in the progress and issue of the war." Spain was concerned, however, to know whether "the return of peace" would restore to her "a great share of the trade with America." In particular, Spain sought "some important discriminations in her favour."[43]

Quickly, Everett now rebuffed the proposal. Since January he had learned that preferential trade arrangements between a mother country and its former colony "did not accord precisely with the President's views." He reminded the Spanish minister that "the New States . . . had bound themselves to each other and to foreign nations by express treaties" forbidding such special arrangements. Although Everett believed Spain "wavering and irresolute," "on the whole inclining towards a better policy," he could press the matter little farther. Instead, he at that time transmitted to Infantado the Colombian request for a prolonged armistice. As civil war erupted in Colombia later that summer, even so-limited a settlement failed to win acceptance.[44]

The administration's pursuit of ideologic goals was thus limited to a nationalistic perspective and, within that focus, was bound by the interests of American commerce. Journalists of seaboard cities from Baltimore to Boston, who generally supported American participation in the Panama Congress, credited the sending of delegates to Adams's decisive commitment to that viewpoint. But congressional critics recognized a new extension of the president's ideological stance. Contending that Adams had, in fact, become "a proselyte" of the secretary of state, William C. Rives agreed with Randolph that Adams had contracted from Clay "this Spanish American fever": "He has started from a caution cold as marble, into the vernal fervors of love at first sight for the South Americans." Adams's Panama message, Rives complained, "made the most copious use" of "certain *cabalistic* phrases" associated with the "American System." The New Englander had even "added some new samples to the original stock. 'The fraternity of freedom,' 'sister Republics'. . . , 'nations of this *hemisphere*,' 'the Powers of America'. . . ."[45]

As president, Adams had moved considerably beyond his narrow nationalism of 1821. In reference to both Greece and Latin America he had pursued a course that was very different from the views that he had espoused even in 1824. If he had not yet specifically committed the United States to react against the use of force by European powers on the Latin-American republics, he had interceded in behalf of peace. He had, moreover, as one analyst has observed, expanded conceptions of the Monroe Doctrine to "a hitherto neglected aspect of the American system, namely the positive principle of inter-American consultation."[46]

In passages of remarkable toughness the president had rejected his opponents' arguments that European powers might take umbrage at United States participation in the Panama meeting and that Washington's Farewell Address had laid down "the great rule of conduct" against the nation's "political connection" with foreign states. He assured critics that his ministers would agree to nothing that could give "*just cause* of umbrage or offence" to Spain or her allies—"for the rest the United states must still, as heretofore, take counsel from their duties rather than their fears." Those duties, he contended, were no longer circumstanced as at the founding of the Nation. Then, this country had been the only independent nation in the hemisphere and had been surrounded by European colonies. Now, most of those colonies had become independent states, "seven of them Republics like ourselves, with whom we have an immensely growing commercial, and *must* have and have already important political connections. . . ." Their "political principles and systems of government . . . must and will have an action and counteraction upon us . . . to which we can not be indifferent if we would."[47]

Adams conceded that his motive for sending a mission to Panama was not primarily related to the announced objectives of the congress—

and, indeed, as his opponents pointed out, that the agenda had been only broadly defined. In response, he voiced the missionary theme. Perhaps not again in centuries would the United States have so favorable an opportunity "to subserve the benevolent purposes of Divine Providence; to dispense the promised blessings of the Redeemer of Mankind; to promote the prevalence in future ages of peace on earth and good will to man. . . ." Cordial "good will," next to *"disinterested-ness,"* was basic to developing friendly relations with the new republics. "Under these impressions," he would have accepted the invitation "had it even been doubtful whether *any* of the objects proposed for consideration and discussion at the Congress were such as that immediate and important interests of the United States would be affected by the issue. . . ." Between nations, he argued, "temper is a missionary perhaps more powerful than talent. Nothing was ever lost by kind treatment. Nothing can be gained by sullen repulses and aspiring pretensions."[48]

Upon leaving office, Adams noted Jacksonian charges that the diplomatic intercourse of his administration had "not been sufficiently courteous and conciliatory. . . ."[49] Such attacks were unwarranted. On the dispute over claims against France, the president had rejected the warlike stance that his successor would subsequently assume. Despite provocations that had led to Raguet's withdrawal from Brazil, Adams and Clay had acted to restore normal relations. Even on the issue of the West Indies trade, their instructions to Gallatin had demonstrated a spirit of concession which British intransigence, stimulated by evidence of partisan divisions within the United States, had carried to the breaking point. Popular forays in support of cherished territorial goals—against Texas, New Brunswick, and the British Northwest—had been discouraged. International consultations, looking to peace within the Western Hemisphere, had been pursued as a major policy concern in the face of partisan opposition to the basic concept. Committed fervently to American nationalism, the administration had, nevertheless, eschewed chauvinism.

Jacksonians closed from both sides upon this middle ground. They decried the president's efforts to seek better West Indian trading arrangements on the argument that these actions had alienated the British. They repudiated the principles of the Monroe Doctrine and the consultations at Panama on the basis that the consequent associations threatened involvement in a war with Europe. At the same time they criticized the ineffectiveness in pressing claims for losses under the

Napoleonic decrees, complained of laxity in protecting United States shipping from violation of neutral rights in South American traffic, and demanded more vigorous assertion of boundary claims from Maine to Oregon. Assailing, on the one hand, what they conceived as rigidity in the administration's diplomacy, they deplored, on the other, its reliance upon the negotiating process.

The discordant voices were damaging to the effective pursuance of foreign policy. The confusion indicated in British response to congressional criticism of the administration's stand on the West Indies trade was only one manifestation of the difficulty. A formal report of a Senate committee chaired by Francis Baylies, calling for more vigorous enforcement of American claims on Oregon, confirmed Canning's determination, in November 1826, to defend Huskisson's program. As Gallatin ruefully noted, the British minister complained that the Baylies report had "almost the appearance of a Manifesto issued on declaring war." Brown, in Paris a year later, commented upon the embarrassment that was occasioned by the "divided State of our Senate and house of Representatives." "These divisions," he warned, "are well Known in Europe and have their influence."[50]

In Brown's view, a wise course would "cultivate peace and increase our resources at home." To have preserved peace in foreign affairs through the turbulent international relationships in Europe and America during the mid 1820s was no small achievement. Divisive politics, however, which had so greatly complicated this effort, proved even more damaging to the administration's pursuit of harmony and economic development domestically.

8

★ ★ ★ ★ ★

THE AMERICAN SYSTEM
AT HOME

If debate on the constitutionality of Adams's diplomacy was surprising to the administration, controversy attending the development of his domestic program was not. In his Inaugural Address the president had acknowledged the existence of disagreements concerning the powers of Congress to legislate upon internal improvements. He contended that in the "nearly twenty years" since the National Road had been begun, "repeated, liberal, and candid discussions in the Legislature" had served to conciliate differences and "approximated the opinions of enlightened minds upon the question of constitutional power," but he could only "hope that by the same process of friendly, patient, and persevering deliberation all constitutional objections . . . [would] ultimately be removed."[1] It was not a program that assured harmony to an administration pledged to pursue unity among diverse political factions.

It was, however, one that combined Adams's strong sense of national responsibilities with Clay's conception of interlocking sectional interests, a domestic American System resting upon governmental support for industrial development, a home market for productions of town and country, with federally assisted transportation and a centralized credit structure designed to facilitate commercial interchange. Expanded under the president's exposition, the agenda also encompassed "moral, political, intellectual improvement" as "duties assigned by the Author of Our Existence to social no less than to individual man." "For the fulfillment of those duties," he continued in his first annual message to Congress, "governments are invested with power, and to the attainment of the end—the progressive improvement of the condition of the governed—the exercise of delegated powers is a duty as sacred and indispensable as the usurpation of powers not granted is criminal and odious."[2]

In the course of his annual reports to Congress, Adams urged the establishment of a naval academy, a national university, and a federal program of geographical and astronomical exploration; continuation of surveys for, and aid in the construction of, roads and canals; federal bankruptcy legislation and vigorous efforts to reduce the public debt; a balancing of "the burdens upon native industry imposed by the operation of foreign laws"; and reform of the Indian policy. "The spirit of improvement is abroad upon the earth," he announced in December 1825:

> While foreign nations less blessed with that freedom which is power than ourselves are advancing with gigantic strides in the career of public improvement, were we to slumber in indolence or fold up our arms and proclaim to the world that we are palsied by the will of our constituents, would it not be to cast away the bounties of Providence and doom ourselves to perpetual inferiority?[3]

In preliminary cabinet discussions, Adams was warned of the dangers inherent in so sweeping a philosophical statement at the beginning of his administration. Secretary Barbour, the president noted, objected to "the whole concluding recommendations on the subject of internal improvements." Clay contended that Congress had the requisite powers and that if it failed to use them, the Appalachian West would break from the Union. He questioned, however, the practicability of pressing the issues at this time. Adams, who viewed the occasion as one for annunciation of goals, responded that he looked "to a practicability of a longer range than a simple session of Congress." Rush "very earnestly urged the communication. . . ." With great reluctance, Barbour yielded. Adams concluded: "The perilous experiment must be made. Let me make it with full deliberation, and be prepared for the consequences."[4]

Clay had particularly questioned the proposal for a national university. He believed that its constitutionality was more dubious than was that of the issue of internal improvements. Adams recalled that President Washington had recommended both the university and a national military academy. The latter institution had been established only after the elapse of a decade. He maintained that the seeds for the related proposal and for a naval academy should be sown.

Neither project made headway during his term of office. President Madison's opposition, on constitutional grounds, to the proposal for a national university had established an argument that rationalized a wide range of negative views. The successful move to charter Columbian College (George Washington University) in the District of Columbia in 1821 and the effort of that institution over the next decade to obtain public funding deflected support from the broader conception. No legislation for a national university even reached the floor of Congress.

Bills for the founding of a naval academy were introduced in both the Senate and the House of Representatives in January 1826. Postponed through the end of that session, the proposal came up for extended debate in March 1827. A memorial from the state of Maryland, urging Annapolis as the site for the institution, offered encouragement, and sections of the navy appropriation bill that encompassed such legislation passed the Senate by a vote of 24 to 22. In the House, however, opposition, predominately Jacksonian, defeated the provisions, by vote of 71 to 65 in the Committee of the Whole and of 86 to 78 before the general body. Proponents of the academy emphasized the importance of scientific education as an adjunct to seamanship in naval training. Opponents criticized its cost, estimated at a total of $7,000 a year for nine "professors," and argued that it would serve as a "vast source of promotion and patronage," threatening democratic virtue by creating an educated upper class. Lemuel Sawyer of North Carolina, alluding to the "annual proselytes . . . to the Administration" produced by the Military Academy, protested that such institutions led to abandonment of the "dull pursuits of civil life" and the denigration of labor. It would "have a tendency to produce degeneracy and corruption of the public morality, and change our simple Republican habits."[5]

Running counter to this political anti-intellectualism, Adams's personal interest in scientific observation had been marked in his able report of 1824 on a uniform standard for weights and measures. Alluding to contemporary research on the subject in Britain and France, he expressed his belief that it "would be honorable to our country if the sequel of the same experiments should be countenanced by the patronage of our Government. . . ."[6] Nothing came of his proposal, but when the disappointments of office increased during the latter half of his administration, the president himself turned increasingly, as an escape, to botanical study. His cabinet members, whether by precept or example, devoted careful attention to expanding their departmental libraries by purchasing the classic and current publications on European scientific investigation. Consular officials carried standing instructions to provide details upon not only commercial and political developments but also the physical and geographic features of the countries to which they were assigned. Even naval officers were directed to procure information about useful seeds, plants, and animals and to import "such as they could conveniently. . . ."

This effort to acquire knowledge of the world beyond the national limits was associated in Adams's view with a responsibility to add this nation's "portion of energy and exertion to the common stock" devoted to "improvement of the species" through science. The country's "engagement to contribute her share of mind, of labor, and of expense to the improvement of those parts of knowledge which lie beyond the reach of individual acquisition" represented a measure of national maturation. The president pointed particularly to the potentialities for American contribution in "geographical and astronomical science." He confessed "no feeling of pride as an American" that Europe maintained some 130 astronomical observatories while the United States had not one of "these lighthouses of the skies."[7] Although the argument fell on ears that were closed alike to the intellectualism of the concept and the stilted phraseology of the effort at popularization, Adams and Secretary Southard, during the final year of the administration, still hoped that a nation of frontiersmen and a constituency of seafarers and traders might respond more favorably to a proposal for "voyages of discovery."

The record of the administration's effort to initiate an expedition for exploration of the South Seas provided in the end but one more illustration of a commitment to scientific progress that was thwarted by bitter partisan opposition. The episode, nevertheless, demonstrates remarkably both the aggressiveness of the executive pursuit of the program and the insensitivity to constitutional restraints which sustained political hostility to it. Support for the undertaking was late in blooming among the president's adherents. Since 1822 Congress had received numerous petitions seeking governmental aid for outfitting an expedition to explore the polar regions, primarily to test the highly publicized "hollow-core" theory of the earth's structure, as expounded by the visionary John Cleves Symmes, Jr. When such a proposal came before the House of Representatives in February 1827, Edward Everett emphasized his support for any project designed to advance science but questioned that the nation was yet ready to pursue this investigation. The Jacksonian James Buchanan then saved the measure by explaining that it was not identified with "the peculiarities of any hypothesis" but, indeed, carried the unanimous endorsement of the legislature of Maryland and of other community leaders, "as cool heads, and as far removed from anything like enthusiasm, or credulty [*sic*], as any that could be found.''[8] A few days later the petitions were referred by House resolution to the secretary of the navy.

Southard interpreted the action as a mandate to support the project. In his annual report the following December he noted that the petitions had come from New York, Pennsylvania, Maine, Virginia, and Ohio and that they had been supplemented by many more after Congress had adjourned. He had accordingly authorized leaves of absence for officers and seamen who chose to join an expedition should one ''be fitted out by private enterprise.'' He emphasized, however, that such action was as much as he could extend, since no appropriation had been provided: ''there was no money which could with propriety be used to carry into execution the object of the reference.''[9]

In March 1828 a bill authorizing the proposed expedition and appropriating funds for it was brought before the House but was tabled. Two months later, amidst the flurry of activity at the close of the session, a resolution was debated briefly and passed, permitting assignment of a small public vessel ''to the Pacific ocean and South sea, to examine the coasts, islands, harbors, shoals, and reefs in those seas . . . ,'' provided it could be done ''without prejudice to the general interest of the naval service; and . . . without further appropriations during the . . . year.''[10] Neither the resolution nor the funding proposal came under Senate review.

On the basis of this questionable authorization, Adams and Southard, drawing upon regular and contingency appropriations of the Navy Department, pressed major preparations throughout the remainder of the administration. The president bluntly advised the secretary of his ''earnest wish'' that the vessel might depart before the reassembling of Congress. He had ''a deep anxiety that this expedition should be undertaken, and as far as possible executed, under the present Administration''; and he thought it ''certain'' that the following year they should not ''have the opportunity.''[11]

Since no naval vessel was deemed, ''in its then condition,'' to be suitable for such an expedition, the sloop *Peacock* was ''repaired and supplied with conveniences suited to the object,'' construction that included double timbering of the hull as protection against antarctic ice floes. Arrangements were also made, conditioned upon congressional approval, for either charter or purchase of a second vessel, of 200 tons burden, to ensure the safety of the enterprise, and of a third, a smaller, vessel to serve in provisioning the party on location. A special agent was sent to the major ports of New England to interview ship captains and to study their logs for information on trading developments and navigational hazards in the area. Astronomers and naturalists were invited to participate. The New York Lyceum of Natural History accordingly assigned nine members of its staff to prepare reports for guidance of the expedition; and one of the institution's leading scientists, Dr. James Ellsworth DeKay, applied for appointment as navy surgeon to accompany the party. The secretary of the navy reported in December that the expedition, "ready to sail in a few weeks," would carry "better guides than are usually possessed by those who embark in similar undertakings."[12]

At the end of the year, however, problems had not only delayed sailing until after Congress convened but had threatened to stall the operation beyond the end of the administration. The Navy Board of Examiners refused to commission Dr. DeKay and others of the scientific staff. Young Lieutenant Charles Wilkes, a member of a family that had long been prominent in New York social and political affairs and the only naval officer who had pretensions to scientific expertise, was bitterly resentful and vocal in his complaints against the role of civilians. Assigned to collect astronomical instruments under the direction of a civilian astronomer, he appears to have deliberately protracted the preparations. Longstanding jealousies, nurtured by the administration's reiterated emphasis upon the scientific deficiencies in the training of naval officers, focused in rivalry for leadership of the expedition. Even Southard's appointment of the ardent Jacksonian Thomas ap Catesby Jones, veteran commander of the Pacific Squadron, failed to silence the criticism.

With the meeting of Congress, opposition surfaced to defeat the aspirations of civilian and service proponents alike. The scale of the project now required an appropriation, but before the bill came to a vote, a proposal was introduced to explore the Oregon country. Introduced by the administration leader John W. Taylor of New York and backed by John Sergeant, now representing Pennsylvania, the latter measure was offered as a substitute for a bill of the Virginia Jacksonian John Floyd, to establish a military post on the Columbia River. It bore no direct association with the South Seas venture, but it engendered bitter animosities that were transferred to the issue of scientific investigations generally. Under a sectional division between East and West, with opposition voiced by most New Englanders, including the administration stalwart Edward Everett, as well as by Floyd and his followers, the project for domestic exploration was narrowly defeated.[13]

Although at mid January the House, by vote of 97 to 59, sustained the South Seas project and provided $50,000 to fund it, political and sectional divisions were sharply evident. Spokesmen from the northern seaboard endorsed the venture; those from the West divided on it; and those from the South opposed it. As the measure came before the Senate in early February, Robert Y. Hayne, chairman of the Committee on Naval Affairs, consolidated the opposition by making a vehement attack. Emphasizing that the Senate had never approved the resolution under which the Navy Department had acted and that the stipulations of the House had been ignored in the elaboration of the preparations, he protested: "The importance of the exploring expedition was nothing, in comparison with the question—(one of the most important that could be discussed)—of the power assumed by the Executive to transfer, at pleasure, appropriations made by law to certain objects, to another and distinct object, not having the sanction of Congress." He deplored the leadership roles accorded to civilians as constituting a derogation of the navy's competence. The naval officers were to be mere navigators: "he [Hayne] would have them at the head of the expedition, and the scientific corps should be their mere agents and instruments." Finally, he assailed the policy that, while there were "unsettled and unexplored regions at home," looked to "the discovery of unknown lands, however rich they may be in resources, however inviting to the enterprise of individuals, or the ambition of rulers." Such an enterprise would tend to the establishment of a colony "in a distant region, which could only be defended at an expense not to be estimated, and which could not be taken under the protection of the United States, without an abandonment of the fundamental principles of our policy, and a departure from those wise and prudent maxims which have hitherto restrained us from forming unnecessary connexions abroad."[14] Again the restrictions of a narrowly defined federal authority were called into force.

On March 2, by a procedural motion, the Senate refused to consider the bill. From the West, only William Hendricks of Indiana, Benjamin Ruggles of Ohio, and William Marks, a Pittsburgh lawyer, supported the proposal. Only Ezekiel Chambers of Chestertown, Maryland, endorsed it from the South. Sectional interests appear to have carried the Jacksonians John Holmes of Maine and Levi Woodbury of New Hampshire into endorsement of the project, as they also swung the administration supporters Dominique Bouligny of Louisiana, David Barton of Missouri, James Noble of Indiana, and Jacob Burnet of Ohio into the opposition.[15] The expedition, which ultimately was led by Captain Wilkes, was not launched until 1838, when it combined investigation of the South Seas with a survey of the coast of the American Northwest.

With similar lack of success, Secretary Southard struggled to win congressional authorization for a coastal survey of the eastern seaboard.

While such a project was manifestly identifiable as an operational concern of the national government, the president and his secretary were again challenging an entrenched opposition to scientific advance. Nearly twenty years earlier, Thomas Jefferson and Albert Gallatin had been interested in bringing into the nation's service the Swiss geodesist Ferdinand Rudolph Hassler, a recent immigrant. A coastal survey had been authorized under a congressional resolution of 10 February 1807, and Hassler had been nominated to superintend it. The disruption during the succeeding period of war had delayed the undertaking, but in the interim, Hassler had assembled the necessary instruments. In 1816 he had been formally appointed and directed to begin operations. Two years later, jealousy that a civilian and a foreigner should direct the project, combined with a demand for governmental retrenchment, had led Congress to require that only army or navy personnel be employed in conducting the survey. Criticism that Hassler worked slowly, that he could not, like land surveyors, produce maps and charts quickly, contributed to his dismissal. The project was thereafter virtually suspended.[16]

The need, nevertheless, remained. During the war with Britain, Americans had seen that British captains, who had better navigational data, dared to sail into inlets where American skippers shied away. In his report of 1825 Southard complained that "scarcely a mile" of the coastline was "thoroughly known." Under legislation of the previous year, surveys of the harbors of Charleston, South Carolina, and St. Mary's, Georgia, had been conducted, primarily to ascertain the practicability of developing naval facilities in those areas. A $10,000 appropriation in 1826 provided for similar studies of the harbors of Savannah, Brunswick (South Carolina), and Baltimore. The work, Southard reported, was performed by "competent officers" and would "furnish sufficient information" to serve the designated purposes. He emphasized, however, that it did not afford "perfect surveys and charts"; harbor approaches could not be accurately charted without the broader coastal survey. Although throughout his term of office the secretary reiterated this plea for a "scientific survey" of the whole coastline, Congress failed to revive the project.[17]

In contrast, projects identified with "practical" benefits and localized constituencies, as distinct from undertakings of generalized scientific import, won ready endorsement. Southard, with difficulty, discouraged the demands of legislators to increase the number of navy yards beyond what he considered to be either necessary or practicable. Governor Ninian Edwards of Illinois, urging that the president introduce into his annual message "some sentiment favorable to the connec-

172

tion of our great Lakes with the Atlantic & Western waters," advised that the demand in his state and in Missouri for a canal linking Lake Michigan to the Illinois River was "indeed a political hobby that supercedes [sic] all other."[18] The administration's advocacy of a lengthy schedule of internal improvements—harbor development, stream-bed clearance, canal and road construction—became its most popular and successful domestic program.

Adams and his cabinet held few of the doubts that had marked Monroe's endorsement of the legislation of 30 April 1824, establishing the Board of Internal Improvements to conduct surveys for roads and canals deemed to be "of national importance. . . ." The president, Clay, and Rush shared a philosophical commitment to the program. Wirt joined Barbour in questioning, as "excessively bold," the statement on internal improvements in Adams's first annual message, but their fears rested largely upon anticipation of political repercussions in Virginia. The attorney general himself found the passage "a noble, spirited thing. . . ."[19]

Monroe had named to the new board Baron Simon Bernard, a French military engineer; Major Joseph G. Totten of the United States Army Corps of Topographical Engineers; and John Langdon Sullivan, former superintendent of the Middlesex Canal. Basing their work on Albert Gallatin's report of 4 April 1808 on "Roads and Canals," they had begun with a survey of the route for the projected Chesapeake and Ohio Canal, advocated by proponents in Virginia and Maryland as well as in the West, since before the founding of the nation. Adams advised Congress, as he delivered his initial endorsement of the activity, that this report, another for a proposed road from Washington to New Orleans, and one for an intraregional canal from Lake Memphremagog, in northern Vermont, to the Connecticut River were nearing completion.

Surveys for a wide distribution of works, designed to meet the demands of numerous local communities and interlocking sectional interests, were brought under review during the next three years. Despite Congress's refusal to yield to reiterated requests for increased personnel, the Engineering Department of the army added to the above-mentioned reports some analyses of routes for extension of the Cumberland Road east to the tidewater within the District of Columbia and west to St. Louis, for rerouting of a post road from Baltimore to Philadelphia, and for construction of roads from Washington to Buffalo; from Zanesville, Ohio, to Florence, Alabama; from the Maumee River to

Detroit and on to Fort Dearborn; from Detroit north to Saginaw Bay; from Little Rock to Cantonment Gibson in Arkansas Territory; and from Missouri across the Plains to New Mexico. Army engineers surveyed for proposed canal development from Lake Pontchartrain to the Mississippi River; from the Atlantic Ocean to the Gulf of Mexico across northern Florida; from Pensacola Bay to Mobile; from the Hiwassee River to the Coosa in Alabama; from the North River to the Neuse in North Carolina; from the James River to the Kanawha in Virginia; from Port Erie to Pittsburgh in Pennsylvania; from the Maumee River to the Wabash in Ohio and Indiana, along the north bank around the falls of the Ohio; from several small streams linking to the Connecticut, the Androscoggin, and the Kennebec Rivers, respectively, in northern New England; and from Taunton to Weymouth in Massachusetts. They also aided independently initiated ventures such as the Ohio State and the Dismal Swamp canals.

Military engineers studied possibilities for opening or improving navigation through the Muscle Shoals of the Tennessee River; along the main streams of the Kentucky, the Wabash, the White, the Allegheny, the Genesee, the Kennebec, the Androscoggin, the Cape Fear, the Apalachicola, and the Red River of Louisiana; as well as an inner coastal passage by way of Roanoke Inlet and Pamlico Sound. They also initiated railroad surveys as early as 1826, in comparison of such routing with canals to link the Kanawha with the James and Roanoke rivers. By 1828 they were surveying railroad routes from the Hudson River to Pittsfield, Massachusetts; from Catskill to Ithaca and from Ithaca to Owego in New York; from the headwaters of the Savannah River to the Tennessee and from the Savannah to the Altamaha. The Baltimore and Ohio Rail Road and the South Carolina Canal and Rail Road Company, private undertakings, were also receiving assistance from the army, "as the work was considered by the Executive of great national importance. . . ."[20]

Such aid was not limited to the planning stage. Either as the supervising authority for letting of contracts or as the construction force directly, the Army Engineering Department engaged in a vast array of civilian operations. The extension of the Cumberland, or National, Road from Wheeling to Zanesville was virtually completed before Adams left office. An act of 2 March 1827, appropriating $30,000 for repair of the old road from Cumberland to Wheeling, permitted improvement of the worst sections in that segment but left about half the distance yet to be done. Construction of a road from Maumee to Detroit, under legislation of May 1824, was well advanced, and sufficient funds had been allotted for its completion. More than fifty miles of an extension west from Detroit, authorized in the spring of 1825, were also constructed.

A policy, pressed by Adams, which opened contracts under competitive bid to small contractors, so that numerous sections could be built simultaneously, contributed to speed and economy of operations. Greater use of local materials also reduced the costs. The technology of the Scotsman John Loudon McAdam, which provided for a roadway of crushed stone to a depth of nine inches and was first put to extensive use in the United States in this work, greatly improved the durability. Without reference to the differences in terrain, Secretary Barbour pointed out that the cost of the National Road averaged less than $4,300 per mile west of Wheeling, compared with $12,900 to the east.[21]

Harbor improvement at Presque Isle (Erie), Pennsylvania, and breakwaters for preservation of Plymouth Beach, Massachusetts, had been authorized as Federal projects under legislation of 1823 and 1824. Between 1826 and 1828, statutes were enacted to extend the construction of piers to thirty additional sites. Facilities were developed along the Great Lakes—at Oswego, Buffalo, and Dunkirk, New York; Ashtabula, Grand River, Cleveland, Huron, and Sandusky, Ohio; along the New England seaboard—at Belfast and Saco, Maine; at the mouths of the Piscataqua and Merrimack rivers, Hyannis, and Provincetown, Massachusetts; at Little Compton, Newport, and Warren, Rhode Island; at Saugatuck and Stonington, Connecticut; along the Delaware River—at Chester, Pennsylvania, and New Castle, Delaware; and at Roanoke Inlet, North Carolina; Mobile, Alabama; and Pascagoula, Mississippi. Engineering Department reports reiterated complaints about the constant struggle to keep up with the demand for services. During the Adams years, rivers and harbors legislation, which was destined to become the "pork barrel" of American politics, provided for the opening of waterways for a rapidly expanding internal commerce and for the expansion of port facilities around the national perimeter from the Great Lakes to the Gulf of Mexico.

Technical assistance was only part of the program. Financial aid was provided, in the West, through grants of public land and, in the East, as governmental subscriptions to corporate stock issues. Congress had earlier initiated the practice of providing the right of way for internal improvements through public lands. Illinois in 1822 and Indiana in 1824 had been accorded such encouragement for canal programs to link the Great Lakes with the Ohio-Mississippi river system. In 1827, with backing from the Adams administration, Congress authorized expansion of this support to encompass the allotment of public lands in alternate sections for a distance of five miles on each side of these works. Ohio received a similar grant in 1828 to aid in extending its Miami Canal to Lake Erie and an additional 500,000 acres to help finance the construction of its two canal projects that were already under way. At this time, Alabama also received a grant of 400,000 acres to finance the construction of a canal and the removal of obstructions to navigation at the Muscle Shoals of the Tennessee River.[22]

A public subscription to the extent of $300,000 for the privately organized Chesapeake and Delaware Canal Company had been authorized on the closing day of Monroe's administration, after a twenty-year struggle to win such support. As financial difficulties engulfed the company, a second subscription, for $140,000, was approved just before Adams left office. Two subscriptions, totaling $235,000, to the stock of the Louisville and Portland Canal Company, for a route around the falls of the Ohio, and two, amounting to $200,000 to the stock of the Dismal Swamp Canal Company, for a project linking the lower end of Chesapeake Bay to Albemarle Sound, were also provided during the Adams years. In 1828 Rush reported that during the past four years some $14 million had been spent "on internal works, designed to improve the condition of the country, or otherwise on objects not belonging to the mere annual support of Government, in its civil, military, and naval establishments." As a program resting upon presidential advocacy, it was not again approached until the 1850s.[23]

Openings of the Ohio Canal from Cleveland to Akron in 1827, the Dismal Swamp Canal in 1828, the Chesapeake and Delaware and the Louisville and Portland projects in 1829, and the Miami Canal from Cincinnati to Dayton in 1830 gave prompt evidence of the value of such effort. Even where completion of works was long delayed, the development hastened settlement and accelerated the transition to commercial production along finished segments of the routes. Political opponents yielded unwilling testimony to the popularity of these works. Congressman George McDuffie of South Carolina, looking ahead to the presidential canvass, assailed the program as a "comprehensive scheme of corruption, which proposes under the form of law and under the assumed guise of patriotic motives to purchase up one half of society with the wealth plundered from another."[24]

Not all the consequences, either political or economic, were beneficial, however. As had been earlier evident in New York, localities that were remote from these projects questioned the expenditures that benefited their competitors. In northwestern Ohio, too, the pressure from land speculators to engross potential sites of routes led the General Land Office in 1828 to introduce the practice of closing large areas to entry. Such exclusion evoked public protests, similar to those that would later be echoed in agrarian outrage against the railway land grants. Elsewhere, long delays in construction were discouraging. The

Wabash Canal, which was mismanaged financially throughout most of its history, never fulfilled popular anticipations. Extended first from Lafayette to Terre Haute and ultimately south to Evansville, it was not fully opened until 1853, when railway development had long since eliminated need for such expansion. The Chesapeake and Ohio project, which gave Adams particular satisfaction, occasioned, in the end, the greatest disappointment.[25]

That undertaking, in which the federal government shared a local interest through the participation of the District of Columbia, had finally taken form as the outgrowth of a Chesapeake and Ohio Canal convention in Washington in November 1823. The massing of public interest that had then been demonstrated had, in fact, induced President Monroe to recommend the legislation under which the Board of Internal Improvement had begun its work. Virginia had provided for incorporation of the company in January 1824; a year later, Maryland confirmed this action. On the basis of the board's preliminary report, Congress had endorsed the corporate arrangement on the final day of Monroe's administration. Pennsylvania finally yielded its agreement, with reservations, in February 1826. The opposition of the rival ports of Baltimore and Philadelphia, which was counteracted by the generalization of the improvement program, had been overcome.[26]

The estimated cost of the venture continued to delay operations. The Virginia charter had provided for a capitalization of only $6 million. General Bernard and the Board of Internal Improvement, under their survey report of October 1826, estimated that the cost for the whole project would run to $22,375,428. In length the canal would be but 341 miles, as compared to the 362 miles of the Erie route, but the technical difficulties of the former would be vastly greater, with lockage amounting to 3,158 feet, as opposed to only 688 on the New York canal.[27]

As Adams was drafting his second annual message, he noted the completion of the engineers' report and prepared an accompanying paragraph including "a most earnest and emphatic recommendation of it to Congress." Clay, whose enthusiasm for internal improvements had made him the foremost exponent of legislation on behalf of the Cumberland, or National, Road, demurred, reluctantly but most decisively, on the canal proposal. He questioned its practicability, "believed that at all events its cost would rather exceed than fall short of the estimates of the Board . . . , and [that] when accomplished . . . it would be, comparatively speaking, of small utility." He doubted that it would greatly benefit the city of Washington and asserted that, except for the areas closely bordering the route, "there was very little interest felt in it anywhere, and none at all in the Western country generally." Barbour, who shared Clay's views, expressed still stronger doubt about the feasibility of the canal. Rush and Adams opposed these contentions, but the president finally decided to strike out his recommendation and let the report of the board "stand upon its own strength."[28]

Learning of the board's cost estimate, supporters of the canal hastily called a second convention, which met in Washington on 6 December 1826. On the ground that the costs of labor and material were estimated too high, they called for a revision of the report. Congressmen Andrew Stewart of Pennsylvania and Charles Fenton Mercer of Virginia, who were among the most active proponents of the undertaking, won the adherence of thirty colleagues to a petition asking that the president submit the board's report to review by civilian engineers. Adams accordingly referred the matter to experts who had worked on the Erie Canal. When their report in 1827 reduced the estimate for the eastern section from a little over $8 million to about $4.5 million, subscription books for the venture were opened.

Congress, in May 1828, authorized purchase of stock by the federal government to the value of $1 million and by the three cities in the District of Columbia to an additional $1.5 million. This action, in turn, validated an earlier Maryland subscription amounting to half a million dollars. With individual pledges exceeding $600,000, the company was formally organized in June 1828. In ground-breaking ceremonies on July 4, the president turned the first shovelful of earth and delivered the brief remarks that he subsequently delineated as one of the major programmatic statements of his administration.

His address, which he described as having "somewhat of a religious character," cited three stages in the development of the American vision. The first was marked by the Declaration of Independence; the second, by the confederation that was at last achieved under the Constitution; and the third, by the adaptation of the powers "of the whole Union" to national improvement: "of its moral and political condition, by wise and liberal institutions—by the cultivation of the understanding and the heart—by academies, schools, and learned institutes—by the pursuit and patronage of learning and the arts; of its physical condition, by associated labor to improve the bounties, and to supply the deficiencies of nature. . . ." The Lord had commanded that man "replenish the Earth, *and subdue it.*" That, the president noted, was "pre-eminently" the purpose of this project. He implored divine blessing upon it "and upon every other similar work in this Confederation. . . ."[29]

What gave Adams particular satisfaction, however, was the rapport that, on this occasion, he established with the audience of some two thousand. Striking a root as he dug, he struggled vainly three or four times to raise a shovelful of earth. Finally, removing his coat, he hacked vigorously through the obstruction, to the accompaniment of "a general shout." The normally formal and reserved New Englander too rarely displayed the emotions of frustration and triumph in labors of common experience. The *National Intelligencer* (Washington), reporting the incident, commented that it "produced a greater sensation than any other that occurred during the day."

Adams's toast in the course of the activities was, appropriately: "The Chesapeake and Ohio Canal: perseverance."[30] That mandate was sorely tested as the construction dragged on for a quarter-century before it reached the peak of the divide at Cumberland, Maryland. Without the fanfare that had marked the beginning of the canal, ceremonies inaugurating commencement of the Baltimore and Ohio Rail Road had also been held on Independence Day in 1828. Legal difficulties over the right of prior location, especially through the narrow passes of the upper Potomac, were to occasion extended delays for both projects. Poor-quality materials, scarce labor, unhealthful working conditions, cost inflation, and renewed financial stringency also caused long interruptions in the work. The canal, which finally cost some $14 million, excluding interest and repairs, never met the goal of providing a short, cheap route to the Ohio. The railroad emerged the survivor.

The internal-improvements program incurred little serious congressional opposition until the spring of 1828. On February 14, Congressman William D. Martin of South Carolina moved to strike the annual appropriation for surveys from the internal-improvements bill. Disavowing all sectional feeling, he nevertheless protested that "not an Engineer had made his appearance in the State from which he came." Philip Pendleton Barbour of Virginia argued that the increasing expenditures of that sort were disrupting the "equilibrium" of power between the federal and state governments and held out "to those States who deny the constitutional power so to apply it, a constant and strong temptation to abandon their principles, or see these benefits lavished upon other States, while they were necessarily excluded." The motion was defeated the next day by an overwhelming vote; but on February 25 Thomas H. Hall of North Carolina moved to strike out the enacting clause of the bill. As his argument, which was based on constitutional grounds, was challenged by a reminder that he was questioning the authority that encompassed the financing of lighthouses and other undeniably federal works, he withdrew the motion. Objections to the bill by other South Carolinians and by Thomas J. Oakley of New York continued the House debate until March 8, when the measure was approved, by vote of 124 to 57.[31]

In the Senate, however, the outcome remained in doubt through April and early May. The debate, as it ranged in both House and Senate, evidenced a sectional division that pitted spokesmen for the South against those of New England and the West, notably among the latter delegations without distinction as to political affiliation. William Smith of South Carolina, the Crawfordite chairman of the Senate Committee on Finance, deplored "the great inequality and injustice" of the internal-improvements program in "its practical operations in the different sections of the Union." There were then, he noted, applications before Congress for some ten million acres to benefit the Western States, all of which had already received large grants of public lands, and for more than $300 million to be spent on internal improvements outside of South Carolina and Georgia. These states were, therefore, to be penalized because their legislatures deemed it neither constitutional nor proper that their representatives "should join in the general struggle for the mere favors of the General Government, and higgle and huckster for a road or a canal, as they would in a market or fair for a bale of goods or an ox."[32]

The Senate finally approved, by vote of 27 to 12, a compromise statement reenforcing the limitation of the survey appropriation to projects "deemed of national importance." For Senator Smith and a hard-core coterie who shared his States' rights views, such a distinction was not easily made. "The term National was a new word that had crept into our political vocabulary," Smith contended, "a term unknown to the origin and theory of our Government." How was an improvement to be identified as "national"? "This question is susceptible of but one definition," proclaimed the Senator. "A road, canal, breakwater, river, or creek, becomes national or not national, in the ratio of its supporters, and the influence of those who ask it."[33]

The wide dispersion of improvement projects won, for that phase of the administration's program, a broadly based support which other measures failed to attract. President Adams's advocacy of a national bankruptcy act followed in the tradition of legislation that his father had espoused and that had been repealed as a Jeffersonian reaction in 1803. Clay, familiar as a lawyer with the problems inherent in state action on the subject, had been urging passage of such a federal statute since 1818. For the administration the issue was primarily a concern to benefit commercial classes, and so the measure was framed when Daniel Webster brought a bill before the House of Representatives in January 1827. That body deferred action, however, as the Senate took up a bill, introduced by a committee chaired by Robert Y. Hayne, which incorporated a provision for "voluntary bankruptcy" that would be applicable to classes other than merchants and traders. With backing from John Branch of North Carolina, John M. Berrien of Georgia, and the Kentuckians John Rowan and Richard M. Johnson, the latter proposal was viewed as particularly helpful to agricultural interests.

Party lines were split on the legislation. Many back-country senators, both for and against the administration, opposed bankruptcy measures generally. A segment of Jacksonian leaders, professing attachment to the proposal, sought an amendment to restrict it to commercial application. Levi Woodbury of New Hampshire, Van Buren of New York, and Littleton W. Tazewell, of Virginia—all former Crawfordites— contended that the bill, as presented, fell outside constitutional authorization and extended a general encouragement to insolvency. Were such a sweeping coverage to be assigned to federal jurisdiction, the powers and the patronage of that authority would destroy the states' sovereignty.

Proponents of the bill contended that bankruptcy legislation in 1821 had been rejected because it was limited to merchants and traders. They hoped that a general bill could be passed. On two separate votes, with tallies of 26 nays to 19 ayes, they beat off attempts to reject the broader coverage. Even so, the bill was defeated, 25 to 15, on January 31. The next day a motion to reconsider was adopted, and a week later an amendment to eliminate the generalizing section was approved, 34 to 12.[34]

This action failed to save the bill. It was finally rejected on February 6, by a vote of 27 to 21. As proponents had feared, the westerners Benton of Missouri, Johnson of Kentucky, and Noble of Indiana, who had supported the bill when it covered agricultural interests, opposed it without that section. The amendment, on the other hand, won the votes of several senators who represented commercial districts—Thomas Clayton and Henry M. Ridgely of Delaware; Nathan Sanford and Van Buren of New York; Johnston of Louisiana; and William Rufus de Vane King of Alabama—who had earlier opposed the measure. The difficulty lay in the fact that fourteen senators, who had gone on record as supporters of agricultural interests, either failed to vote or opposed the bill on *both* occasions when it came to a final vote. This group, only three of whom were identified with the administration, joined a cadre of nine consistent opponents of bankruptcy legislation. The debate reflected not only the festering resentments of sectional economic cleavage but also the development of a partisan obstructionism that played upon such concerns.[35]

The administration's support of commercial and financial interests evoked a somewhat similar effort by its foes in the House of Representatives, during the same session, to rally an opposition to the Bank of the United States, based upon an alliance of States' rights extremists and agrarians. The movement failed decisively, but it was significant as an opening barrage in the coming struggle over renewal of the bank's charter. The controversy developed as an outgrowth of recommendations by the president and by Secretary Rush for refunding the public debt.

Under legislation of 1817, a sinking fund had been established, into which revenues of $10 million annually were pledged "to the payment of interest and charges, and to the reimbursement or purchase of the principal of the public debt." For several years during the depression period, surplus sums to that amount had not been available; but notwithstanding the administration's heavy expenditures for internal improvements, Rush reported that the Treasury, from the beginning of 1826 through 1828, "countervailed" that deficiency "by such an excess of annual payments towards the principal of the debt, as to leave . . . no arrears . . . due to the sinking fund, or none of importance."[36]

In actuality, Rush had achieved that accounting by the inclusion of payments for interest charges, as authorized, under the $10 million annual allotments. But he had struggled vainly to effect a refunding that would have considerably reduced the costs that cut into the proportion available for bond retirement. Upon entering office, he had found that some $16,270,797 of the public debt, contracted at the high rate of 6 percent during the War of 1812, was redeemable in 1826. He requested authorization to refund that loan to the amount of $9 million at a rate not to exceed 5 percent, redeemable in 1829 and 1830, with the expectation that from funds on hand the remainder of the 6 percent bonds that were currently redeemable could be liquidated. When the House Committee of Ways and Means demurred, Rush reluctantly paid some $7.067 million of the redeemable debt and interest amounting to almost $4 million. In 1826 he returned to Congress with a request to be allowed to refund $16 million of the debt, again with the hope of liquidating the whole amount of the 6 percent bonds that would be redeemable during the ensuing year.[37]

Still the Congress failed to act. Rush accordingly, in 1827, paid off some $6.507 million more of the 6 percent bonds, but continued to pay over $3.5 million in interest on the balance of the public debt.[38] Why the reluctance to reduce this interest burden? A report by the House Committee of Ways and Means in February 1826 and brief debate the following year in the House of Representatives make evident that the opposition to refunding rested primarily upon the government's ties to the Bank of the United States and to the role of that institution in relation to the public debt.

Refunding legislation had been enacted previously, in 1820, 1822, 1824, and 1825. The security transfers had not been readily negotiated. During the last two years the Bank of the United States had taken up $10 million in government bonds, issued at 4.5 percent interest, partly to finance the Florida purchase, partly to refund 6 percent bonds. In recommending that further refunding be initiated, Rush proposed that the rate of interest on the issues of 1825 be raised to 5 percent: "Those who were willing to accede to the terms of the Government at an early day in this transaction, should not be left in a worse situation than those who may have held back in the hope of better offers," he argued. The Ways and Means Committee on the other hand, opposed annulling the earlier arrangement, "as it is fairly to be inferred that the exchange was not made without satisfactory evidence with the individual creditor, that it was his interest to make it, and without reference to the views or circumstances of others. . . ."[39]

The 1827 debate brought repeated and overt attacks upon the bank. The Jacksonite Gulian C. Verplanck of New York proposed to amend Rush's proposal to provide for paying off the 6 percent bonds through the issuance of Treasury notes in small denominations, which, Verplanck maintained, would enable the government to get the necessary funds at a much lower rate of interest. He knew of but one bidder on government bonds "this side of the Atlantic." That was the Bank of the United States, which could consequently dictate the terms. Treasury notes, on the other hand, offered "a chance of competition."[40]

C. C. Cambreleng, another New York Jacksonian, supported his colleague with the observation that since the bank would take up a large proportion of the proposed security issue, "the effect would be to diminish the amount of the circulation in the country, and transfer a large part of it to an overgrown institution." Edward Livingston, a Jacksonsite from Louisiana, viewed the notes as a means of "remitting funds through the country, and avoiding the premium now charged by the Bank of the United States, which had a monopoly of that business." McDuffie of South Carolina and Willis Alston of North Carolina expressed similar views.[41]

Nicholas Biddle's development of the bank as the regulating force of the national banking system, controlling the market for both domestic and foreign exchange, depended in no small degree upon use of government securities. As the Treasury acted to recall the redeemable 6 percent bonds in the fall of 1825, Biddle had met the demand for release of public deposits by selling some $3 million of the bank's bond portfolio. In part the purchases probably drew some cash from hoards. They also, however, put pressure on state banks at a time when a commercial crisis in England threatened to have international repercussions. Biddle subsequently contended that the bank's increase in discounts to state banks during this period maintained confidence and forestalled financial difficulties in the United States. In actuality, the action merely counteracted the effect of the bank's sales of bonds; the total credit expansion through this difficult time was relatively slight.[42]

Foreign-exchange rates were high from September 1826 through December 1828, partly as a consequence of the retirement of the public debt but primarily because of heavy imports preliminary to upward revision of the tariff. To avoid exports of specie, Biddle again sold government securities, beginning in January 1828. Criticism, which had marked the bank's earlier selling program, increased. Biddle hoped that private purchases of bonds would lessen the demand for imports, but he moved also to curtail loans for merchants and brokers. From February through April the offices of the bank called upon state banks to redeem their notes. Persistent pressure finally fostered the desired contraction, not, however, without generating bitter animosities.

The administration's concentration of public deposits from state banks into the Bank of the United States added to the unpopularity of this last institution. Rush, who reported his activities to the president in the form of a journal during Adams's absence in the fall of 1825, noted that he, Rush, had ordered transfer to the bank of all remaining public moneys in the western country, except $25,000 each at the Tombecbee Bank and the Bank of Mobile, in Alabama, where holdings had been previously reduced from $100,000. At about the same time, as a means of increasing the resort to specie, he had issued directions that receivers and collectors of public revenue should reject payments in notes of any state bank in denominations of less than five dollars.[43]

That old hostilities to a national bank were not dead became evident. In December 1827 Philip Pendleton Barbour proposed to the House of Representatives a resolution calling for the Committee of Ways and Means "to enquire into the expediency of providing by law for the sale of that portion of the stock of the Bank of the United States . . . held by the Government . . . , and the applications of the proceeds thereof to the payment of the public debt." Noting that the bank's stock was currently worth "about 23½ percent advance above its par value," he anticipated a profit of $1.6 million "above the nominal amount of the stock." Were that sum applied to retire public debt, a savings of about $100,000 might be effected in annual interest costs, Barbour contended.[44] The secretary's argument for reduction of the interest was thus to be deflected into an assault upon the administration's support of the bank.

Beyond "a merely pecuniary view," the Virginian emphasized a concern of greater moment. In nine years the bank would be petitioning for renewal of its charter. He did not believe "that the Government to whom such a petition was presented, ought, while listening to and deliberating upon it, be placed under the unavoidable bias arising from the Government itself being a joint stockholder with those who were petitioning." Disclaiming any partisan interest, he conceded that he would oppose the move to recharter. For the present, however, he argued only against the participation of the government "as a stockholder in any joint stock company like a bank." Incorporation was "an exercise of high political power, and so long as the Government continued to have a pecuniary interest in such an institution, it could not but feel all those considerations which address themselves to that interest."[45]

Debated over three days, the resolution was finally overwhelmingly defeated, 174 to 9. The gist of the expressed opposition centered upon fear that so large a disposition of bank stock would depress its value and thus eliminate the anticipated revenue. While denying that there would be such a consequence, Barbour scorned the argument that withdrawal of the government as a stockholder constituted an injustice to the institution: "Obligations of gratitude! And are we, as stockholders, to be bound on this consideration? The benefits have at least been fully reciprocated." He considered the use of the public deposits "an abundant compensation." Under its charter the bank held a twenty-year privilege of receiving 6 percent on all notes that it discounted. The government, he contended, could borrow at 5, perhaps even as low as 4, percent elsewhere. Above all, the bank held "a kind of monopoly of the advantages derived from Government. . . ."[46]

Here was the groundwork for the approaching legislative war on the bank. In 1827 the Virginians Barbour, Floyd, John Roane, and Mark Alexander; the North Carolinians Daniel Turner and Thomas H. Hall; Tomlinson Fort of Georgia; and the Kentuckians Henry Daniel and Joseph Lecompte—all Jacksonians—were eager to begin the assault. Secretary Rush's profuse praise of the bank's service to the government, voiced in his report for 1828, delineated the administration's stand and the sentiment that, for the time being, prevailed. Citing not only the bank's agency as a depository for public moneys, Rush also emphasized its service to state banks in receiving their notes, "paid on public account in the interior, as well as elsewhere," and "placing it to the credit of the United States as cash." He noted the confidence with which its stock was accepted "as a medium of remittance abroad" in lieu of external flows of specie. Finally he acclaimed the bank's operations as a regulator of the currency. State banks, "following or controlled by, its general example," had shaped their policies "towards the same salutary ends," proving "that, under the mixed jurisdiction and powers of the State and National systems of government, a National Bank is the instrument alone by which Congress can effectively regulate the currency of the nation."[47]

That the House Committee of Ways and Means rejected Rush's refunding proposals in contemplation of a broader programmatic attack upon the administration is doubtful. Although Louis McLane, the committee's chairman, held little love for Adams, he was a strong proponent of internal improvements, and the committee was then dominated by administration supporters. In arguing, however, that the extension of bond maturities under a refunding program would limit flexibility in debt reduction, the committee prepared the way for those who, in the Twentieth Congress, demanded general retrenchment and revision of the sinking-fund schedules to promote earlier retirement of the debt.

Sam Smith of Maryland, chairman of the Senate Finance Committee, raised the issue somewhat tentatively as early as January 1827, with a bill to appropriate $1 million from an anticipated $2 million Treasury surplus, as an addition to the regular sinking-fund allotment. Nathan Sanford of New York and Josiah Stoddard Johnston of Louisiana, administration supporters, opposed the measure as a budgetary restraint that would foreclose the customary practice by which Congress added projects in excess of Treasury estimates. Johnston explained that over the past two years, Rush had already paid into the sinking fund $3 million in excess of the $10 million annual allotments. That was as much as Johnston thought proper, "with a just regard to other objects." He claimed any surplus "for improvements of various kinds," now being urged upon Congress. "We have ports to open, channels to deepen, break-waters, roads, canals, and various other subjects of great concern to this country. If this sum may be safely touched, why apply it to the sinking fund?"[48] Protesting that the bill, reported by his own committee, "had come up unexpectedly," Smith then moved to table it, and so the matter rested until the Twentieth Congress.

Proposals in both Houses of Congress in 1828 called for paying over all Treasury surpluses to the sinking fund and for the adoption of measures "to hasten extinguishment of the public debt." Neither legislative body carried the issue to action. The House bill, introduced by the Committee of Ways and Means, was never debated. The Senate resolutions, introduced by Benton of Missouri, remained in committee through 1828, and at the following session were reported unfavorably. Reports by a House Committee on Retrenchment in May 1828 and February 1829 endorsed the concept but also failed to win support. Collateral debate made clear, however, that for such opposition leaders as Congressmen Floyd and Randolph of Virginia, as well as Senator Benton, the issue of debt liquidation had become an assault upon the administration's whole domestic program, and specifically a concern to eliminate a justification for tariffs.[49]

Josiah Stoddard Johnston protested the "ulterior views" of Benton's project: "The object seems to be, to force the revenue to the highest point, to stop the progress of all our improvement, to press the payment of the public debt in five years, in order that, when that is accomplished, we may remove protection. . . ." They set forth principles forming "the distinctive lines between the great parties that are to divide the politicians of this country."[50]

The president's priorities in domestic policy had centered upon recommendations for scientific development, internal improvements, and bankruptcy legislation. He had also publicly and strongly endorsed Rush's proposals for management of the public debt. The agenda had expressed Adams's personal interests and, to a considerable degree, those of his constituents. That he had not opposed the generalization of the bankruptcy proposal testified, nevertheless, to a flexibility in intersectional adjustment. Similarly, the dispersion of internal improvements had served to counteract localized rivalries. The program had encompassed expanded benefits in promotion of general harmony.

But the linkages of the home-market argument required regional sacrifices as well as benefits. Within the South and amidst Adams's own constituents, the divisions on tariff policy ran deep. The South and West held strongly discordant views from those of New England on land and Indian policy. These issues represented political flash points that Adams approached warily. As late as 1833, in claiming paternity for the "American System," he yet defined it primarily in relation to internal improvements.[51] How fully he conceptualized its integrative features during his presidency was, at least, obscure. The cabinet—Clay, Rush, and Barbour in particular—moved to the fore as expositors of these components of the program.

9

TARIFF, LAND,
AND INDIAN POLICIES:
THE POLITICAL FLASH POINTS

That President Adams opposed protective tariff legislation as a feature of the administration's program is highly questionable. Notwithstanding his equivocal stance on the issue during the political campaign of 1824 and his assurance of satisfaction with existing impost levels, as expressed to James Barbour that December, there is no record that he sought to deter the vigorous advocacy of stronger protective measures by his cabinet officers or by the administration's leaders in Congress. Privately he testified that Secretary Rush's recommendations for increased duties not only on woolen manufactures, fine cottons, and bar iron but also on the raw materials hemp and wool carried his "entire approbation." In diary entries he noted that the policy would "outlive the blast of faction and abide the test of time." Himself a vigorous adherent to the retaliatory features of reciprocity policy, he viewed protective tariffs as a necessary response to foreign barriers against American exports:

> Is the self-protecting energy of this nation so helpless that there exists in the political institutions of our country no power to counteract the bias of this foreign legislation; that the growers of grain must submit to this exclusion from the foreign markets of their produce; that the shippers must dismantle their ships, the trade of the North stagnate at the wharves, and the manufacturers starve at their looms, while the whole people shall pay tribute to foreign industry to be clad in a foreign garb; that the Congress of the Union are impotent to restore the

balance in favor of native industry destroyed by the statutes of another realm?

He hoped that "more just and more generous sentiments" would prevail.[1]

But Adams delayed this public pronouncement until his final presidential message. He had refused earlier to incorporate such a statement in his annual message to Congress because "the friends of the Administration in the South were . . . urgent that nothing should be said upon the subject. . . ." He was well aware, too, of similar sentiments in coastal areas of New England. In 1814 Daniel Webster had protested against rearing manufactures "in hot-beds" and as late as 1824 had delivered the principal antitariff argument. One of Clay's New England friends, who held no love for Adams, reminded the secretary of state of those divisions as late as 1826, noting that the Kentuckian's adherents in the North were the manufacturing, rather than the president's commercial, supporters.[2]

With presidential endorsement in abeyance, Secretaries Clay and Rush provided the initial identification of the administration in advocacy of protective tariffs. The Kentuckian, as a leading proponent of the tariff of 1824, had been prepared to pursue such a policy even if it should occasion temporary decline in public revenue and delay in retirement of the public debt. The unusually high level of foreign imports in 1825 was encouraging. Although in value that record declined some 8 percent during the following year, Secretary Rush attributed the change to falling price levels abroad, rather than to a decline in volume. Cotton exports, for which data by bulk as well as value were available, indicated that the quantity of foreign sales was steadily increasing—from 176 million pounds in 1825 to 192 million in 1826, even as the value had sharply declined, from $36 million to $24 million. The principal arguments in opposition to the program on economic grounds appeared to have been met.[3]

From the beginning of the administration, Secretary Rush's annual reports expounded the interlocking economic relationships of the home-market argument. Hailing the exports of domestic manufactures in 1825 as the largest in the nation's history, he acclaimed the development as "the commencement of an epoch in the national resources, since an intimate connexion is believed to exist between the full encouragement and success of domestic manufactures and the wealth, the power, and the happiness of the country." Agriculture, he argued, could never achieve full prosperity without the demand of a home market. Foreign commerce could never expand to its full limit without an active home trade and diversified exports. "By numerous manufactures, in fine, we shall see reared up in the state that additional pillar, which, standing in the middle, is indispensable to the stability of the other two; for the state must be in a false position, lying perpetually at the mercy of extrinsic events, when reposing only upon foreign commerce and agriculture." In planning for the public revenue, therefore, nothing was "more likely to prove salutary" than to "look to the fostering of manufactures."[4]

Returning to the theme in his second report, the Treasury secretary again provided an integrative defense of aid for domestic manufactures. He estimated that already the home market was absorbing fully a quarter of the raw cotton grown in the United States. Towns and villages were developing rapidly in proximity to factories, "in resorting to which the rural population of the vicinity find ready and profitable sales for the various productions of farming enterprise and labor." "It is then," he emphasized, "that the farmer, the artisan, and the merchant, give support to each other, each enlarging the occupations and the gains of each; the State, meanwhile reaping the fruits in fiscal prosperity and political power."[5]

From Virginia came the response—one that turned aside from arguments of economy and national interest alike. On 29 January 1827 William Branch Giles introduced resolutions in the House of Delegates, defining the issue primarily as one of States' rights. He protested "the claim or exercise of any power whatever, on the part of the general government, to make internal improvements within the limits of the state of Virginia . . ."; "any claim or exercise of power, whatever on the part of the general government, which serves to draw money from the inhabitants of this state, into the treasury of the United States, so as to disburse it for any object, whatever, except for carrying into effect the grants of power to the general government, contained in the constitution of the United States"; and "the claim or exercise of any power, whatever, on the part of the general government to protect domestic manufactures. . . ." Specifically, he condemned the tariff act of 1824, which, in his view, distributed "the proceeds of the labor of the community, in such a manner as to transfer the property from one portion of the United States to another" and took "private property from the owner for the benefit of another person, not rendering public service. . . ." The act was, he maintained, "unconstitutional, unjust, unequal and oppressive."[6]

Robert Barrand Taylor, for the administration's supporters, answered by offering a substitute proposal, which he defended in a four-day address, running to March 1. On the following day the Taylor amendment was rejected, by the vote of 131 to 48. The Virginia delegates then approved the Giles resolutions, and on March 5 the state senate upheld this action. Virginia had announced her stand, not only upon the tariff but on the whole conception of an American System.[7]

The president's fears of southern opposition had been fulfilled, but those concerning the views of his New England constituency were allayed. Wool manufacturers had suffered heavily under competition from British imports during the first two years of the administration. With duties on imports of raw wool into England reduced in 1824 from 12 pence to a penny a pound, British manufacturers had been able to sell cheaply in the American market. The Massachusetts legislature, spurred by a manufacturers' meeting in Boston, now passed resolutions requesting greater protection. Prodded by a delegation of these constituents, Webster himself brought the issue before the House of Representatives. On January 10 the chairman of the Committee on Manufactures, Rollin Mallary of Vermont, introduced legislation to aid domestic producers of both wool and woolens.

This joining of raw material and fabricating interests constituted a basic modification in the premises of the American System. Agricultural districts, whether of the South or of the back-country North and West, were expected, under the "home-market" argument, to find relief for declining foreign trade and a resulting domestic surplus through growth in domestic industry and urban employment. Their rewards were to accrue only indirectly, as manufacturing prospered. A protective tariff that would project higher production costs violated the theoretical tenets. By such a concession to sheep raisers, the administration's forces expanded the range of political appeal but laid the basis for massive distortion of their program.

As the wool bill came before the House in 1827, the Jacksonians Charles A. Wickliffe and T. P. Moore of Kentucky called also for protection of hemp and distilled spirits made from grain. When those amendments were summarily rejected, James Buchanan of Pennsylvania described the issue as one of protection for a corporate manufacturing monopoly centered in Boston and Salem, to the damage of infant industry and of farmers generally. He contended that Pennsylvania wool growers would not be able to compete with those of New England for the market, that they ought to "have some equivalent in the increased price of their grain"; and alluding to their pivotal political position, he called upon Pennsylvania to "vindicate her own rights." "She has but to will it," he asserted, "and her farmers shall be protected. Without the vote of her Representatives, this bill cannot pass."[8]

Buchanan's amendment demanding a wider range of protection was rejected, 110 to 90. Samuel Ingham, the Philadelphia Calhounite, then sought modification of the proposed classification schedules to minimize the gains for manufacturers. With that effort also defeated, the bill passed the lower house by a vote of 106 to 95.[9]

In the Senate, however, opponents of the bill were successful. Calhoun, as presiding officer, cast a tie-breaking vote for tabling. The action showed split votes for Missouri and Illinois, aligned with a united South, including Maryland and Kentucky, against the tariff. All the senators from Indiana, Ohio, and Pennsylvania and the only voting senator from New York joined with the New Englanders, including the Jacksonians of the northern hill country, in support of the measure. Manufacturers and sheep raisers had been won to the proposed legislation; agricultural interests generally had not.[10]

The tariff was clearly an issue that transcended partisan lines, and the degree of response was just as evidently related to the immediacy of the anticipated benefits. The indirect gains of the "home-market" argument held limited appeal. The movement for tariff revision was becoming, like that for internal improvements, a scramble for particularistic interests. But in the view of administration leaders, the blending of Adams's and Clay's political bases rested upon consolidation of the programmatic interests from New England through the Middle States into the Ohio Valley. The changing economy, which had attached New England to tariff revision, generated support, too, in southwestern Pennsylvania and the transmontane counties of Virginia. If modest concessions were made to sheep, wheat, and hemp growers, the linkage might yet be effected.

On March 18 Clay wrote to his friend Benjamin W. Crowninshield of Pennsylvania concerning plans for political organization. He projected a series of meetings, perhaps to begin at Philadelphia, focusing on a union of the supporters of the administration and the friends of domestic manufactures and internal improvements, "without regard to party denominations heretofore existing." He urged that Mathew Carey, the tariff publicist, be brought out and that "the proceedings in the Virginia legislature agt the American system" be featured in the agenda. Six weeks later, Peter B. Porter, discussing the founding of an administration journal at Albany, again stressed this political emphasis, as he reported that the editors were "given distinctly to understand . . . That the pole star of its policy must be the encouragement of domestic manufactures & support of the tariff. . . ." As members of the cabinet took to the hustings in the Middle States that summer, the twin topics of "D.M. & I.I." became their themes.[11]

The Philadelphia gathering met from May 14 to 19, under the formal sponsorship of the Pennsylvania Society for the Promotion of Manufactures and the Mechanic Arts. It was only one of a series of local meetings, which led to a state convention at Harrisburg on June 27 and finally to a national convention in that city from July 30 to August 3. State meetings throughout New England and in New York, New Jersey, Delaware, Maryland, Virginia, Ohio, and Kentucky also sent delegations to the national assembly. Public addresses and resolutions of support for protective tariffs were a standard feature of these sessions. The resolutions of the national convention, culminating in a memorial to Congress, provided detailed recommendations for duties against imports of raw wool and woolen goods and more general suggestions for protection of domestic producers of flax and hemp, distilled spirits, iron and steel, and printed cottons, "although not in such crying need of . . . immediate assistance."[12]

The movement was issue oriented, but so clearly was the administration identified with the issue that the meetings represented the nucleus of political organization. The tariff bill that was brought before the Jacksonian-dominated Twentieth Congress during the winter of 1827/28 was accordingly carefully structured to counteract this design. As early as July 1827 Buchanan was reported to have announced: "We will next session bring before Congress a tariff bill so *larded* with other than protection to wool growers and manufacturers of wool, and involving principles which we know the East will not agree to [that] we will . . . throw the odium of its rejection off the South on . . . the East." Charles Hammond, editor of the Clay-oriented *Liberty Hall and Cincinnati Gazette*, warned the secretary of state on August 10 that local Jacksonians, meeting two days earlier, had "resolved to support a tariff, such an one as no sensible man can support, and hope[d] to throw the blame of rejecting it on the North."[13]

The stratagem was simple and, in part, had been presaged in the amendments offered by Buchanan and Ingham to the woolens bill of 1827. Schedules were proposed which, first, narrowed the limits of valuation classes on woolen goods, thus reducing the margin of benefit for American producers of low grade cloths, and, second, set duty rates that would afford little aid to manufacturers but, by heavily protecting raw wool and molasses, would greatly increase their costs. Support for Middle State and northern New England sheep growers and for distillers in the West, on the other hand, attracted the interest of those groups. The Jacksonians, with a majority on the committee that drafted the measure, could claim credit for a tariff that was desired in the regions of crucial political contest. They anticipated that Adams's New

England constituency would find the measure unacceptable. Southerners, agreeing to force the bill to final vote without amendment, believed that in combination with this opposition, they could defeat the legislation. The opprobrium of inconsistency to party policy would redound against the administration.[14]

Hezekiah Niles, in September 1828, published a series of statements from the congressional debates, supported by an analysis of votes, showing that southern representatives had cooperated with northern Jacksonians to reject limiting amendments which would have served their own interests. Without such consolidated backing, the sweeping provisions of what came to be called the "tariff of abominations" would not have been accepted. Congressman George E. Gilmer of Georgia conceded that he found "difficulty in coming to the determination of pursuing this kind of legislation." He believed that increasing the molasses duty was "not only injurious to our commerce, but oppressive upon our People. . . ." Not, however, more so than the increased duties that the administration was proposing for woolens and cottons. He concluded that there was "but one way of satisfying the People of this country of the iniquitous and calmitious [sic] consequences of the falsely styled American system; and that is by extending its operation to every part of the Union." Edward Livingston of Louisiana, Thomas R. Mitchell of South Carolina, and C. C. Cambreleng of New York echoed these views. Cambreleng, noting that one of his opponents "seemed to be 'horror-struck' at the idea of his voting for some features of the bill—knowing them to be injurious," commented that he "did not wish to be misunderstood—his motive in doing so was to defeat the bill."[15]

Writing of the tariff proposal to his friend John J. Crittenden in mid February, Clay commented: "The Jackson party is playing a game of brag on that subject. They do not really, desire the passage of their own measure & it may happen, in the sequel, that what is desired by *neither party*, commands the support, of both." Clay himself found the bill "the vilest of cheats." "With the professed purpose of protecting our Woolen manufactories," he continued, "it demolishes them. With the purpose avowed of encouraging the growth of wool it destroys the Home market." Unless it could be amended, he hoped that the bill would not pass.[16]

The popularity of the measure in the farming districts of New England, New York, Pennsylvania, and the Ohio Valley could not, however, be denied. The administration dared not oppose it. In April, Clay advised that Adams's supporters in the House approve it. On the twenty-second the measure passed that body by a majority of 105 to 94. Administration forces provided 61 of the affirmative votes, as opposed to 35 of the negative. Jacksonians, on the other hand, repudiated their own measure, 59 to 44. The bill won only three votes from representatives of the area south of the Potomac, all from administration supporters. Twenty-three New Englanders also opposed it; sixteen, however, all but one an Adamsite, accepted the bitter medicine.[17]

In the Senate the measure passed by vote of 26 to 21. Here an amendment setting a somewhat higher ad-valorem rate for woolens enhanced the attractiveness of the measure to manufacturers. The Jacksonians Van Buren of New York and Levi Woodbury of New Hampshire, responding to constituent interest, broke from the "system of legislation" to approve it, thus shifting the vote to 24 ayes, as opposed to 22 nays, when earlier amendments that they opposed had been as narrowly defeated. Even with the changes, New Englanders split on the final proposal, 6 to 5. Webster evoked heavy criticism by Jacksonians when he voted to strike out the section affording protection for what was described as almost every article of interest to the West— hemp, flax, molasses, sail duck, cotton bagging, and distilled spirits; but in the end, his influence carried a majority of his regional colleagues for the bill, despite the objectionable section. All but four southern senators—two from Kentucky and one each from Tennessee and Louisiana— rejected the measure. Votes from the Middle States and the West, drawn to this legislation as they had not been in 1827, provided most of the support in both branches of the Congress.[18]

Throughout the contest the president continued to remain publicly aloof. Friends of Rush and Clay had urged that he include in his annual message of 1827 "an earnest recommendation of protection to domestic manufacturers." The governors of Pennsylvania and Ohio had issued such statements, and administration supporters throughout the Middle States had looked to the president for leadership in the campaign. From New York, Jabez Hammond explained that they had "meant to have charged the Jackson party with hypocrisy in pretending friendship for the American System while at the same time they supported a party in the nation hostile to it." "Why should the President omit giving an opinion on so important a Measure?" he queried.[19]

To all such complaints the secretary of state responded that the views of the president and his cabinet were so well known that "to multiply proofs of that disposition was perhaps unnecessary." It would be interpreted as "electioneering" and would invite Jacksonian charges of insincerity. Adams himself expressed concern that he should not "appear to interfere improperly for the purpose of exercising an influence over the House."[20]

To the politically cynical the explanations sounded specious, yet they accurately reflected the president's reluctance to assume a partisan role publicly during the election year. He was content that his stance on the issue, like his campaign, should be promoted through his cabinet officers and his congressional allies. His lingering personal concern for the views of older constituencies, "the agricultural interest of the South and the commercial interest of the North," supported his inclination for anonymity in the institutional structure of the "Administration." The president did not set forth his own endorsement of the tariff program until after the election. Perhaps more significantly, he withheld it until after southern threats of secession reasserted the issue as one of national unity.

In his annual message of 1828 the president conceded that the recent tariff legislation "was in its details not acceptable to the great interests of any portion of the Union. . . ." It had been designed "to balance the burdens upon native industry imposed by the operation of foreign laws, but not to aggravate the burdens of one section of the Union by the relief afforded to another." If experience should prove that aid for the manufacturer had been attained at the cost of the planter, he would urge revision. He saw no grounds for protest "so long as the duty of the foreign shall operate only as a bounty upon the domestic article; while the planter and the merchant and the shepherd and the husbandman shall be found thriving in their occupations under the duties imposed for the protection of domestic manufactures. . . ."[21]

The American System, in its design to bond the nation as an integrated economy, rejected particularistic demands for easing the program of distributing public land. While President Adams regularly endorsed the extension of relief legislation for debtors under the rescinded credit system of public-land sale, he had anticipated with manifest pleasure the approaching time when, with public-land revenues increasing and the national debt retired, "the swelling tide of wealth with which they replenish the common Treasury" could "be made to reflow in unfailing streams" of internal improvement. In his view the establishment of the public-land holdings, "made at the expense of the whole Union, not only in treasure but in blood," created "a right of property in them equally extensive." They represented a capital base against which the nation might borrow in time of financial crisis and a revenue source for benefits that the nation might share generally.[22]

Clay applauded this view, although he warned that "there were parts of the country where it would not be approved." Shortly after entering the administration, Clay had been advised from Booneville,

Missouri, by Finis Ewing, one of a large family of westward-moving Virginia-Kentucky pioneers, that a gradual reduction in the price of public lands was "one particular subject which the people of the West, particularly the States of Missouri, Illinoise, Indiania [sic] &c, &c. feel a deep, very deep interest in." If the president would but recommend it to the next Congress, the proposal "would fasten him in the affections of tens of thousands of the citizens of the West. . . ." A year later, Clay's Missouri friend John Scott, whose vote for Adams had been critical to the president's election, warned that the graduation proposal "had stimulated all the people of the Western country to madness for the public lands."

On this issue, too, however, intraregional divisions complicated the strategy for intersectional adjustments. As a spokesman for the West, the Kentuckian represented a district that had been settled nearly two generations earlier than the Missouri frontier. To his Bluegrass constituents, cheap public lands signified a disruptive influence upon the value of established local interests. Reporting Scott's correspondence to the president, Clay described it as a view that was limited to Missouri—"in Ohio the sentiments of the people were perfectly sound." Clay rejected the suggestions as being "treasonable in their character."[23]

Since the early 1820s Thomas Hart Benton of Missouri had been pressing for such legislation. In the spring of 1828 he finally got a bill to the Senate floor, calling for reduction in the price of unsold lands over three years to a minimum of 25 cents an acre, with cession of the residue after another two years to the states in which the lands lay. Adams and Rush officially opposed the legislation. The president, in his annual message, had reminded the Congress that not only were the proceeds of land sale "pledged to the creditors of the nation" but also that the amount paid to the Treasury for land purchases was "not yet equal to the sums paid for the whole. . . ." The secretary of the Treasury, arguing for legislation to encourage manufactures, bluntly spoke of the land laws as "a bounty . . . in favor of agricultural pursuits," which contributed to the dispersal of the population into less-productive enterprise. If the tide could be stemmed, as would probably result from "extending the motives to manufacturing labor," the nation would gain doubly, "by the more rapid accumulation of capital" and "by the gradual reduction of the excess of its agricultural population. . . ." Again he urged that legislators look to "the whole good of the nation. . . ."[24]

Benton's Missouri colleague David Barton, an administration supporter, spoke at length against the graduation bill. Arguing that it served primarily speculative interests, he proposed, instead, that the price of lands be lowered only slightly, to a dollar an acre, and if they remained unmarketed for five years, that they be patented without charge in quarter-section units to those who proved five years' residence and cultivation. He contended that the agitation had been stimulated as a political maneuver, and while he exonerated Jackson, Barton attributed it to lesser opponents, who would bribe the public in an election year by using its own, the national, treasure.[25]

Since the Congress was then completely dominated by Jacksonians, the defeat of Benton's measure on the question of engrossment, by a vote of 25 to 21, could not be attributed solely to pressure from the administration. Eastern Jacksonians, excepting only Berrien and Cobb of Georgia and Tazewell of Virginia, joined eastern adherents of the administration in opposition; western supporters of Adams, excepting only Barton, advocated the proposal. But Barton's solitary western dissent, in conjunction with his definition of the issue as a political measure, emphasized the administration's stand in opposition to the regional interests. The Jacksonian press, trumpeting the geographic division, called upon the West generally to "examine how far that system, which . . . made them tributary to the other States, is sanctioned by the Constitution, and the treaties of cession through which the Federal Government claims title to the soil of the new States." The issue was costly to the administration in the votes of Missouri and the newly settled districts of Indiana and Illinois.[26]

Western land hunger, identified as the cause of States' rights in opposition to the federal government's handling of the public lands, evoked still more bitter controversy in connection with Indian holdings. In its cession of western charter claims the state of Georgia had stipulated that the United States extinguish Indian titles within its boundaries as soon as practicable. While no other state had demanded so formal a commitment, pressure for access to Indian reserves prevailed wherever the red man and the white man lived in close conjunction. Indian removal, however, as effected under the "moderation" policy outlined by Secretary of War Calhoun in 1818, had been a slow process.

The plan contemplated that the United States would cease to treat the tribes as independent nations; would extend over them the white man's "laws and manners"; would reduce Indian holdings to an "appropriate" size, with assurances that no further demands would be made for their land; would inculcate the white man's concept of individual ownership through a program of education; and would remove Indians who chose not to submit to a distance remote from white settlements. "By a proper combination of force and persuasion, of punishments and rewards, they ought to be brought within the pales of law and civilization," Calhoun had argued. He repeatedly pledged that military action would not be used to force removal.[27]

The Adams administration, in generally adopting this agenda, introduced some major shifts in emphasis. In the spring of 1826, despite doubts shared by all the other cabinet officers as well as by Adams himself, they endorsed an outline for legislation as proposed by Secretary of War Barbour in response to congressional request. The Virginian urged a bill that would: (1) set aside the country west of existing states and territories as an "exclusive abode" for the Indians; (2) establish a territorial government there under federal maintenance; (3) remove the Indians as individuals, "in contradistinction to tribes"; (4) if "circumstances . . . [should] eventually justify it," extinguish tribal organization, amalgamate the Indians "into one mass," and distribute the property severally; but (5) leave unaltered the condition of the remnant that rejected the program. Nothing was to be done without the Indians' "*own consent.*" The secretary believed that those who chose to remain in the East would be "so few that their condition . . . [could] be regulated without committing violence on their wishes or their interests, and yet reconciling their residence with the prosperity of the whites." Time alone, he concluded, would induce them "to surrender their distinction of race for the resemblance of the white man, and accept, as an equivalent, the blessings" of that transformation.[28]

The program thus emphasized the establishment of a barrier to white settlement over a large segment of the West, and it expressed a far-more-limited perception than Calhoun's regarding the practicability of Indian integration in their current locations. Reacting in frustration to a refusal of Creek Indians to negotiate cession, Barbour, at a cabinet session in December 1825, had proposed to cease all such efforts and to bring the tribes under American law in existing jurisdictions. Adams had objected on constitutional grounds; Clay, on the basis of practicability. The latter thought it impossible to civilize Indians: "He believed they were destined to extinction, and, although he would never use or countenance inhumanity towards them, he did not think them, as a race, worth preserving." Adams conceded that he feared that these opinions had "too much foundation."[29]

Somewhat "shocked" by his colleagues' views, Barbour abandoned the recommendation for incorporating the Indians within the state jurisdictions and pressed ahead with the removal program. The concept of a giant reservation along the western frontier accorded with the administration's general focus upon more intensive economic development in older areas rather than expansion onto new lands. The more limited vision of Indian absorption "within the pales of law and civilization" responded to a course of events that had carried the administration into a major political confrontation in the South.

On all fronts, white pressure for Indian removal and for congressional support of those demands was posing difficulties. In the Northwest, incursions onto Winnebago lands by lead miners, who poured into the Galena district in the mid 1820s, led to attacks by a small band of the tribe under Red Bird in the spring of 1827. When reports reached Washington in September that several whites had been killed while traveling up the Mississippi River, Clay hastily recalled Barbour from his vacation in Virginia and alerted the president in Quincy. But the incident had by then been resolved. Thomas L. McKenny, chief of the Bureau of Indian Affairs, with a force of army troops, militia, and friendly Indians, had trailed the warring tribesmen to the Fox-Wisconsin portage, where Red Bird surrendered. Tried and convicted of murder, but not yet sentenced, the Indian leader died in prison the following February. President Adams pardoned his companions after the election in November 1828. Meanwhile, the episode had led to negotiations and an agreement for cession of some 5.36 million acres in western Illinois.

The problems in dealing with the southeastern tribes were more complicated. The Creeks, shattered by Jackson's victories during the winter of 1813/14, had been fragmented. Some had fled southward, where they merged with the Seminoles in a plight that even the military and governmental leaders of the region found unconscionable. In 1826 Governor DuVal of Florida complained that Indians were hunting in the settlements and thus supplying themselves with cattle and provisions. His home had been crowded with Indians for the past six months, he lamented, yet they had come to him in sickness, and "common humanity" required that he provide for their care. Col. G. M. Brooke, explaining an unusually high account for rations, reported that six hundred to seven hundred Indians, most having traveled nearly a hundred miles, had gathered at the subagency: "The major part of the nation are and have been suffering for some time; in extreme want some have died from *Starvation,* and many have lived on the roots of the sweet briar, as a substitute for bread." "It is impossible," he continued, "for me or any other officer, who possesses the smallest feelings of humanity to resist affording some releif [sic] to men, women and children who are actually dying from the want of something to eat."[30]

Confronting these circumstances, Secretary Barbour urged that the Indians be relocated. He conceded that the previous holdings had been exchanged, "as is usually the case, by treaty, doubtless with an ignorance on their part of that [area] to which they consented to emigrate; and erroneous information on ours, as to its fitness." Convinced that their location in Florida was unsuited "either in soil, or salubrity, to their preservation," he sought the Indians' assent to their removal west of the Mississippi.[31]

Removal was not, however, a program to which a majority of the Indians readily agreed. A part of the Cherokee nation had purchased a tract beyond the Mississippi in 1817; the remainder, under the leadership of John Ross, were resisting efforts to induce them to move. On 26 July 1827 they adopted a written constitution, patterned after that of the United States, and insisted upon their national sovereignty, with full jurisdiction over their territory. The authorities of Georgia now found themselves confronting an organized government within borders to which the state professed residual claim. Arguing that the Indians were merely tenants at will, the Georgia legislature in the following December, adopted resolutions that asserted the state's right to extend authority over the territory and threatened to use force to uphold its claims. Shortly thereafter the legislature enacted a statute declaring that all whites within the Cherokee nation were subject to Georgia law and providing that the Indians, too, should come under such jurisdiction after 1 June 1830.[32]

The difficulties posed by the Cherokee were less immediately pressing upon the Adams administration than were those centering upon the plight of the Creek remnants in northern Georgia. Under the Treaty of Indian Springs, negotiated shortly before Adams had entered office, several subordinate chieftains, led by William McIntosh, a mixed-blood spokesman for the Lower Towns who was a cousin of Georgia's Governor George M. Troup, had committed their people to cession of the remaining tribal lands in that state. By the terms of the arrangement, the tract was not to be surrendered until 1 September 1826; but Governor Troup immediately opened negotiations with McIntosh to permit an earlier survey. In the midst of this activity, on 29 April 1825, McIntosh and two others who had entered into the treaty were killed, under an execution decreed by the tribal council as the penalty for violating their law against unauthorized sale of tribal lands. Charging that the federal Indian agent, John Crowell, had incited the violence, Troup demanded that Crowell be discharged. Meanwhile, President Adams directed Gen. Edmund Pendleton Gaines and Maj. Timothy Patrick Andrews to investigate the manner in which the treaty had been negotiated. When their findings indicated that the cession had been made by minority leaders, Adams refused to authorize the survey;

202

directed that General Gaines be instructed to prevent it, "by force" if necessary; and called for renegotiation of the treaty.[33]

After first rejecting any discussions, the Creeks finally agreed at Washington, in January 1826, to yield all their lands south of the Chattahoochee River. The Georgia legislature and its congressional delegation, meanwhile, reasserted the validity of the earlier Treaty of Indian Springs and insisted upon the state's vested right to the full territory thus acquired. Questioning how to present the issue of treaty revision to the Senate, Adams received conflicting advice from his cabinet. Clay advised submitting the new treaty with all the related documents, thus revealing the fraudulent nature of the original cession and bringing the controversy before the legislative body. Barbour reported a Georgia senator's warning that the state "would necessarily be driven to support General Jackson" if the administration failed to make concessions. Adams retorted that he had little concern about the threatened support for Jackson; he "had no more confidence in one party there than in the other." He believed, however, that the federal government "ought not to yield to Georgia, because . . . [it] could not do so without gross injustice." Finally, desiring that the arrangement should be completed in conformity to the views of Barbour, the president agreed to withhold the inflammatory correspondence until the revised treaty had been ratified.[34]

Georgia's governor was not to be appeased. Although the new treaty delayed the cession until 1 January 1827, he ordered that the survey be begun on September 1, the effecive date of the Treaty of Indian Springs. When Secretary Barbour protested, Troup replied on October 6 that the work had been virtually accomplished. A month later the governor informed the Georgia legislature of his radical disagreement with the federal government concerning the rights of sovereignty and jurisdiction that the state claimed by charter over the Indian lands. The General Assembly, in turn, after bitterly denouncing "a force and power" in the national authority "which should have formed the subject of concern, if not alarm, to . . . sister States," adopted resolutions asserting Georgia's exclusive ownership of "the soil and jurisdiction of all the territory within her present chartered and conventional limits," denying that she had ever "relinquished said right, either territorial or jurisdictional to the General Government," and terming "the attempted abrogation of the Treaty of Indian Springs . . . illegal and unconstitutional." Warning that the stationing of armed force on its borders tended "to the complete annihilation of State sovereignty," the legislature called upon Congress and the other states to disavow the president's assertion that Georgia had no right to enter the Indian country without the consent of the Indians.[35]

Troup now ordered his surveyors to move into the area northwest of the Chattahoochee. There they were challenged by the Creeks and by the federal authority. On January 29 Barbour informed the Georgia governor that the president would "employ, if necessary, all the means under his control to maintain the faith of the nation by carrying the treaty into effect." On the next day the federal attorney, Richard W. Habersham, was ordered to obtain a warrant for arrest of the surveyors. Habersham initiated the process so that the interests of the government would be represented, but then he warned that if the case were pressed to prosecution, he would resign out of loyalty to his higher duty "to his native State." Clay, with the president's approval, promptly replaced the attorney.[36]

Troup, in turn, announced that he would resist "any military attack which the Government of the United States . . . think proper to make on the territory, the People, or the sovereignty of Georgia. . . ." "From the first decisive act of hostility," he wrote to Secretary Barbour, "you will be considered and treated as a public enemy, and with the less repugnance because you, to whom we might constitutionally have appealed for our defence against invasion, are yourselves the invaders, and, what is more, the unblushing allies of the savages, whose cause you have adopted." He thereupon ordered the militia into readiness "to repel any hostile invasion of the territory of this State."[37]

Adams and his cabinet were now in agreement that the correspondence should be sent to Congress. Rush and Wirt proposed that some accompanying statement should disclaim any intention of an immediate resort to armed force. Clay urged a simple transmittal of the papers. Tempted "to show by a very summary exposure the prevarication of Troup," the president accepted the course of silence. On March 2 Troup's response was delivered to both houses of the national legislative body, without comment.[38]

Already, however, measures were under way which were to resolve the impasse. On January 31 Barbour had urged that Crowell reopen negotiations with the Creeks, looking to a cession of their remaining lands. On March 3 a select committee of the House also advised such action, while at the same time calling for enforcement of the Treaty of Washington. A Senate committee, chaired by the Jacksonian Thomas Hart Benton, concluded that no evidence indicated Georgia's determination "to resist the civil authority of the United States." The committee rejected "any measure in anticipation of an issue which they . . . [did] not apprehend . . ." and called upon the president to continue exertions to obtain from the Creeks a relinquishment of all claim to lands within the limits of Georgia. Pressure upon the Indians for cession was continued throughout the summer of 1827. On November 15 the aged chief Little Prince finally directed that an agreement be signed.[39]

Outside the lower South the administration appears to have lost little ground from the controversy. Throughout the episode, Adams's consideration for the delicacy of Barbour's position had drawn the secretary increasingly into support of the administration's program. While the Jacksonian press criticized the president's response as evincing "the insolent and tyrannical tone of a despot," his pursuit, first, of the Chattahoochee boundary settlement and, then, of negotiations for final removal led many people elsewhere in the nation to look upon Troup's intransigence as "madness."[40] The issue of States' rights was thus defused to the point that the legislature of Georgia complained bitterly of the "cold, if not . . . reproachful indifference" of its sister states. Virginia, which received the Georgia resolutions as it was debating the Giles protest against the administration's tariff proposals, ignored the theoretical context of the Georgia appeal.

However, across the southern tier of states, where Indians were still blocking the advance of settlement, the delays of the "moderation policy" had become intolerable. On that matter, Georgia was not alone in her demand for a changed approach. In 1820 the Choctaw Indians had relinquished some five million acres of their Mississippi holdings for an area of undetermined size in western Arkansas, but within three years they were under pressure to cede the remainder of their Mississippi tract, as well as to readjust the Arkansas boundary. The latter difficulty had been negotiated in January 1825, shortly before Calhoun resigned as secretary of war. Barbour and Indian Agent Thomas McKenney struggled unsuccessfully over the next four years to effect Indian removal from Mississippi.

Meanwhile, Congress had taken no action upon Barbour's proposed package of Indian legislation. A resolution that called for information on the willingness of the tribes to accept his recommendations had died in a House committee. In April 1827, delegates from North Carolina, Georgia, Florida, Alabama, Mississippi, and Tennessee, led by Senators Thomas B. Reed of Mississippi and Thomas W. Cobb of Georgia, joined in demanding total removal of the Indians from the area east of the Mississippi and recommended extension of state jurisdiction over local Indian reservations if the federal government failed to act. In the following December, representatives from Georgia and Tennessee introduced further resolutions directing the House Committee of Indian Affairs "to inquire into the expediency and practicability of establishing some mode by which all the Indians" east of the river might be moved to the West, or, if such a plan could not be devised, "of extending the laws and municipal regulations of the United States, and, also, of the several States wherein said Indians reside, over them." Congressman John Woods of Ohio subsequently offered a counterproposal, requesting the committee to devise means to protect the Indians against white encroachment "and to secure to them a permanent right to the lands which they now possess." With the adoption of both sets of instructions, the stage appeared to be set for a major debate on federal Indian policy.[41]

Instead, the controversy emerged only indirectly, in the discussion over a proposal in the appropriation bill to allot $50,000 for treaty negotiations with the Cherokee "and such other Indians" as might be disposed to emigrate. Woods warned that the legislation signified the extermination of the Indians: "Those who now prey upon them as vultures, will follow them to their new abode." When his effort to strike out the appropriation was defeated, an Ohio colleague, Samuel F. Vinton, moved to bar use of the funds for transfer of Indians south of the line of 36° 30' into areas north of that latitude and west of the Mississippi. Both Vinton and Woods bitterly assailed Secretary of War Barbour's proposals for removal.[42]

Vinton's action, as well as the arguments of Ambrose H. Sevier, the territorial delegate of Arkansas, made clear, however, that much of the opposition centered upon the barrier that was being posed to the settlement of whites in the trans-Mississippi West, rather than upon the plight of the Indians. Congressman William McLean, also of Ohio, who was chairman of the Committee on Indian Affairs and supported the administration, upheld the legislation and contended that it had been offered out of "the best feelings of the human heart." John C. Weems of Maryland agreed that the move was humanitarian. Two sovereignties, he argued, could never exist together—"the weaker must certainly go to the wall."

In the end the appropriation bill was approved, with an allotment of $50,000 to enable the president to extinguish the Cherokee claims within the chartered limits of Georgia. Provision for continuation of the policy was encompassed under a separate measure to allot $15,000 for deputations by the Choctaw and Chickasaw, legislation that was later amended to include the Cherokee, Creek, and any other tribes that were disposed to send delegations west of the Mississippi for exploration of the unoccupied public lands, "preparatory to the final emigration of said Indians."[43]

In December 1828 Peter B. Porter, as Barbour's successor, emphasized "the absolute necessity" of redefining Indian relations by law. "Nothing can be more clear, to one who has marked the progress of population and improvement, and is conversant with the principles of human action, than that these Indians will not be permitted to hold the reservations on which they live, within the States, by their present tenure, for any considerable period." Restating the removal policy as the most important feature of the current program, he criticized the influence of missionaries in counteracting the movement for emigration among the eastern tribes and proposed that federal funds for Indian education be restricted to the "new colony exclusively." Whether there or within the states to the East, Indian lands should be apportioned to the tribesmen as "individuals in severalty . . . , with perhaps some temporary and wholesome restraints on the power of alienation." Let the remainder of the tribal holdings of those who refused to emigrate "be paid for, by those who hold the paramount right, at such prices as shall be deemed, in reference to the uses which Indians are accustomed to make of lands, reasonable. . . ." The proceeds should then be used "for the benefit of those of the tribe who emigrate . . . or . . . divided between those who emigrate and those who remain, as justice may require."[44]

Endorsing Porter's report, President Adams, in his final annual message, also warned that the Indian situation demanded "a remedy." In appropriating their hunting grounds the nation had incurred "the obligation of providing them with subsistence," he argued, but he also recognized a new aspect of the problem, which for his administration had elevated the issue to a climax: "when we have had the rare good fortune of teaching them the arts of civilization and the doctrines of Christianity we have unexpectedly found them forming in the midst of ourselves communities claiming to be independent of ours and rivals of sovereignty within the territories of the members of our Union."[45] Georgia had laid the basis for a jurisdictional confrontation when it should attempt to apply its law to Indians in 1830. After a Choctaw delegation, having inspected the region to the west, determined to remain in Mississippi, the legislature of that state, on 4 February 1829, likewise announced the extension of its law over the reservations within its borders.

Challenged by the competing pressures of States' rights and Indian nationalism, the policy of removal under a program of "moderation" had run its course. While the Whig party, with Adams as a leading spokesman, was later to protest the brutality of Jackson's removal operations and to defend the Cherokees' claims to Georgia land, the New Englander's administration had afforded little more as an alternative than a holding action in defense of federal jurisdiction. Congressman Woods had stood virtually alone in his plea for recognition of the Indians' reservation claims in the East.[46]

Despite persistent confrontation, the Adams administration had developed a groundwork of domestic nationalism. The president had failed in his attempt to advance governmentally sponsored educational and scientific institutions, but he had brought the issue of such support forward as a standard of national maturity. He had achieved significant progress in the advancement of internal improvements. Notwithstanding such expenditures, the national economy was strong; the public debt had been nearly retired; and the financial structure, which had been developed in cooperation with the centralizing operations of the Bank of the United States, had maintained solidity in the face of foreign economic crisis. The protective tariff had been extended to an expanded range of interests. It had not destroyed United States commerce, and it had not, in fact, reduced foreign imports of southern cotton. The administration's land policy had asserted the public claim to a commonly shared resource, and its Indian relations had upheld a commitment to national polity. After surveying in detail the powers delimited under the Constitution, Adams, in his first annual message, had called upon Congress "to give efficacy to the means committed to you for the common good." Until the Civil War, no other administration attempted to effect so broadly integrated an approach to that goal.

But the tariff, land, and Indian policies had alienated large segments of the South and the West. Only the strong support for internal improvements and the reluctant advocacy of tariff extension to raw materials had counterbalanced the president's identification with the economic interests of the Northeast. Writing to Webster in June 1827, Clay noted the rapidly increasing population of the West and reemphasized the need for sustaining the regional linkages. He was insistent that internal improvements "should be supported in New England, and that the West and Pennsa. should be made *sensible* of that support." "You have your equivalents in other forms, if not in that of I. Improvements," Clay reminded his friend. "We must keep the two interests of D.M. & I.I. allied, and both tend to the support of that other great & not less important interest of Navigation."[47] Neither the Bluegrass Kentuckian nor his political associates to the eastward had yet conceded that frontier land interests should be brought into the American System. Of the administration leaders, only Rush recognized that these interests represented a significant factor in the regional balance, and it was not one that he sought to foster. Programmatic nationalism would come ultimately by alliance of the East and the West, but not until a broader-based awareness of shared interests had forged the ties.

10

★ ★ ★ ★ ★

PROBLEMS OF GOVERNMENTAL ADMINISTRATION

Historians of governmental administration, emphasizing the theme of continuity in such development, nevertheless recognize that occasionally events have accelerated the trends toward structural change—as at the founding of the nation and during the war years of 1812-14—while in other periods, philosophical or budgetary restraints have had a depressing effect. The Adams years, a period of enormous expansion in economic and social growth, at the same time bore the lingering influence of an emphasis on retrenchment. The administration's program of expanded governmental activity required major reforms in institutional structure and operation. But in some degree sharing the prevalent public concern to free the nation of wartime debt, the president and his colleagues found little support, where they recognized the need, for bureaucratic innovation. The fact that major administrative changes—continuing trends that had been initiated early in Monroe's presidency and were to be accelerated under Jackson's—were not achieved during this period was damaging operationally as well as politically to the record of the administration.

Mechanisms had yet to be established for deflecting minor personnel grievances from executive and even congressional review. The harmony that prevailed within Adams's cabinet did not always extend into lower echelons of staffing, and behind every administrative conflict lay the threat of bitter partisan attack. The president's open door to visitors, which was mirrored in the arrangements of his secretaries, immersed the principal heads of government in the routine complaints of a discharged messenger or copyist; a suitor for office or contract; a pensioner, patent applicant, or land claimant; a visiting journalist, "mendicant clergyman," or disgruntled politician—forty to fifty such encounters a day, as Adams wearily lamented at midterm: "I was from ten this morning till ten at night never five minutes without one or more of these marginal notes. And I can scarcely conceive a more harassing, wearying, teasing condition of existence. It literally renders life burdensome."[1]

The president's personal staff, apart from the cabinet officers, included only his second son, John, as private secretary, and domestic servants. Young John, who had been reared during the formative years from six to twelve by doting grandparents, had a fiery temper and imperious manners. Expelled from Harvard on the eve of graduation, in 1823, for leadership in a student protest of college disciplinary action against a classmate, he had been called to Washington to assist his father.

It was not a happy experience for either the parent or the son. The youth was responsible for the error in reporting to Congress, as expenditures on "Furniture of the President's House," a billiard table, billiard balls, and a set of chessmen. The president subsequently explained that these purchases, totaling less than $80, had been paid for personally and had been mistakenly listed in the account. But Jacksonians, who demanded a congressional investigation, made political capital of the spending of public money "for purchase of gaming tables and gambling furniture."[2]

John embroiled his father in further difficulties with the politically hostile Congress in the spring of the election year, 1828, by his involvement in an affray with a reporter for the Jacksonian *United States Telegraph*. When Russell Jarvis attended a White House levee in early April, young Adams, in an audible aside, remarked that if the journalist "had the feelings of a gentleman he would not show himself" in the Adams home. Learning of the comment, Jarvis dispatched a friend to demand "explanations." John repeated the statement but refused to continue the discussion. Two weeks later, as he was passing through the rotunda of the Capitol after delivering papers from his father to the House of Representatives, he was set upon by Jarvis and punched in the nose. Witnesses hastily intervened as the young man attempted to retaliate.

The president did not learn of the episode until that evening, when Congressman Everett related the details and questioned whether it should be brought before Congress. Adams at first proposed to leave the matter for action by the legislative bodies within whose hall the attack had occurred. On the following day, however, Secretaries Rush and Barbour advised that "the members of the Administration all thought it would be proper to send a message to Congress concerning the assault. . . ." In a subsequent cabinet discussion of the proposed message, they agreed that under the present political composition of Congress, little action was apt to result, but Clay argued that the executive had a duty "to maintain his own dignity and security in the performance of his functions." Such violence "had a tendency to introduce assassination into the Capitol." Forbearance, although laudable, could be carried "to an extreme." For a time, Wirt questioned whether dignity might not be better served by ignoring the incident but, with the President, finally yielded to the views of the others.[3]

By a partisan vote of 24 to 22, the Senate on April 18 deferred action to the House. The latter body appointed an investigatory committee, composed of five opponents and two supporters of the administration. Nearly a month later, on the verge of congressional adjournment, they filed majority and minority reports. The former concluded that there had, indeed, been a violation of congressional privilege which merited censure but that inasmuch as Jarvis had not intentionally transgressed the dignity of the House, it was not "expedient" to take any action. The minority report denied that the House had any authority touching the matter. A second minority, who had demanded some punishment for the insult to the House and the president, abandoned the struggle without filing a brief. The reports, in turn, were tabled without further consideration. The Jacksonians scored their point in a long editorial by Duff Green, editor of the Telegraph, criticizing Adams for bringing "a private affair" before Congress. Jarvis, he twitted, "could not have anticipated that the baby, who was considered old enough to take charge of the contingent fund, and bear messages to Congress, would run blubbering to tell his daddy that he had had his nose pulled and his jaws slapped for his impudence."[4]

The State Department, which at that time encompassed a wide diversity of duties both at home and abroad, was perhaps the most unwieldy office to organize. It operated in 1825 with only a chief clerk and eleven subordinate clerks, apart from a maintenance staff of two messengers and two watchmen. Translators, additional copyists, and special messengers were hired and paid from small contingency funds as occasion required. This staff conducted correspondence with 14 United States embassies, 4 United States consulates that performed diplomatic duties, 110 additional consulates abroad, from 10 to 14 foreign legations in the United States, an unspecified number of foreign consulates serving as diplomatic agencies in this country, numerous United States citizens inquiring about claims, passports, and miscellaneous foreign concerns; federal marshals and district attorneys; governors of the states and territories; and members of Congress and their constituents, often on matters that were not applicable to departmental matters, but were channeled through this central governmental agency.[5]

Apart from foreign policy, the State Department was responsible for issuing passports and sea letters, registering seamen and attending to the needs of those who were "distressed" abroad, compiling returns of arriving passengers, and distributing general commercial information; for preserving the rolls and manuscript journals of Congress and the public papers of the federal government, recording the laws and arranging for their circulation, supervising the administration of the territories, and coordinating relations with the states; and· for issuing patents and copyright certificates, making out commissions for public officers under its jurisdiction, recording executive pardons and remissions of penalties, and superintending the enumeration of the federal census. Beyond all this, Adams had revived and gave considerable attention to the reassembling of a departmental library, which had been instituted by Jefferson but had been scattered during the intervening period. The accounts for all these operations had to be examined and cleared within the department. Small wonder that consuls in remote ports and even occasionally ministers in major posts lamented their lack of direction from Washington!

Adams, as secretary of state, had already brought innovations. He had complained during those years of "the want of method in the arrangement of business . . . ," of the "continual confusion and embarrassment" arising from "the want of order in keeping the files of papers in the office." He had accordingly begun a minute book of letters received, an index of diplomatic and consular correspondence (which was in use as late as 1915), and a systematic listing of changes in personnel, with dates of employment and salary detail. Having discovered that the statute that required the recording of federal laws had long been ignored, he had issued instructions that this work be undertaken.[6]

Clay found, however, that this transcription had advanced no farther than the collection of "some blank record books which were wanted for its execution." In January 1826 he informed the House Committee of Ways and Means that there was "scarcely a record in the office made in compliance" with the legislative mandate. Nothing had been attempted in the effort since the beginning of Jefferson's administration, "except an inconsiderable essay . . . begun since the fourth of March last." Inasmuch as records prior to the turn of the century had been destroyed, the work had to be done "almost for the whole period of the present Government."[7]

While publication of the laws might, as some had argued, substitute for having them recorded by the State Department, no system provided for preservation of the registration of patents. Clay reported in 1826 that all the patents except those for the past year remained to be listed. "The business of the Patent Office had increased to an Extent so far beyond the capacity of the Superintendent and his Assistant to execute it," Clay explained, that he had authorized the temporary employment of two additional clerks "for the necessary transaction of its business until the pleasure of Congress could be known." When the legislative body adjourned without taking any action, he halted the work. His annual report covering the year indicated that he had paid from the contingent fund $350 for the extra services of a translator, $150 for an alphabetical index of the laws of the last Congressional Session, and $6,723.46 for assistance to the department, including the Patent Office, in transcribing and translating documents of current relevance and in arranging the records "of the old confederation," which had fallen into "great confusion and disorder."[8]

Clay was also concerned that diplomatic archives be better preserved. Ministers who were sent abroad had to be supplied with laboriously copied files of background instructions and correspondence relating to their assignments. The secretary of state's instructions in April 1825, upon replacing Hugh Nelson as minister at Madrid and Richard Rush at London, required that they leave the legation papers for transfer to their successors. Both complied; but Everett, as Nelson's successor, did not, and neither did Albert Gallatin upon leaving London. William Beach Lawrence, who temporarily took over the latter post in October 1827, and his successor, James Barbour, in the following year, complained that the record of instructions was incomplete and that the texts of congressional enactments over the past two years were lacking. Raguet, upon returning from Brazil, presented a receipt for transfer of the consular files to his successor but added that he had retained both the copies of his correspondence as chargé and "all the original notes of the Brazilian Ministers to him." Clay then conceded that this was "customary."[9]

Although in 1821 Adams had lamented the "inaptitude" of Daniel Brent, the chief clerk, neither Adams nor Clay moved to replace Brent. Incidents of misplaced documents continued to plague the department, most seriously when Clay had to request Poinsett, in Mexico, to supply duplicates of dispatches reporting assurances that had been extended to that government in connection with the movement of the French fleet in 1825. Opponents of the Panama mission accused the administration of deliberately withholding correspondence relating to the secretary of state's instructions referring to the Monroe "pledge."[10]

Reluctance to discharge entrenched officeholders was, as Jacksonian critics asserted, occasionally a problem for the administration; but given the niggardly allowance for additional personnel, the experience, continuity, and general integrity of those on hand carried countervailing advantages. Brent had attempted to subdivide the overwhelming labors of the office with a view to economies of specialization. Each of the clerks had regularly assigned responsibilities of record keeping. George E. Ironside, an expert in the Spanish language, served primarily as a translator, although his duties also included the "conservation" of treaties and the law rolls and superintendence of the publication and distribution of the laws. The labor of the last operation also fell heavily upon William Browne, who handled the departmental accounts, including the payroll and requisitions for supplies, with the attendant correspondence. Another clerk recorded instructions to United States ministers abroad and reports to the president and to committees of Congress. A fourth clerk dealt with correspondence to and from foreign functionaries inside the United States. A fifth handled the consular correspondence and the compiling of supportive documents on United States claims against foreign governments. Another summarized and filed the letters of application for office, prepared the commissions of appointment, and, perhaps because of his exceptional penmanship, transcribed the formal letters of credence, powers to negotiate, and social notes to foreign courts. The remaining clerks performed a variety of routine chores. All, however, were expected to assist in special copying as needed. That the department, in five months during 1827, besides routine operations, was able to transcribe 24 manuscript volumes, "averaging each about 250 pages of close writing," and prepare 42 copies of maps, to meet the request of Governor Enoch Lincoln, of Maine, for documents relating to the northeastern-boundary controversy, indicates both diligence and a fair degree of efficiency.

The limiting of staff operations primarily to filing and copying is noteworthy. Brent himself answered the most-routine inquiries, usually in accordance with brief directives from the secretary. Clay, like Adams before him, drafted not only the instructions to diplomatic and consular personnel and the notes to foreign emissaries but also most of the responses to domestic correspondents. This procedure kept the reins of planning and administration highly centralized, which had attendant advantages in correlating program. At the same time, the department head assumed a crushing burden of detail which, as Adams had earlier noted, could not be "committed to clerks or performed by them. . . ." "Business crowds upon me from day to day," he had lamented, "requiring instantaneous attention, and in such variety that unless everything is disposed of just as it occurs, it escapes from the memory and runs into the account of arrears."[11]

Management analysts have questioned why the operations of the department were not shared with an assistant secretary and why they were not subdivided into geographic desks, freeing the secretary to concentrate on the formation of policy. Augustus Brevoort Woodward, judge of Michigan Territory from 1805 to 1824 and thereafter of Florida until 1827, recommended this plan in a publication issued early during the Adams administration. He advised, further, that the domestic functions of the department be separated under a new cabinet post as a Home Department.[12] The history of the latter proposal explains in large part why such reorganization was not effected.

The plan for such a department had been urged in a paper drafted by the secretaries of the Treasury, War, Navy, and State departments in 1816, as an approach to the arrearages in assigned operations that were already evident throughout the executive branch. While President Madison had endorsed the proposal, Congress had accorded it little attention. Monroe, as secretary of state, had, indeed, been reluctant to part with responsibility for administering the patronage channels in the federal court system and the census enumeration. President Adams, in his first annual message, alluded to the nine-year-old recommendation and again advised that it be adopted. A month later, Clay also urged the proposal upon the House of Representatives. Writing to the chairman of the Committee of Ways and Means, he pointed to the longstanding arrearages in the work of the State Department, the "increase of business proceeding from an augmentation of the population and wealth of the Country," and the "great recent addition to the labors," occasioned by the developing relations with Latin America, which had doubled the number of foreign missions and greatly increased the necessity for translation of correspondence. To Daniel Webster, chairman of a House Select Committee directed to consider that portion of the president's message, Clay, in the following month, argued at length the "incongruity" of indiscriminately blending the domestic and foreign duties. "The necessary consequence of this variety and extent of business is," he contended, "that it lessens responsibility or renders the enforcement of it unjust." Unless a Home Department was established, authorization for appointment of three additional clerks and a translator was "necessary."[13]

Adams realized that any reorganization so comprehensive as the one proposed by Judge Woodward would fail to win congressional approval. He had "no expectation" that a Home Department would be accepted, "even upon the simplest plan." The House Select Committee, on May 22, shortly before adjournment, reported a bill for establishing an additional department, but the proposal was tabled. On April 29 Clay had again urged upon the Committee of Ways and Means the "urgent necessity of an authority to appoint . . . additional clerks. . . ." That plea also went unanswered.[14]

Through succeeding months, Clay pressed the need upon his congressional friends. He or some member of the administration inspired Congressman Edward Everett, editor of the *North American Review*, to publish, in October 1826, a review that was critical of legislative colleagues who made much of the extravagance of the executive branch but neglected their own responsibility "to *look into* and *examine* the state of those departments, rectifying what is wrong and supplying what is wanting."[15] Clay renewed his plea for a Home Department in January 1827, and the report was now referred to the Committee of the Whole in the House of Representatives; but again no action was taken.

The secretary of state still hoped, without success, into the spring of 1828, that such a reorganization might be effected. Instead, the Congress, after requesting a special report on the "neglect or omission to record . . . patents," had approved, in March 1827, the employment of three additional clerks for the general duties of the department and another clerk for the Patent Office. Although William Thornton, the superintendent of that office, had urged, for his work alone, the provision of three additional clerks, organization, and a salary scale comparable to those in the General Land Office, the Auditors, and the Pension Office—and Clay had argued in favor of at least a salary increment—administration of the patents remained structurally the function of a lesser clerk.

Thornton, whose "many-sided near-genius" as architect, painter, novelist, poet, horse fancier, and advocate of politically controversial causes had earlier posed problems for Adams and Monroe, was a liability as an administrator. As early as 1807 Senator William Plumer had concluded that "Dr. Thornton . . . has too long been guilty of great negligence." In 1823 a House committee had reported that many of the models stored in his office "were in a decayed or injured condition."[16] Now nearing seventy years of age, Thornton was opinionated, stubborn, and autocratic.

On the day that Clay was commissioned secretary of state, he received a bitter complaint from Peter A. Browne, corresponding secretary of the Franklin Institute of the State of Pennsylvania for the Promotion of the Mechanic Arts, asserting that the patent officers were ignorant of the law, partial, and inconsistent in their application of regulations. By the end of March, Browne had added "extortionate" to the allegations. The Franklin Institute, at this time of rapidly increasing invention, had undertaken to examine and report on all new designs, a survey that was to develop the journal of that body into one of the most important scientific organs of the period. The institute requested access to the specifications of patented inventions and objected to the copying charges of 20 cents for a sheet of 100 words. In mid April, Clay sought the attorney general's ruling on the issue. Wirt noted the ambiguity in the law and conceded that it "might well receive the strict construction" that Thornton had given. Browne, in turn, presented countering legal opinions.[17]

Adams and Clay, as interested exponents of American science and invention, were in a quandary. While rejecting Browne's demand that Thornton be removed, the secretary of state agreed to review the case. Four months later he authorized the copies of the specifications. Thornton then protested to the president that "by misconstructions of the Law, some have contended for a knowledge of the patented Secrets before the expiration of the patent Term." He also proposed that a council, "which might be comprised of any three heads of Departments," be established as a review board to whom he might refer applications for patents which he knew "to be not new."[18]

Uncertainty concerning the nature and security of patent rights remained a problem. Congressman Everett, in commenting on the operation of the Executive Department in 1826, recommended that certification of the legality of patent licenses be removed from the office of the attorney general, where, under the statute, it existed more as a testimony to fulfillment of the formalities of registration than as an evaluation of inventive achievement. He proposed that it be assigned to the superintendent of the Patent Office or the head of the proposed Home Department. Thornton protested, however, that his office lacked funds for prosecuting cases of infringement of patents. Instead, he took the course of repudiating an inventor's claims by means of newspaper publicity.

During the spring of 1827 the patent officer published a statement criticizing the pretensions of Michael Withers as the developer of a "winged gudgeon" for use in milling. The inventor, who had been awarded a patent in 1804, had successfully upheld his rights in federal court in 1817. Now, as his certification was about to expire, he was encountering difficulty in marketing it, and he believed that Thornton's comments were effectively curtailing his protection. He demanded a public retraction by the officer, disavowal by Clay of the superintendent's "authority and competency," and certified copies of the patent, which Thornton had denied him. The secretary of state authorized the authentication of the patent but interpreted Thornton's publication as "the exercise of the common rights of every citizen" and refused to intervene. Both Clay and Attorney General Wirt, the latter as a private legal service, advised that recourse be taken through the courts. Withers, for whom such delay would be defeating, appealed to Adams, by letter and personal visit, and finally to Congress. In January 1828, however, he withdrew his memorial—perhaps because his patent was no longer applicable, or perhaps because he was near death.[19]

The episode had involved the administration in extensive and highly publicized correspondence. As a consequence, the secretary of state himself subsequently intervened to stipulate that an applicant be granted patent and to direct that the certification be issued. One more duty had devolved upon the secretary.

The limited role of the attorney general left many responsibilities under other cabinet heads which would much later be transferred to a Department of Justice. From the founding of the government, the attorney general had been viewed as a member of the cabinet, but his activities had not been considered a full-time operation. Not until 1814 had he been expected to reside in Washington, and Wirt, during the Adams administration, was frequently absent from the city on personal business. When present at cabinet discussions, he provided a dependable voice of moderation and balance. He was methodical and conscientious in the performance of his duties. He won distinction for being the first to establish a visible office and a written record of opinions as a body of precedent in the conduct of its operations. One scholar, applauding Wirt's achievements, notes that he formulated a series of significant technical rules by which he "chopped his way through a wilderness" in defining his functions.[20] But the restraints with which he viewed his public duties afforded no pressure for institutional development of a governmental legal department.

Wirt confined his public legal services to the requirements of the president and the cabinet. He would provide no opinions directly to Congress or its committees or even to subordinate branches of the executive departments, such as collectors of customs or courts martial.

Moreover, he demanded that the department heads themselves justify their requests as being essential to the performance of their specific functions. He represented the federal government before the Supreme Court, but only with great reluctance did he do so before the lower courts. Jacksonian critics, observing that in one instance Clay had negotiated an arrangement for the attorney general's assistance to the government in the Maryland District Court, complained that Wirt had been paid a private consulting fee. The secretary of state himself issued the directives to subordinate legal officers by which prosecutions were initiated for violations of international commitments. The secretaries of Treasury and War and the postmaster general exercised a similar mandate in reference to offenses on matters under their departmental oversight. Recommendations for appointments of district-court officers—attorneys and marshals, as well as judges—were channeled to the president through the Department of State.[21]

Wirt's restricted approach to the office rested in part upon narrow interpretation of his powers under the law. To a congressional committee, which in 1820 had sought his advice, he explained that the attorney general was sworn to act *"according to law"* and that any action he might take to enlarge his sphere of official duties would violate that oath. But this view also reflected the attorney general's personal desire to limit his public role. Shortly after taking office, he had written to a friend concerning the rigors of his office and concluded: "Much of this is not properly my duty. . . . I shall find ways and means to put an end to it, *prudently,* and do only *my own duty."* At about the same time he had advised the chairman of the House Judiciary Committee of his "strong objection" to any provision for increasing the duties of his office, *"as now organized."* The proposed operations, Wirt protested, could not be performed satisfactorily unless he devoted himself to them "solely and exclusively."[22]

Wirt did not seek an expansion of his staff or an extension of his own position to full-time status. He preferred to continue a very active, independent legal career. As he noted, he had "no taste for political contention." That "taste" was a very important requisite for administrative development during the Adams presidency.

Both Barbour and Southard, as heads of the military and naval establishments, pursued their roles more assertively. Upon assuming office, Barbour took over a department which, under Calhoun's direction, had achieved an organizational structure that has been ranked as "one of the major administrative contributions of the Republican period."[23] It rested upon a bureau system—specialization of functions, with authority delegated to supervisors operating under the secretary's oversight through dual chains of command, encompassing both the military and civilian services. On the military side the office of chief of staff, which was held by a major general and had been established in 1821 with headquarters in Washington, had brought the field operations directly under the inspection and control of the government. A general staff, developed during the War of 1812, provided a corps of officers to relieve the secretary of much administrative detail. Paralleling this structure on the civilian side, a chief clerk directed sixteen subordinate clerks, a messenger, and an assistant messenger, most of whom had specific assignments in office routine. Additionally, there were central offices that administered the operations of the subordinate departments of Adjutant General, Engineers, Quarter Master, Purchasing, Military Store Keeper, Ordnance, Subsistence, Paymaster General, Surgeon General, and Indian Affairs, each of which had one to four civilian clerks. Armories and arsenals at major posts in the field were staffed with supervisory military personnel. Accounts, since 1816, had been transferred to the Auditor's Office under the Treasury Department.

The War Department, as Barbour assumed the secretaryship, thus constituted an administrative component which was considerably larger than that accorded to the combined foreign and domestic concerns of the State Department. He obtained authorization for one additional clerk in the secretary's office, another in the Subsistence Department, and two more assistant quartermasters. Congressional critics found, with some outrage, that in 1827 he had also applied contingency funds, to the extent of $753, for the employment of an additional clerk in the Office of Indian Affairs.

Through the application of the professional skills of the engineers in civilian construction the War Department became the focal point of the administration's program of internal improvements. So great were the rivalries for priority of development of these projects that Barbour reported in 1826 the detailing of officers from other units to engineering service. He therefore asked for a gradual doubling of the force of military engineers and an immediate expansion and organization of the topographical engineers into a separate corps. The combined units—projected ultimately to total forty-five officers in the military engineers and thirty-four in the topographical—along with the Military Academy, would then comprise the equivalent of a brigade, over which Barbour proposed to place "a chief engineer, with the pay, rank, and emoluments of a brigadier general." With Adams's endorsement, Barbour and his successor in 1828, Peter B. Porter, continued to urge these changes, but the legislation was not approved. The civilian staff of construction superintendents was more than doubled between 1825 and 1829, but the number of army engineers was actually reduced by one during that period. The ranking officer of the Engineering Department remained a colonel.[24]

Barbour's proposal for major revision of the militia system also failed to win congressional support. In personnel the recommendation entailed only appointment of an adjutant general of militia, to serve as a Washington-based liaison officer. The program, however, called for extension of a federally structured organization throughout the nation.

The secretary of war's recommendation resulted from a resolution presented by Congressman Samuel C. Allen of Massachusetts, in March 1826, urging that better training be given to militia officers. While he disclaimed any hostility to the provision for military education at West Point, Allen deplored the fact that graduation from the Military Academy had become the only avenue for promotion, that militia officers were superseded in command on active service, and that the militia no longer held public confidence. By joint action of the House and Senate on May 17, the War Department was requested to have manuals prepared for instruction in cavalry and field-artillery tactics. Barbour thereupon appointed a board of three officers each from the state militia and the United States Army, together with the chief clerk of the War Department, to review the state organizations, to assess their defects, and to recommend remedies.[25]

Studying responses to a War Department circular which was widely distributed over the summer of 1826, as well as proposals which at various times had been presented in Congress, the board in October concluded that the primary problem rested in the enrollment of excessive numbers of militiamen, as required under legislation dating from 1792. With a population that had trebled since that date, the requirement for service of all able-bodied white males between the ages of eighteen and forty-five seemed no longer necessary in peacetime. While the costs to the national government were nominal, the board noted, those to the individuals or to the local authorities who must purchase the arms, ammunition, and equipment operated "as heavy burdens on the most productive class of the community, without the acquisition, except in the cities, and a few other highly peopled districts, of any adequate degree of military instruction or efficiency." The vast majority of letters to the board had described ordinary militia musters "as useless, or worse than useless; as so many occasions for hurtful practices, instead of martial exercises. . . ." The board made no reference to the costly loss of time from employment caused by such maneuvers, but it recognized that neither officers nor men would, unless the nation were threatened by war, participate without remuneration in a prolonged encampment for instruction. Meanwhile, vast numbers, in some states equaling the total of active militiamen, were obtaining exemption from duty.[26]

The board proposed that the entering age be raised to twenty-one, that the minimum enrollment for each state be set at one brigade for each member of its delegation in the United States House of Representatives, and that maximums be left to the discretion of the respective states. No exemptions, except for conscientious objectors identified with religious groups, would be approved. Under such recommendations it was estimated that the reduction in force would be about 50 percent, providing a militia of about 400,000 men, with a maximum age limit of twenty-nine or thirty. Under the proposed plan, this body would be organized according to a prescribed table of command, parallel in all states. Officers would be trained, and paid for that period of duty, in a series of encampments under manuals prepared by the War Department.

In his annual message to Congress, Adams transmitted the recommendations of the board as an accompaniment to the report of the secretary of war. The president noted that the occasion of the preparation of the manuals had been "thought favorable for consulting the same board . . . upon the acknowledged defective condition of our militia system and of the improvements of which it is susceptible."[27] His remarks indicate that the initiative for the proposed reorganization had come from the administration, rather than from Congress. Barbour had, in fact, sent out his circular to the states several months before the board was instructed to report upon the manuals.

Lack of serious congressional interest in the suggested changes became evident. The House Committee on the Militia in 1827 hailed the new training manuals as certain to produce "most favorable and beneficial results" and found itself "at a loss to conceive of any other plan that could have been devised, so likely to attain the grand object in view." The Senate Committee on the Militia introduced legislation in accordance with the board's report. But no action was taken on the recommendations. Even the proposal of standardized training manuals was rejected by the House of Representatives in May 1828. House committees, in February 1827 and again in February 1829, cited a constitutional conflict of authority which opposed any intrusion by the federal government in the training and discipline of the militia.[28]

States' rights had again risen as a barrier to the administration's course. At the same time, resentment of the elitism associated with the dominance of military education and leadership from West Point rang in the congressional debates. Congressman James C. Mitchell of Tennessee was only one of several who, in the spring of 1828, criticized that institution. He questioned that the "orphan son of a widowed mother" was ever recommended for appointment. "No, sir," he continued, "we recommend a boy, whose father is abundantly able to educate him, and we do it because that father is also able to aid us in our election to this House." He rejected the argument that the school was conducted with "republican simplicity." It was, he contended, "a monarchical institution," "one of the very creatures of royalty." Jackson's laudatory reference, in his Inaugural Address, to the "patriotic militia" as "the bulwark of our defense" identified the political context of the debate.[29]

A residue of problems growing out of the reorganization of the army in 1821 occasioned persistently worrisome difficulties for Adams and Barbour in the administration of the War Department. Neither Calhoun nor the General Staff of the army had wanted to have a single commanding officer in charge of military operations, but the legislation had established the rank of major general at the head of the line of command, without defining his duties. Jacob Brown, the first to hold the post, had actively participated in the political discussions preliminary to Adams's election, and he continued to maintain a close personal relationship with the president. Ignoring the chain of departmental communication on military policy, the officer conversed directly with Adams about appointments, the relocation of units, command instructions, and the policy of army centralization. The fact that the commanding general never accepted status subordinate to the secretary of war, which was attributable basically to the vagueness of the statutory provision for the military office, developed, on the basis of the Adams-Brown relationship, into more serious problems of dual authority under Jackson and into a civilian-military conflict that extended into the twentieth century.[30]

On the issue of authority over military appointments, which Monroe had contested with the Senate throughout his second term, Adams was at first conciliatory. The Senate had twice rejected the nominations of Nathan Towson, as colonel of a newly established artillery regiment, and of James Gadsden, as adjutant general, on the ground that their elevation ignored the prior claims of officers who had been dismissed under the Reorganization Act. Adams's nomination of Col. Roger Jones of Virginia to the latter post satisfactorily removed the difficulty in that case, for the officer had been the choice of Senate proponents. Upon Barbour's recommendation, the president also nominated Daniel Bissell for the artillery colonelcy, again as the officer who had the most Senate support, despite reports that the alternative was better qualified. The Senate, however, requested that Bissell be appointed with "retrospective rank," dated from his active service. Adams, like Monroe, now chafed at the Senate's assumption "that the President is to act according to the Senate's opinion of the law, and that the Senate are to inform him how he *may* perform his duty." With the controversy centered primarily as one of authority and identified with the newly developing political opposition, Adams became as inflexible as Monroe had been.[31]

The president first sought a ruling from the attorney general on interpretation of the legislation of 1821. Wirt saw the situation as "unfortunate" but contended that Adams could not yield "without getting wrong." If the issue were merely a matter of expediency, the surrender might well be made in the interest of peace. As a question of power, the sacrifice became one "to conscience." Wirt suggested the proposal of a new statute, "giving to the officer or officers so to be arranged all the advantages of rank which he or they would have possessed, if they had been arranged under the original act. . . ."[32]

Adams offered no compromise. On 11 April 1826 he advised the Senate that he could not concur in their request, and he inquired whether they approved the nomination notwithstanding. The Committee on Military Affairs reiterated its approval of the appointment but under a commission dating from the war period. When that proposal was defeated, John H. Eaton moved to take no further action on the Bissell nomination. Under leadership from administration forces, that motion was tabled. On May 22, as the committee reasserted its original stand, that motion, also, was tabled. The issue was revived in the second session of the Nineteenth Congress, when Jacksonians sponsored bills in both Houses supporting Bissell's appointment, with pay retroactive to his dismissal in 1821. Administration opposition was continued, and so was the stalemate. The colonelcy remained vacant throughout the remainder of Adams's incumbency.[33]

With less congressional involvement, an even more rancorous and aggravating controversy over military appointment developed out of the rivalry between Brigadier Generals Edmund Pendleton Gaines and Winfield Scott for second rank under Jacob Brown and for succession to his office. Here, too, the dispute had originated under the secretaryship of Calhoun. Gaines, the elder officer, had a longer service record, but both he and Scott had been elevated on the same dates, successively, as major, lieutenant colonel, colonel, and brigadier general during the War of 1812. Scott's claim to precedence hinged upon the fact that he had been brevetted to the rank of major general twenty-one days earlier than his rival. The bitterness had become so intense by 1824 that Scott, in violation of army regulations, had challenged Gaines to a duel. The latter, citing the regulations and his personal opposition to the dueling code, had rejected the challenge. A board of army officers, which considered the problem during the closing days of the Monroe administration, had determined that Gaines held the senior commission as brigadier general; but its members had been unable to agree on the relevance of the brevet ranking.

Upon assuming office, Adams protested that Calhoun had "evaded" the problem "on the pretence that it was merely an *abstract* question!" For the new president, the issue was pressing. Brown was in ill health. The commanding general urged the cause of Gaines, and Barbour, in a long letter of 18 July 1825, supported this view. Scott, on the other hand, produced a letter from Calhoun, promising Scott the command in the event of Brown's death. Over the succeeding months correspondence from both the divisional officers, setting forth their arguments, appeared in pamphlet form. Presumptions were strong that they were equally guilty of violating army regulations against publication of private quarrels. After lengthy discussion at a meeting in March 1827, Adams and his cabinet decided to side-step court-martial proceedings against either officer, on the ground that direct evidence was lacking to indicate their personal involvement in the publication; but Barbour was directed to express the president's disapproval.[34]

Brown's death in February 1828 brought the issue to a climax. Before the funeral had taken place, Gaines renewed his claims. Adams requested that Gaines submit a written statement of his pretensions, warned that equal consideration would be given to the views of Scott, and promised to "finally settle the point upon full advisement with those associated . . . in the Government." When six weeks later the matter had still not been settled, Gaines threatened to leave the service, an action that the President deemed "neither seasonable nor delicate."[35]

Underlying partisan pressures surfaced. Scott had been politically active since 1822 and was known to be an Adams supporter. Gaines, denying to the president that he had ever spoken disrespectfully of him, conceded that he was attached to Jackson. Some of the president's backers charged that the investigation by Gaines and Maj. T. P. Andrews on the Creek negotiations at Indian Springs had, in fact, been deliberately conducted so as to antagonize Governor Troup against the administration. Adams promptly rejected the idea that personal considerations should influence his views. But Clay, who in 1825 had brought to the attention of both Brown and Gaines an affront by the latter's aide, Edward George Washington Butler, Jackson's godson and former ward, was less tolerant. On April 12, as Clay and Barbour discussed with the president the problem of the appointment, the secretary of state alluded to the Butler incident and warned "that if Gaines should be appointed he could not serve with him." Adams then agreed that Gaines would not be nominated.[36]

Two days later, when for three hours the cabinet debated the problem of Brown's replacement, Clay, Barbour, Southard, and Wirt united in support of Scott; no one endorsed Gaines. Ignoring the fact that both officers were sons of the Old Dominion, Adams somewhat naïvely attributed the stand to "the Virginian sympathy." He himself objected to Scott for his "outrages upon the discipline of the army" in issuing the challenge to a duel.[37]

The president finally resolved the problem by broadening the range of choice. The proposed alternatives were Alexander Macomb, commander of the Engineering Department, who had accepted the rank of colonel under the reorganization plan but had been the senior brigadier general, with brevet rank as major general, at the conclusion of the War; and William Henry Harrison, who had held full rank as major general upon his resignation from service in 1814. Both had strong political support—Macomb by the New York congressional delegation; Harrison as former territorial governor of Indiana and congressman and, at this time, senator from Ohio. Clay, Adams noted, "had also Western biases inclining him towards Harrison." Macomb, however, had the support of Rush and perhaps, if Scott is to be believed, of a bevy of Washington ladies who were intent upon advancing the career of a young army lieutenant as Macomb's aide. Whether or not "petticoat influence" was effective, Adams joined the secretary of the Treasury in endorsing the appointment of Macomb. That nomination was submitted to the Senate on April 15 and was promptly approved.[38]

Gaines readily acquiesced in the decision, but Scott refused to recognize Macomb's authority. Charging that Macomb, in assuming the office, displayed "contempt & insubordination" towards "his senior, & therefore, commanding officer," Scott requested that the new appointee be brought to court-martial. Upon Adams's instruction, Southard, then acting secretary of war, responded that Macomb's assumption of the command was at the president's "express" order and directed that Scott return to his post. The irate Scott thereupon requested an extension of furlough so that he might "seek relief in some form from the Congress of the U.S. at its next session." Adams, who brought the matter to cabinet discussion on June 24, was outraged. He considered the proposal to appeal to Congress "an insult; for in what manner could Congress control these orders and decisions?" "Certainly," Adams argued, "by no other mode than by impeachment of the President, or by an ex post facto law to annul a purely Executive act." Yet, in deference to Scott's military record, the president was reluctant to dismiss him. Scott's petition for an extension of the furlough was denied, and he was again ordered back to duty.[39]

The general returned to his headquarters in Cincinnati, but there he prepared yet another lengthy pamphlet, reasserting his claims to rank above Macomb. By November, both the new chief of staff and Peter B. Porter, who had become secretary of war, were prepared to take action. Macomb proposed to bring the recalcitrant general before a court-martial. Porter, in turn, advised Scott that a brevet rank was "a mere honorary distinction," conveying no right to command except in certain clearly limited cases. Porter also ominously expressed hope that Scott's services should not be lost to the nation.[40] On November 26 the general was relieved of his command and ordered to Washington.

Scott seized the opportunity to appeal to Congress. Stating his case on December 9, he petitioned for legislation to define the rights and privileges of brevet rank. In both Houses the memorial was rejected. Both upheld the authority of the president to make the appointment, regardless of brevet ranking, and the House further concluded that "without any interference of the Executive, the regular army . . . would at this time be subject to the command of Major General Macomb, he being the officer highest in rank of the line. . . ."[41] Journalistic comment, while frequently sympathetic to Scott, likewise viewed him as being in the wrong.

In mid January, Adams was prepared to publish his own views upon the significance of brevet rank but Wirt dissuaded him from doing so. Ruefully, the president noted that he had lost "two months of painful labor" in composing the essay; but he found in it "so much of sarcastic bitterness and indignation" that he suspected he had mistaken "resentment for patriotism." Perhaps, he concluded, by withholding the paper he had spared himself "some additional and unnecessary enmities." "Of these," he added, "I have already more than enough."[42] The problem of Scott's intransigence was left with other unfinished business to be settled by the incoming administration.

Southard, as secretary of the navy, confronted a similar and, for the nation, a more serious problem of insubordination. The major outlines of organizational reform that marked his administration of the service had been evolved under Presidents Madison and Monroe. The Board of Navy Commissioners, established by legislation of 1815, had relieved the secretary of considerable official detail. Under his supervision, this board was charged with directing the construction and armament of vessels, the procurement of stores, the deployment of ships, the administration of navy yards and stations, and the preparation of service regulations and the annual budget. Their administrative staff included a secretary, who had served in the department since 1798; a chief clerk, who also had long experience; five subordinate clerks; a draftsman; and a messenger. Southard retained direct authority over appointments and disciplinary proceedings. He, too, was provided with a chief clerk and a staff of six subclerks, which was increased by one during the Adams administration. Under such an organization the naval secretary was in large measure freed for program development.

Southard's record, despite the restraints imposed by highly politicized congressional opposition, was good, conspicuously so in contrast to the laxity that had marked the role of his predecessor. Southard undertook to broaden the geographic representation of service personnel through apportioning appointments to midshipman training. He instituted training vessels at the principal recruiting stations, partly to reduce the hazards of disease and desertion pending assignment, as well as to introduce recruits to the regimen and to make better use of manpower. He also sought, unsuccessfully, the establishment of a naval academy; legislation for a criminal code to ensure consistency in disciplinary requirements; incorporation of the marines on shore duty, as at sea, under regulation by the navy; and improvements in promotion and salary for career officers. He was particularly concerned that no provision existed for elevating navy captains to the rank and pay equivalent of generals in the army.[43]

Southard, who had begun his administration when a serious malaria outbreak was raging at the Thompson's Island navy base, directed much attention to the health arrangements in the service. He obtained removal of the Florida base to the more healthful environs of Pensacola. He also won, in 1827, increased compensation for surgeons and surgeons' mates and, in the following year, provision for appointment of a "Surgeon-of-the-Fleet" for each squadron. He made some progress toward the establishment of navy hospitals.

This last effort indicated both his conscientiousness as an administrator and his attention to personnel concerns. Under legislation of 1799, Congress had required a 20-cents per month pay deduction from all navy and marine servicemen for a hospital fund. For twenty-five years those payments had been incorporated in the navy appropriation accounts and at various times, notably during the War of 1812, had been expended on general operations. No hospital had been provided. Upon assuming office, Southard directed that the fund be segregated, and by his order, over the next three years, part of the deficiency was repaid out of regular naval appropriations. However, a sum due to the fund from the period before 1811, when Congress had previously called for repayment, had not yet been restored. Southard devoted a large segment of his report for 1827 to contention that the earlier accounting had been inaccurate and that the sums due should be repaid with interest. Between 1823 and 1827, hospital commissioners had purchased sites for four buildings. Two of these establishments were under construction, and the funds were needed for their completion. By an act of 24 May 1828, Congress appropriated the remainder of the 1811 allotment and finally, on 2 March 1829, $125,000 more, a total of $175,000 on an account that Southard calculated, including interest, should total $262,000.[44]

A program of naval construction, begun in 1816, was nearing completion as the Adams administration began. In his first annual message the president urged continuance of the regular $500,000 appropriation for maintenance of the naval establishment and suggested that the funds could be profitably expended in acquisition of seasoned timber for future construction, building of docks, or establishment of a naval academy. While the last of these projects was disapproved, the full annual appropriation was authorized in 1827, to the president's particular personal gratification. Forest reserves for naval use were established, and construction was begun on dry docks at Charleston and Norfolk, the first of the United States Navy, before the end of the administration.

Southard initiated a thorough review of naval establishments. As a consequence he closed the stations on the Great Lakes and Lake Champlain and at New Orleans and Barataria. He effected major structural changes in the yards at Brooklyn and Gosport, and he completed long-range plans for systematic development of all the yards, except the newly built one at Pensacola. In conjunction with this program, the navy shared the administration's commitment to internal improvements. Need for deeper water at the Gosport yard led to a survey for additional flow from Lake Drummond or from the Dismal Swamp Canal. The navy also supervised the erection of a breakwater near the mouth of the Delaware, which was designed to improve the harbor at Philadelphia.

Fleet assignment was reorganized. With the virtual elimination of piracy from the Caribbean, vessels of that squadron were directed to make more frequent sailings to the southward, off the eastern coast of South America, as a protection to merchant vessels that were being menaced by violations of neutral rights during the conflict between Brazil and Buenos Aires. Termination of the Spanish-American revolutions, which had necessitated protection of United States commerce along the western coast of South America, permitted extension of Pacific cruising outward to the vicinity of the Sandwich Islands, where whaling was rapidly developing. To facilitate communication between the Atlantic and Pacific squadrons, Southard repeatedly urged the establishment of a regular passage and mail route across the Isthmus of Panama, a facility that foreign-service personnel and merchants who were active in Peru and Chile also persistently requested; but Congress failed to act on the proposal. Reflecting Adams's interests, the navy at this time initiated an annual sailing into the waters off Newfoundland, in aid of American fishing vessels. The Mediterranean Squadron was also expanded to provide convoy for merchant ships as warfare in that area increased the threat of piracy. The navy's role thus reflected and assisted in the broadening range of the nation's foreign commerce.

It was not, however, a service that during this period occasioned many swashbuckling exploits, and not all fleet commanders were prepared to subordinate their personal ambition to the staider operations of peacetime duty. Such frustrations may have contributed to the petty bickering over the command of the South Seas expedition; they were very clearly evidenced in the actions of Capt. David Porter. For Southard, the insubordination of Captain Porter, who was brought to court-martial during the early weeks of Adams's presidency, posed a major challenge to administrative authority. The episode provided one of the opening skirmishes of the 1828 presidential campaign, and the officer's subsequent activities as commander of the Mexican navy continued to embarrass the administration's foreign relations throughout the intervening years.

Porter, who had had great success in raiding British shipping in the Pacific during the War of 1812, had been a member of the Board of Navy Commissioners from 1815 to 1822. As the Monroe administration undertook a major assault upon Caribbean piracy during the following year, he had requested and had been assigned to command the West India Squadron. The duty was unpleasant and, from the standpoint of health, exceedingly dangerous. Outbreaks of yellow fever and malaria were regular summer occurrences. During the summer of 1823, Porter had nearly died of yellow fever, and he had had to spend months recuperating in the United States. In the following February he had returned to the Caribbean, and in May he had again contracted the disease. He had then returned to Washington, so rapidly that he had arrived before the notification of his withdrawal from his post.

As piracies increased while Porter was directing the fleet from his home throughout the summer, Southard, in October, had finally ordered the commander to return to the squadron. Porter argued, in reply, that Washington was closer than was Key West to the center of his command; he could see no need to return to the West Indies. Complaining that he was being harried by "almost . . . daily" demands for explanation, he had concluded with a request to be relieved of the assignment. A few days later he had related his "mortification after mortification" to President Monroe. Terming Southard's treatment of him "unexampled . . . in the Annals of our Navy," Porter expressed "hope that such will never be repeated." "My convenience, my comfort, my feelings, nay my life are therefore entirely held at his mercy!" he lamented. The president had made no reply.[45]

Porter's choleric and tactless acts had repeatedly occasioned criticism. During the winter of 1823 to 1824 he had preferred charges in court-martial against one of his squadron officers who had commented unfavorably in print about the commander's arrangements for return of a Spanish vessel that had been seized during an attack upon the Americans. When the officer was acquitted, Southard had reminded Porter of the departmental policy to avoid legal action insofar as practicable. Shortly thereafter the British chargé in Washington had formally protested Porter's sanctioning of a challenge to a duel, which had been issued by one of Porter's officers against a British captain. Again Southard had rebuked the commander of the West Indies Squadron.

Upon this record, Porter's assignment to return to his post was unwise. His instructions had, however, warned him of the delicacy of international relations in the Caribbean area. He was to "observe the utmost caution not to encroach upon the rights of others." He was to notify Spanish authorities of his arrival off their coasts and to seek their "favorable and friendly support." Pirates might be pursued into uninhabited areas, but never if the privilege were denied by local authorities. While Vives, as governor of Cuba, had cooperated in the struggle against piracy and had permitted Porter's fleet to take shelter on the uninhabited coast, he had insisted that such recourse should be "conformable to the laws of nations." Manuel de la Torre, governor of Puerto Rico, had assumed a thornier stance. Recalling the expedition of Ducoudray-Holstein and Baptis Irvine against that island during the previous year, Torre had expressed little sympathy when, in 1823, his officers had killed one of Porter's lieutenants as an American party entered San Juan harbor for consultations. The episode had brought Torre's pledge that he would grant no more letters of marque to privateers, but he had persisted in refusing to permit United States landings.[46]

Porter had barely returned to the squadron in November 1824 when he learned that two of his officers, Lieutenants Charles T. Platt and Robert Ritchie, had been arrested and briefly detained by Puerto Rican officials at Fajardo (or Foxardo). Investigating the theft of some $5,000 worth of goods from the store of Cabot, Bailey, and Company at St. Thomas, the officers had landed on October 27 near the Puerto Rican town, where missing property had been previously found. Dressed as civilians, they had been arrested and held for several hours while they sent for their credentials. Later that day they had been released, but they ''left the village mortified very properly, hissed at by the ruff scuff of the place . . . ,'' Platt reported.[47]

Upon learning of the incident, Porter set sail for Fajardo. With two hundred men he landed there on the morning of November 14, overran and spiked several batteries en route to the town, and demanded from the captain of the port an apology for the insult to his officers. The alcalde promptly complied, and Porter withdrew with his force. He reported the affair to the Navy Department the following day, with anticipation that he would be commended for his defense of the ''national honor.''

Instead, he was relieved of command and ordered home, where he faced, first, in May 1825, a naval board of inquiry and, through the following July and early August, court-martial proceedings. Two charges were involved in the indictment. The first concerned ''disobedience of orders'' in making the landing, with force and military array, upon the territory of a friendly power. The second was ''insubordinate conduct and conduct unbecoming an officer.'' He was convicted on both counts and was sentenced to a six-months' suspension from duty, but was permitted to retain full pay and allowances.

That both the Monroe and the Adams administrations should have reacted strongly to the Fajardo incident is understandable in view of the delicacy of the international relations then prevailing. Porter had been aware of the commitments expressed in the Monroe pronouncements of December 1823 and of the sensitivity of the Spanish officials to Caribbean adventurism. His justification of his actions by comparing them to those of General Jackson in taking Pensacola, while the latter was in hot pursuit of Seminole Indians in 1818, was neither apt nor judicious. Of Monroe's cabinet, only Adams had condoned Jackson's considerably more defensible course, and the New Englander had been then pursuing diplomatic initiatives that could be served by the general's demonstration of Spanish weakness. In 1824 Adams was attempting to reassure Spain and the European powers that the United States held no designs on Spain's island colonies. Indeed, while Porter's court-martial was under way, the president and his secretary of state were extending their good offices to win recognition of Latin American independence through assurances of Spanish hegemony over the islands. In Adams's view the Fajardo incident was "one of the most high-handed acts . . . ever heard of." His administration not only discountenanced Porter's action but also invited Spanish diplomatic representation at the naval inquiry.[48]

For Southard, however, the issue was even more seriously a concern over Porter's insubordination. On 2 December 1824, shortly before news of the Fajardo affair reached Washington, the cabinet had reviewed Porter's instructions, with particular attention to the restriction against landing in settled areas. The officer's march with military force upon a Spanish town, and particularly his spiking of the guns en route, represented "acts of war" that could not be condoned. "Had the Ex[ecutive] not made an enquiry into the facts a broken const[itution] & an offended people would have demanded a better reason than could have been given for the neglect," Southard commented.[49]

Porter had, moreover, demonstrated wreckless disrespect for both civilian and naval authority. He had delayed his return for three months and had reached Washington in the midst of the change of administration. Then, on March 17, he wrote to Southard a bitter letter complaining that he had been forced to wait two weeks without new instructions. Informed that he was to face a court of inquiry, he protested that the immediacy of his recall had prevented him from acquiring the necessary testimony and charged that the administration was using the incident to displace him from command. He questioned the competency of two of the three judges who sat on the board of inquiry, because they were junior to him in captaincy. Reprimanded because of his personal attacks upon Southard during the hearing, he walked out and refused to attend further sessions. Two days after the proceedings were publicly released, he published his own justification of the actions at Fajardo. When Southard criticized the statement, Porter responded so angrily that his letter, along with three others to the secretary and one to the president, was offered before the court-martial as evidence to the charge of insubordination.

Porter's defense of his actions rallied strong popular support. For some people the response was patriotic. Senator Sam Smith of Maryland wrote in July: "I understand that the Foxardo business is generally approved by the people. They think that it was Spirited and had a proper influence on the Governor of Porto Rico. and induced him to execute the Pirates." Charles Hammond, editor of the *Liberty Hall and*

Cincinnati Gazette, warned of the reaction in the West: "The conviction of Commodore Porter does not Set well with our folks— They are resolved to consider him a persecuted man, and to curse the administration. . . . They are determined to misunderstand it."[50]

But partisan considerations swelled the chorus. The *Washington Gazette,* the *National Gazette* (Philadelphia), the *United States Gazette* (Philadelphia), the *Enquirer* (Richmond, Va.), the *Herald* (Lynchburg, Va.), the *Mercury* (Charleston, S.C.), the *New York National Advocate,* the *Statesman* (New York), the *Evening Post* (New York), and the *Salem* (Mass.) *Gazette*—most of which were to be distinguished as Jacksonian organs over the next four years—strongly criticized the administration's course in the case. "Insubordination" was, they chanted, a "frivolous" charge. A "faithful servant" who had "devoted the morning and noon of his years to the public weal" was now forced to "submit to the supremacy of a civil officer, whom accident faction and intrinsic matters" had made his "nominal superior." The "good fame of an honest man" was being "blasted and destroyed by the magic potency of individual prejudice. . . ."[51]

Adams's supporters responded as vigorously in arguing that military leaders must accept civilian control. Clay commented that "the factious" had endeavored "to make something" out of Porter's case. Clay's own reaction, focusing upon generalized civil responsibility, was not without political connotations. "It was time to neutralize the effect of the bad precedent furnished in Genl. Jackson's case," he argued. "If Porter had been acquitted, or had not been brought to trial, hereafter the peace of the Country would have been in the hands of every military and naval commander of an expedition."[52]

Porter's resignation of his commission and his assumption of appointment as captain in the Mexican navy, in July 1826, removed the recalcitrant officer from Southard's charge but aggravated his nuisance to the administration. Throughout the winter and spring of 1827 the Mexican force raided Spanish shipping in the Caribbean while it also claimed asylum in United States territorial waters at Key West whenever the Spanish admiral, Angel Laborde, threatened to take counteraction. Fearing Spanish protest, which was in fact registered in June, Clay directed that Poinsett file a complaint with the Mexican authorities. The secretary of state explained to the Mexican, as also to the Spanish, government that Porter had been accorded the hospitality "which the United States are ever ready to dispense alike to the public Vessels of all friendly foreign Countries" and had been permitted to remain because he was blockaded. Clay emphasized, however, that the president would not condone violations of neutrality.[53]

Early in October 1827 a second Spanish protest pointed to advertisements run by Porter at New Orleans for recruitment of American seamen. Clay, in response, cited a countering advertisement by the federal attorney, warning of the penalties for citizens who made war on a friendly power. Some seventy sailors were shortly afterward arrested by United States marshals as the recruits were attempting to join the Mexican fleet, but a hundred others reportedly made the rendezvous successfully. To a friend, Porter boasted that he was accorded an "ovation" at a banquet honoring him during his recruitment efforts.[54]

The administration reacted to Porter's operations cautiously. At a cabinet meeting in February 1827, it was agreed that United States naval officers should be directed to protect American neutrality, but at the same time, Spain was to be warned against invading territorial waters in attacking the United States renegade. When Captain Charles Ridgely of the West Indies Squadron notified Porter of the Spanish protest, the latter responded with effrontery, promising to leave Key West if he were officially informed that the Mexican fleet was unwelcome and if he were "also officially informed that the blockade . . . [was] raised, and the Squadron . . . in pursuit of . . . [him had] retired to a Spanish port, and the sea left free. . . ."[55] Although Ridgely's report, which was received while Adams and Southard were vacationing, was copied and dispatched to the secretary of the navy, Ridgely was given no formal orders to take further action. Holiday inertia and Porter's popularity in the West contributed to the delay.

By October the commander of the Mexican fleet, who was in need of funds, sailed to Veracruz. Finding that his government was no longer able to support the operations of the fleet, he announced the issuance of letters of marque for privateering and in mid November put forth a blustering proclamation stating that his forces would seize every vessel found carrying contraband goods. While he commissioned a few privateers to enforce his edict, diplomatic protest by Poinsett and the signing of a commercial treaty at Mexico City the following February counteracted his efforts. Individual vessels raided commerce with some success over the next year, but Porter's command disintegrated. He himself fled in secrecy back to Washington after there were political upheavals in Mexico in 1829.

Personnel difficulties, which had proved so annoying to Barbour and Southard, also plagued Rush's administration of the Treasury. That department, under reforms of 1817, had been given increased staff and general responsibility for governmental accounting. As Rush assumed office, he commanded a bureaucratized Washington organization that included two comptrollers, five auditors, the commissioner of the General Land Office, the treasurer, and the register, each with a chief clerk, ten to twenty or more subordinate clerks, and attendant messengers. Beyond that administrative cadre were the army of customs collectors, land-office registers, and receivers of public moneys, scattered over the country.

Under that establishment, current accounting operations within the Treasury seem to have been relatively well organized, but serious problems remained. Cabinet officers retained responsibility for reviewing and approving vouchers within their own departments. Moreover, while requirements for submitting the accounts had been tightened, procedures for clearing the records of delinquent, even hopeless, accounts were deficient. In February 1825 Tobias Watkins, as fourth auditor, had urgently requested legislation to permit purging the files of delinquents long deceased or insolvent. Congress failed to act on the matter then or over the next four years.[56]

No investigative mechanism provided for routine supervision of customs-house operations. Rush complained of the inadequacy of customs records and instituted changes designed to collect data on the basis of volume, as well as valuation. His principal difficulties, however, centered on the control of customs personnel. Collectors and surveyors, who hired and directed large subordinate staffs of measurers, weighers, gaugers, and similar functionaries, dispensed extensive political patronage. Secretary William H. Crawford, during his years of presidential campaigning, had developed this service as a major repository of personal support. Adams yielded to the importunities of his New England backers by removing the collector in Bath when malfeasance could be proved, but the president resisted persistent pleas by Rush, with Clay's backing, for removal of political opponents who frequently were not only hostile but incompetent.

John Steele, a veteran of the Revolution, who had been serving in the Pennsylvania Senate immediately prior to his appointment, had held the collectorship at Philadelphia since 1806. Seventeen of the twenty inspectors under him were also long-term employees. In November 1825 Steele reported that Edward Thomson, a Philadelphia tea merchant, had gone bankrupt, owing $857,247.60 in unpaid duties on five shiploads of tea which had been certified for entry on general bond. As the case developed, it was revealed that the tea had not been promptly warehoused and that parcels of it had been shipped directly from the wharf to merchants at New York. The residue had been stored without inspection or recording of the amount. Moreover, the customs inspector had freely lent the storage key to the local importer, permitting him to withdraw a large number of the chests unobserved. The government lost not only the unpaid duties but over $250,000 in claims and legal costs when a New York merchant and an insurance company won litigation based on prior lien to part of the tea that had been seized by federal agents. Both Judge William P. Van Ness of the Federal District Court and Judge Bushrod Washington of the Supreme Court openly criticized the customs officials' handling of the shipment.[57]

Federal Attorney Charles J. Ingersoll, who had grandiloquently brought indictments directed against several hundred individual chests of tea, compounded the embarrassment to the administration. Losing the first case before the Supreme Court, he entered nolle prosequi actions on each of the remaining indictments in April 1827. Only Adams's leniency, Webster complained bitterly, had kept Ingersoll in office, yet it was doubtful that "he would now walk round one square of the City to prevent Genl. Jackson from turing [sic] the President out of Office." Meanwhile, "his 700 ridiculous Indictments, not only brig [sic] great expense to the Government; but what is much worse, expose it to censure & reproach."[58]

The president appointed Samuel Harrison Smith, Jeffersonian founder of the National Intelligencer (Washington) and a former revenue commissioner, to investigate the incident. Smith's report indicated that there had long been inefficiency both in the warehousing system and the service of the employees, but he found no corruption, a judgment that was "qualified by the information . . . of a departure, in some cases, from the provisions of the law." Other statements reaching the president were less reassuring. An anonymous "friend of the Administration" had warned in December 1825 not only of the laxity in customs operations but also of "presents" to the officers "for making out bills." A year later, while the tea cases were under adjudication, Adams noted that "strong representations" had been made for removal of the principal officials at Philadelphia and Charleston and that the surveyor at New York had been discharged from an indictment "for a conspiracy to cheat" only because of a "hung" jury, eight men having voted for conviction, with but four for acquittal. The president concluded that it was "best to wait some time longer before making any removals." He saw "yet no reason sufficient to justify a departure from the principle . . . of removing no public officer for merely preferring another candidate for the Presidency." Steele, who purportedly because of ill health was out of the office throughout 1826, was not replaced until he voluntarily resigned at the end of the year.[59]

George Graham, who served as commissioner of the General Land Office, was a retrenchment-minded Virginian. He had succeeded John

McLean in the post in 1823 and had found heavy arrears in the clerical functions of recording certificates, noting the prices bid and the payments made at land sales, entering subsequent partial payments on accounts, and finally issuing patents—operations that were complicated by the series of relief measures that, throughout the decade, had authorized the extending of requirements for payment on earlier credit sales and permitted the patenting of fractional entries. By 1826 Graham had sufficiently overcome the backlog to warrant recommending that the number of clerks be reduced from twenty-three to seventeen, and Congress responded with alacrity. Graham also curtailed general office expenses by seeking bids on contracts for supplies, but the reform evoked some complaint, at least from the president, who found that only with difficulty could he sign the parchment that was being used for patents.[60]

Accounts in local land offices were subject to review under a system instituted in 1816, but examiners frequently found records in the field offices in disarray—partly from ignorance of registers and receivers on accounting procedures but more generally in consequence of the low pay and excessive work. Richard Call and George Ward, who were appointed to the newly opened Tallahassee Land Office in 1825, noted at the end of a year that "the Compensation falls very far Short of all reasonable expectations. . . ." Secretary of the Treasury Crawford had earlier reported that in only one office did the amount come to $2,000 annually and that it averaged but $850, yet Congress had refused to increase the compensation. Call and Ward, estimating their out-of-pocket costs at $1,160 annually merely to maintain the office, could not afford adequate clerical help.[61]

William McRee, who assumed the duties of surveyor general for the district covering Illinois, Missouri, and Arkansas, found an office with three clerks unequal to the task of supervising the annual surveys, recording them, meeting calls for renewal of plats issued previously, and overcoming "near ten years arrearages of other work on hand; which must be performed before either accuracy or promptness can characterize the operations of this office. . . ." Despite pressure from Senator Benton and a request from Commissioner Graham, however, Congress rejected legislation for a $1,700 increase in appropriation for clerical hire.[62]

Harried by the demands of settlers under an accelerating westward movement and by the continuing congressional call for retrenchment, Land Office administrators and the examiners who verified their records too frequently fell into the plight described by McRee a year later. He found but two ways to "get along"—either receive adequate funding to operate according to law or "secondly (and which is much the most convenient for him who chooses to have recourse to it) to receive the work, without examining it—And sign his name, without Knowing what is above it."[63]

Postmaster General John McLean, who ranked as the prime instance of Adams's toleration of political dissent, did establish an excellent administrative record. To the extent that work performance was influenced by increased staff, McLean's administration should have been notable. Under legislation of 3 March 1825, his force had been increased by two clerks, to a total of two assistants, a chief clerk, and twenty-six subordinate clerks. By the close of the Adams administration, he had been accorded nineteen additional clerks and two unclassified workers to open "dead letters." He was thus able to organize the department into three distinct branches—finance, appointments, and contracts. The finance unit, in turn, was subdivided into the specialized functions of bookkeeping, examining accounts, payment of contracts, prosecution of delinquents, and registering generalized records for the Treasury. The appointments branch was subdivided into three geographic sections for the collection of data on applications, examination of bonds, and preparation of letters of appointment. The contract branch advertised for bids, filed contracts, and checked on compliance. The chief clerk acted as general supervisor. He also handled much of the correspondence, including statements prepared for the president and Congress, and kept the accounts with banks.

By careful attention to accounts and greatly expanded routing, postal revenues under McLean's administration were increased from $1,114,344 in 1823 to $1,598,134 in 1828. Adams reported to Congress in 1825 that for the first time in many years, the revenues of the department exceeded its expenditures. That trend continued over the next two years but fell in 1828, as the president explained, largely because of a marked expansion of the range of service. The increased income permitted, and provided justification for, the elevation of McLean's salary to the level of a cabinet officer in 1827. It also financed a 41 percent addition to the number of post offices and a 30 percent extension in the mileage of post roads within the period 1823 to 1828.[64]

McLean not only expanded routes into the rapidly developing West; he also improved deliveries in frequency and dependability over the remainder of the nation. The legislation of 1825 had authorized personal delivery of city mail, at an additional charge of three cents an item—a practice that was already prevalent. At the same time the postmaster general introduced "Express Mail," a form of "Special Delivery." Poor roads, flooding streams, and washed-out bridges had long afforded excuses for delays of the mail. McLean alleviated the problem by allotting surplus revenues to road repair. Then, rejecting excuses, in 1826 he imposed penalties for "every failure, without regard to the cause producing it." Fines were to be increased for each seven minutes of delay, and failure to make a connection with a dependent line carried a threat of contract forfeiture. Quarterly review of accounts and careful check on such matters as franking records and newspaper transportation marked the close control over local offices. Theft was reduced by requiring that mail be carried in large portmanteaus, under special locks, which remained unopened between major distribution centers. In 1828 McLean proposed that "at some future time" the government might insure mail, "being authorized to charge a higher rate of postage in such cases. . . ."[65]

Contractors and postmasters were held answerable for public criticism of service. McLean was conscious of the value of good publicity upon the work of his department. The detail on the operations of the Washington staff, reported by "a friend" to the editor of the *National Intelligencer* in 1826, could have come only from an official source and suggests that at least one clerk must have devoted much of his time to counting the activities of personnel. Adams noted that the postmaster general's report of 1827 was "not backward in setting forth all these improvements. . . ."[66]

The promotional effort was effective. Adams himself praised McLean's administration so highly at that time that Barbour and the cabinet, generally, protested. The postmaster general's political allies in Congress needed little encouragement to laud his performance. He was the only department head who was not sweepingly criticized in the administrative review presented to Congress and the nation by the Jacksonian dominated Committee on Retrenchment in the spring of 1828.

The president, in his annual message of December 1827, had emphasized the need for "the strictest economy in the application of the public funds," if progress in retirement of the public debt were to be maintained. Using the recommendation as an introduction for summation of the administration's record in reduction of the debt, Adams in effect provided the basis for the opposition's demand for retrenchment. But the formation of the House Select Committee that prepared the highly critical report developed as a political aberration, which the Jacksonians themselves initially found embarrassing.

Thomas Chilton, a young physician from Elizabethtown, Kentucky, who had just entered the House of Representatives after winning a special election against an administration candidate, set out, apparently without organizational blessing, to prove the validity of the propaganda that was being bruited by his Jacksonian backers. In his maiden speech on January 22, he introduced resolutions calling upon the Committee of Ways and Means to report "what offices, in their opinion, . . . [could] be most advantageously discontinued, what salaries . . . [would] reasonably bear reduction, and such other means of retrenchment as to them seem[ed] necessary," so that the national debt might be discharged "without unavoidable delay." In his accompanying remarks he pointed to the long list of public officeholders, men, he had been informed, "who, to give the plain English of the matter, . . . [were] feasting and fattening upon the Treasury: rendering, in the mean time, no services, nor, indeed, having any to render to the country." Specifically, he cited the "crowded" Navy list, thirty to fifty West Point cadets, "educated at the expense of the government" but "destitute of employment"; "a fifth auditor," appointed for service no longer needed; and "in most of the public offices, more clerks . . . than . . . necessary to transact the business. . . ." He thought the salaries excessive, notably for members of Congress, "sitting . . . at their ease, receiving eight dollars per day for their services, and eight dollars for each twenty miles travelled, in reaching and returning from the seat of the General Government." A per diem of six dollars, he believed, would be quite ample. He deplored, too, the excessive use of public printing, especially in presentation of private claims, evidenced in documents that were piled each morning on "upwards of 200 tables" in the congressional hall. The nation, which currently could "just struggle on, gaining nothing upon the current," would be ill prepared, he concluded, to cope with any threat of war.[67]

His fellow congressmen did not welcome this attack upon their salaries. Criticism of the extent of public printing was no more popular with the Jacksonian leadership, since their editor, Duff Green, had garnered that political plum during the Twentieth Congress. Members of longer standing realized that Congress had itself authorized the hiring of the clerks and had fixed their salaries. Moreover, of the principal officers in government, the postmaster general alone had received an increase in salary during the Adams years. With some amusement, Barbour commented to the absent Clay on the Jacksonian reaction to Chilton's speech. Warning that "young Doctors always killed their patients," a colleague had complained that the parties were too evenly divided to permit "experiments—and he should not be surprised that by this tampering if Chilton killed them."[68]

The Jacksonian James Buchanan defended "with pride and pleasure the Third and Fifth Auditors, and the Postmaster General," as well as the Military Academy. He was opposed to the investigation. So, also, were George McDuffie, chairman of the Committee of Ways and Means, Samuel Ingham, John Floyd, and John Randolph—all of whom were hostile to the administration. Indeed, all but six of the forty-seven members who sought on January 24 to table the resolutions were identified with that opposition. Jacksonians readily seized upon the opportunity to air in open debate an assortment of political "scandals" that had been journalistically reported over the past three years— Adams's expense account in removing from St. Petersburg to London in 1815; his purchase of the billiard table and chessmen for the White House; the payment of expenses for the administration editor John H. Pleasants on an aborted errand as bearer of dispatches to South America, which had ended as a junket to England; the authorization of an outfit for John A. King as his father's successor in London; and the transfer of the stationery account of the Philadelphia customs house to John Binns. But throughout two weeks of unseemly wrangling, some four hundred columns of reported "debate," the administration's forces emerged as the proponents of a full inquiry, while the Jacksonian chairmen of the standing committees protested that they were too busy to undertake the task.[69]

However lightly Chilton's resolution was viewed as an item "for mere home consumption," it could not be ignored. Few congressmen of either party dared go on public record to table the proposal. Two such motions were overwhelmingly defeated. Finally, the Jacksonian leadership, through James Hamilton, Jr., of South Carolina, moved to substitute a resolution establishing a Select Committee to conduct the investigation. With passage of this amendment, Hamilton was named chairman of a seven-man committee which included only John Sergeant and Edward Everett of the administration forces and, conspicuously, excluded Chilton among the Jacksonians. The committee did not report until May 15, nine days before the close of the session, when majority and minority statements were filed. Both were designed to be carried to the hustings in the approaching campaign. They were never debated, but nine thousand copies were ordered to be printed for distribution.

Given the Jacksonian majority in the Twentieth Congress, the administration's early confidence that the committee must "find the most economical administration of the public offices since the establishment of the government" was a delusion. Complaining that the secretaries of the executive departments had been uncooperative by denying that they were overstaffed, the committee majority concluded that "at least one-third of the present number of clerks . . . might be reduced with safety to the public interest." The minority, on the other hand, saw no lack of cooperation in the fact that heads of departments who were frequently compelled to hire extra copyists from contingency funds should conclude that they could not reduce the permanent staff. The minority report pointed to excessive congressional calls for information as a heavy burden on the executive branch. Increased public services, which the Congress had also authorized, necessarily entailed expanded administration. Notwithstanding the immense growth of the nation, the per capita cost of government remained no greater than that of thirty years earlier or, indeed, of any intervening period. The expenses of the executive branch had increased much less than those of Congress over the years.[70]

The majority report, which assailed the administration, department by department, was answered by the minority with the same specificity. Criticisms of the State Department centered upon Clay's use of the contingency fund for foreign missions, out of which expenditures for secret service, bearers of dispatches, and the younger King's salary had been met. The institutional framework of this political attack upon the appointments of Cook, Pleasants, and King provided a ready mode of defense. Secret service, as an aspect of executive operations, dated from the founding of the nation and by its essence could not be publicly discussed. The dangers confronting the nation over the past decade had been "neither trifling nor remote." Therefore, the minority found it not surprising that there had been "a somewhat increased expenditure" from that fund. They had been defeated by the majority of the committee in efforts to extend the review to determine whether the engagements of such service had been initiated by the previous administration, and Clay's offer "to communicate in confidence to the Committee" the amount paid to Cook had been similarly rejected. The minority therefore "confidently" pronounced "their deliberate conviction" that the fund had been used properly.[71]

Use of bearers of dispatches, they explained, was a form of diplomatic courtesy in handling the exchange of treaties; hence, the increased number of such functionaries pointed to the activity of the administration in expanding the commercial role of the nation. Pleasants's accounts had, moreover, been adjusted to accord with his service performance—traveling expenses and a per diem which were limited to the period when he would have returned if he had come directly home. He had not been compensated as bearer of the dispatches that he had brought from Rufus King. The younger King's activities had been initiated and terminated during a congressional recess; hence, his appointment, which had been occasioned by the emergency of his father's "sickness," had been an appropriate exercise of executive authority. The majority of the committee, nevertheless, assumed the niggardly stance of demanding that John King refund his outfit and salary for 62 days' employment.

The "tedious process of auditing and adjusting" accounts in the Treasury, War, and Navy departments was criticized. Abolition of the Second Comptroller's Office, which litigated delinquent claims, was recommended, with a proposal that the attorney general assume the direction of all suits involving the national government. The minority, in response, pointed to the efficacy of the long-established system of checks, established by Congress, as security in Treasury operations. Conceding that a law officer should be attached to that department, they questioned whether the broad legal capabilities of the attorney general were required for that function. Since the fourth auditor, Tobias Watkins, was Adams's personal friend and a political "legman" for the administration, the committee focused attention on his record. His "extraordinary" contingency expenses, reckoned by the committee majority at $6,726.69 over the four years, were explained in the minority statement as a necessity occasioned by the hiring of extra clerks to handle accounts for expanded naval operations. The "most extraordinary" expenditures for newspapers and printing, cited by the majority in reference to the Treasury, were attributed to the costs of advertising the liquidation of the outstanding government bonds.

The Navy and War departments shared with State and Treasury criticism for expenditures on stationery, newspapers, and books—all in amounts so small as to be readily represented as the consequence of minor exigencies. The State Department had run advertisements in several journals—too few, indeed, to please the opposition editors—informing Santo Domingo claimants of French arrangements for their compensation. The Navy and State departments had provided newspaper subscriptions for their personnel abroad, two to each naval squadron. A War Department book purchase of $310, described by the majority as encompassing "politics, statistics, history, biography, and, theology," was identified as a file of *Niles' Register* and journals of religious and charitable associations for use in the Office of Indian Affairs. Expenditures of $1,000 for a medallion of President Adams, $3,190 for Indian portraiture, and $215 "for boot and shoe blacking for Indians" were attributed to the necessary and traditional outlays for Indian parlaying. Reference to the Winnebago and Creek crises countered particular criticism of Thomas L. McKenney's bill for $6,412, "for six months' service" in traveling to Green Bay and among the tribes of the South and Southwest, including distribution of presents to the amount "of something over 2,000 dollars" for which he submitted no vouchers.[72]

The reports yielded little groundwork for institutional revision. The majority called upon the executive officers themselves to institute "a judicious system of reform," which would reduce their staff but extend their hours of public access. Beyond that, the majority projected the introduction of legislation to abolish use of State Department contingency funds for secret service in peacetime, to provide for a more efficient system of accounting and collection of public moneys in the Treasury, to regulate the forage allowance in the army, to charge expenses for interpreters and Indian agencies to Indian annuities, and to encourage shorter sessions of Congress. Their report was particularly critical of the "pecuniary censorship of the press" that was exercised through the State Department, and it proposed a series of "reforms" to bring that patronage under congressional control.[73] For the most part, these were political recommendations which contemplated no major changes in administrative structure.

None were adopted. Late in April the committee reported resolutions that urged increased accountability in the Indian Department and the termination of congressional sessions on the last Wednesday in March. Both proposals were tabled. During the second session of the Twentieth Congress, which met after Jackson had been elected, the reports of the Retrenchment Committee were returned to that committee for development of the projected legislation. Eight bills, touching on many of the reforms that had been recommended by the majority, were subsequently reported. None were even debated. The final report of the committee, which was again brought before the House near the close of the session, recommended three resolutions emphasizing the importance of retrenchment, generally, so that the public debt might be paid "with all convenient despatch." That report, after brief discussion, was left in suspension as the session ended.[74]

The retrenchment investigation had been a partisan maneuver without relevance to the serious problems of administrative development for a growing nation. No legislation for restructuring the duties of the State Department or for expanding the office of the attorney general was introduced. Even the committee bill in reference to Treasury accounting ignored the manifest need for better customs supervision. The minority report, in countering with a point by point rebuttal of the majority's allegations, accorded a measure of legitimacy to the superficiality of the attack. The defense was on stronger ground when it protested the criticism of continuing Navy and War Department expenditures in time of peace as an attack upon basic policy decisions, centering upon the administration's commercial and internal-improvement efforts, which Congress had itself espoused. The committee majority was unprepared, in either 1828 or 1829, to endorse more than a general plea for speedier reduction of the national debt. The investigation indicated, more than anything else, that the political campaign of 1828 was to center in partisan-slanted criticism of disparate incidents rather than in debate upon coherently defined programmatic issues.

11

THE ART OF POLITICS

The heterogeneity that scholars have found in the Jacksonian attack upon the Adams presidency points, not to a lack of conflict over basic issues, but to the myriad forms of its expression. States' rights, as an ideologic ground of concern, was becoming increasingly important in southern regionalism. In the absence of an administration stand on slavery, States' rights surfaced in criticism of the Panama mission, Indian removal, and the domestic program generally. While the attachment of the Western States and the Middle States to *localized* improvements and to *specific* forms of tariff protection limited the range of this opposition to the administration's program, the qualifying adjectives were significant. In the same geographic areas, credit restraints of the Bank of the United States, land policy, and the marketing problems occasioned by commercial nationalism in the West Indies were counteractive irritants. Everywhere diverse social discontents, many but vaguely identified with generalized programmatic themes, surfaced out of the contemporary liberalization of the suffrage. Anti-intellectualism; criticism of the president's life style; protest against governmental authority, whether against the militia system or the disciplining of popular heroes; desire to rid the executive departments of entrenched officeholders, regardless of their merit—these were manifestations of the social unrest as expressed in Congress during the Adams years. At state and local levels, widely pervasive disestablishmentarianism assumed more varied forms. And individuals, with their coteries of supporters, very frequently pursued more personal ambitions that were unrelated to any attachment to policy.

Yet a common denominator of particularism characterized these disintegrating forces. Sectional or localized, group or individualistic, they were fundamentally antithetic to subordination under the generalities of nationalism. Even the egalitarianism that marked the social discontents expressed, for the most part, constricted perspectives, hostile toward the well-being of the "haves" but as yet projecting few alternatives for the "general good." The administration was not free from such special interests, but it repeatedly yielded them to the requirements of programmatic harmony—most notably, in foreign policy, on the West Indies trade and the protection of Cuba and, in domestic affairs, on the bankruptcy proposal and tariff legislation. The American System, which was designed to assure benefits for all, at the same time entailed sacrifices by all. It was vulnerable to particularistic attack, at some point in the blend, under every aspect of its program. Herein lay the issue conflict of 1828.

The triumph of so negative, querulous, and fragmented an opposition on such grounds in the years of the nation's jubilee required a masterly counterstructuring of discrete interests. John H. Eaton had set the pattern in his "Wyoming" letters of 1823. Eschewing programmatic stands, he had fixed upon a personality. Only Jackson of the "Leading Men of the Country" had achieved distinction as "a private citizen," untrammeled by ties of "party," "system," "intrigue," and "prejudice." "On nothing is he committed, and to none is he under obligation. . . . No parasite claims rest against him; he will be left free to administer the government, as his judgment and prudence may direct. . . ."[1] The issue conflict was to be resolved, for many participants unwittingly, as a "blank check" in a contest that evidenced newly developing skills in the art of politics.

A Calhounite endorsement of Jackson's candidacy had been projected months before Adams had assumed the presidency. It was evident in Duff Green's editorial comment of October 1824; in the pressure of Ingham, Isacks, and McDuffie to win Cook's vote in the House election; and in Richard M. Johnson's warning to Adams in January 1825. It was but thinly veiled in the February 11 prediction by Calhoun's friends that if Clay were named secretary of state, an opposition "would be organized from the outset; that the opposition would use the name of General Jackson as its head. . . ." On February 27 Rufus King commented to his son: ". . . a party is forming itself here to oppose Mr. Adams' administration. South Carolina is headquarters, and I understand that a Dinner takes place today [at] the Quarters of this

Delegation, when Gen'l Jackson, Mr. Calhoun . . . and others are to be guests. . . . This first step may serve to combine the malcontents."[2]

Jackson himself had joined with thirteen other Senators—his followers with those of Calhoun and Crawford—in opposing on March 7 the nomination of Clay to the State Department. All the way from Washington home to Nashville, the Tennessean reiterated charges of bribery and corruption, sealed, in his view, by Clay's appointment. A Nashville committee to organize Jackson's campaign for the next presidency was established during the summer of 1825. On October 6 the Tennessee legislature placed him in nomination for the campaign of 1828, and eight days later he accepted.

At the same time he once more resigned from the Senate, "a situation," he observed, "where temptation may exist and suspicions arise in relation to the exercise of an influence tending to my own aggrandisement." Earlier in its session the Tennessee Senate had begun consideration of a measure requesting the state's congressional delegation to work for adoption of a Constitutional amendment providing for popular election of the president and vice-president, "and thereby preclude all idea of fraud and combination in these elections." Jackson proposed an additional section that would bar any member of Congress from holding office, other than judicial appointment, under the federal government during the term for which he was elected and for two years thereafter. In presenting his recommendation, the general pointed specifically to the need that Congress be freed "from that connection with the Executive Department," which currently was giving "strong ground of apprehension and jealousy on the part of the people."[3]

The so-called Tennessee Amendment, under a variety of texts, was heatedly debated in both the House and the Senate throughout the first session of the Nineteenth Congress. On April 1 a select committee was named in the House to draw up the proposal, but six weeks later the committee, through McDuffie as chairman, reported its inability to agree upon any specific plan and asked to be discharged from further consideration of the matter. Motions for similar legislation in the Senate were finally tabled. Alexander Smyth of Virginia revived the recommendations in the House of Representatives in December 1827, but they were not debated until after the presidential election. Supported then by administration adherents, they remained under debate at the close of the session. The proposals had served their primary purpose in directing public attention to the Jacksonian campaign theme.

The addition of Van Buren's New York Regency forces and Crawford's Radicals to the Calhoun-Jackson alliance entailed complicated maneuvering. The Regency's blundering "over-kill" in removing

Clinton as one of the New York canal commissioners in the spring of 1824 had produced a reaction that carried "the father of the Erie" to the governor's chair in the popular acclaim that accompanied the opening of the waterway. Clinton had been one of the first to endorse Jackson's candidacy for the election of 1824, and if his own pretensions to the White House were to be set aside, Clinton stood among the general's principal adherents. Clinton's rejection of the proposal that he go to London as an Adams appointee made clear this stand. On the other hand, the anger of Regency supporters who had backed Crawford against Adams in the bitter New York electoral campaign forestalled their becoming attached to the administration. For nearly two years, advisers of the president pondered with uncertainty the strange reports of an opposing Clinton–Van Buren coalition.

Van Buren's course did not, in fact, remain so long undetermined. Outraged by the president's inaugural plea for political fusion, he bided his time until the reconvening of Congress and Adams's first annual message in December 1825. The president's espousal of the program of nationalism, particularly his focus upon federal aid for internal improvements, provoked Van Buren to action. He introduced resolutions stating that Congress lacked "the power to make Roads and Canals within the respective States" and calling for an amendment to the Constitution to define the authority of the legislative body on the matter and to subject it "to such restrictions as shall effectually protect the sovereignty of the respective States, and secure to them a just distribution of the benefits resulting from all appropriations made for that purpose." Since he quickly discovered, as he later observed, "that there was no reasonable hope for their success," he never brought the resolutions to debate.[4]

Whether the New Yorker's basic motivations were those of a pragmatic politician or a States' rights ideologue, he exploited the latter issue in developing the basis for assault upon the administration. On constitutional grounds also, he marshaled the attack upon the president's acceptance of the invitation to the Panama Congress. As a Crawfordite, Van Buren had not been on good terms with Calhoun, but shortly after Adams's announcement, the New Yorker approached Calhoun to discuss their mutual opposition to that project. Finding themselves in agreement and, through their control of the Senate Committee on Foreign Relations, in a position to assert their views, they initiated upon that proposal the first organized assault against the administration. In view of the mission's general popularity, they could hope for little more than delay in approving it; but in the course of debate, by blending the arguments of constitutional limitation and threat to slavery, they elaborated a basis of ideological harmony. By

January 1827, when Van Buren invited the collaboration of Thomas Ritchie and the Richmond Junto of Old Republican "Radicals," the fruit had ripened.

Local politics fed the developing alliance. In New York the announcement of Regency support for William B. Rochester's gubernatorial candidacy against Clinton, in the fall of 1826, served to win backing for Van Buren's reelection to the United States Senate but divided the considerable body of adherents that Adams had held among Federalist Clintonians. In Virginia, administration aid for John Tyler over John Randolph in the senatorial election of January 1827 contributed to Ritchie's determination to respond favorably to Van Buren's overture. By the following March, as Van Buren headed south to renew his old Crawford ties, Ritchie's *Enquirer* (Richmond, Va.) echoed the call to "Radical" supporters for union behind Jackson's candidacy, "upon the high grounds of the Constitution, and the interest of the country. . . ."[5] The New Yorker had small difficulty in winning Crawford's adherence. If Van Buren then relaxed his Calhoun ties, he merely sacrificed an opportunistic personal association for the broader base of a more longstanding regional commitment to his political organization.

While Van Buren contemplated this structure as a revived Jeffersonian alliance between the "planters of the South and plain Republicans of the North," Jackson's complaint of "bargain and corruption" carried an appeal to political outcasts generally. In the West the charge held special significance, not only as a direct assault upon the general's principal regional rival but also as a rationalization for the collapsing "relief" movement. Kentuckians, recalling Jackson's harsh criticism of their militia at New Orleans, had not been predisposed to his candidacy. Their legislature had nominated Clay for the campaign of 1824, and the instructions sent to Washington as an alternative after he had been eliminated from the race connoted little more than a preference for a regional candidate. They had not then known of Clay's endorsement of Adams. Moreover, the impetus for their action had been generated by relief partisans, who had been repudiated in the elections of the following summer. If Jackson were to carry Kentucky and Clay's northwestern adherents in 1828, the secretary of state must be discredited and his local opposition must be expanded.[6]

Generated primarily as a protest against judicial interpretation of the contractual protection under the federal Constitution, the relief agitation had been inherently identified with the cause of States' rights. Despite his avoidance of a public stand in the local conflict, Clay, by his Bluegrass political associations, his long business relationship with the second Bank of the United States, and his basic commitment to nationalism, personified the countering forces. By the fall of 1826, when the relief movement had been again repulsed in Kentucky, it posed a threat chiefly, as one of Clay's supporters warned, because "the Jackson interest is considered a kind of floating capital to be taken up by the party that will fight under his flag."[7]

Clay's erstwhile friends Amos Kendall and Francis Preston Blair, cast adrift politically and financially by their sympathy for the relief cause, turned to that banner during the closing years of the administration. In the fall of 1827 Kendall, as editor of the *Argus of Western America* (Frankfort, Ky.), began to publish a series of open letters, addressed to Clay, contending that the Kentucky delegation had been seduced to vote for Adams under assurance that Clay would become secretary of state. Blair even then professed "affections" for his old friend, but he lamented: "Alas! Alas! you have made sad work for the poor Republicans. Here we have been vanquished by division & the main body of us subjected, without a limitation on their power to the same masters who had driven us into a sort of rebellion."[8]

The defection of Kendall and Blair marked an expansion of Jackson's support into Clay's home base. Personal rivalry, States' rights, and social protest were thus blended in the Jacksonian opposition, blanketed under an assumption of old partisan identifications that concealed the novelty of the association. Unifying themes had been developed upon which to found an intersectional opposition of seemingly diverse and incompatible leadership.

Adams's response to this skillful honing of political knives was inept. Some analysts have seen his reluctance actively to seek reelection as a carryover of traditional ideals that "the office should seek the man." Nathan Sargent contemporaneously attributed the course to a difference in cultural attitudes of the North and the East from those of the South and the West. Jacksonian sympathizers, also identifying a moral imperative, have found that Adams was suffering from a guilty conscience in the aftermath of the 1824 election. More sympathetic interpreters have suggested that the president yielded to a fatalism that operated to discourage his active pursuit of the goal.[9]

Adams did have a strong sensitivity to ethical considerations and an exaggerated awareness of his own failings. He recognized his overweening ambition, and he had fervently craved the presidency. He had courted the support of cabinet colleagues Barbour and Southard during the months before the election. He had provided the necessary assurances to woo the wavering Federalist congressmen of New York and

Maryland. He had undoubtedly cemented Clay's proffered support by agreeing upon programmatic goals, and perhaps upon an official role for the Kentuckian. Yet, in all this, there is no evidence that he had surrendered his personal views on public policy.

Neither sense of moral guilt nor fatalism was necessary to indicate that his administration stood little chance of extending beyond a single term. Since December 1824 it had been apparent that whoever assumed the presidency would serve as a minority choice; he would necessarily embrace some coalition, *in the national interest*. Adams had hoped to win cooperation from all the rival candidates, yet before he entered the White House he knew that Jackson, Calhoun, and Crawford were consolidating in opposition. The attack upon Adams's first annual message made clear that there was to be no balanced assessment of his program. He had concluded by the summer of 1826, as he was planning for the disposition of his father's property, that he would have need "within two or three years" for "a place of retirement." With deteriorating health throughout the spring of 1827—sleeplessness, habitual constipation, indigestion, lack of appetite, "uncontrollable dejection of spirits"—he conceded that Van Buren had "now every prospect of success in his present movements. . . ." Adams's "own career" was "closed." "My anticipations for the two succeeding years call for more than Stoic fortitude."[10]

Had he believed counterattack feasible, it is questionable that Adams possessed the will or the skills to organize such a movement. His father's rejection in the presidency haunted John Quincy's memory. ". . . I will sooner turn scavenger and earn my living by clearing away the filth of the streets, than plunge into this bottomless filth of faction . . . ," young Adams had written in 1801. And the old man had reinforced those sentiments in warnings against a public career as his son advanced in diplomatic attainments. The Adamses, John Quincy had been reared to believe, were a breed apart, whose values the world did not share. His wife, Louisa, commiserated with their son in February 1829, by reiterating the lesson: "Our tastes, our tempers, our habits vary so much from those of the herd that we can never be beloved or admired, but," she exhorted, "we may and must be respected—unless we forget the respect we owe ourselves."[11]

During his brief experience as the recipient of popular mandate for public office, from 1803 to 1808, John Quincy had demonstrated a reckless independence of outlook, an appeal to reason in defense of his views, a restraint toward those who opposed him, and a proud withdrawal in the face of defeat. In the presidency he pursued much the same course. Viewing his first annual message to Congress as the appropriate occasion for an all-encompassing "avowal of general principles," he had not hesitated to embrace the controversial issue of the constitutional powers of the federal government. His plea that popular representatives "in the career of public improvement" rise above political constraints, unrestrained by regard for the will of their constituents, evidenced little responsiveness to popular criticism. When Clay warned that "misrepresentations" of the president's Ghent accounts were undermining the administration's support in Kentucky, Adams declined to clarify the matter to an "electioneering committee":

> I was aware that it is the usage in Kentucky for candidates to offices conferred by the suffrages of the people to offer themselves and solicit votes—a natural consequence of which is, that they are called to account before the people, and to answering charges against them, or enquiries made of them, respecting their conduct or principles. But this has not been customary with reference to the office of President of the United States, and I should not be willing to set the precedent.[12]

Clay, but not Adams, assumed the burden of responding, in public statement as well as by duel, to the charges of their joint involvement in "bargain and corruption."

Always the president held himself stiffly, awkwardly, aloof from the political hustings. In the months before his election he had known of the partisan efforts in his behalf in the factionally divided Middle States and had rallied his supporters to stand firm, but how little control he maintained over such friendly interests was evident in their abandonment of his vice-presidential preference and their belated explanation of the decision. While he had visited with Boston backers nearly every day during the summer of 1824, he had refused to permit the honor of a public dinner. Despite pleas from friends along the route on his annual return to Quincy, he continued to decline such ceremonies until his father's death occasioned the justification of a memorial homage. Although he acknowledged his authorship of the anonymous article explaining the colonial-trade issue for the *American Quarterly Review,* published by his friend Robert Walsh, Jr., he never admitted participation in the political journalism, commonly attributed to him, by which "Patrick Henry" in the summer of 1826 assailed Calhoun's partiality as presiding officer of the Senate.

Adams not only rejected but also found difficulty in projecting popular communication. He had had laboriously to explain his obscure allusion to "Ebony and Topaz" at a banquet in Baltimore, where he likened the coat of arms of a British officer who had been killed in the

Battle of Bladensburg to the symbolism of good and evil in a work by Voltaire. Like his metaphoric reference to astronomical observatories as "lighthouses in the sky," the phrase became the subject of journalistic ridicule. His diary account of his performance at the dedication of the Chesapeake and Ohio Canal revealed his self-consciousness during such appearances: "As has happened to me whenever I have had a part to perform in the presence of multitudes, I got through awkwardly, but without gross and palpable failure." The incident with the stump, he noted, had "struck the eye and fancy of the spectators more than all the flowers of rhetoric . . . and diverted their attention from the stammering and hesitation of a deficient memory."[13]

His announced approach to counteract his minority status had been to draw upon all factions, "discarding every remnant of rancor against each other, of embracing as countrymen and friends, and of yielding to talents and virtue alone that confidence which in times of contention for principle was bestowed only upon those who bore the badge of party communion."[14] With the offer of cabinet appointments having been rejected by Crawford and Jackson, he had yet wooed their supporters to public office—notably such Crawfordites as Barbour, Sam Smith, Louis McLane, Bartlett Yancy, John Williams, Shadrach Bond, and Burgess Thomas and the Jacksonians Samuel R. Overton, Francis W. Armstrong, and De Witt Clinton. Other Clintonians called to the administration effort included John W. Taylor, Jacob Brown, and Alfred Conkling; but in responding to Clinton's rejection of the diplomatic post at London, Adams turned to Rufus King, the New York governor's bitter opponent. The appointment of King, above all, however, accorded recognition to a Federalist leader, and subsequent appointments to half a dozen other prominent Federalists further upheld the president's preelection commitment. Calhoun partisans—Southard, McLean, Poinsett, and Beaufort T. Watts—likewise found tolerant acceptance.

The patronage of Federalists posed particular problems. Long stripped of power, Federalists pressed their demands ubiquitously. Yet the bitterness of old party divisions and the factional splits among Federalists themselves raised controversy in all efforts to appease them. Adams complained that "upon the occasion of appointments to office . . . all the wormwood and the gall of the old party hatred ooze[d] out." Wherever there was a vacancy to be filled, he found that some distinguished Federalist was being urged as a candidate—"always well qualified, sometimes in an eminent degree, and yet so obnoxious to the Republican party that he cannot be appointed without exciting a vehement clamor against him and against the Administration."[15]

The appointment of the Federalist Rufus King was bitterly assailed by Clintonians, as well as by Republicans generally. The subsequent naming of the Clintonian and former Federalist Alfred Conkling to the judgeship of the Northern District of New York mollified leaders like Ambrose Spencer and John W. Taylor, who shared his factional identification, but further outraged Republicans who had given Adams the vote of the Empire State. Lieutenant Governor James Tallmadge, in disgust, observed to Thurlow Weed that Adams was pursuing a steady course of buying up old enemies; but, Tallmadge asked, would he thus ''succeed to keep old friends. . . ?''[16]

Perhaps because of the vehemence of the protest over the New York appointments, the president named to office only one other Federalist, John Sergeant, delegate to the Panama mission, before the closing months of his incumbency. Adams yielded to moderates of the party, who warned that the elevation of extremists like James Kent, a former judge of the New York court of chancery, would be politically disastrous. Charles King advised: ''tho' no one can more heartily approve the principle promulgated by you, of choosing your officers without reference to party, than myself—I would not desire to see it pushed too far or on occasions when some harm & no particular good may result from its application.'' King and Alexander H. Everett blocked support also for Joseph Blunt, who had been among Adams's most ardent New York adherents. Despite the important role of Henry Warfield in conveying the Maryland vote, he pled his cause vainly to both Adams and Clay over the next three years. Webster himself had to relinquish hope for appointment as minister to England, because the administration, as Joseph Hopkinson dourly observed, considered the Boston Federalist ''perfectly secured in the service.''[17]

The delay in recognizing the judicial merits of Hopkinson, a Philadelphia lawyer, former congressman, and Federalist leader, occasioned bitter recriminations. Entreaties in his behalf had been pressed early in Monroe's administration, and they increased with the declining health of Richard Peters, judge of the eastern district of Pennsylvania. Such illustrious Federalist jurists as John Marshall, Joseph Story, and Bushrod Washington urged Hopkinson's cause. Walsh, editor of the influential National Gazette (Philadelphia), a Federalist organ, had himself earlier hoped for nomination to a foreign post, but in the spring of 1827 he came to Washington to plead on behalf of his friend. Webster, noting that some forty to fifty thousand former Federalists in Pennsylvania were greatly influenced by the editor, also brought the matter to the president's attention. But Clay, upon the advice of Pennsylvania Republicans, discouraged the appointment, and this view prevailed. Both Hopkinson and Walsh were outraged.[18]

Adams finally proffered the judgeship to Hopkinson, in October 1828, when the action could no longer affect the election. Sending the nomination to the Senate for confirmation in December, Adams submitted with it proposals to appoint two other Federalists, Nathan Smith as district attorney of Connecticut and Clay's friend John J. Crittenden as a member of the Supreme Court. All were challenged. The first two were finally carried, that for Hopkinson only after three attempts; the Crittenden nomination was tabled.

Disappointed Federalists frequently turned to the Jacksonians. Elias Kent Kane, who was active in opposition to the administration as senator from Illinois after 1825, had earlier that year failed in an effort to win the New York postmastership for his father. Richard Stockton and his son Robert, leaders of the New Jersey Federalists and owners of the *New Jersey Patriot*, had vigorously campaigned for Adams in 1824 and for administration candidates in local elections during the summer of 1826; but when the elder Stockton failed to win appointment to the district judgeship in the autumn of the latter year, they promptly endorsed Jackson's presidential candidacy. As they left the administration camp, they carried most of the remaining Federalists in the state to the opposition.[19]

Federalists were not, of course, the only disgruntled office seekers. Dabney Smith Carr, Samuel Smith's nephew and a grandnephew of Jefferson, failing as a candidate to replace Christopher Hughes at Stockholm, founded the *Republican and Commercial Advertiser* (Baltimore, Md.) as a Jackson organ in 1827. James G. Brooks, a poet and literary editor, unsuccessfully solicited the post as secretary of legation in Colombia before joining the staff of the strongly Jacksonian *Morning Courier* (New York). Gideon Welles, who had supported Jackson's candidacy in 1824, sought to become either a bearer of dispatches or a secretary to Gallatin. When Welles's services were rejected, he acquired part ownership of the *Times and Advertiser* (Hartford, Conn.) and pledged it as early as 1826 to Jackson's cause. Amos Kendall, Clay's erstwhile journalistic henchman, was among the more venal of these petitioners. With pledges that if "employed in the Administration, . . . [he] should certainly not write against it" and that with sufficient funding, either by loan or public appointment, he would retire from involvement as a leader of the Kentucky relief movement, he finally declined the secretary of state's unsatisfactory proposal. Stiffly Clay responded that "unless a clerkship should be created or become vacant," he could offer Kendall nothing other than that which had been rejected.[20]

Administration supporters, more dedicated to the cause, remained in the fold but also voiced chagrin. Those from New York and Pennsylvania, states that had long resented the dominance of Virginians in the

Republican party, introduced a strongly factional demand extending beyond mere resentment over Federalist appointments. Henry Wheaton had applied for the judgeship that went to Conkling. Wheaton's friends suggested also that he might be named to the missions at Mexico or Brazil: "He has been useful, in our late struggles to sustain ourselves in this state and he ought to be sustained for future usefulness." He was finally sent as chargé to Denmark in 1827, but he had no great enthusiasm for so minor a post. Thurlow Weed, to whom went much of the credit for Adams's defeat of the Crawfordites in the New York electoral campaign, sought only a contract to publish the laws in his *Rochester* (N.Y.) *Telegraph* and a minor postal appointment. Despite a visit to Washington, he found the president cool to his pleas. Lieutenant Governor Tallmadge, in recommending both Wheaton and Weed, reminded Adams of the importance "that firm & fast *friends* of the present administration be timely posted advantageously before public observation, to act as centinels [sic] to aid in the formation of public opinion."[21]

When Tallmadge further pursued the matter in a letter to Clay, the latter responded for himself and the president, expressing regret "that any conception should be taken up in N. York that he intended to neglect or abandon his friends and woo his enemies." Arguing that the nomination of Clinton represented a "complement [sic] . . . as much to the State as to the person," Clay begged, in the spring of 1826, "that there should not be formed any precipitate judgments." Six months later he was still explaining, in reference to the administration's awareness "of the unfriendly dispositions of some of the Federal officers" at Philadelphia and elsewhere, that the president had been "very unwilling to exercise his dismissing power merely from the fact of the indulgence of individual opinion without some malfeasance." Clay agreed that "moderation and forbearance . . . was the true policy for him [Adams] at the commencement of his administration, as it would be throughout, if violence and intemperance should not render a departure in some instances necessary." By October 1826, the secretary of state believed it time for "serious consideration, if some examples . . . [were] not called for in Philada."[22]

His correspondent, Richard Peters, Jr., himself of Federalist background, agreed. So, also, did Peter Paul Francis Degrand, a Boston merchant and banker, one of the president's personal adherents, who, as early as the summer of 1825, reported encountering complaints all the way from Boston to Washington that only opponents of the administration were receiving its countenance. By 1827 Degrand had established correspondence with Clay and was pressing upon him, with particular reference to Pennsylvania, the urgency of a more vigorous political stand: "The Genl. Govt. have C. House Officers & Post Masters, in every part of the state.—*Let their course demonstrate that they look to their open & avowed friends, to fill the Places.* . . ." Unless the administration dared to produce "excitement in the State," it would be assumed to support Jackson. If they were accused of partisanship, so much the better: "It animates all to become 'partisans.'—& it is but fair we shd. meet 'Partisans' of Jackson, by 'Partisans' of Adams."[23]

Samuel Foot, in Connecticut, warned that Federalists should not be "forgiven, without some evidence of Repentance & reformation, neither of which have been shown or even professed. . . ." Governor Kent of Maryland, who himself complained that his state had "received nothing from Mr. Adams . . . during his administration . . . ," forwarded the plea of a member of the Maryland Executive Council: ". . . we never shrink from Enemies or abandon our friends, but we expect sometimes to be gratified in preference to our Enemies and the Enemies of our administration." A North Carolinian noted that Adams's neglect of his friends was harmful, "particularly so, as Executive favors have always been dealt out sparingly and unequally in this State." A South Carolina supporter argued: "If the Administration *would have friends*, it *must make friends.*" Georgians called for cleaning out the Crawfordite customs collectors at St. Mary's. George Poindexter, in Mississippi, who had campaigned actively for Adams's election in 1824, lamented that one of but two or three people he knew who were opposed to the administration had just received an executive appointment. Ninian Edwards, in Illinois, announcing his determination to remain uncommitted on the next election, protested that the time was at hand "when the wisdom of Mr. Jeffersons course in regard to the patronage of the administration must become too obvious to be any longer neglected." Friends of the administration, as one correspondent summarized the situation, felt neglect "from one end of the continent to the other."[24]

In this situation, Clay was becoming increasingly restive. Appeals to him from Adams's adherents, as well as from his own, voiced, with mounting urgency, the demand for a more partisan stance. From Lexington, Clay's long-time friend and colleague at Transylvania University, Dr. Benjamin W. Dudley, warned that the administration could not hope for "a fair trial of its policy" when its local officials were arrayed against its measures: "The correct policy of vacateing [sic] all offices held by individuals hostile to the administration, & who take advantage of their situation to prejudice the public mind against its measures cannot be questioned." Another former Lexington associate, William W. Worsley, founder of the *Kentucky Reporter,* Clay's home organ, who was now about to establish the *Focus* (Louisville) in support of the administration, stressed the "immense importance" of giving patronage "to its *decided* friends in place of its enemies or its lukewarm friends." "A contrary course," he continued, "has in no instance within my knowledge conciliated an enemy, but has, I am apprehensive, in many cases made friends who would otherwise have been ardent and enegertic [sic], a good deal cold in the cause." In the summer of 1826 Henry Shaw, a Clayite Republican from western Massachusetts, who never had liked Adams and continued to distrust him, revived a correspondence with the Kentuckian which was highly critical of the president and his Federalist ties. Some of Clay's adherents were deserting the cause, partly because they disapproved of such connections, partly "because they . . . [thought] Mr. Adams' re-election doubtful or impossible and wish[ed] to be on the strong side." By 1827 others were talking of running the secretary of state in place of Adams in the coming election.[25]

Still, Clay refused to countenance defection. In January 1827 he expressed concern to one of his Kentucky supporters, at the "attempt which is there making to separate the case of Mr. Adams" from himself: "We are both guilty or both innocent of the calumnies which have been propagated against both. . . ." He should "be compelled to regard a decision of K. against Mr. A." as a personal condemnation. Later that spring, Clay rejected the suggestion that he might replace Adams as the candidate of New York adherents. The actions of the Jacksonians had left him "no wish but for Mr. Adams's re-election," he maintained. "By their calumnies they have completely identified us; and I hope every friend I have will see in Mr. Adams re-election my interests as much involved, as if by [sic] name were directly held up for the Presidency."[26]

Clay's identification with the issue did, however, induce him to seek a more active political stand. His long service as Speaker of the House of Representatives had made him well aware of the congressional contribution to a successful administration and of the importance of politics in congressional operations. With his and Webster's support, John W. Taylor had been elected Speaker of the Nineteenth Congress, by a margin of five votes on the second ballot. In view of Taylor's Federalist antecedents and his pronounced opposition to slavery, evidenced during the Missouri controversy, his election had not been easy. Through his control of the speakership and the committee appointments that it dispensed, he represented the administration's power in the lower house as it entered office. There was little margin for increased dissatisfaction if that control were to be preserved.

In the Senate there was none. Vice-President Calhoun, as presiding officer, used his authority effectively to counter the administration. His refusal to curb outrageous personal abuse in debate having culminated in the Clay-Randolph duel, the Senate, on 15 April 1826, rescinded the rules that placed under his control the supervision of the "Journal" and the power of appointing committees. He had previously assigned to the administration a majority on eight of the fifteen standing committees; but the important Foreign Relations, Finance, Agriculture, Military Affairs, Naval Affairs, Indian Affairs, and Judiciary committees were controlled by the opposition. A very large preponderance of Jackson's supporters comprised the Select Committee on Constitutional Revision. After the change in rules on committee selection, midway in the Nineteenth Congress, the administration gained a majority on all standing committees; but its hold was tenuous, with support from only twenty-three of the forty-two senators. The defection or absence of but a few members could produce, as on the woolens bill in February 1827, a tie vote, giving the vice-president the power to block action. The elections for the Twentieth Congress would be crucial to any further program development, whatever they might bode for the presidential conflict of 1828.

Reporting a "general conviction" in the cabinet that the time had come when "the principle ought to be steadily adhered to of appointing only friends to the Administration in public offices," Clay discussed the policy with the president. Adams reiterated his opposition "to giving any public pledge" on that course. He protested the "tendency of our electioneering to venality . . ."; he would "not encourage it." Shortly thereafter he also declined to appear at the celebration of the beginning of the Pennsylvania Canal, where his supporters anticipated that his fluency in German might have good effect. "Electioneering," he explained, suited neither his taste nor his principles. Without apparently recognizing the significance of the imminent congressional contests, he complained fretfully that although the presidential campaign was "still more than eighteen months distant," "politics and electioneering topics appear to be almost the only materials of interesting discourse to men in the public service."[27]

The adjournment of Congress in March 1827, nevertheless, signaled the beginning of a more vigorous reaction. Van Buren's departure for the South gave warning of his developing intersectional alliance. The administration, having gained ultimate victory on the Panama issue in both houses during the first session of the Nineteenth Congress, had lost crucial contests during the second session—notably its recommended legislation on the colonial trade, a naval academy, bankruptcy, and the woolens tariff. It had also suffered defeat in several early midterm elections. As a final precipitating event, during the closing days of the session, Jacksonians had shocked their opponents by rejecting renewal of the contract with Gales and Seaton, editors of the *National Intelligencer* (Washington), as printers for the Senate. In doing so, Van Buren and his allies had boasted of the power that anticipated majorities in both houses of the ensuing Congress would give them to control journalistic patronage. During the course of the debate, the New Yorker's advocacy of "judicious revision of the laws relative to the public printing at large" became the basis for a strong journalistic counterattack.[28]

The editors of the *National Intelligencer*, discounting personal interest and withholding formal endorsement of Adams's candidacy, began a series of articles that specifically criticized Van Buren and his leadership in generating "an organized Opposition" to the administration, with the object of putting it down, "right or wrong." The editors published a report from Harrisburg stating that the *Pennsylvania Intelligencer* had been assured of "patronage . . . increased to double its extent" if it would support Jackson; "if not, that . . . $2000 should be applied to establishing a Press to answer those purposes, and crush them." The *True American* (Trenton, N.J.) was also quoted in a warning that Jacksonians had $50,000 available for such employment. "It is thus," the Trenton journalist had advised, "that the leaders of the Opposition (not the People) are determined to control public opinion, and corruptly elevate themselves to office, over the ruins of those who now preside over the Nation." Commenting upon these reports, the Washington editors observed that, if true, they made clear "where the epithets of Coalition, corruption, &c. *properly* belong." Only "veteran traders in politics . . . could contrive such a plan for subsidizing the press, where it is venal, and breaking it down where it cannot be seduced."[29] Charges of corruption and thwarted popular will were a refrain that was not to be limited to Jacksonian voices.

The secretary of state was not prepared to abandon political effort, and he had not given up hope for success. During the spring of 1827 he received an apparently concerted range of reports on the views encountered by congressional adherents en route to their home districts. Webster delayed his journey at Baltimore, "mainly for the purpose of seeing some of our friends. . . ." "Indeed," he added, "some pains were taken to bring them together."[30] Over the succeeding weeks, Clay maintained a close correspondence with the Massachusetts congressman, who had served as the administration's majority leader, and with John Sergeant, who at this time was a candidate for the Twentieth

Congress, where he would take over Webster's role as the latter moved into the Senate. Clay sketched not only the organizational framework for the Harrisburg Convention but also, the following September, a plan for setting up local and state committees to collect and disseminate political information. He was himself supplying such data and editorial copy to friendly journalists. His annual return to his home that summer encompassed a particularly heavy speaking schedule directed to advocacy of a stronger protective tariff. Diverted from this theme by renewed Jacksonian charges of corrupt bargaining, he responded with a ringing demand, in a major address at Lexington, that the general produce his evidence. At the end of the year, Clay published the first of two lengthy compendia documenting his defense.

Barbour, Southard, and Rush joined this political activity. Despite the secretary of war's earlier Crawford ties, his support of the administration was enthusiastic. In November 1826 he had voluntarily undertaken a defense of the president's first annual message, for insertion in the *National Intelligencer* (Washington) as a response to persistent criticism by Ritchie's *Enquirer* (Richmond, Va.). Honored by a public dinner at Annapolis in June 1827, Barbour again attacked the "public journals" which had "become mere vehicles of unfounded slander." Like Clay, he rallied friends in Virginia and Kentucky to organize for Adams's reelection. When a Virginia State convention of Adams supporters in January 1828 sought to enlist Madison's consent to head their list of electors, Barbour urgently reinforced their appeal, as a measure to "save the Republic" in its hour of "greatest danger."[31]

Southard maintained particularly close contact with local political developments in New Jersey and Virginia, where his brother in the former state and a brother-in-law in the latter kept him abreast of events. His longstanding personal rivalry with Mahlon Dickerson, prominent as a Jacksonian senator, gave added impetus to Southard's activity. Congressional elections as early as 1826 in New Jersey had centered upon the presidential alignments, and Southard's efforts contributed to a reversal of the Jacksonian victory of 1824. The navy secretary kept up an extensive political correspondence, generated funding for New Jersey editors sympathetic to the administration, occasionally himself wrote items for inclusion in local newspapers, and, as an adjunct to his official tours of port facilities, found a wide range of opportunities to enter into partisan gatherings outside Washington. As Barbour sought to draw Madison to the administration cause, Southard undertook, by personal visits and letters, to win Monroe's endorsement.

Rush also wrote voluminously in public defense of the administration. Shortly after entering the cabinet, he had published a piece under the pseudonym "Fox," which appeared first in the *National Journal* (Washington) and subsequently as a pamphlet, hailing the election of Adams by the House of Representatives as an institutional expression of the popular will. Throughout 1827 Rush supplied anonymous newspaper articles upholding the administration's program and, upon George Canning's death that summer, issued a pamphlet, "Sketch of the Character of Mr. Canning," which attributed the suspension of the West Indies trade to the British foreign minister's intransigence. Under Rush's exposition the American stand was applauded as a commitment to reciprocity in trade and to international justice. With his nomination to the vice-presidency early in 1828, the secretary of the Treasury abandoned campaign journalism as inappropriate to his position, but during the following summer he again returned to the *National Journal*, now under the pseudonym "Julius," to respond to slanderous personal attacks by John Randolph in congressional debates over the previous two years.

Rush's most notable efforts were the extended comments that he incorporated into his annual Treasury reports in explication of the American System. Adams acclaimed them as "very well written," the first since Hamilton's that were of "marked superiority." The German political economist Friedrich List, in an address before the Pennsylvania Society for the Encouragement of Manufactures in 1827, praised Rush's 1826 report extravagantly: "all those who are friendly to American prosperity, estimate the Finance Report of this gentleman as a worthy counterpart to Hamilton's celebrated work. . . ." Rush, who greatly admired and publicly endorsed the first Treasury secretary's efforts as a "guiding light over the path of his successors," had the political wisdom to withhold those views until after the presidential election.[32]

The emerging political role of the secretaries brought them under attack in congressional debate as early as February 1827. The editor of the *United States Telegraph* (Washington) some months later castigated Adams for permitting "his Secretaries to quit their official posts, and neglect the business of the nation, for the purpose of making electioneering journies, attending barbecues, and addressing inflammatory addresses to the people." Clay's and Southard's ill health during the summer of 1828 was described as a *"political phthisis,"* an excuse for campaigning outside Washington. "The present perambulating cabinet have most *convenient* constitutions," railed Duff Green, the editor. Ritchie, of the *Enquirer* (Richmond, Va.), dubbed them "the travelling Cabinet," and under that headline the Jackson press made much of the fact that in August of the election year, Adams was in New England, Southard in New Jersey, and Barbour and Clay in the West. By

September the *Eastern Argus* (Portland, Me.) found the cabinet "scattered up and down, here and there, in this State and that, from the President down to most of the Secretaries, sub-Secretaries, and under clerks, for the *ostensible purpose of visiting friends!*" "Certain it is," ran the tune, "that the public interests have been most shamefully neglected. . . ."[33]

Clay's patronage arrangements were, however, the focus of the electioneering criticism. At the urging of Thomas Hart Benton, a specially formed Senate Committee on Reduction of the Patronage requested in 1826 that the heads of departments supply information on the number of their employees (a regular statement in the course of events); their salaries, distinguishing the "compensation prescribed by law, and that which . . . [was] dependent on the will of the President, or the Officer at the head of either of the Departments"; the amount spent for printing over the current and the past three years; and a list of the newspapers that carried the laws or public advertisements "by authority." On the basis of their investigations, the members of Benton's committee proposed half a dozen bills to regulate governmental publication; the appointments of postmasters, cadets, and midshipmen; and the dismissals of army and navy officers by the executive. The legislation was tabled, but the responses to the resolutions were published, thus serving to emphasize the patronage opportunities of the administration.[34]

Clay's report, listing the publishers of the laws comparatively between the Eighteenth and the Nineteenth congresses, revealed that the printing had been shifted from ten of seventy-six journals, while several had been added to the list. Most notably, John Binns's *Democratic Press* (Philadelphia) had been substituted for John Norvell's *Franklin* (Pa.) *Gazette*, an organ partially owned by Samuel Ingham; in Charleston, South Carolina, the *City Gazette* had supplanted the *Patriot*, backed by Hayne and McDuffie; in Washington, the *National Journal*, Adams's organ, had replaced the *National Intelligencer*, which had supported Crawford's presidential candidacy; and in Tennessee the *Sparta Review* and the *Nashville Republican*, both Jacksonite, had given way to the *Jackson Gazette* and the *Nashville Whig*, which endorsed the administration.[35]

To a degree, those alterations in patronage represented a normal shifting in response to electoral results, but Clay's addition of six more changes during the fall of 1827 was retaliatory for persistent abuse of the administration. In Portland, Maine, the *American Patriot* replaced Todd and Smith's *Eastern Argus*; in Concord, the *New Hampshire Journal* supplanted the Hills's *New Hampshire Patriot*; the *Western Virginian*

(Charleston), founded as an administration organ, took over from the *Intelligencer* (Clarksburg); in South Carolina, the *Winyaw Intelligencer* (Georgetown) replaced the *Messenger* (Pendleton); in Indiana, the *Western Register* (Terre Haute) was substituted for the *Western Sun* (Vincennes); and at Frankfort, Kentucky, Amos Kendall's *Argus of Western America* gave way to the *Commentator.* Congressman Romulus Saunders of North Carolina, in proposing a resolution that Clay report the alterations of newspaper patronage for 1827 with "the reason for each change," precipitated a bitter month-long debate.

Admittedly the payment for public printing was a slight sum. Including the supplementary advertising of governmental notices, it amounted to from $20,000 to $30,000 in total amount for the eighty-two newspapers then publishing "by authority," an average of about $240 apiece. Supporters of the administration argued that no journalist of integrity would sell his endorsement for so paltry a benefit. But Saunders contended that the existence of such favoritism posed a threat to all who hoped to obtain printing contracts: "It was thus calculated to operate, and did actually operate, so far as it went to control the freedom of the press, and to enlist throughout the country that powerful instrument in behalf of the views of the State Department."[36]

Even the president's attempt to relax partisan distinctions and his general restraint on removals from office became, in this context, a suppositious basis for criticism. Emphasizing the minority status of the administration, James Hamilton, Jr., of South Carolina explained that "should there be three parties in the country, one of superior force, or of nicely balanced strength with their own, and a third of inferior numbers," such a government would cast their appointments, "even to the exclusion of their friends, in the ranks of this third party." Whenever there was an office to be filled or patronage to be dispensed, there would be found "great hesitation and delay, a perfect survey of the whole ground, and, very often, after a procrastination greatly prejudicial to the public interests, distinguished talents and long tried service . . . made to give way . . . , and sometimes even a zealous, constant, and faithful friend . . . compelled to yield to a mushroom apostate, that may have been purchased but yesterday."[37]

The debate ended without action. It had served only as an additional sounding board for partisan argument. It did not deter Clay, who, before the sitting of the Twentieth Congress, shifted the printing from six more journals and, in 1828, from four others. In this way he promoted the development of an administration press, as in the support of Thurlow Weed's *Rochester* (N.Y.) *Telegraph* and of William W. Worsley's *Focus* (Louisville, Ky.); he also repudiated the defectors, notably Simon Cameron's *Pennsylvania Intelligencer* (Harrisburg).

Opposition criticism of departmental subscriptions pointed to another, though certainly minor, form of journalistic patronage. On Clay's order the State Department, in the spring of 1825, started subscribing to the *Kentucky Reporter* (Lexington), the *Morning Post and Commercial Advertiser* (Louisville, Ky.), the *Supporter* (Chillicothe, Ohio), the *Intelligencer* (Petersburg, Va.), the *Indiana Journal* (Indianapolis), the *Nashville* (Tenn.) *Whig*, and the *Village Record* (West Chester, Pa.). In 1826 he added two subscriptions to Sylvester S. Southworth's *Literary Cadet* (Providence, R.I.).

The political motivation in such action was apparent in Webster's efforts in behalf of the *Patriot* (Baltimore, Md.). Isaac Munroe, editor of that journal, had been so greatly distressed at his failure to obtain a contract to publish the laws that he had requested to be informed who had successfully pressed the claims of the rival *American* (Baltimore). Clay refused to release such information; and the *American*, which was backed by Samuel Smith, Peter Little, John Barney, and Joseph Kent, among other Maryland political leaders, retained the printing throughout the administration. In March 1827, however, Webster urged Adams personally to subscribe to Munroe's journal: "The giving of such a direction would, I think, be a useful thing and have a healing tendency." Two days later, Webster, reminding Clay of the resentment that was prevalent in Baltimore over the closing of the West India trade, elaborated upon this explanation: "The Proprietors & Editors of the Public Journals are, generally, well disposed; but they are not willing to *take a side*, & to make their papers political papers." The grievances of Munroe, on being deprived of the public printing, had *"neutralized"* him as well, "& all the rest were *neutral* before." Webster had acted "to change this *neutrality* of the *Patriot* into active support. . . ."[38]

Through his ties to New England commercial and manufacturing interests, Webster had access to financial support, which Clay in the fall of 1827 sought to channel to needy journalists who were backing the administration. A year earlier, John H. Pleasants, editor of the *Constitutional Whig* (Richmond, Va.), had begged the president for funds to pay his debts, amounting to some $3,000 in numerous small obligations. The *Whig*, Charles Hammond's *Liberty Hall and Cincinnati Gazette*, and "some others to the West" figured in Clay's plans as he reminded Webster in October that they had discussed, during the previous winter, the raising of "a fund for the purpose of aiding [th]e cause. . . ." Clay proposed that "struggling presses" be extended assistance in return for circulation "gratis" of a number of papers, in proportion to the contribution received.[39]

Webster's response, a promise of $250 for Pleasants "if no more should be obtained to ensure the accomplishment of the object," was not very encouraging. Webster subsequently agreed to double that sum and even to quadruple it, if necessary, but protested that there were so many calls for funds, "& so few persons who feel the importance of aiding objects so distant," that he feared the burden would "fall too heavily on the willing few." He therefore urged that some part of the grant be "looked for elsewhere."[40]

In New England the Everetts, Alexander H. and Edward, had established the *Massachusetts Journal* (Boston) in January 1826, in order to promote the views of the administration. In the following year the *Butterfly* (Dover, N.H.) and the *New Hampshire Journal* (Concord) were founded to combat the Jacksonian organs of Isaac Hill and Levi Woodbury. Clay's friend Sylvester S. Southworth set up the *Literary Cadet* in Providence, Rhode Island, in April 1826. Elsewhere, Thurlow Weed's purchase of the *Rochester* (N.Y.) *Telegraph* in the summer of 1825 and the founding of Mason Campbell's *Western Virginian* (Charleston) in July 1826 and of W. W. Worsley's *Focus* (Louisville, Ky.) the following November represented notable exceptions to the general lag in organization of an administration press.

In several critical areas the problem of developing adequate journalistic support remained serious throughout the campaign for midterm elections. In the summer of 1826 Edward Ingersoll had seen the need for a broader popular appeal in Pennsylvania and accordingly had distributed "a short plain manual so familiar in language and illustration" that the "well meaning but not acute"—elsewhere in his account described as "well inclined but benighted"—might resist the "sophistry" of their opponents. From western Pennsylvania, one of Clay's correspondents in the spring of 1827 dismissed such efforts with the report that the Jacksonians' "purchasing up presses, and controlling the publication of the News Papers, had proved deeply injurious to the General's prospects in that quarter." By autumn, however, administration forces were advertising for editors to present their cause in the state.[41]

In New York, also, the lack of an Adams paper at Albany weakened the organizational effort. Throughout 1827, reports of the imminent establishment of such a journal had buoyed the hopes of administration leaders. Funding difficulties had, however, been complicated by disagreements on editorial policy. The Kings and their friends in New York City, "very zealous & liberal in their efforts to get up this paper," were proponents of free trade. Informed that "the polar star of its policy must be the encouragement of domestic manufactures & support of the tariff," they assented; but other backers questioned the independence of the journal under such auspices. An observer, describing the disarray in the New York legislature some months later, shortly before the fall elections, noted that the friends of the administration lacked "a paper & a leader." He had "urged them to establish the one—and agree upon the other." "Had they done so," he contended, "Van Buren might have been kept at bay."[42]

At the nation's capital the administration was ultimately supported by both David Force's *National Journal* and the *National Intelligencer* of Gales and Seaton, but neither organ was a match for the hard-hitting and well-financed *United States Telegraph*, which was reconstituted out of the *Washington Gazette* as a Jackson paper in February 1826. Duff Green, Calhoun's son-in-law, who had edited the *St. Louis Enquirer* as a Calhoun and later as a Jackson journal during the presidential campaign of 1824, joined the staff of the *Telegraph* in the spring of 1826 and assumed the proprietorship the following autumn. As he himself testified, he had entered upon his work with the determination to demonstrate that Clay had sold his vote upon the promise of the secretaryship. While he published summaries of congressional proceedings and occasionally an address that served his partisan interest, his paper offered little general news and concentrated almost exclusively upon opposing the administration. As a Jacksonian press was more widely developed, the *Telegraph*, through its exchanges, became a virtual clipping file of editorial diatribe, with Green selecting and organizing a patterned attack that reverberated throughout the nation. By the spring of 1828 he claimed a circulation of some forty thousand copies weekly for the regular edition and was then promoting a special weekly extra of twenty thousand copies for campaign purposes.[43]

Neither the *National Journal* nor the *National Intelligencer* devoted comparable space to such coverage. Both published relatively full reports of congressional debates. The former, as the official organ for publication of the treaties and laws, necessarily filled many columns with those records as well. The *Intelligencer*, having lost that source of revenue, had begun in 1824 the project of compiling for commercial sale a comprehensive *Register of Debates in Congress*, with extended reporting of all major speeches. This material, with general and foreign news, crowded its columns until Congress adjourned. Both journals continued to carry a wide range of miscellaneous news, despite the pressure of the campaign. Neither viewed its operations as being primarily political.

The editorship of the *Journal* was criticized as ineffective throughout much of Adams's administration. John Agg, who held the post into the spring of 1827, was then replaced by Samuel Lorenzo Knapp, formerly an editor of the *Boston Gazette*. Knapp's departure from the latter journal and his assumption of the Washington employment without regard for political attachments greatly amused Duff Green, who regaled his readers with the fact that the *Telegraph* had earlier received and rejected the editor's application. George Watterston, Librarian of Congress and later editor of the *Journal*, was also writing for the paper in April. For a time the editorials reflected "more spirit and ability," Clay noted, but Force was again seeking another editor by the following September. As late as April 1828, Fourth Auditor Tobias Watkins, who had already been handling much of the administration's political publication, proposed that he himself take over the *Journal*. At this time the president agreed that Force had been "unfortunate with it" and lacked funds or credit to sustain it longer. Presumably, some of the support that Webster supplied in succeeding months relieved the financial problem, for Force continued, at least nominally, as the proprietor of the administration's designated organ in the capital. Watkins and Philip R. Fendall, a clerk in the State Department, reputedly provided much of the political copy during the campaign of 1828.[44]

The editors of the *Intelligencer*, stripped of their official status in June 1824 after a disagreement with Adams over some omissions in documents published for the State Department, had thereupon announced their support for Crawford in the election of that year; but more importantly, they had strongly opposed Jackson's candidacy. Throughout the first year or two of Adams's administration, they remained relatively neutral; but following Van Buren's efforts to shift the Senate printing to Duff Green in the spring of 1827, they bitterly attacked the "caucus" activity of the Jacksonians in Congress. In mid August they formally announced their opposition to Jackson as the alternative candidate to Adams. Their criticism, as the historian of the journal notes, gave more space "to tearing Jackson down than to building Adams up," but "compared to a number of the country's newspapers, the *Intelligencer* conducted a relatively high-level campaign." Defining their editorial guidelines in the midst of their efforts, Gales and Seaton emphasized that they sought to present "all facts truly upon the evidence . . . and misrepresent no man or measure" because of political opposition. "It cannot be said of us, that, during the course of our public life, we ever acted upon a malevolent feeling, knowingly misrepresented a fact, or invaded the sanctuary of private life."[45] That was not the style of journalism that set the tone of the campaign, on either side, in the election of 1828!

The difficulty of developing and maintaining partisan commitment under the administration's policy of discountenancing old affiliations had been evident in those states that held congressional elections in 1826. Inertia and lack of a sense of organizational urgency were widespread. Charles Hammond complained that in the Cincinnati district of Ohio, William Henry Harrison and other influential supporters of the administration backed the candidacy of the Jacksonian James Findlay because of business and family ties, while in another district of the state, three Adams supporters opposed one Jacksonian.[46] As a consequence, both seats were lost, although the remainder of the delegation backed the president.

In Illinois, Governor Edwards, while announcing his own refusal to take a stand on the presidential succession so long as he was "impudently" assailed by officers under administration appointment, insisted that the defeat of his son-in-law Daniel Pope Cook "was not produced by his vote on the Presidential election." The latter had been ill "and could visit but few of the counties," while his opponent "had done nothing for many months previously, but ride through the state, and visit the people at their own houses." Neither Cook nor his friends had foreseen the danger. They had "felt too secure." The result had "surprised every body."[47]

From Kentucky, Clay's brother warned in February 1827: "the friends of Jackson are desperat [sic] and clamerous [sic] and consequently active while the friends of the admn. are inactive and luke warm and with out any concert."[48] In the ensuing election the administration lost three seats, and thereby its majority in the Kentucky congressional delegation. As in Ohio, the problem in one district developed through the competition of multiple administration candidates against a single Jacksonian.

From New York in December 1826, Peter B. Porter presented a similar account of organizational weakness. He believed that "two thirds, & probably three fourths of the citizens of this state," supported the administration. "And yet I am fully of opinion that, by the manouvres [sic] of Clinton & Van Buren, whether in concert or not, the state will be represented in the Senate by the latter, who is the decided enemy of that administration." The leader of the Regency forces had been "very active in concerting & maturing his plans," while the supporters of the administration had done "little or nothing."[49]

Van Buren's machinations had been astute. Confusing the administration's local leaders, who had earlier noted the developing Van Buren–Clinton relationship, the Bucktails at the Herkimer Convention had nominated William B. Rochester as gubernatorial candidate against Clinton. The move, heralded as a reunification of the Old Democratic party, had garnered support from friends of the administration for Van

Buren's reelection to the Senate but had failed to assure Rochester's election, and it had alienated Adams's many adherents among the Clintonians. Rochester contritely explained to Clay that he had been nominated "without pledges being asked." From Washington the secretary of state responded that Van Buren was playing an "obvious game": "He is inculcating *neutrality* as to the general administration, which means ultimate hostility, to be gradually approached." "How can the Citizens of N. York be neutral as to *measures* which affect them in common with other Citizens of the U.S.?" Clay asked in protest.[50]

By the fall elections of 1827 the effect upon the administration's forces was evident. Rochester reported that the state senate stood 16 to 14 in favor of Jackson, with 6 Clintonians for the general and 4 against—in short, a tie vote among Republicans, with Clintonians tipping the balance. The "doctrine of non-committal" prevailed in the New York Assembly. Peter B. Porter's explanation reflected the disorganization among adherents of the administration. Van Buren had attempted "to keep the presidential question, as much as possible, out of sight." He had "succeeded in several instances, in getting Jackson men nominated for the Legislature, when a majority of the nominating convention were administration men; but who did not think it worth while to enquire, and perhaps did not care what the opinions of the candidate were in regard to this particular question." He had attempted "to get Jackson candidates nominated when he could—&, when he could not, to take such as he deemed most promising subjects of *conversion*." The "extraordinary result" had been produced "*in the country,* by strategem [sic] & party discipline on the part of the Jacksonians, and by apathy a [sic] want of concert among the friends of the administration." Webster concluded that the administration's cause had nowhere else been "so badly managed" as in New York.[51]

In New York City the lines were sharply drawn and the fight was bitter, but the effect was the same. Charles King's *American* (New York) rebuffed the Clintonians, while the Tammany Society split on the issue of support for the administration. After elections to the Tammany Council of Sachems in May 1827, the president's friends were slightly outnumbered. Through the summer the feuding leaders squabbled over retaining the Adamsite *National Advocate* (New York) as a party organ, but Tammany continued to place its advertising in the journal. For two weeks during the following October the Adams faction, acting in the absence of the Jacksonite majority of the council, held possession of Tammany Hall, forcing the opponents of the administration to hold their nominating convention in the basement. The Jacksonians finally resolved the problem by calling an assembly of the general membership and carrying their proposals, thus recovering the Hall and sending two senators to Albany. Thereafter the Adams supporters, lacking control of the established organizational framework, failed to develop an alternative.[52]

Organizational difficulties were also apparent in Pennsylvania. In the summer of 1826 P. P. F. Degrand described the whole Adams "party" as inert, much of it "paralised" by the notion that Jackson was so strong that effort to combat him was useless. Degrand and John Sergeant then proposed to issue a circular as an appeal from New England Republicans for support of the president in the Keystone State. Republicans alone, however, could not carry the day. Sergeant's predicament in the election that autumn pointed to the problem. A majority of the politically dominant Democrats (in Pennsylvania, Republicans still carried the old Jeffersonian designation) endorsed Jackson. Federalists, "with few exceptions," were opposed to him and, united with the administration's Democratic adherents, constituted a majority. Sergeant's election depended upon fusion of those forces.[53]

Clay repeatedly reminded his correspondents that there were only two parties, the one supporting the administration and the other opposed to it; but in Philadelphia the hostility between his Democratic editorial friend John Binns and Adams's Federalist supporter Robert Walsh, Jr., was inveterate. And both reflected large constituencies. Federalists clung "to their old name & discipline," as Robert Peters, Jr., explained in October 1826, out of "Private griefs—dissappointed [sic] ambition, a conviction that the entire surrender of the *name* will deprive some of the consequence they still retain as leaders, even of a broken corps. . . ." They retained the old "pride of party," commitment to leaders who claimed "to have been the martyrs to their principles," and, above all, suspicion that the apostate Adams, in his pursuit of neutral rights and Jeffersonian reciprocity, did not share their views of "general policy." Walsh himself led a bitter criticism of the interruption of the West Indies trade.[54]

When a tie vote resulted between Sergeant and his Jacksonian opponent, the issue was deferred, pending a special election in the fall of 1827. Meanwhile, conflict between Democrats and Federalists continued. The Clay adherent Philip Swenk Markley, who had been defeated for Congress in 1826, was named navy agent at the Philadelphia Customs House. In a position where he might have been expected to support administration candidates, he strongly opposed "amalgamation." Writing to Clay in May 1827, Markley argued: "all the movements in Penna in relation to the reelection of Mr. Adams in order to produce the desired effect, must be identified with the Democracy of the state—to malgamate [sic] with the federalist in our Meetings would be fatal. . . ." Webster, on the other hand, reflecting the dissatisfaction of Federalists over the failure to elevate Hopkinson, voiced their reciprocal outrage over the appointment of Markley. While Webster conceded that Markley was "entirely well qualified for his office, & was probably recommended by a great Country interest," he found it "too evident that warm & zealous friends here are, some disappointed, & others disgusted." The feeling was prevalent "that to be active & prominent in support of the Administration, *is the way to throw one's self out of the chance of promotion, & the sphere of regard.*" Those seeking office had concluded that policy favored holding back, "in the ranks of opposition," until they were "offered their price."[55]

Webster concluded that "a distinct majority of the City" favored the administration "and that if there could be a proper spirit infused, and a just degree of *confidence* excited, not only might the City return . . . a favorable member, but it might act also, *efficiently,* on the State." Yet the organizational problem was unresolved. With the second election but a month away, Sergeant found that they continued "in the same disjointed state. . . ." He had a "great many well wishers[, some] zealous friends, and, no doubt, a large majority in the City, but no organization." The old political divisions persisted, "so that there is no effective mode of operating in mass, or even of encouring and animating each other." He had hoped that "before this time some thing would have been done at Harrisburg. . . ."[56]

The failure of tariff proponents to develop the political framework that had been contemplated in the organization of the Harrisburg Convention in the summer of 1827 had deflected the issue orientation which might have consolidated Pennsylvania's fragmented party structure. P. P. F. Degrand, writing to Clay of the initial meeting in Philadelphia, reported that only one Jacksonian had been named as a delegate: "His being in arrises [sic] from there [sic] inexperienced hands—not knowing that he was a Jackson Man.—However, we have all but one & all will go right." Jacksonians of the Middle States knew well, however, the importance of the tariff issue to their constituencies and promptly undertook to counteract this development. John Tod of Bedford and Henry Baldwin of Pittsburgh, both of whom were strong proponents of a tariff, declined to serve as representatives to the Pennsylvania state convention, because they rejected its political associations. Residents of Buck and Lancaster counties in Pennsylvania, after hearing addresses by Ingham and Buchanan, resolved not to send delegates, on the ground that the convention was a plan to array the states against each other, on a geographical basis. In Delaware, Louis

McLane, elected as a delegate to the national gathering, also refused the appointment, after carefully explaining that while he advocated protection, he considered the woolens bill "partial, unequal and extravagant." Following his remarks, "party spirit" so disrupted the Wilmington gathering, according to reports, that a second state meeting, which Jacksonians refused to attend, met a month later to select a new slate of delegates. Van Buren, at the state meeting in Albany, similarly professed concern for protection of home industry but deplored "the feverish attempts of designing partisans, and the artful contrivances of those who seek to pervert a great national question to their own personal and political advantage."[57]

Jacksonian journals further elaborated upon the partisan focus. "The Harrisburg Convention is considered in its true light, as a contemptible political stratagem, to bring over Pennsylvania to the Adams party," railed the editor of the *New-York Evening Post*, a Jacksonian advocate of free trade. The *Pittsburgh Mercury* reiterated the charge, terming the convention "a contemptible maneuver to operate on public sentiment in your state." Both journals reported the adoption of a resolution at a Harrodsburg, Kentucky, meeting, which repeated the theme that "the real design of this convention at Harrisburg is not to advance American industry, but to organize a political club under the direction of the administration of the general government, to direct and controul public sentiment, and particularly to operate upon the election in the state of Pennsylvania."[58]

Confronted by such denunciations, leaders of the sponsoring organization, the Pennsylvania Society for Promotion of Manufactures and the Mechanic Arts, had carefully eschewed all reference to political associations in the proceedings of the Harrisburg convention. John Binns argued editorially in the *Democratic Press* (Philadelphia) that tariff proponents "would have been madmen to break down their strength by mingling the economical plans with political matters." Mathew Carey had long opposed politicization of the tariff agitation and, while conceding his personal preference for Adams, specifically renounced identification of the issue with the presidential campaign. Hezekiah Niles expressed similar views.[59] In closing the convention, George Robertson of Kentucky, James Tallmadge of New York, and Charles J. Ingersoll, the federal attorney at Philadelphia—all active proponents of the administration—had introduced a range of complimentary resolutions honoring individuals and the state of Pennsylvania for assistance in the effort, but none had cited President Adams or his secretary of the Treasury, Pennsylvania's native son, who had brought the issue before the national legislature. Nothing had been done to organize a political force to sustain the memorial to Congress that was adopted by the convention.

Despairing of organizational assistance, Sergeant fought his congressional campaign in September 1827, more on the strength of his own personal following than as the candidate of Democrats or Federalists. Thomas I. Wharton, who had earlier provided the Fourth of July address at the festivities held by friends of the administration, noted that only *"one* officer under the government" had subscribed to that political rally. Markley was "out of town" through mid September. While Democrats remained inactive, Sergeant's Federalist allies, angered by his acceptance of the nomination under Democratic auspices, refused to endorse him. They did, however, leave the post open on their ticket. On September 18 Sergeant finally described the "friends of the Administration among the democrats" as organized. He won the election three weeks later by a vote of 2,702 to 2,557 over his Jacksonian opponent.[60]

Returns in the fall elections elsewhere in Pennsylvania were confusing. Considering their previous defeats in the state, administration supporters were encouraged by victories in several counties; but their boasted triumph in Montgomery County consisted of a narrow win in the state senatorial race while losing three assemblymen to the Jacksonians. The status of the dominant German vote in the southeastern counties remained uncertain.

Traditionally Federalist, the Germans had long held the governor's chair in Pennsylvania. With the splintering of Federalism, John Shulze had attained that office with support from the Calhounite-Federalist combination headed by the so-called Family party of Richard Bache and Samuel Ingham. Restive under their control, the governor, in the fall of 1826, appeared to be bending toward the administration. In his annual message to the legislature he had applauded the peaceful resolution of the presidential election in 1825. Administration supporters interpreted this stand as favorable, and they believed that a majority of both branches of the Pennsylvania Assembly were also friendly to their cause. But, as B. W. Crowninshield reported, "no one is hardy or strong enough to come out & take the field, each thinks the Jacksonians so strong, that they are be [sic] overwhelmed [sic] if any one comes out to oppose. . . ." He believed the governor was "a *little hurt at it.*"[61]

Nevertheless, Shulze continued to support the administration. In his annual message the following December, he specifically endorsed the program of internal improvements and domestic manufactures and pointedly warned against those who were criticizing "their public functionaries": ". . . we owe it to ourselves . . . to avoid everything which may shake the confidence of mankind in the competency for self-government or wastefully diminish the stock of our national reputation, by detracting from the distinguished reputations of which it is composed." Even Jacksonians conceded that the state's executive favored Adams.[62]

In March 1827, however, Clay had been warned that Joseph Ritner, the German Speaker of the Pennsylvania House of Representatives, looked "to political promotion." When no plums fell his way from the Adams administration, Ritner, late in August, publicly announced that he would vote for Jackson. Immediately after the fall elections the *Pennsylvania Intelligencer* (Harrisburg), which was edited by Governor Shulze's brother-in-law Simon Cameron, also swung to the general's cause. Sergeant explained that Cameron's "somerset" was dictated "by the threat of losing the Legislative printing." In succeeding months a wave of removals of administration supporters who were under legislative appointment told the story of resurgent Jacksonian strength.[63]

Even in New England the Adams forces reflected serious organizational weaknesses during the elections of 1827. While Jacksonians were in fact gathering accessions of the splintered Federalists in all areas of the country, the opprobrium of "amalgamation" was brought against the administration with particular force because of the president's antecedents, his Federalist appointments, and the prominence of men like Webster, Sergeant, and Taylor among his congressional supporters. His Republican adherents reacted with marked sensitivity in areas where they had felt most severely the proscription of earlier Federalist domination. At a public meeting in Faneuil Hall, Boston, in April 1827, Webster urged unity among those who approved "the general course of the government . . . , without reference to former party . . ."; but Clay's Republican friend Henry Shaw of Lanesborough, Massachusetts, expressed widespread reservations concerning Webster's elevation to the Senate. He believed the former Federalist to be "too strong a Man to be made too independant [*sic*]. . . ." Moreover, Shaw continued, it was "too soon to commit so great a violence upon the Old Republican feelings of the State." Old feelings, he warned, "are to be respected, and we are to be brought not in a lump but by degrees, to amalgamate."[64]

Federalists reciprocated the feeling. Resenting the plea for "union" with friends of the administration, they met separately to draw up their own list of candidates for the Massachusetts General Court and called for the backing of party members who were "not yet ready to be transferred, bargained, assigned, and sold by a few individuals. . . ." As a result, with five separate tickets in an election that required a majority vote, only eight of the thirty allotted representatives could be chosen from Boston. When the Republican Administration Committee of Boston called a nominating convention for July 15 to select a congressional candidate to fill Webster's vacant seat, the Federalists again met separately, three days earlier, and nominated one of their own. The Federalist candidate won comfortably over three opponents, including a Jacksonian; but again the administration's coalition had split factionally.[65]

Such differences were not critical in the Bay State, but similar discord in New Hampshire occasioned the election of a Jacksonian governor and defeat on a major test of the administration's strength in the state assembly in 1827. Believing that the New England legislatures, particularly that of New Hampshire, where there was, among the states of that region, the "most show of opposition," ought "to take occasion to express their opinions, respecting Mr. Adams' election, the merits of his Administration, and the conduct of the opposition," Webster proposed that Samuel Bell, an administration senator and editor of the *Butterfly* (Dover), initiate appropriate resolutions. "They would pass, by a large majority," Webster argued, "& friends would then be known from foes."[66]

Bell, however, ignored the amalgamation effort. He called the drafting body as a meeting of the "Republican friends of the Administration." The proponents of the resolutions "vindicated" Adams of his earlier Federalism and defended the administration as being "strictly democratic." Federalists, who constituted one-third of the legislature, were angered. By combining with Jacksonians, they voted, 137 to 70, to table the proposals. With exasperation, Webster concluded that Bell's "good sense" had "strangely forsaken him." Dependent himself on Federalist support, Bell yet prated of *"exclusive caucusses* [sic], & *party discipline."* "This *party* confidence, & *party* blindness, which are so unworthy of so wise a man, will assuredly defeat all his objects," Webster warned.[67]

The lesson had been learned in New Hampshire by December 1827, when Bell finally called a broadly defined convention of the "friends of the Administration"; but the healing process was slow, and many Federalists in the interim had made the shift to Jackson. While the problem was less serious elsewhere in New England, amalgamation was not easy anywhere. From Rhode Island, Southworth explained that at a political supper in March 1827, the toasts had been designed to honor the secretary of state, "but as it was afterwards considered inexpedient, to make any distinction between the friends of the administration generally and Mr. Clay, they were, upon after consideration supplied" on a broader basis. In Connecticut, as elsewhere in New England, a majority of Federalists supported the administration, but the Republicans openly split on the issue of such endorsement in 1828.[68]

In Maryland and Delaware, too, there was deep division within former Federalist ranks. There, however, the administration was able to organize fusion more effectively. The breakdown of formal organization by Maryland Federalists as early as 1821 contributed to their acceptance of new partisan affiliations with less defensiveness. While many of their leaders followed Virgil Maxcy in his attachment to Calhoun and thence to Jackson, the popular majority had voted for Adams in 1824 and remained loyal to his administration. Strong personal ties between the president and cabinet members with both the Federalist former senator Robert H. Goldsborough and the Democratic governor, Joseph Kent, maintained leadership connections. Goldsborough was invited to deliver the official address to the state convention of friends of the administration at Baltimore in July 1827. The combined forces had won five of the nine congressional seats in 1826 and, in the following year, carried control of the House of Delegates, replacing a Jacksonian senator with an administration adherent. Six counties in southern Maryland and the Eastern Shore strongly supported Adams, while only three, in the north and west, voted consistently Jacksonian. The remainder were deeply divided.[69]

The defection of the Federalist-Crawfordite Louis McLane of Delaware stemmed from longstanding dislike of Adams, but his strong support for internal improvements and a protective tariff had masked a growing hostility as he cooperated in developing the administration's program while he was chairman of the Committee of Ways and Means in the Nineteenth Congress. By the summer of 1826 the thwarting of his personal ambition for the Speakership under the administration and a desire for a seat in the Senate, which was attainable through cooperation with Delaware Jacksonians, led him to espouse the opposition openly. The state sent two Jacksonian senators to Washington in 1827, but McLane's efforts to carry the Federalists into his Jacksonian alliance divided his local power base. Working with the Federalist Clayton faction, which had long been hostile to McLane, the administration forces won election of the Federalist Kensey Johns, Jr., to McLane's vacated congressional seat. In the process, the withdrawal of the Democratic candidate, Dr. Arnold Naudain, as an alternative anti-Jackson competitor, evidenced an organizational discipline that was generally lacking among administration forces.[70]

With victories in Philadelphia, Maryland, and Delaware, the sanguine Clay was still optimistic about ultimate triumph after the fall elections in 1827; but the administration had lost control of both houses of Congress, "a state of things," Adams gloomily noted, which had "never before occurred under the Government of the United States."[71] When the legislative body assembled in December, the Jacksonian and antitariff Virginian Andrew Stevenson defeated the administration-supported Taylor for the speakership of the House of Representatives by ten votes. Stevenson accordingly named four opposition but only three administration supporters on each of the standing committees. In the Senate, all committees, chosen by ballot with majorities of 25 to 19, consisted of four members of the opposition to one for the administration. Duff Green became the official printer for the Senate. The Twentieth Congress thus became a national forum that was directed toward Jacksonian political expression. The early hope for a nonpartisan assessment of program development; the attempt to woo opponents, rather than friends, by political patronage; the delay in organizational structuring; and finally, the difficulty of amalgamating Federalists and nationalistic Republicans had brought the administration into the campaign year 1828 under heavy odds.

12

★ ★ ★ ★ ★

THE CAMPAIGN OF 1828

Viewed in retrospect, the presidential election was anticlimactic. The Jacksonians had shaped their strategy and initiated the media to give it structure by the spring of 1827; the friends of the administration were still struggling to develop such an organizational framework during the following autumn. The composition of the Twentieth Congress, as the immediate consequence of this lag, established the mechanism for destroying the programmatic record on which the administration sought judgment. Even in routine diplomatic negotiation its ministers found the impact damaging. Treaty ratifications were suspended; negotiations, deferred. Adams's stand for reciprocity in indirect trade survived as a program legislated by his opponents, more to express annoyance with, rather than approbation of, the administration's efforts. The concept of mission in international relations—the hope for instrumentality in effecting Spanish recognition of Latin-American independence and the dream of hemispheric influence—was denigrated to the status of partisan rhetoric as a goal of national policy. Jacksonians were later to translate it as "Manifest Destiny" in rounding out physiographic boundaries. The domestic program of federal support for science and education, internal improvements, and domestic industry was attacked as a system of benefits for the few at the expense of the many. Retrenchment, it was argued, would restore "republican simplicity." The opposition was calling the tune.

Adams himself saw the outcome of the New York election in the autumn of 1827 as "decisive upon the next Presidential election." The increasingly acerbic comments in his diary in reference to his opponents reflected his mounting abhorrence of the political brouhaha, his conviction that the administration cause was lost, and his personal suffering in the defeat. Categorically rejecting suggestions that Crawford be wooed by nomination for the vice-presidency, he described the Georgian as "more like one of Milton's fallen angels" than anyone he knew, "excepting that Milton . . . made his devils true to each other," while Crawford's character rested upon "treachery of the deepest dye. . . ." The chief executive was indignant that Jacksonian congressmen, "bitter as wormwood in their opposition, indulging themselves in the warmth of debate in personal reflections as ungenerous as they were unjust, . . . yet came to the drawing-rooms and, when invited, to the dinners; always ready to introduce their friends . . . , to partake of his hospitality, and to recommend candidates for every vacant appointment." He found such social gatherings "becoming more and more insupportable." By March 1828, observing that the majority of the people were "inveterately opposed to the Administration" he lamented that there was "scarcely any condition so mortifying as that of being in a minority at home."[1]

Although he had yielded to Barbour's plea that his third annual message should "avoid controvertible matter," Adams continued to hold himself aloof from active electioneering. He persisted in the policy of reappointing public officers, despite their attachment to the opposition, "unless official or moral misconduct . . . [was] charged and substantiated." He refused to permit his son to contribute to the founding of a German newspaper, and he himself rejected a proposal that he provide five to ten thousand dollars to assure the election of administration candidates in Kentucky during the summer of 1828. Such expenditures for "the circulation of newspapers, pamphlets, and handbills," in his view, rendered elections "altogether venal." He still noted, with bemused amazement, the western practice which required that the Kentucky congressman, as a candidate for the governorship, must "before the election travel round the State and offer himself to the people and solicit their votes."[2]

Meanwhile Adams's friends and supporters struggled to approximate the organizational efforts of the Jacksonians. Clay's plan for developing a local political structure, which he had outlined to the defeated Kentucky congressman John F. Henry in the fall of 1827, noted that they must learn from their adversaries and emphasized that "organization . . . [had] been the efficient cause" of the latters' recent success. He called for public meetings of friends of the administration and of the American System in every county of the state and for the adoption of supportive resolutions. Those who attended the meetings were to appoint committees of a dozen or so persons to conduct correspondence with similar bodies locally and nationally and to collect and distribute "political essays, tracts, and newspapers, calculated to advance the success of the cause." The presidents of these committees would form "so many rallying points, to which could be transmitted, from friends in other States, useful documents and information." "Committees of Vigilance," consisting of a hundred or more persons who would be representative of every neighborhood, were also to be named at the county meetings and were to serve as channels for distributing the available information. They would also have the responsibility "to animate their neighbors, and to stimulate and encourage them to attend the elections."[3]

Clay also urged that a central committee be established for the state, to coordinate local efforts and, particularly, to act in conjunction with friends in the legislative assembly. He did not mention the activities of a national central committee, although one was set up at Washington. He made no reference to the possible development of a national nominating convention.

As the Jacksonians assembled throughout the nation on January 8, in commemoration of the Hero's victory at the Battle of New Orleans, Adams's supporters held an array of state meetings, extending through New England, the Middle States, the West, and even into the South, in Mississippi, North Carolina, and Virginia. The Virginia delegates attempted to bring Madison and Monroe out as electors for the president, but both declined to take a partisan role in the campaign. The Louisiana legislature, at the same time, attempted to counteract the political connotations of the New Orleans celebration by adopting a resolution emphasizing that the invitation for Jackson's participation had been given "*solely* in compliment to the military services rendered . . . in defence of Louisiana, and not for *political* purposes, or in any way to express an opinion on the approaching election of president of the United States. . . ."[4]

Prolonged uncertainty over selection of a vice-presidential running mate on the Adams ticket was also resolved in early January 1828. New York friends, reflecting the bitterness of the amalgamation issue, had strongly urged the secretary of state to permit his name to be run. William B. Rochester had argued that some eight or ten electoral votes depended upon Clay's placement on the ticket. "Our people will not come out with such hearty goodwill and Spirit for A. & Schultz [*sic*] or for A. & Barbour—Even now our friends have to call their meetings by inviting such as are '*opposed to Jackson*.' " But Clay, while deferring the decision to the "good of the cause," had demurred. With backing from Virginia and Maryland as well as Pennsylvania, Governor Shulze had been offered the nomination at the end of December but on January 4, he, too, had declined it. The Harrisburg convention of Adams's adherents thereupon endorsed Richard Rush, and on January 8 Virginians, who had also been urging Barbour or Southard for the position, endorsed the Pennsylvanian. Rush, with Jeffersonian credentials and a Middle-State commitment to the home-market domestic program, was chosen so as to appeal to the "vast many of the more influential democratic Republicans," who, as Rochester maintained, did not like Adams, would not support Jackson, and "would not stir an inch one way or the other" for either of them.[5]

The administration also undertook to counteract the Jacksonian advantage with the press. In October 1827 the *Pennsylvania Gazette* (Philadelphia) and the *Reporter* (Lancaster, Pa.) had appeared as administration journals, and the *Marietta Pioneer,* also of Lancaster County, had pledged its support. At about the same time, two Bucks County journals were brought into the campaign. In November a long-established Federalist organ, the *Oracle of Dauphin County and Harrisburg Advertiser,* was renamed the *Harrisburg Argus* and identified as "a democratic paper, friendly to the administration." Edited by Francis Wyeth, the son of the earlier proprietor, it was accorded the contract for publishing the laws, as Cameron's *Pennsylvania Intelligencer* defected to the Jacksonian cause. In December, administration backers established the *Berks County Adler* (Reading) and a second German paper, probably that at Aaronsburg, *Der Centre Berichter.* The editor of the *Berks and Schuylkill Journal* was supplied with German type. Belatedly, Adams's adherents were attempting to retrieve their waning strength in the German districts. In January 1828 they also finally succeeded in establishing an organ, the *Morning Chronicle,* at Albany, emphasizing the "democratic" commitment of the president's supporters in New York.

Notwithstanding the president's distaste for the activity, one of the principal functions of the organizational effort was to raise funds for campaign publications. Numerous pamphlets supplemented the editorial effusions that were published, reprinted, excerpted, and distributed across the country. Publication of the resolutions and statements adopted at various conventions was a major phase of the local program. The Virginia convention, for instance, assessed its two hundred members five dollars each to cover the printing and distribution of thirty thousand copies of its "Address." The New Hampshire friends of the administration brought out a collection of *The Wise Sayings of the Honorable Isaac Hill,* quoting from the Jacksonian leader's earlier endorsement of Adams and Clay, and printed ten thousand copies of the report of their state convention. Delaware adherents published a series of essays entitled *The Political Primer: or, a Hornbook for the Jacksonites*, which focused on the political reversal of Louis McLane. John Binns's "Coffin" handbill, recounting Jackson's order for the execution of six militiamen, with supplementary data on other similar incidents, was sent out by the boxload for distribution throughout the country.

The scandalous charges and countercharges of the campaign need not be here reviewed. Hezekiah Niles contemporaneously denounced them, in reference to both sides of the controversy, as "derogatory to our country, and detrimental to its free institutions and the rights of suffrage, with a more general grossness of assault upon distinguished individuals" than he had witnessed even during the bitter era of 1797 to 1804. Whether they were directed against the "pimp" in the White House or the "adulterous murderer" at the Hermitage, whether they pointed to the illegitimacy of Louisa Adams's mother or the prostitution of Jackson's, they reflected at its worst the "new politics" that characterized the rebirth of the American party system.[6]

With "bribery and corruption" as the primary focus of the Jacksonian attack, Clay's *Address to the Public*, published at the end of December 1827, was a central feature in the administration's countering effort. It included statements rejecting allegations that there had been undue influence in the House election. Testimonials to this effect had been supplied by all but two of the congressional representatives of the West, one of these being Daniel Pope Cook, who had since died, and the other, David White, Jr., of Kentucky, a Jacksonian. When the latter's cohorts emphasized this significant omission, White himself, on 17 February 1828, issued a public denial that he had had any connection "in the alleged *management, bargain, sale, &c.* in the election of the President, and in the formation of his cabinet." He professed belief that his vote for Adams had conformed to the will of his constituents and explained that his possible opposition to Adams's reelection grew out of "circumstances foreign from, and entirely unconnected with," the president's election by the House of Representatives. Clay's pamphlet also provided testimony on the numerous occasions when, prior to his arrival in Washington in the fall of 1824, he had indicated his personal intention to support Adams should the alternatives be Jackson or Crawford. In June 1828 the Kentuckian supplemented this documentation with yet another publication, presenting evidence that Jackson had developed the account of the bargain as he returned from Washington, in the spring of 1825, after having said nothing about it during the congressional investigation.[7]

Jacksonians had revived the charges in a slightly variant form in the spring of 1827, asserting that the general himself had been approached prior to the election to provide assurances that Adams would not be named as secretary of state, the presumption being that Clay was the logical alternative. When Jackson named James Buchanan as the intermediary, the latter publicly conceded that he had "had no authority from Mr. Clay, or his friends, to propose any terms to General Jackson in relation to their votes" and that, in actuality, he had never made such a proposition. The general's supporters had then shifted to a further allegation—that Clay's congressional friends had blocked a full investigation in 1825.[8] The Jacksonian-dominated Twentieth Congress offered little hope for a fair review, but the existence in the Kentucky Senate of a majority that was sympathetic to the administration encouraged Clay's adherents there to accept the challenge to a second investigation in January 1828.

The result was disastrous—not because evidence supported the Jacksonian contentions but because Francis Preston Blair refused to testify or to produce the correspondence that purportedly cited the offer of the State Department post as an inducement for the Kentucky delegation to follow Clay in his alignment with Adams. Repeated allusions to the existence of such a letter or letters merely confirmed popular suspicion. Clay, who was himself unwilling to publish the correspondence without Blair's consent, could make it available only for private review by the investigating committee. Its report, which exonerated him, but without public documentation, appeared to be a mere political whitewash. "How will your indignation rise on seeing the disgraceful conduct of the Jackson party of the Senate in the late investigation?" wrote a friend to Clay in mid February. Describing the outcome as "a Complete abortion," he concluded that Blair "had been studying the part of Iago in Othello."[9]

For the administration, the charge that Jackson's unruly passions as a military chieftain threatened the security of the Republic provided the basis of a countering personal attack. The general's prolongation of martial law in New Orleans in 1815, his execution of Ambrister and Arbuthnot at St. Marks and subsequent seizure of Pensacola in 1818, and his assumption of judicial powers as governor of Florida in 1821—all had occasioned strong opposition to his candidacy, particularly among Crawford's adherents, in 1824. The editors of the *National Intelligencer* (Washington), in rejecting Jackson's pretensions three years later, reprinted, in support of their argument, comments from the *Enquirer*

(Richmond, Va.), the *New York National Advocate*, the *New York Evening Post*, the *Delaware Gazette*, and the *New Hampshire Patriot*—all journals that at one time had been scathingly denunciatory of Jackson's high-handed exercise of authority but now were actively supporting his cause.[10] John Binns's "Coffin" handbills dramatized this line of criticism. The "Qualifications for the Presidency" was a campaign theme which afforded discourse that descended from the intellectually elevated to the scandalous.

Also, however, this theme furnished grounds for assault upon the president. Adams's European education, his long association with monarchical courts, his Federalist background among the "New England Aristocracy"—all had, Jacksonians argued, stripped him of appreciation for republican simplicity. His "dandy dress of 'nankeen pantaloons and silk stockings,'" his billiard table and ivory chessmen, his Unitarian religious associations, and his purchases of foreign books and newspapers appeared in opposition accounts as evidence of his aristocratic tastes. "We hold this truth to be incontrovertible," wrote Mordecai Noah of the *New York Enquirer*, "that no person can have a correct knowledge of mankind who has led a life of entire abstraction from the great body of the people, and who relies for this information on the books he has read, and the scholastic theories that are taught."[11] That Adams was the son of the Federalist second president was an additional disqualification. This election, Duff Green informed his readers, was a struggle against "a system, which is fast tending to monarchy . . . , a struggle between the honest yeomanry of the country, and an aristocracy, that with monied influence and patronage for its aid, seeks to make every thing subservient to its own views, and to perpetuate *in certain families*, all the offices and honors of the government." The "deadly rancor" with which the supporters of "John the first" had contended against Jefferson was now being "extended to *Jackson* in his contest with John the second."[12]

Notwithstanding the diversion into personalities, the administration sought to maintain its issue focus upon the American System. Recognizing the popularity of the program, the Jacksonians, in turn, sought to minimize and to distort the record. When Clay emphasized the support for internal improvements, Duff Green challenged the claim to merit for appropriations made by representatives, "a great many of whom . . . [were] opposed to Mr. Clay, and to Mr. Adams. . . ." It was, moreover, "but another attempt at bargain." Reports in the *National Journal* that Jackson criticized the subscription to Chesapeake and Ohio Canal stock were promptly denied in the *Telegraph*, and were as promptly reiterated in the administration organ.[13]

The same contradictions marked the editorial pronouncements regarding Jackson's views upon the tariff. Indeed, the Jacksonians' success in defusing that issue stands as the apex of their defensive strategy. The key to their effort lay in the divisions that were created by separating protection for farmers from that for developing manufacturers. The Jacksonian argument—that eastern proponents of the tariff, in opposing proposals to broaden the relief for agricultural products, rejected the legislation when it raised the cost of their raw materials— promoted western regionalism. The contention that the administration centered its benefits upon Adams's New England constituency nullified the values of a program to which many in the crucial electoral districts of the Middle States and the West professed continuing ideological commitment. At the same time, the administration, in accepting the compromise of the woolens bill and, ultimately, the agricultural provisions of the tariff of 1828, failed to communicate the essential sectional linkages of the home-market argument—the point that Hezekiah Niles stressed as he reviewed the tariff debate. Protected woolgrowers could not compete abroad, he argued, and they would have no market if domestic wool manufacturers could not survive.[14] The protection for agriculturalists that Jacksonians proposed offered little in the absence of encouragement for internal improvements and industrial development, which they opposed.

The inconsistencies of the Jacksonian position were not altogether unnoticed. Andrew Stewart and Joseph Ritner, both of whom were tariff proponents of southwestern Pennsylvania, renounced their endorsement of Jackson when they saw the measure that was introduced by his followers in the Twentieth Congress. The *Harrisburg Intelligencer,* after Cameron had relinquished the journal, also denounced the Jacksonian tariff proposals. One Pennsylvanian discussed his dilemma at some length in a letter to a friend: "The great mystery of the case to me is that the South should support Gen. Jackson avowedly for the purpose of preventing tariffs & internal improvements & that we should support him for a directly opposite purpose." The writer doubted that Pennsylvania would have more influence upon the general than would the eight Southern States, and he suspected that voters in the Keystone State were being "deceived by the ambiguity or double intent of his past acts & declarations."[15]

In February 1828 the administration-dominated senate of Indiana sought to force a clarification of the general's stand by noting the dichotomy in the views of his supporters of the West and the South and by requesting a commitment that he would, if elected, "recommend, foster and support the American system." Demurring against any further exposition than his advocacy of a "judicious" tariff, as expressed in his letter to Littleton H. Coleman of North Carolina in 1824, Jackson responded by pointing to his Senatorial vote "for the present tariff and appropriations for internal improvement." He noted that his position had been thus defined "at a time when the divisions of sentiment . . . were as strongly marked as they now . . . [were], in relation both to the *expediency* and constitutionality of the system. . . ." As for an American system, he continued, "every prudent administration" should seek to fulfill that object by preserving the Constitution and by preparing against invasion by foreign foes—through "the practice of economy, and the cultivation, *within ourselves*, of the means of national defence and independence. . . ."[16]

Such vagaries clarified little. As the general's advisers had intended, they were carefully designed to mask the profound disagreements that existed among his diverse partisans. On the other hand, the president's own failure to man the guns in defense of tariff legislation weakened the administration's stand. In a virulent Fourth-of-July address in South Carolina in 1827, George McDuffie had contended that Adams had not supported the tariff and internal improvements in 1824 but had espoused the program subsequently as a political ploy, "under the assumed guise of patriotic motives to purchase up one half of society with the wealth plundered from another." The remarks were echoed when the editor of the *Mercury* (Pittsburgh) responded to charges that Jackson was equivocating on the issue: "A reward of a suit of homespun will be given to any man who will produce any evidence that Mr. Adams ever gave any public pledge that he was in favour of *any tariff* at all." From New York, Peter B. Porter warned that Jacksonians were placing their candidate's "superior claims to the presidency on the ground of his having publicly advocated & voted for the tariff, while Mr. Adams . . . maintained a profound silence on the subject." The issue was "so much the favourite policy" in the North that if the president was "really friendly to the American System," he ought to "give some decided & unequivocal expression of his views. . . ." From Pennsylvania, Thomas McGiffin also voiced the doubts and partisan divisions that Jacksonian propaganda was exploiting. Had Clay been the candidate, he noted, no question would have arisen concerning Clay's views on the tariff. "But Mr. Adams never has in any public official act placed his opinions on these questions before the nation in an *unquestionable* shape."[17]

The president's expressions of concern for congressional initiative in financial legislation and his desire to avoid antagonizing "friends in the South" afforded but weak explanations. They betrayed his ignorance, if not indifference, about the structure of the political campaign in which his adherents were engaged. Neither he nor Clay had attracted strong southern support outside Louisiana in the election of 1824. Since the spring of 1827 it had been apparent that the coming struggle must center upon the Middle States and the Ohio Valley West. Yet Adams showed limited perception of the interests of that area. He had even, in reference to tariff proposals for 1828, suggested to Clay that concessions might be offered to the British by yielding to their arguments for dropping discrimination against rolled iron, which competed with the American hammered product.[18] Suspicion was widespread that the New Englander's concerns were bound by those of his regional constituency and, indeed, that they remained closely limited to those of the shipping interests in that seaboard base.

Administration leaders also failed to counteract those perceptions when they were unable to exploit a developing protest against the auction system in the port cities of New York, Philadelphia, and Baltimore. Stemming from the period when American markets were flooded with British goods after the Treaty of Ghent, sales at public auction, rather than through normal mercantile channels, were fostered by state governments, which appointed the auctioneers and profited from the licensing fees. Local merchants and traders, however, bitterly protested the irregular and highly promotional system. They emphasized that imported goods upon which unpaid duties were carried under bond at the customs houses were brought to sale in competition with domestic manufactures. If the imports were sold, the duties were paid from the profits; but stocks could be supplemented by additional entries several times prior to the lapse of the original bond. The capital requirement and the consequent costs in such ventures were thus held to a minimum, with the option left of withdrawing the goods for transshipment, as indirect commerce, out of the country if sales weakened. The competition accordingly extended beyond local merchants to domestic producers as well. The antiauction argument was inherently protectionist, and its proponents professed to speak in behalf of "mechanics."[19]

In December 1827, New Yorkers organized the American Institute to advocate measures "favorable to domestic industry." Directing public attention to the auction system, the institute held a mass rally the following May and found an enthusiastic popular response. Although the organization was nominally nonpartisan, Adams's friends James Tallmadge and Joseph Blunt were prominent in its development. When the Jacksonian congressmen, Gulian C. Verplanck, C. C. Cambreleng, and Jeromus Johnson, refused to press an antiauction memorial during the closing days of the congressional session, there seemed to be grounds that the issue might revive the flagging administration cause.

Yet the memorial had included a paragraph which discounted the protective tariff as an approach to the program by arguing that "the existing duties would be more than a sufficient protection, in the absence of auctions, which, alone, are fatal to native industry." In mid October 1828, as the fall elections approached, a large antiauction assembly in New York adopted resolutions upholding protective tariffs and federal aid for internal improvements, but at the same time nominated as their congressional candidates two Tammany Jacksonites and a friend of Adams. When the Jacksonians rejected the nomination on the ground that it had not been sanctioned by the Tammany Society, one was ultimately replaced by an Adamsite. The leaders of the movement then, however, stressed a nonpartisan stance. The cause had been lost as an administration issue.[20]

The antiauction effort was one of several localized but dynamic protest agitations by means of which Adams's adherents might have broadened their political base. They failed also to project their program through the developing labor movement. As one scholar has noted in reference to the auction debate, the Jacksonian *New York Evening Post*'s argument that the cause of mechanics could not "be identified with that of manufacturers" went unchallenged in the administration press.[21] The Bank of the United States, in striving for monetary stability, made little effort to relate the program to workingmen's complaints that rising prices were outstripping wages. Tight credit brought bankruptcy to rural and urban workers, but the administration's proposal for bankruptcy legislation had stressed relief for mercantile interests, not for the farmers and artisans who were also suffering imprisonment for debts. Barbour's concern for modification of the militia system was directed primarily to the need for more adequate training, and only incidentally to the removal of the inequities recognized to exist in the current program. Adams's plea for governmental support of scientific investigations and higher education ignored the growing rate of illiteracy that fostered anti-intellectualism. Artisans in eastern cities shared with relief advocates in the West the demand that extension of public education take precedence.

Recent scholarship has emphasized that Jacksonian leadership, no less than that of the administration, encompassed representatives of the wealthy and the socially elite. On the other hand, both Jackson and Adams attracted adherents in the nascent workingmen's movement in the city and county of Philadelphia during the summer and fall of 1828.

Labor presented no candidates in the presidential election of that year, and in a state that Jackson carried on general ticket by more than fifty thousand votes, the impact of so local a political movement was probably minimal. Yet candidates who carried the support of the Working Men's party, which was organized in July 1828, outdistanced their nonaligned colleagues on both major party tickets by from 300 to 600 votes in the elections for local and state offices that autumn.[22] Labor was a constituency that no developing political organization could well neglect.

Again, however, the administration forces lagged in the effort. In numerous instances they appeared to turn aside from it. They viewed Jacksonian "talk about *aristocracy & the oppression of the poor*" as a demagogic seduction of the "very ignorant." Such propaganda, they recognized, must be counteracted: "The ignorant and degraded class of our population are all against us—and the number of that description of people who push forward to the polls are really formidable." But Adams's supporters smugly counted among their own ranks "all the Merchants and nearly all the principal mechanics," "mostly quiet moral people—men of weath [sic] and influence; and this remark is general through the nation." Whether or not either extreme of the categorization was valid, it reflected attitudes that operated against development of a broadly based political organization and fed the egalitarian propaganda of the Jacksonian press. Clay's friend Isaac Russell of Cincinnati spoke for too many of the administration's adherents when he wrote: "There was a great stir or fuss here, a few days ago; carriages gratis, filled with the halt, the lame & & [sic] the blind; nearly all drunk, to vote for Jackson, or to try his strength in the State Appointments of Ohio; such as these preponderated. . . ." The president's friends, he added, "make no display, they are above imitating the vociferations of the rabble."[23]

The development of the Anti-Masonic movement in western New York presented perhaps the most favorable opportunity for the administration to delineate a popular stance. Generated as a protest against the presumed murder of William Morgan, a brick and stonemason who had exposed the secrets of the order, the attack upon Masonry acquired connotations as a protest against the all-pervasive influence of a secret society that was identified with entrenched political authority. Governor Clinton was a prominent Mason, as also were many of Van Buren's Regency leaders. Moreover, their presidential candidate, Jackson, ranked high in the order. By the winter of 1827/28, administration leaders, notably Thurlow Weed and Francis Granger, were guiding the Anti-Masonic movement into partisan channels on behalf of the president. The following April, Adams, in a rare manifestation of political expression, announced that he was not, never had been, and never would be a member of the lodge.[24]

The death of De Witt Clinton in February 1828, had brought major political repercussions, however. Among them was the fact that it severed the embarrassing linkage between the Masonic governor and the inconclusive investigation of Morgan's disappearance. Clinton's successor, although himself a Mason, promptly called for appointment of a special public prosecutor to act on the Morgan affair.

Meanwhile, Van Buren, recognizing the danger in the politicization of the protest, publicized the fact that Clay, like Jackson, had long been a prominent Mason, the grand master of the Grand Lodge of Kentucky as recently as 1821. The information fostered the determination of the Anti-Masonic forces to maintain a separate political identity. Having carried five counties and elected fifteen members of the state assembly in the fall of 1827, they called a state convention to meet in August for nomination of candidates in the elections of 1828. In July the friends of the administration nominated Smith Thompson for governor and Granger for lieutenant governor. The Anti-Masons, in turn, proposed Granger for the first office. When he refused to withdraw from the Adams ticket, they substituted Solomon Southwick as the Anti-Masonic gubernatorial candidate.

Van Buren resigned from the United States Senate in order to run for the Jacksonians. The split between the Anti-Masonic and administration forces contributed to his election and to Jacksonian victory in the legislative contest. Its relevance to the concurrent presidential election is, however, uncertain. The Anti-Masonic counties formed a core of Adams support in western New York, but not all the consequences of Anti-Masonic backing were to be credited positively. A majority of Masons recognized the focus of their opponents' political interest and, reportedly, reacted in support of the Jackson ticket. The relationship of the movement to the presidential campaign was most significant as evidencing the continuing organizational problems in the administration's effort.[25]

The death of Governor Clinton had been of primary importance in that it had resolved the issue of primacy between Clinton and Van Buren in the Jacksonian movement of New York. With the followers of the former cast adrift and their leverage reduced in the Jacksonian organization, the event appeared "favorable to the administration," Clay optimistically predicted. The contemporary political analyst Jabez Hammond estimated that three-fourths of the old Clintonian party favored Adams and that many of those who had followed their leader into the Jackson camp now returned to support of the administration.[26]

They were not, however, welcomed into political leadership. When the friends of Adams convened at Utica in July 1828 to nominate electors, all their officers were chosen from the anti-Clintonian faction. The wounds of the divisions in the gubernatorial election two years earlier still rankled. Although Charles King remained committed to the Adams administration, Clinton's death opened the way for a strong minority of the "High Minders" to follow James Hamilton and Josiah Hoffman into the opposition. Some former Federalists of New York City, concerned about the preservation of shipping interests, found Jackson's equivocation on the tariff issue preferable to the administration's emphasis upon it. With this group, too, the declining West Indies traffic also had an influence. The administration's problem of bringing together the Republican–Clintonian–Anti-Masonic forces of western New York with the Federalist-Clintonians and "High-Minders" to the north and east reflected in that state, as in the nation generally, the enormous difficulties in trying to coalesce the fragmented interest groups of sectional, economic, social, and partisan affiliation.

The president, during the closing days of the campaign, contributed to the problem of attracting former Federalists to his support. In an attempt to refute Jacksonian criticism of Adams's Federalist background, as well as to develop the record of his relationship with Jefferson, one of the president's supporters obtained the publication of a letter from the great Virginian, written in December 1825 when his mind was no longer clear, which implied that Adams had accused New England Federalists of treasonous association with the British during the War of 1812. As the editor of the *National Journal* (Washington) printed the correspondence, on 21 October 1828, he provided an accompanying statement, "authorized" by Adams, clarifying the dating of Jefferson's recollection but, at the same time, indicating that the New Englander had in fact informed Jefferson of the existence in 1807 of a letter from the governor of Nova Scotia "to a person" in Massachusetts, discussing a French plot "to effect the conquest of the British Provinces on this Continent" by first producing a war between the United States and England. Adams noted further that he had also advised his then senatorial colleague William Branch Giles of the great opposition to the embargo legislation in Massachusetts and had warned that its continuance "would certainly be met by forcible resistance, supported by the Legislature, and probably by the Judiciary of the State." Were counteractive force used by the federal government, he had predicted, "it would produce a civil war; and . . . , in that event, he had no doubt the leaders of the party *would* secure the co-operation with them of Great Britain." For several years, "he knew from unequivocal evidence," they had had as their objective "dissolution of the Union, and the establishment of a separate Confederation. . . ."

Federalist cries of outrage were vehement and immediate, heightened perhaps by the growing national reaction to the contemporary South Carolina protest over the new tariff law. The editor of the *Salem* (Mass.) *Gazette* promptly announced his shift to support of Jackson. Even Charles King expressed disgust. Sergeant informed the president that his "federal letter" had occasioned "a very extensive and unpleasant effect." Ezekiel Webster, who was still prominent as a New Hampshire Federalist, complained to his brother Daniel that there never had been a publication he "so regretted" as the president's piece. Duff Green's *United States Telegraph*, after long deploring Adams's Federalist associations, now criticized his apostasy: "The course which Mr. Adams had pursued towards the federal party of New England, cannot fail to open the eyes of all honorable men to his true character."[27]

Nationally, the Jacksonians carried the electoral vote for the presidency in November 1828 by 178 to 83. The popular majority was 56 percent, 647,276 to 508,064. The administration was defeated decisively. It was repudiated not only in the South but also in the nation's heartland, the Middle States and the West, the area for which its campaign had been most particularly designed.

Although lagging organizational effort had continued to handicap the administration forces through 1828, it was not, in the final balloting, the critical factor that it had been during the congressional elections of the previous two years. The margin of Jackson's victory was close in Louisiana, New York, and Ohio—53, 51, and 52 percent respectively; but in none of these states was there such limited voter participation as to suggest that greater activity by the friends of the administration in the later stages of the campaign could have changed the outcome. If, as has been estimated, only 47 percent of the adult white males in Louisiana could vote, the percentage of the electorate that went to the polls must have been very high. In New York, 63 percent of the electorate voted; in Ohio, 67. While relatively low rates of popular interest were marked in Georgia, Alabama, Tennessee, and Illinois, the strong endorsement of Jackson by voters in each of those states indicates the stability of the outcome. In most states, voting by general ticket conveyed the whole of the electoral block to the leading candidate. Of the few that allotted the votes by district, Maine's single vote for Jackson might have been garnered had more than 39 percent of the electorate been drawn out; but in New York and Maryland the high levels of voting pointed to a political concern that, on election day, must have been firmly committed. Accretions of one or two electoral votes could have made little difference.

Despite its record of maladroit tactics, the administration won the Anti-Masonic and most of the Federalist districts—all but one of the votes of the New England States, sixteen from New York, Delaware's three, and six of Maryland's eleven. The Federalist counties of the upper Hudson Valley and central New York and areas settled by New Englanders in northern and western New York, northwestern Pennsylvania, northern and southeastern Ohio, and northern Indiana and Illinois backed the president. Not all the political errors had been committed by Adams's adherents—McLane's ineptitude in alienating local factions split the Federalist swing to Jackson and contributed to his defeat in Delaware. Southard's influence successfully countered the defection of the Stocktons in New Jersey.[28]

Above all, however, the administration needed to have carried the general-ticket votes of the upper Ohio Valley—Pennsylvania and Ohio, with either Kentucky or Indiana. That of the Keystone State was crucial. Sixty-seven percent of its voters supported Jackson, but only 51 percent of those who were eligible went to the polls. The Quakers, who disliked Jackson's identification with the army and with slavery, supported the administration; but the German farmers, who were predominantly Federalist but politically inactive, did not. The president won only Adams, Bucks, and Delaware counties in the German district. An estimated half of the Pennsylvania Federalists supported Jackson, including the German followers of Kremer and Buchanan.[29] Even the city of Philadelphia—together with New York and Baltimore—fell to the Tennessean.

Repudiation of the president personally was very evident when viewed in relation to local elections in the West during the fall of 1828. Friends of the administration that year won the gubernatorial offices in Ohio, Indiana, Kentucky, and Louisiana and held control of the state legislatures in Ohio, Indiana, and Louisiana. They retained a two to one majority in the congressional delegation of Indiana; that of Louisiana was equally divided; the Ohio delegation was lost narrowly, eight to six. In none of these States, however, could they carry the presidency for Adams.

Professing disbelief in the charges of bargain and corruption, Governor Ray of Indiana wrote of the administration: "Its *measures*, I found to be good, wholesome for the people of the Union, and particularly Indiana." Yet he also discredited "the charge upon General Jackson, that he is hostile to internal improvements and the protection

TABLE 2

The Presidential Election of 1828

State	Electoral Votes		Popular Vote			Electorate[a]	
	Adams	Jackson	Adams	Jackson	Jackson's Percentage	Total	Percentage Voting
Maine	8	1	20,733	13,927	40	89,970	39
New Hampshire	8		24,134	20,922	46	62,651	72
Vermont	7		25,363	8,350	25	65,501	51
Massachusetts	15		29,876	6,016	17	150,573	24
Rhode Island	4		2,754	821	23	22,060	16
Connecticut	8		13,838	4,448	24	71,826	25
New York[b]	16	20	135,413	140,763	51	436,058	63
New Jersey	8		23,764	21,951	48	69,386	66
Pennsylvania		28	50,848	101,652	67	296,272	51
Delaware[c]	3						
Maryland	6	5	25,527	24,565	49	70,501	71
Virginia		24	12,101	26,752	69	150,055	26
North Carolina		15	13,918	37,857	73	97,276	53
South Carolina[c]		11					
Georgia		9		19,363	100	62,782	31
Alabama		5	1,938	17,138	90	40,962	47
Mississippi		3	1,581	6,772	81	16,762	50
Louisiana		5	4,076	4,603	53	25,886	34
Kentucky		14	31,460	39,397	56	108,695	65
Tennessee		11	2,240	44,293	95	104,833	44
Missouri		3	3,400	8,272	71	25,149	46
Ohio		16	63,396	67,597	52	194,860	67
Indiana		5	17,052	22,257	57	66,888	59
Illinois		3	4,662	9,560	67	32,667	44
Total	83	178	508,074	647,276	56	2,261,613	51

[a] Computed on the basis of free white male population over the age of twenty-one, according to the federal census of 1830. Suffrage restrictions in the form of property-holding or tax-payment qualifications disenfranchised about half of the totals listed for Rhode Island, Virginia, and Louisiana. See Richard P. McCormick, *The Second American Party System: Party Formation in the Jacksonian Era* (Chapel Hill: University of North Carolina Press, 1966), pp. 77, 179, and 312. Although tax-paying requirements applied in a number of other states, they were not generally a seriously limiting restriction.

[b] The electoral vote was actually closer, for two at-large electors were chosen by the Jacksonian district majority, 18 to 16. *Niles' Weekly Register* 35 (22 Nov. 1828): 194.

[c] Electors named by state legislature.

of *home* industry. . . ." Ray had therefore "determined to occupy *neutral* ground." The so-called friends of the administration in Missouri sought similarly to disassociate themselves.[30]

Although the forms of organizational structure had finally been developed by the president's adherents in the West, too often they had been put in motion with ritualistic apathy. The central committee of the friends of the administration in Indiana had met only once, while their Jacksonian organizational counterpart sat six times. From Kentucky, Worsley had lamented that Adams's supporters remained on their farms, but Jacksonians were "swimming rivers and risking their lives to get to the polls." Robert P. Letcher had warned in late August 1828: "They have their forces better disciplined, and can bring them to the pools [*sic*] with greater facility than our party can. . . ." In September, Clay's friends from Lexington and Frankfort reported meetings at which they had finally "matured a system of organization," which they hoped would "bring to the polls the whole of our strength. . . ." The higher-than-average voter participation in Kentucky, Ohio, Indiana, and Louisiana during the presidential election testified to the excitement that had been stimulated by the Jacksonian challenge; but for the friends of the administration it represented a response, not an initiative.[31]

Why had Jackson won so decisively throughout much of the nation? Adams's adherents had been slow to organize politically, thus permitting Jacksonians to gain congressional leadership and, consequently, to blunt or distort the administration's record of programmatic achievement. Historians have disagreed on the merit of the amalgamation approach inherent in the organizational effort. It was repugnant to Jeffersonian Republicans, but whether the gains attainable in Pennsylvania and the West without Federalist ties could have offset the attendant losses is questionable. The problems, under either strategy, pointed up the internal tensions among the administration's forces.

Sergeant, explaining the defeat in Philadelphia, noted that "Local dissensions . . . had some influence. . . ." The opposition of Republican supporters that had long blocked the judicial appointment of the Federalist Joseph Hopkinson struck at a leader who was identified as "the moving cause of the junction of the two parties, in those counties, heretofore known, as federal—Such as Delaware Chester, Lancaster & the City of Phila." Clay's adherents were also highly critical of the president's friendship with Robert Walsh, Jr., the Federalist editor of the *National Gazette* (Philadelphia), whose editorials, Adams himself noted, exhibited "constantly a hostile spirit to Mr. Clay. . . ." The president had finally intervened to push Walsh into grudging endorsement of the administration. Disclaiming any desire to influence the journal's policy, Adams had informed the editor that "the savage and profligate character of the war waged against the Administration," not only by Jackson, his partisans, and his press, but also by Walsh himself, "could not be met by moderation and magnanimity. . . ."[32]

Throughout the nation, fragmented Federalists were affiliating with the forces of both Jackson and Adams, but the president's identification with Federalism was a major ground of criticism in the Ohio Valley West. There, where the settlement stream had been predominantly southern, the Jeffersonian tradition was strong. Political rallying cries that recalled the partisan struggles over the Alien and Sedition Acts, the annexation of Louisiana, and the coming of the War of 1812 struck responsive chords. Rumors of the president's assurances against Federalist proscription, as projected in Webster's Warfield correspondence of January 1825, circulated during the campaign and aggravated Republican sensitivities. Clay, who had long played upon those themes, now found them turned against his new associations. Kendall and Green bared the record of Clay's earlier attacks upon Adams, and Blair complained that where once Clay's voice had "rallied the power of the democratic party to defeat the domestic enemy arrayed . . . by foreign influence during the second war . . . for Independence," the Kentuckian had now "made Webster & Sergeant 'the lords of the ascendant.'" To lend his "mantle to those men" was "withering to the hopes of many" who had once followed him "as the great Champion of their Cause."[33]

That personal as well as political attachments also proved divisive became apparent in the postelection lamentations of the respective partisans. In his most important campaign speech, at Cincinnati at the end of August 1828, Clay had turned aside the "flattering partiality" of his adherents to reiterate his endorsement of the course of the administration. Had he himself been the chief magistrate, "the measures . . . would not have been, in any essential particular, different from those . . . adopted." The Kentuckian's friends, however, subsequently attributed the defeat to his association with Adams and assured their favorite of his future triumph as "the great head & hope of the great mass that constitutes the present administration party." Louisa Adams, on the other hand, recorded that "among the respectable portion of the party" there was "something more than suspicion of foul play in a great Western leader whose intimate connection with the P. ought to have kept him [Clay] steady had he ever possessed one principle of honor." The president, observing the enthusiastic plaudits for the secretary of state by his western friends, bitterly reflected that the election outcome had resulted from the desertion and betrayal of that leader's own particular adherents. The New Englander had expected a consolidated opposition from the "disappointed candidates"—Jackson, Crawford, and Calhoun—but "did not foresee that the supporters of the fourth, Mr. Clay, would have joined in the chase, the first object of which was to hunt him [Clay] down." They had "clustered to strangle him whom they had crawled ineffectually to raise, and transferred their homage to the quarter where thrift might follow fawning."[34]

Both leaders saw the explanation in the corrosive impact of sectional divisions. The president noted, in reference to Clay's western opposition, that "sectional feeling" had proved "more powerful than personal attachment. . . ." In a New Year's Eve conversation with the chief executive after the election, the Kentuckian also voiced alarm for the country in the combination of "threats of disunion from the South, and the graspings after all the public lands, . . . disclosing themselves in the Western States."[35] The theme of southern and western political bargaining, soon to be fully explicated in the famous Webster-Hayne debate, was already operational.

For some critics of the administration, States' rights provided an ideologic basis of opposition to programmatic nationalism. Southern leaders—the "Old Republicans" of the Richmond Junto, the South Carolinians who were already threatening secession, the Georgians and Mississippians whose land hunger fueled the controversy, even such Kentucky relief proponents as Francis Preston Blair—staked their position upon grounds of old constitutional argument, "the great divisions which marked the era of 1798."[36] Demands for restraint upon the extent and cost of federal enterprise, for restoration of power to the states, and, in its most extreme demagoguery, for preservation of democracy over aristocracy filled the congressional debates and, as Jackson's latest biographer demonstrates, shaped the general's philosophy.

But Van Buren, in initially pressing Jackson's candidacy upon Ritchie, had rested it upon "personal popularity." "Indeed," the New Yorker had argued, "Genl. Jackson has been so little in public life, that it will be not a little difficult to contrast his opinions on great questions with those of Mr. Adams."[37] In the crucial Middle States and Ohio Valley States there was scant desire to forego the benefits of expanded federal activity. From Pennsylvania to Louisiana the demand for a protective tariff and for governmental aid to internal improvements was so strong that Jackson dared not unequivocally propound programmatic views. The measures of Kentucky's relief advocates, who comprised the base of Jacksonian support in that state, had been decisively repudiated as an alternative to conservative credit controls. Even the issues of individual liberty were at least as powerfully addressed in the administration's warnings against the dangers of military despotism as in the Jacksonian alarms over Adams's Federalist antecedents. Here the mixture of the opposition's concerns was less programmatic and ideologic than cultural.

The element of personal charisma, Adams's lack and Jackson's abundance of it, evoked a multifaceted sectional distinctiveness. It was not Anti-Masonry, and perhaps not even Federalism, that carried into support of the administration the districts into which New England settlement had expanded and into the opposition those throughout the Midwest that had southern antecedents. The president's personal popularity had not been enhanced by his years in the White House. Even in New Hampshire, Ezekiel Webster commented, in reference to the defeat of 1828, that voters "always supported his cause from a cold sense of duty, & not upon any liking of Mr. Adams."[38] Adams's aristocratic tastes, intellectual interests, and social insecurity appeared as coldness, craft, and superciliousness. In the West, such attributes were identified as Yankee, with all the opprobrious connotations conjurable by a population of southern background. The extremes of congressional and journalistic criticism of the president's dress, life style, and intellectual pursuits marked one aspect of this problem. Yet another appeared in the contemporaneous attack by Kentucky Presbyterians upon Transylvania University and its Unitarian identification, an assault upon both the president's reported spiritual beliefs and upon Clay's Bluegrass adherents.

Ethnic associations, closely related to such distinctions, have also been frequently noted in the voting patterns. A heavily Scotch-Irish derivation of voters hostile to the New Englander was evident not only in the West but also in the one district of Maine that opposed his reelection. Irish population centers, in New York City as well as the New York counties of Sullivan and Delaware, voted overwhelmingly for Jackson. Adams, it had been charged, was hostile to Catholicism, as evidenced in his message to Congress justifying the Panama Mission as an opportunity to counteract the "bigotry, prejudice, and oppression" of the established religion in Latin America. Revelation of the variety and scope of cultural concerns encompassed in such particularistic fragments affords one of the most fruitful areas of current historiography. It clarifies the magnitude of the internal divisions that political organization was required to embrace.

The persistent charges of "bribery and corruption" undoubtedly influenced many voters, yet evidence abounds that leading Jacksonians—Benton, Blair, and even Van Buren—saw nothing in them as a fundamental issue stand. The New Yorker, writing his *Autobiography* some thirty years later, extended his repudiating testimonial beyond the issue of corruption in Adams's election to the broader Jacksonian argument of dishonesty in the administration. Adams, he commented, "was an honest man, not only incorruptible himself, but . . . an enemy to venality in every department of the public service."[39] That assertion ignored the record of dishonesty, evidenced in the Treasury and War departments under Monroe's administration, which had not been eradicated because of Adams's reluctance to press for removal of political opponents. The New Englander was to be mortified by the revelation, under his successor, that his own political lieutenant, Tobias Watkins, left the office of fourth auditor with a shortage of $3,300 in his accounts. But the defalcations during the Adams administration appeared as mere peccadilloes to those who later looked back upon the theft of more than $1,250,000 by Jackson's appointee Samuel Swartwout, during his eight years as collector of New York, and the widespread Land Office and post-office corruption revealed during the latter years of the general's administration.

The argument which Clay could not refute in the Jacksonian attack was that he had made the decision to commit his support to a New Englander rather than to a westerner. Clay, like Adams, had become an apostate to regional mythology. He had been prepared to forget that Adams was the son of the old Federalist leader, that at Ghent the New Englander had given primacy to fishing privileges over exclusivity in Mississippi River navigation, that he had been slow to appreciate the importance of expanding western boundaries and western trade. Clay had found, instead, that Adams, alone of the contending presidential candidates, upheld the views which he, Clay, shared of the course for national development.

Critics, then and since, have contended that, whether or not bribery was involved, the Kentuckian's was a self-centered judgment, dictated by his personal hopes for political advancement. The argument need be pursued here only to note that Clay's views reflected the fact that his own Bluegrass political base was more closely affiliated with eastern mercantile, financial, and manufacturing interests than with the indebted farmers "south of Green River." He retained the endorsement of his local constituency and regularly returned as their spokesman in the national councils throughout the remainder of his life. Clay's "corruption" was the error of political misjudgment in generalizing the trends of intrasectional change.

In focusing its program upon nationalism through economic adjustments honed to sectional interests, the administration had oversimplified its analysis of the instabilities of American development. For many voters, as the Georgia and Virginia resolutions had showed and as those of South Carolina would soon replicate, the nation was not the entity of governmental preeminence. Sectionalism itself was many faceted and as yet had imperfectly coalesced. States had not been consolidated into consistently definable sectional units and, within themselves, encompassed divisive aspirations. Moreover, economic interests were not—sectionally, locally, or individually—solely the motivating concern.

Finally, in their reliance upon dispassionate evaluation of their program, the Adams forces displayed an attachment to policy-oriented leadership that was no longer viable in the changing political context of the period. The president's closely reasoned messages, Clay's forensic argument, Rush's expository papers—all were anachronistic as a technique for generating support. Men like Duff Green pronounced them false, and a cloud of doubt confused popular judgment. Attitudinal responses, more emotional than reasoned, blinded voters to Jackson's manifest evasions on issues to which they professed a firm commitment. Resting upon particularism and widespread anti-intellectualism, and new-found power for evocation of such sentiments, the art of politics had become the communication of cultural catchwords and their consolidation under personal symbolism, with tenets but incoherently defined.

13

★ ★ ★ ★ ★

AFTERMATH

Little governmental action occurred during the closing months of the administration. Jacksonians at the second session of the Twentieth Congress, convened in December 1828, were disinclined to pursue retrenchment proposals that would be applicable to their own activities. They centered their spleen on the few measures that were urged by administration supporters, most notably the appropriation for the South Sea expedition, proposals for additional funding of internal improvements, a call for publication of the instructions to the Panama commissioners, and approval of Adams's final nominations for appointment. After extended debate, an appropriation of $100,000 for repair of the Cumberland Road was finally approved. Clay's hope for incorporation of the Panama instructions in the official congressional records, a matter of personal pride, was denied. On January 17 the president was informed that the majority of the Senate Judiciary Committee had decided to oppose any further appointments during the session, unless "cases of special necessity . . ."; and on February 12, after two months of controversy, his nomination of Clay's friend John J. Crittenden to the Supreme Court was rejected. Adams had advised suspension of diplomatic instructions to Brown in France on January 16 and shortly thereafter recommended interruption of pending negotiations for a commercial treaty with Prussia, leaving such matters to the succeeding administration. In mid February he directed that activity under all Treasury and Indian accounts also be postponed.[1]

Such a course was the more necessary because most of the secretaries—Clay, Rush, and Southard—were ill during much of the period. Louisa Adams, writing to her son Charles Francis in late January, described them as "the weakly Administration." But the president's "constitution," she also commented, appeared "to be quite renovated. . . ."[2]

Adams's failing health throughout the extended election campaign had induced him to pursue exercise and relaxation with almost desperate determination. Regularly he had enjoyed summer morning "baths," in the Potomac while at Washington or in the ocean when at Quincy. Warnings about the dangers of swimming in the channel, the embarrassment of losing his clothes when the boat tipped, and the doctor's caution that a persistent pain in his side might be aggravated by the effort had deterred him only briefly. As an alternative, he walked for an hour or more, to the Capitol Square or to College Hill above Georgetown. In the spring of 1828 he had begun daily horseback riding. Although at first he had experienced "such extreme lassitude through the greater part of the day" that he was "unable either to write or read," he continued to ride ten to fourteen miles regularly, usually in company with his son John.[3]

During the stressful months of the tariff debate, he had slept somewhat later than usual, rising "two or three times in broad daylight"; but by the winter of 1828/29 his routine had returned to normal. He arose around five o'clock, built his fire, wrote until breakfast time, between nine and ten, read newspapers for an hour or so, then received visitors, consulted with cabinet members, and handled mail until three-thirty or four. He rode for two hours or walked for one before dining between five and six. Since Louisa was unwell, he spent "an evening hour or two" in her chamber and then returned to his own to write again for two or three hours until eleven o'clock or midnight. He rarely left home for social gatherings. A large weekly dinner party, fortnightly receptions, and "occasional company of one, two, or three to dine . . . in the family" broke the monotony. It was a routine "so habitual," he wrote, "that it forms part of the comfort of my existence, and I look forward with great solicitude to the time when it must be totally changed."[4]

The writing for which he strained to find uninterrupted hours during his final weeks in office focused on three extended papers. One was the subsequently withheld brief defining the authority pertaining to a brevet military title, which was directed specifically to counteract the pretensions of General Scott. The others were responses to thirteen prominent Federalists who, immediately after the election, had publicly demanded proof of the conspiracy and identification of the conspirators mentioned in Adams's campaign statement on Massachusetts Federalism during the embargo controversy. All were closely reasoned documents, entailing great care in documentation and analysis. The Federalists who had challenged the president's allegations were, in some instances, his longstanding personal friends. Seeing himself under a "double persecution," he anticipated a hostile reception upon his return to Boston and lamented the bitterness that had been engendered. Yet he was determined to prove the validity of his charges.

Adams published his first *Reply* to the Massachusetts Federalists on December 30. Denying that his criticism applied to the whole Federalist party or that the thirteen who had challenged him represented that constituency, he refused to name to them the leaders of the alleged plot. While he could cite no "overt act of treason," he pointed to a repudiation of federal authority and to an emphasis upon States' rights that had dominated the thinking of *"certain leaders"* of the Federalist party from the annexation of Louisiana until the Hartford Convention. He rejected the theory that the authorities of a state could authorize resistance to the acts of Congress: ". . . the *people* of a State . . . have delegated no such power to their legislatures or their judges. . . ." Indeed, he denied "the right even of the people" constitutionally "to secede at pleasure from the Union." Such an act "presupposes a departure from the principle of compact and a resort to that of force." The controversy was thus identified with the issue of South Carolina's mounting protest against the tariff, and he meant for his paper to respond to both sources of contention.[5]

His Federalist critics returned to the attack at the end of January 1829. The president, they averred, had brought into disrepute not only "their ancient friends" in the Federalist party but also the state of Masschusetts. Adams aggrievedly complained that the respondents had attacked him "at the very moment when . . . the public favor seemed to have deserted him,—at the close of his career of public service, when he had no longer any power to exercise, or favors to bestow,—at the very moment when the favor of the successor to his station might best be propitiated by a rancorous and unrelenting persecution of him." He thereupon began yet another "reply," in this case virtually a history of the struggle between the Federalists and the Republicans from his father's presidency to the Hartford meeting. Throughout the spring he searched for supporting data and continued his writing. But when he consulted various associates concerning the draft manuscript, he was generally advised to withhold it or, at least, to moderate its severity. Later in the year, some of the documentation was appended to a pamphlet edition of the previous correspondence. The notes on the early party conflict were supplied to Philip R. Fendall to use in a proposed historical account of the period. As with the response to Scott's demands for a more elevated military status, Adams abandoned months of literary effort, in this instance a manuscript of some 84,000 words. The exercise had, at least, busied him through the transition to private life: "I have found that occupation suspended the pains of disappointment," he noted in reference to his defeat for reelection, "and has even filled with enjoyment time which would otherwise have been distracted with anguish and agitation."[6]

Adams did feel acutely the repudiation implicit in what he saw as "the overwhelming ruin of the Administration." Like his father before him, he would not endure the agony of attending his rival's inauguration. In retrospect, however, he perceived nothing in his conduct of the presidency that he "could have avoided" and nothing that he "ought to repent." He took consolation in the "prosperous condition of the country" and remarked that it removed "from the load of public care all its pain, and almost all its weariness."[7] The last of his annual messages to Congress included sweeping passages of prideful assessment of the work of his administration.

In reference to foreign relations, he reported a partial settlement of United States claims upon Denmark and Brazil and an expectation that the remainder would shortly be adjusted. With unwarranted optimism, he also voiced an anticipation that those upon France would "ere long receive a favorable consideration." While commercial difficulties with Great Britain required "the serious consideration of Congress," he concluded that "the exports, the revenue, the navigation of the United States . . . [had] suffered no diminution by . . . exclusion from direct access to the British colonies." Those dependencies were paying dearly in charges for "double voyages, freight, insurance, and commission," as alternative channels were substituted for the "indispensable" trade with the United States. With some bravado, he warned that the general Anglo-American commercial convention could be terminated if other British measures, "more pointedly bearing upon the navigation of the United States" and "manifestly incompatible with the positive stipulations" of that arrangement, were not "modified" in their interpretation.[8]

Emphasizing the longstanding national commitment to liberalism and reciprocity in commercial arrangements, he noted that the United States now had "free trade" throughout the Western Hemisphere and "even with the insular colonies of all the European nations," excepting only the British possessions. He anticipated an acceptance soon of the principles in negotiations with other states and cited the pendency of the treaties with Austria and Mexico. He also alluded vaguely to his desire for commercial ties with Turkey, even as he expressed hope that the Russian war upon that country would give opportunity for the ultimate "triumph of humanity and of freedom" for the "suffering Greeks."

Writing of the domestic program, Adams stressed the interrelationship of agricultural, commercial, and manufacturing interests, "so linked in union together that no permanent cause of prosperity to one of them can operate without extending its influence to the others." All were "alike under the protecting power of the legislative authority," and the "representative bodies" bore the responsibility "to conciliate them in harmony together." While the necessity for meeting the revenue needs of the nation "should be adapted as much as possible to suit the burden with equal hand upon all in proportion with their ability of bearing it without oppression," he noted that sometimes the interests of other nations pressed "most unequally upon the several component interests" of their neighbors. Britain, for example, had excluded "the great staple of productions of our Middle and Western States" and had proscribed "with equal rigor the bulkier lumber and live stock of the same portion and also of the Northern and Eastern part of our Union." It accepted southern rice only "aggravated with a charge of duty upon the Northern carrier." Its partiality to cotton, received "almost duty free," was dictated by the needs of its looms "to the destruction of our own manufactures, which they are enabled thus to undersell." This, then, was the basis upon which the tariff legislation had been designed. "To the great principle sanctioned by that act—one of those upon which the Constitution itself was formed," he hoped that "the authorities of the Union" would "adhere."

He pointed, too, to another of "these cardinal measures of policy," in the provision for "great and lasting works of public improvement"—the surveys of roads; examinations for canal routes; removal of obstructions to rivers and harbors; subscriptions to the Delaware and Chesapeake, the Louisville and Portland, the Dismal Swamp, and the Chesapeake and Ohio canals; appropriations for the Delaware breakwater; and land grants for other improvements in Ohio, Indiana, Illinois, and Alabama. At the same time, the more traditional measures of national defense had not been neglected; there had been "steady and progressive" advances in naval preparedness, land fortifications, and officer training. Acclaiming the West Point Academy as "the living armory of the nation," he stressed its "beneficial results . . . already experienced in the composition of the Army, and their influence . . . in the intellectual progress of society." Adams had not surrendered to the anti-intellectualism of his critics.

Much of the president's message was keyed to the theme of prosperity. He had found Rush's annual "Report" particularly "pleasing." Incorporating a summation of the progress achieved during the whole period of the administration, the secretary's accounting showed that public revenue had increased by more than $18 million over that for the preceding four years. More than $30.3 million had been paid on the principal of the public debt and nearly $15 million as interest on the debt. Apart from such payments, public expenditures had been increased by less than 10 percent, the bulk of that increase being encompassed in the sum of about $14 million for internal improvements. For the current year the Treasury report indicated receipts nearly $2 million greater than had been estimated when the appropriations were requested. Nine million dollars had been paid on the principal of the debt, and an additional $3 million for interest on the balance. Interest charges, through liquidation of the outstanding 6 percent securities, had been reduced during the year by over half a million dollars annually.[9]

Most of the increased revenue had come from higher tariff rates, but the *value* of merchandise imports during the past four years exceeded that of the previous quadrennium by 13 percent. The value of merchandise exports, despite the severity of depression in Europe, was also greater than for the earlier period, by 16 percent. Surpluses in the balance of payments had been achieved in two years of the last four, a record that had not been equaled in the previous administration and was not again to be matched until the 1840s. With a mercantilistic concern that "the real value of exports should by a small . . . balance exceed that of imports, that balance being a permanent addition to the wealth of the nation," Adams emphasized the commercial record and particularly the opening of new markets. Ignoring the declining commodity prices, which apart from a brief period in 1825 had been marked throughout the decade, he pointed instead to the admittedly "accidental and temporary" increase in returns to farmers of the Middle States and the West, which had been occasioned by short European harvests in the late summer and fall. The lifting of normal interdictions against American wheat and flour might last only one year, he conceded, but optimistically he alluded to the experience "in the revolutions of time" frequently marked by "scarcity harvests in succession." Hastily, then, he added a "consolatory reflection" that "the sufferings of scarcity in distant lands" were not attributable to this nation, that they came "from the dispensation of Him who ordains all in wisdom and goodness, and who permits evil itself only as an instrument of good; that, far from contributing to this scarcity," the United States had acted "only to the alleviation of its severity," that in so doing the nation reduced its surplus but added to the price of its own bread, "so as in some degree to participate in the wants which it will be the good fortune of our country to relieve."[10]

Adams's reasoning balanced regard for the profit motive with Puritan moralism to a degree that well illustrated why he had been so strongly identified as "the candidate of *all New England*—of the universal Yankee nation wherever dispersed throughout the Union."[11] It was an outlook that had incurred the derision of his political opponents; but as with his program of domestic development generally, it expressed policy concerns that were to have more extended application at a later period in the nation's history.

From its inception the Adams administration had been politically vulnerable to particularistic pressures. Elected as a minority candidate, the president had pledged to continue the nonpartisan stance and the harmonizing programmatic trends of his predecessor, but he had inherited a climate of change in which the myth of "good feeling" had already broken down. The economic instabilities of postwar readjustment had not been resolved. New sectional interests had engendered shifting focuses of concern and, within even so delimited a framework, a variety of local and individualized sensitivities. Institutional fragmentation, mirroring the flux, had invited realignments—economic, social, and political.

Out of such regrouping had come the alliance between Adams and Clay, as the champions of the "American System." Although the program had been initiated under Monroe, its genesis was peculiarly identified with the new leaders, who brought to it a conceptual enthusiasm that had been lacking in the Virginian's tentative endorsement. In foreign affairs they had aimed to combine expansion of the carrying trade with opening of new markets, a blending of the older New England shipping interests with the developing demands of agricultural sections for a broader range of trading outlets. In their emphasis upon relationships with the newly independent Latin-American states, Adams and Clay had joined pragmatic considerations with those of an ideologic glorification of the nation's republican, even specifically of its federal, governmental form. Domestically, they had looked to a merging of regional interests by correlative promotion of the home-market economy—through governmental aid to internal improvements, a centralized credit structure, and protection of domestic manufactures. In essence the plans projected aggressive nationalism.

Such an integrated agenda had enhanced the vulnerabilities. The diplomatic goals challenged the Old World generally and, in their commercial aspects, Britain particularly. They also rested upon perceptions of Latin-American development which were, at best, idealistic and, at worst, presumptuous. On the one hand, they assumed that the new governments were sufficiently stable to operate with responsible independence. On the other, they anticipated that these states would submerge their aspirations under the hegemony of a northern neighbor which was unprepared to assist in their fulfillment, or perhaps even to tolerate that outcome.

The foreign policy also presented problems at home. Attainment of the commercial goals rested upon a proffered reciprocity, which inherently entailed the obverse relationship, discrimination. Yet the United States' definitional boundaries to "reciprocity" were not acceptable to the British, and as Americans had learned under Thomas Jefferson, economic sanctions could be mutually hurtful. When British concessions on the West Indies trade split the interests of American marketers from those of American shippers, the policy agreement had been jeopardized. That Adams, a New Englander, had attempted to uphold concerns that were most applicable to his constituency required a commitment to nationalistic pretensions which suffering farmers and traders of the Middle States and the West found questionable. The concept of mission proved similarly divisive when southerners, increasingly defensive of their reliance upon slave labor, protested relationships that threatened to identify the nation with criticism of their regional institution. Ideological nationalism in American politics of the 1820s foundered upon pragmatic interests, most of them yet too localized for generalization.

The domestic program posed similar sectional—even intrasectional—challenges. Despite the breadth of the approach to internal improvements, such development was of uneven impact. It was of far greater importance and greater practicability for the Middle States and the West than for New England or the South. The last region, blessed with numerous deep-flowing waterways to convey its productions east and south from the Appalachian crescent, could afford to reject national assistance. Heavily dependent upon depressed European markets, southerners saw far greater gain by removing the tariffs under which highways and canals must be financed. Segments of New England, however, now had the incentive of protecting infant industries as an offset to the limited potentiality for transportation development. The *linkage* of the tariff and improvements issues in bonding the regional constituencies of Adams and Clay was vital to the administration's concerns.

The centralized credit and monetary controls of the Bank of the United States also evoked disintegrating reactions. The availability of capital in coastal commercial centers and its scarcity in the back country, a creditor/debtor relationship of perennial tension, was heightened in the 1820s by the bank's efforts to meet the calls of financially embarrassed European lenders and to liquidate the national debt. Relief agitation in the Ohio Valley States, Anti-Masonry in upcountry New York, Pennsylvania, and New England, and labor and antiauction movements in eastern cities expressed growing dissatisfaction with the dominance of established institutional elites. The surfacing of antibank sentiment in the debates of the Twentieth Congress pointed to the danger in these yet localized protests as a threat to a major component of the American System.

Finally, the administration's concern to conserve the public lands as a national capital—a security for public indebtedness and a resource from which to generate revenues for public improvement—set the framework of countering sectional alliance between the South and the West, already marked since the Confederation period. In the balancing of regional interests, the West cared little about the preservation of slavery and, under the agricultural provisions of the tariff of 1828, actually opposed southern views; but the promise of cheap land offered more general benefits than even the largesse of internal improvements. Adams was to write bitterly in 1837 of the Jacksonian repudiation of "the system of internal improvements by National means and National Energies":

The great object of my life . . . as applied to the administration of the Government of the United States has *failed*— The American Union as a moral Person in the family of Nations, is to live from hand to mouth, to cast away, instead of using for the improvement of its own condition, the bounties of Providence, . . . to rivet into perpetuity the clanking chain of the Slave, and to waste in boundless bribery to the west the invaluable inheritance of the Public Lands.[12]

To maintain that the campaign of 1828 was devoid of issues is to ignore the tenets of the Adams administration. It had presented a balanced, cohesive, and focused program of nationalism—positive, forward looking, perceptive in its vision of the country's future course of growth—a worthy agenda on which to celebrate the jubilee of independence. The Adams-Clay alliance had rested upon commitments to that program, and both leaders had adhered to it with remarkable harmony.

Adams was certainly more attached to New England shipping interests than was his secretary of state, and less interested in projecting ideologic democracy beyond hemispheric bounds; but their counteractive pressures were more moderating than negative. Their goals in domestic policy were similarly compatible. Whatever the president's reservations on the tariff revision of 1828, he had held no doubt about congressional authority to act on the matter. Rejecting the western cry for relaxation in the public-land policy, Clay had joined him with the voice of a constituency that had already found its interest in the maturation of the national, rather than the regional, perspective. Adams and Clay's focal strategy was the American System, in foreign and domestic policy a program that elevated nationalism.

As yet, however, proponents of the administration had had few data on which to measure what they saw as a healthily growing national economy. Treasury statistics vindicating the effort had not been the stuff of campaign journalism. When noted, they had been misinterpreted, presented as half-truth, or rejected by Jacksonian journalists. Duff Green had cited the debt-refunding project as an attempt to befuddle the voters. He had denied that payments for debt service could properly be credited as additions to the sinking fund. He had centered his discussion of governmental financial operations on the distorted conclusions of the Jacksonian congressional majority's "Retrenchment Report." "The waste of eight millions is admitted," he asserted. "We say admitted, because the charge rests upon the assertion of a member of Congress, solemnly made in debate, sustained by official reports, and unanswered by the administration presses."[13] Green did not name the congressman nor cite the reports. Presumably his summation rested upon the approximate difference between the expenditures of the Adams administration and those of Monroe's second term, without consideration of the capital investment in internal improvements.

The president's adherents could point only to the broad conceptual impulse marked in pursuit of expanded foreign commercial arrangements, in the support of a stable financial structure, in the stimulation of domestic productivity under tariff protection and aid for internal transportation—in the climate of encouragement for economic growth. Unreliable as aggregate statistics yet are for the period before 1840, they reveal that the percentage of private production income realized from manufacturing increased from 7.5 to 10.3 between 1819 and 1829. The size of the agricultural labor force during the 1820s increased by 17 percent, while that of the nonagricultural sector increased by 46 percent. The decade marked the most rapid acceleration in the number of workers engaged in nonfarm occupations prior to the Civil War. The expansion of employment in cotton-textile manufacturing was greater then than at any other time prior to the 1880s, and the increase in the number of iron and steel workers was greater than it would be again until the 1860s. The growth in the proportion of nonagricultural employment, amounting to 8.2 percent during the 1820s, compared with but 7.5 percent during the succeeding decade, ranks with 8.3 percent during the 1840s, 8.6 percent in the 1880s, and 8.8 percent from 1900 to 1910 as the highest in the nation's history.[14]

At the same time the percentage of production income that was derived from agriculture had also increased somewhat during the 1820s, from 34.4 to 34.7 percent, a rate slightly greater than would be marked for the succeeding decade (34.6). The beginning of a home market was reflected not only in the growing number of non-agricultural laborers but also in the rising number of urban residents, an increase amounting to 63 percent for urban as opposed to but 31 percent in rural population. Allowing for the decadal expansion of total population, the incremental rate of urbanization changed from a decline of 0.1 percent during the period 1810–20, to an increase of 1.6 percent during the 1820s, continuing at 2 percent during the 1830s and 4.5 percent during the 1840s and 1850s. The commercialization of agriculture in the West was evident in a doubling of the tonnage of vessels trafficking on rivers of that section between 1825 and 1828.[15]

Except for the rates of growth in manufacturing income and urbanization, these trends were all diminished during the succeeding decade, as the programs that had fostered them were abandoned under Jacksonian administration. Adherents of the American System found, in the economic travail of the years from 1837 to 1843, a manifest consequence of the "war" on the Bank of the United States, a decade of declining tariffs, and abandonment of the role of the national government in generating internal improvements. Modern analysis has challenged such perceptions by a variety of arguments. The distortions of decennial census data, reflecting changes that elevate the Adams record after the depression of 1819 and diminish that of the Jacksonians as measured in 1839, must certainly be conceded. But the acceleration of economic growth during the years of Adams's presidency is evident, a phenomenon of major signifi-cance in the nation's developmental history. And in numerous aspects it was distinctively associated with the policies of his admin-istration.

Most notable was the impact of canal development and of river and harbor improvement in the Northwest. With the opening of the Portland Canal around the falls of the Ohio, the cities of Pittsburgh,

TABLE 3

THE CHANGING STRUCTURE OF THE LABOR FORCE

	NUMBER OF AGRICULTURAL WORKERS (IN THOUSANDS)	NUMBER OF NONAGRICULTURAL WORKERS (IN THOUSANDS)	PERCENTAGE OF CHANGE IN NUMBER OF AGRICULTURAL WORKERS	PERCENTAGE OF CHANGE IN NUMBER OF NONAGRICULTURAL WORKERS	NONAGRICULTURAL EMPLOYMENT AS PERCENTAGE OF TOTAL LABOR FORCE	PERCENTAGE OF CHANGE IN RELATIONSHIP OF INDUSTRIAL EMPLOYMENT TO TOTAL FORCE
1800	1,400	500			26	
1810	1,950	380	28	− 24	16	− 10.0
1820	2,470	665	21	43	21	4.9
1830	2,965	1,235	17	46	29	8.2
1840	3,570	2,090	17	41	37	7.5
1850	4,520	3,730	21	44	45	8.3
1860	5,880	5,230	23	29	47	1.9

SOURCES: Compiled from Stanley Lebergott, *Manpower in Economic Growth: The American Record since 1800* (New York: McGraw-Hill Book Co., 1964), table A-1, p. 510; column 6 is adapted from Eric E. Lampard, ''The Evolving System of Cities in the United States: Urbanization and Economic Development,'' in *Issues in Urban Economics* . . . , edited by Harvey S. Perloff and Lowdon Wingo, Jr. (Baltimore, Md.: Published for Resources for the Future, Inc., by Johns Hopkins Press, 1968), p. 117.

Cincinnati, and Louisville entered upon major growth. Steamboats, which had previously operated with difficulty on the upper Ohio except at periods of high water, by the mid 1830s had largely supplanted barges. Similarly, the rise of Cleveland dates from its linkage, via the Ohio Canal, to Akron in 1827. The area from Dayton was opened to the Ohio by the Miami Canal in 1830, and that along the lower Wabash underwent similar development as work progressed on the Indiana Canal between 1829 and 1831. Road building by the army, which was virtually terminated after 1830, had permitted stage travel from Fremont and Maumee, Ohio, to Detroit and, in conjunction with improved harbor works along Lake Erie, had generated expansion into southern Michigan.

Agriculturally and industrially, regional growth ''took off.'' Wheat and corn prices in interior Ohio nearly tripled between 1825 and 1833, and land values rose accordingly. Wheat receipts, primarily by way of the Ohio Canal, increased at Cleveland by 800 percent, to 2 million bushels, between 1827 and 1840. Shipments of merchandise from that port to the interior doubled, to about 20 million pounds. Coal mining was opened with the construction of the Hocking Valley branch of the canal; and water power, developed in conjunction with these waterways, permitted the establishment of some eighty factories by 1839. During the same period, iron manufacturing expanded greatly in southern Ohio and northern Kentucky, primarily as a consequence of the discovery of new ore deposits, but also under stimulus from the availability of shipping facilities and tariff protection. The area began to produce steam engines, milling machinery, wagons and carts, farm implements, tinware, printing presses and type, saddlery, shoes, hats, and books for external markets. Such activity and the expenditures for construction projects brought an increased flow of money into the region, leading Hezekiah Niles to comment in March 1827, with allusion to past "manufactories of paper-money," that no section of the Union now had "a better *circulating* medium, than Kentucky, Ohio, Indiana, Illinois, and Missouri."[16]

For National Republicans and their Whig successors of the Jacksonian era, the domestic agenda of the American System set the course and defined the program for national development. A Kentuckian, writing to Clay in the spring of 1828, had identified the issue and sensed, too, its continuing import:

> It is quite obvious that "the American System" has in its turn obtained the ascendency over all other Subjects of conversation & Legislation. The "System" and the "opposition" to it forms [sic] the two elementary principles of the two parties. . . . The measures in favor of the System *Stand first* among Measures of Public and National utility. The Country is divided—I hope not equally—upon it. The parties for and against it are embodied, and will not be disbanded for many years.[17]

The president's personal friends did not share that conceptualization. After Adams's defeat, John W. Taylor expressed the view "that the two recent parties" were "virtually dissolved—that of the Administration irreversibly." Clay, he added, could never again "take a lead in the affairs of the nation." Adams at this time, as he had consistently over the past two years, contemplated his own retirement. He agreed that the old political divisions were dead, but he predicted that Clay's leadership was not. Already, he noted, Edward Everett had reported the Kentuckian's inquiry "whether he [Clay] might depend upon the support of the Eastern States at the next Presidential election. . . ." Adams hazarded that Clay would reemerge as the spokesman of "the opposition."[18]

Despite his protestations, the president had not closed the door completely upon his own return to public life. As early as December 11 of the election year, while informing a friend that he should "seek no public employment in any form, directly or indirectly," he had concluded with the confidential proviso that if his fellow citizens should ever again seek his services, he should not be "at liberty to decline repairing to any station which they may assign . . . , except for reasonable cause." As he closed his diary upon his administration, he had progressed still farther toward his return: "The cause of Union and of improvement will remain, and I have duties to it and to my country yet to discharge."[19]

Both Adams and Clay were to come back to Washington as members of the Twenty-Second Congress, in December 1831. The Kentuckian, then a Senator, held the stance of presidential nominee and party leader. The former president assumed the unhistoric role of return to public life as a congressman, "turned boy again," as Clay teasingly twitted. Over the next decade these leaders demonstrated an independence in their emphasis upon policy issues that indicates how strongly they had worked to achieve harmony during Adams's presidency.

On land and tariff proposals, the political flash points of the American System, they came to sharp disagreement on various occasions. In further support of his presidential bid in 1832, Clay attempted to mollify the western demand for cession of the public lands. Fearful of the growing alliance of the South and the West on the issue, he introduced a bill providing that 10 percent of the revenue from public land should go to the states in which the sales were made, with the remaining sums to be distributed among all the states proportionally according to their congressional representation. Land prices would not be reduced, but funds would be made available to the states for education, colonization of freed Blacks, internal improvements, or reduction of state debts, as each might choose. The effect would be to continue deterrence of overly rapid western expansion, preserve the protective tariff as the basic source of federal revenue, and provide funding for a variety of worthy local objectives.

To Adams the compromise was unacceptable—then, when, with westerners opposing even such a division of the spoils, the measure was postponed; in 1834, when, in partial payment for Clay's support of the compromise tariff, Calhoun endorsed such a distribution of the Treasury surplus; or in the fall of 1837, when, despite failing revenues as depression gripped the land, Clay still demanded payment of the fourth installment to the states under the distribution program. In the view of the New Englander, the relinquishment of public moneys to state administration represented a surrender of the public treasure and an abandonment of federal responsibility. He was finally to relax his opposition to the distribution proposal in 1841 only as a feature of the Whig response to the States' rights attack upon the nationalist program generally.

The differing views of Adams and Clay on revision of the tariff in 1832 precipitated open controversy in the party councils. The New Englander, as chairman of the House Committee on Manufactures, fathered a measure that not only placed coarse woolens, used for slave clothing, on the free list but also greatly reduced duties on hemp and on pig and bar iron. Clay vigorously opposed the bill, but when its passage failed to mollify the South, he himself sponsored across-the-board reductions under the compromise proposal of 1833. For Adams, who believed that the act of the previous year had adequately responded to southern grievances, the resulting acclaim to the Kentuckian as the "Great Compromiser" was particularly galling. In opposition to the arrangement, Adams wrote a minority report of the House Committee, which he categorized as his "Legacy" to the country, his "Epitaph of the American System." To his son he lamented the "monstrous concessions" of Clay's proposal. Over the past two years, he noted, the National Republicans had meant "Henry Clay, High Tariff, and the American System." "But now—Where is high tariff? —Where is Henry Clay? —Where is the American System?" The Kentuckian's measure had given "the Show of Victory to nullification at the very moment when it was at its last gasp."[20] In the years that followed, as Adams established his strongest claims to eloquence in defense of the Africans of the *Amistad* controversy and the right to read abolitionist petitions before the House of Representatives, his fierce denunciation of "the slave power" and of southern sectionalism at times carried him far from political association with Clay. They did not resume a close relationship until the revival of the struggle for the American System following the Whig victory of 1840.

How influential the old nationalist leadership might have been had William Henry Harrison survived is uncertain. His death, a month after assuming the presidency, brought to power John Tyler, a States' rights proponent whose vetoes of Whig banking and tariff proposals countered the program of the party under whose standard he had been elected. Adams and Clay worked together in 1841 to obtain the passage of bankruptcy legislation, accepting a bill for general coverage as an appeal for southern support. The Whig leaders also reversed their longstanding opposition to permanent legislation for preemption in public-land sale, as a bargain for western support of the Kentuckian's project for distribution of land revenues. Adams was won to the proposal because it also included grants of 500,000 acres to each new state in aid of internal improvements. The bankruptcy and distribution measures were enacted, but with a conditional amendment to the latter providing that it be suspended whenever tariff rates were raised beyond 20 percent ad valorem. With establishment of much-higher rates under tariff legislation of 1842, a bill endorsed by both Adams and Clay in view of revenue deficits, the provisions for distribution of receipts from the sale of public lands and the accompanying grants for internal improvements were repealed. Because of the abandonment of these features, Adams in the end voted against the tariff, although it established schedules that were not greatly different from those of his own 1832 proposal.

The Whig victory of 1840 had yielded temporary tariff protection, but neither the banking nor the internal-improvements features of the American System. And the hope for public-land revenues as funding for projects of national betterment had been abandoned. The bankruptcy act was to be repealed in 1843. The tariff, too, was to be lost in 1846, when Polk's triumphant Democrats enacted the Walker bill, which lowered rates on the major items of protective concern to 25 and 30 percent ad valorem. In 1857 they were to be dropped still lower.

Frustrated, Clay resigned his senatorial seat in March 1842. "In what a sad condition has our unfortunate Country been brought . . . during the last thirteen years," he wrote to Adams from Kentucky that summer. But, Clay continued, "in looking back upon the gloomy state of things, now existing in Washington, my hopes concentrate more upon you than on any other man." Adams reciprocated the sentiment when in November 1843, after traveling west to speak at the laying of the cornerstone for an observatory erected by the Cincinnati Astronomical Society, he crossed into Kentucky at Covington and Maysville and lauded "that great man, . . . my associate and friend, Henry Clay." "And here," he then added in his diary, "I solemnly declare that the charges of corrupt bargaining which had been trumped up against him and me are utterly without foundation." He publicly supported the Kentuckian's presidential campaign of the following year.[21]

Over the period 1835 to 1846 Adams reasserted his sense of national responsibility for scientific improvement by a prolonged fight to win acceptance and restricted utilization of the Smithson grant. He found great satisfaction in the funding that led to establishment, in 1842, of the National Observatory and, in 1846, of the Smithsonian Institution. He did not live to see the latter facility restricted, in 1857, to museum, rather than research, functions.[22] His death, in 1848, while still a sitting member of Congress, had closed the lifelong commitment to public service in promotion of the goals of national maturation as he had enunciated them in his first annual message during his presidency.

Clay's return to the Senate in December 1849, to direct the struggle for political compromise of the dissensions generated by the westward movement, expressed once more the attachment to national unity that had marked their joint effort. But neither leader, through their extended careers, was able to restore the grand design of the Adams administration. The New Englander had correctly identified, in Jackson's fourth annual message, a sweeping attack upon every aspect of the American System and of the ideological nationalism upon which it rested. Over the thirty years that Democratic leadership, with but two brief interruptions, controlled the presidency, Jackson's dictums prevailed against national banking and protective tariffs. Even the western demand for aid in developing internal improvements was sharply restricted until the mid 1840s and was strongly opposed by Franklin Pierce as late as the mid 1850s.[23]

Adams and Clay had diverged in their motivations for policy development under their shared nationalism. For the New Englander the dominating consideration was ethical, a commitment to responsibilities seen as basic attributes of government for the general welfare. Such an approach gave small ground for flexibility of response. Concessions were soul wrenching. A southern protest against tariff clauses that could be judged excessively damaging might warrant amelioration, but nullification, which challenged the established law, could not be tolerated.

That he occasionally yielded to the exigencies of political compromise was always remarkable. He had done so in turning to Clay and Webster for support in gaining the presidency. The action revealed a character flaw of personal ambition that he himself recognized and privately castigated. At the same time, he, like Clay, had found in his rival an attachment to common interests. His "Epitaph" to the American System in 1833 revealed his concern for the broad package of protective tariff, internal improvements, the Bank of the United States, and the public lands. These programs, in his conception, constituted the responsibilities of national authority.

He had not, however, so fully integrated these disparate features into the broader home-market conceptualization as had Clay and Rush. Thence had arisen occasional tensions even within his administration, notably in his delayed endorsement of tariff revision. For Adams, internal improvements held overriding primacy. "I mourn over it [the American System] as over my own child," he lamented in 1833, "for I and not Henry Clay was its father— It was mine as the record of its birth in the Journal of the Senate of the United States of Monday the 23rd of February 1807 will testify."[24] He referred to his initiation of the resolution that had led to Gallatin's "Report on Roads and Canals." This emphasis indicated a priority that explained his eventual concession to preemption and distribution legislation in 1841, but it also dictated that he finally reject the tariff legislation of that year when it jeopardized the land donations for internal improvements.

For Clay, nationalism connoted a stronger ideologic essence. Adams had verged on the conception in emphasizing the governmental dichotomy between Europe and the Americas, but it was Clay who had pressed foreign-policy concerns that ranged beyond the interests of trade and commerce. Urging recognition of Greek independence as also that of the South American states, he had pointed to "another view of the subject, infinitely more gratifying." The United States "would constitute the rallying point of human freedom against all the despotism of the Old World." He had seen his compromise efforts in close reference to this ideal, an adjustment "to be mainly ascribed to those strong feelings of attachment to the Union . . . , to the deep conviction, that without it, our country would be exposed to the greatest calamities, rent into miserable petty states, and these convulsed by perpetual feuds and wars. . . ." Domestic policy required an accommodation of diverse interests if the nation was to fulfill its broad destiny. Compromise to achieve harmony was, therefore, legitimate and inherent in the unifying process. The American System of domestic policy, in Clay's view, represented such an adjustment, the composite of the home-market argument. A recent analyst has commented that Clay "has been overrated as a politician and underrated as a statesman." This is true. His statesmanship evolved, however, as the approach of a politician who was seeking a common denominator.[25]

Ethically or ideologically nationalistic, the views of both leaders called for a moral commitment, a disciplined submersion of individual and localized partialities in the general good. Commerce, foreign and domestic; agriculture; and industry—all were to have a place. As Rush had written in his "Report" of 1827, expounding the implications of the program more comprehensively than any other exposition of the administration's effort: "The eye of legislation, intent upon the whole good of the nation, will look to each part, not separately as a part, but in conjunction with the whole."[26]

The South of the 1820s still had incentives to participate in that enterprise—a growing domestic market for its cotton, revival of regional textile and iron manufacturing under tariff protection, and the offer of federal assistance for the development of canals and rivers, support that was rejected by decision of the state authorities. Instead, southern spokesmen had assailed the American System on the specific ground of its nationalizing impulse. The groundwork for integrated development under governmental stimulus was set aside by their influence until after the Civil War. The slavery issue, which Adams had carefully avoided throughout his presidency, became a symbol of self-consciously regional differentiation.

How much the Adams administration's efforts generated the prosperity that extended through the early 1830s; how greatly the absence of this directing force contributed to the decline marked from the end of that decade into the early 1840s and again for a brief interval in the late 1850s; and how significantly the renewal of governmental support stimulated the economic expansion of the 1870s and 1880s are questions that are still subject to debate. Controversies centering specifically upon the impact of the national government's aid to internal improvements in the "transportation revolution" of the period, on the role of Biddle's management of the Bank of the United States as a regulating force in the interregional and foreign movement of money, and on the efficacy of tariff regulation in the growth of the nation's infant industries reach to the roots of the historiography of United States economic development. Few, however, would deny that a climate of fostering governmental concern was a major ingredient in that growth, that it underlay the Adams administration's programmatic conception, and that it was repudiated by their Jacksonian successors. The Republicans of 1860 returned to the formula of the American System as the unifying theme of counterattack, and it prevailed throughout the national maturization of postwar development.

Only one significant alteration—homestead legislation—was introduced in the program. It was an area of bargaining that Adams and Clay had resisted vigorously. It was, however, one that both had approximated in their response to preemption legislation in 1841. The balancing of concessions had brought forward a demand that could not be longer denied. In the end, both had yielded to the integrating force of their basic nationalism.

NOTES

CHAPTER 1

A TIME OF READJUSTMENT

1. Robert William Fogel, *Railroads and American Economic Growth: Essays in Econometric History* (Baltimore, Md.: Johns Hopkins Press, 1964), p. 229; Douglass C. North, *The Economic Growth of the United States, 1790–1860* (1961; reprint ed., New York: W. W. Norton & Co., 1966), pp. 62–134, 179–203 passim; Richard C. Wade, *The Urban Frontier: Pioneer Life in Early Pittsburgh, Cincinnati, Lexington, Louisville, and St. Louis* (1959; reprint ed., Chicago: University of Chicago Press,

1964), pp. 302–3; Vernon L. Parrington, *Main Currents in American Thought: An Interpretation of American Literature from the Beginnings to 1920,* 3 vols. (New York: Harcourt, Brace & Co., 1927, 1930), 2:318; John William Ward, *Andrew Jackson, Symbol for an Age* (1955; reprint ed., London: Oxford University Press, 1968-2), p. 169; Frederick Jackson Turner, *Rise of the New West, 1819–1829,* vol. 14 of *The American Nation* (New York: Harper & Brothers, 1906), p. 3.

2. Harry Ammon, *James Monroe: The Quest for National Identity* (New York: McGraw-Hill Book Co., 1971), p. 529.

3. Levi Woodbury, "Cotton Manufacture and Foreign Trade," U.S. Congress, *House Docs.*, 24th Cong., 1st sess., no. 146, p. 51.

4. U.S. Congress, *Annals of Congress,* 14th Cong., 1st sess., col. 1352; 15th Cong., 1st sess., cols. 1740–41, 1743; 18th Cong., 1st sess., cols. 2429–30.

5. Jefferson to Benjamin Austin, 9 Jan. 1816, Thomas Jefferson Papers, Presidential Papers Series, Microfilm (MR48).

6. Madison to William Eustis, 22 May 1823, in James Madison, *The Writings of James Madison,* ed. Gaillard Hunt, 9 vols. (New York: G. P. Putnam's Sons, 1900–10), 9:135–36; see also Madison to Joseph Cabell, 18 Sept. and 30 Oct. 1828, *Daily National Journal* (Washington), 25 and 27 Dec. 1828.

7. *A Compilation of the Messages and Papers of the Presidents, 1789–1897,* comp. James D. Richardson, 10 vols. (1896–99; reprint ed., New York: Bureau of National Literature and Art, 1901–6), 1:379, 409–10, 567–68; Drew R. McCoy, *The Elusive Republic: Political Economy in Jeffersonian America* (Chapel Hill: Published for the Institute of Early American History and Culture, Williamsburg, Va., by the University of North Carolina Press, 1980), p. 245.

8. U.S. Congress, *Annals of Congress,* 14th Cong., 2d sess., col. 296; Robert E. Shalhope, "Thomas Jefferson's Republicanism and Antebellum Southern Thought," *Journal of Southern History* 42 (Nov. 1976): 542–45, 552–54; Ammon, *James Monroe,* pp. 387–92; cf. Richard E. Ellis, *The Jeffersonian Crisis: Courts and Politics in the Young Republic* (New York: Oxford University Press, 1971), p. 282.

9. William W. Freehling, *Prelude to Civil War: The Nullification Controversy in South Carolina, 1816–1836* (New York: Harper & Row, 1965), pp. 26–27, 31, and app. A, pp. 361–64.

10. *Columbia* (S.C.) *Telescope,* 27 Nov. 1829, quoted in Freehling, *Prelude to Civil War,* p. 106.

11. Alfred Glaze Smith, Jr., *Economic Readjustment of an Old Cotton State: South Carolina, 1820–1860* (Columbia: University of South Carolina Press, 1958), pp. 153, 201.

12. Charles Henry Ambler, *Sectionalism in Virginia from 1776 to 1861* (1910; reprint ed., New York: Russell & Russell, 1964), pp. 116–25 and passim.

13. Paul Wallace Gates, *History of Public Land Law Development* (Washington, D.C.: Government Printing Office, 1968), p. 341; U.S., *Statutes at Large,* 4:22–23, 32–33, 128 (30 Apr. and 24 May 1824 and 3 Mar. 1825).

14. Alvin Kass, *Politics in New York State, 1800–1830* (Syracuse, N.Y.: Syracuse University Press, 1965), pp. 101–2; cf. Martin Van Buren to B. F. Butler, 25 Dec. 1825, Martin Van Buren Papers, Presidential Papers Series, Microfilm (MR6).

15. Pennsylvania Senate, *Journal*, 1815/16, p. 18, 1819/20, pp. 14–15, 231, 457–58, 1820/21, p. 13, 1821/22, p. 15, 1823/24, p. 502; Pennsylvania House, *Journal*, 1816/17, p. 464, 1819/20, pp. 413–16, 1823/24, p. 449; *Annals of Congress*, 14th Cong., 1st sess., cols. 102, 681, 1352, 18th Cong., 1st sess., cols. 207–8, 1744, 2429, 3109–12.

16. *Village Record* (Westchester, Pa.), 1 and 29 Dec. 1819, 9 and 23 Feb. 1820; Pennsylvania House, *Journal*, 1815/16, p. 563, 1821/22, p. 1114, 1823/24, pp. 447, 449; Pennsylvania Senate, *Journal*, 1815/16, p. 354, 1819/20, pp. 457–58.

17. *Annals of Congress*, 14th Cong., 1st sess., cols. 331, 1273, 16th Cong., 2d sess., cols. 1653–81, 71st Cong., 2d sess., cols. 893–905, 18th Cong., 1st sess., cols. 1546, 1565, 1711, 1742. Similar ambivalence on the issue in New York at this time is discussed in Kass, *Politics in New York State*, pp. 102–3.

18. *Niles' Weekly Register* 16 (17 Apr. 1819): 132; 21 (2 Feb. 1822): 367–68.

19. Clay to Langdon Cheves, 19 Apr. and 13 Dec. 1819, in Henry Clay, *The Papers of Henry Clay*, ed. James F. Hopkins, Mary W. M. Hargreaves, and Robert Seager II, 8 vols. to date (Lexington: University Press of Kentucky, 1959–), 2:688, 729–30.

20. Ralph C. H. Catterall, *The Second Bank of the United States*, Decennial Publications, 2d ser., vol. 2 (Chicago: University of Chicago Press, 1903), pp. 52, 64–65, 88–91; U.S. Supreme Court, *Reports* 17 (4 Wheaton): 316–437; 22 (9 Wheaton): 738–903; 23 (10 Wheaton): 47–48.

21. *Niles' Weekly Register* 16 (3 July 1819): 311; Murray N. Rothbard, *The Panic of 1819: Reactions and Policies* (New York: Columbia University Press, 1962), pp. 98–109.

22. *Niles' Weekly Register* 10 (27 July and 10 Aug. 1816): 365, 386; 11 (1 Feb. 1817): 379; 12 (24 May, 28 June, 2 and 16 Aug. 1817): 208, 287, 368, 396; 13 (6 Sept. 1817): 18 (10 and 31 Jan. 1818): 320, 376.

23. Great Britain, *Hansard Parliamentary Debates*, 1st ser., 33:1099; U.S. Bureau of the Census, *Historical Statistics of the United States, 1789–1945* . . . (Washington, D.C.: Government Printing Office, 1949), ser. M42–55, p. 245.

24. *Niles' Weekly Register* 16 (7 Aug. 1819): 385; 17 (23 Oct. 1819): 117; *American State Papers, Finance*, 3:641–42; James F. Hopkins, *A History of the Hemp Industry in Kentucky* (Lexington: University of Kentucky Press, 1951), pp. 126–28; James Flint, *Letters from America* . . . (1822; reprinted in Reuben Gold Thwaites, *Early Western Travels, 1748–1846* . . . , 32 vols. (Cleveland: Arthur H. Clark Co., 1904–7), 9:274 and passim.

25. John Bach McMaster, *A History of the People of the United States from the Revolution to the Civil War*, 7 vols. (New York: D. Appleton & Co., 1903), 4:341–44, 347–49.

26. Frank A. Cassell, *Merchant Congressman in the Young Republic: Samuel Smith of Maryland, 1752–1839* (Madison: University of Wisconsin Press, 1971), pp. 215–17, 228, 235–36; Smith to Clay, 25 June 1825, in Clay, *Papers*, 4:468–75.

27. Percy Wells Bidwell and John I. Falconer, *History of Agriculture in the Northern United States*, Carnegie Institution of Washington Publication no. 358 (1925; reprint ed., New York: Peter Smith, 1941), p. 191; Thomas Senior Berry,

"Wholesale Commodity Prices in the Ohio Valley, 1816-1860," *Review of Economic Statistics* 17 (Aug. 1935): 24.

28. *Annals of Congress,* 14th Cong., 1st sess., cols. 681, 1352, 16th Cong., 1st sess., cols. 2155-56, 18th Cong., 1st sess., cols. 2257, 2287-88, 2337, 2429; Pennsylvania Senate, *Journal,* 1819/20, p. 457; Pennsylvania House, *Journal,* 1815/16, pp. 364, 563, 1819/20, p. 846, 1821/22, p. 279, 1823/24, p. 449.

29. Ronald E. Shaw, *Erie Water West: A History of the Erie Canal, 1792-1854* (Lexington: University of Kentucky Press, 1966), pp. 262-63; *Washington* (D.C.) *Gazette,* 21 Oct. and 9 Dec. 1825; Frank L. Owsley, "The Pattern of Migration and Settlement on the Southern Frontier," *Journal of Southern History* 11 (May 1945): 168-70.

30. Paul C. Nagel, "The Election of 1824: A Reconsideration Based on Newspaper Opinion," *Journal of Southern History* 26 (Aug. 1960): 315-29.

31. The Transylvania controversy provides the theme for Niels Henry Sonne, *Liberal Kentucky, 1780-1828* (New York: Columbia University Press, 1939); see also Clement Eaton, *The Freedom of Thought Struggle in the Old South,* rev. and enl. ed. (1940; New York: Harper & Row, Harper Torchbooks, 1964), pp. 303-20; and John B. Boles, *The Great Revival, 1787-1805* (Lexington: University Press of Kentucky, 1972), pp. 188-93.

32. Reported in John Quincy Adams, *Memoirs of John Quincy Adams, Comprising Portions of His Diary from 1795 to 1848,* ed. Charles Francis Adams, 12 vols. (Philadelphia: J. B. Lippincott & Co., 1874-77), 5:128.

33. Rothbard, *Panic of 1819,* pp. 32-111.

34. Kentucky, *Acts,* 1824/25, pp. 44-56. On the controversy see Arndt M. Stickles, *The Critical Court Struggle in Kentucky, 1819-29* (Bloomington: Indiana University Press, 1929).

35. David Walter Krueger, "Party Development in Indiana, 1800-1832" (Ph.D. diss., University of Kentucky, 1974), pp. 81-89, 120-21, 126, 132-33; Donald J. Ratcliffe, "The Role of Voters and Issues in Party Formation: Ohio, 1824," *Journal of American History* 59 (Mar. 1973): 857-61; Kim T. Phillips, "The Pennsylvania Origins of the Jackson Movement," *Political Science Quarterly* 91 (Fall 1976): 490-93, 496, 499, 503.

36. On the general movement for electoral reform see Richard P. McCormick, *The Second American Party System: Party Formation in the Jacksonian Era* (Chapel Hill: University of North Carolina Press, 1966); Chilton Williamson, *American Suffrage from Property to Democracy, 1760-1860* (Princeton, N.J.: Princeton University Press, 1960), pp. 138-207.

37. Otis K. Rice, *The Allegheny Frontier: West Virginia Beginnings, 1730-1830* (Lexington: University Press of Kentucky, 1970), pp. 359-66; Ambler, *Sectionalism in Virginia,* pp. 93-96, 137-46; Williamson, *American Suffrage,* pp. 225-34.

38. Philip S. Klein, *Pennsylvania Politics, 1817-1832: A Game Without Rules* (Philadelphia: Historical Society of Pennsylvania, 1940), p. 195; James A. Kehl, *Ill Feeling in the Era of Good Feeling: Western Pennsylvania Political Battles, 1815-1825* (Pittsburgh: University of Pittsburgh Press, 1956), pp. 245-46n.

CHAPTER 2
THE MINORITY ELECTION

1. Monroe to unidentified correspondent, 24 Sept. 1821, cited in Marquis James, *Andrew Jackson: The Border Captain* (New York: Grosset & Dunlap, 1933), p. 355.

2. Chase C. Mooney, *William H. Crawford* (Lexington: University Press of Kentucky, 1974), pp. 7, 26, 196–207, 342–44; Harry Ammon, *James Monroe: The Quest for National Identity* (New York: McGraw-Hill Book Co., 1971), pp. 494–97, 501, 543–44.

3. Ammon, *James Monroe*, pp. 506–7; [John H. Eaton], *The Letters of Wyoming, to the People of the United States, on the Presidential Election, and in Favour of Andrew Jackson . . .* (Philadelphia: S. Simpson & J. Conrad, 1824), p. 28; Paul C. Nagel, *Descent from Glory: Four Generations of the John Adams Family* (New York: Oxford University Press, 1983), pp. 73, 137.

4. John Quincy Adams, *Memoirs of John Quincy Adams, Comprising Portions of His Diary from 1795 to 1848*, ed. Charles Francis Adams, 12 vols. (Philadelphia: J. B. Lippincott & Co., 1874–77), 1:249, 250, 256.

5. Fisher Ames to Christopher Gore, 24 Feb. 1803, in Fisher Ames, *Works of Fisher Ames . . .* , ed. Seth Ames, 2 vols. (Boston: Little, Brown & Co., 1854), 1:321; Adams, *Memoirs*, 1:252; *Independent Chronicle and Boston Patriot*, 27 May 1828; Marie B. Hecht, *John Quincy Adams: A Personal History of an Independent Man* (New York: Macmillan Co., 1972), pp. 142–81.

6. For a well-balanced evaluation see, in particular, Dexter Perkins's essay in Samuel Flagg Bemis, ed., *The American Secretaries of State and Their Diplomacy*, 17 vols. (New York: Alfred A. Knopf, 1927–67), 4:108–11.

7. John Braser Davis to Adams, 2 Dec. 1824, MHi-Adams Family Papers, Letters Recd. (MR466).

8. Mooney, *William H. Crawford*, pp. 161–68, 256–58; Norman K. Risjord, *The Old Republicans: Southern Conservatism in the Age of Jefferson* (New York: Columbia University Press, 1965), pp. 229, 249–53.

9. William W. Freehling, *Prelude to Civil War: The Nullification Controversy in South Carolina, 1816–1836* (New York: Harper & Row, 1965), pp. 108–33 passim.

10. Calhoun to Virgil Maxcy, 23 Jan. 1825, Calhoun to James E. Colhoun, 26 Aug. 1827, and Calhoun to Sam Smith, 28 July 1828, in John C. Calhoun, *The Papers of John C. Calhoun*, ed. Clyde N. Wilson and W. Edwin Hemphill, 15 vols. to date (Columbia: Published by the University of South Carolina Press for the South Caroliniana Society, 1959–), 9:514–15, 10:304, 404.

11. Jackson to L. H. Coleman, 26 Apr. 1824, in Andrew Jackson, *Correspondence of Andrew Jackson*, ed. John Spencer Bassett and John Franklin Jameson, 7 vols. (Washington, D.C.: Carnegie Institution of Washington, 1926–35), 3:250–51; Charles G. Sellers, Jr., "Banking and Politics in Jackson's Tennessee, 1817–1827," *Mississippi Valley Historical Review* 41 (June 1954): 81–83; Herman Hailperin, "Pro-Jackson Sentiment in Pennsylvania," *Pennsylvania Magazine of History and Biography* 50 (July 1926): 233–34.

12. See M. J. Heale, *The Presidential Quest: Candidates and Images in American Political Culture, 1787–1852* (London: Longman, 1982), p. 53; Kim T. Phillips, "The Pennsylvania Origins of the Jackson Movement," *Political Science Quarterly* 91 (Fall 1976): 499–501.

13. Leonard D. White, *The Jeffersonians: A Study in Administrative History, 1801–1829* (1951; reprint ed., New York: Free Press, 1965), pp. 421–22, 546–50, 558–59.

14. *Niles' Weekly Register* 13 (24 Jan. 1818): 345; White, *Jeffersonians,* pp. 415–20.

15. These and other episodes are reviewed as evidence of an "Era of Corruption," in Robert V. Remini, *Andrew Jackson and the Course of American Freedom, 1822–1832* (New York: Harper & Row, 1981), pp. 12–38.

16. See [Everette] Wayne Cutler, "The A.B. Controversy," *Mid-America* 51 (Jan. 1969): 24–37.

17. [Eaton], *Letters of Wyoming,* pp. 4, 5, 11–13, 23, 28, 45, 51, 54–55, 103. See also Robert P. Hay, "The Case for Andrew Jackson in 1824: Eaton's Wyoming Letters," *Tennessee Historical Quarterly* 29 (Summer 1970): 139–51.

18. Adams to Lloyd, 1 Oct. 1822, in John Quincy Adams, *Writings of John Quincy Adams,* ed. Worthington Chauncey Ford, 7 vols. (New York: Macmillan Co., 1913–17), 7:312; *Daily National Intelligencer* (Washington), 15 July 1824, reprinting *Torch Light* (Hagerstown, Md.); George A. Lipsky, *John Quincy Adams: His Theory and Ideas* (New York: Thomas Y. Crowell Co., 1950), p. 146.

19. Adams to Walsh, 1 Mar. 1824, quoted in Samuel Flagg Bemis, *John Quincy Adams and the Union* (New York: Alfred A. Knopf, 1956), p. 26; *Delaware Gazette* (Wilmington), 20 July 1824, quoted in Paul C. Nagel, "The Election of 1824: A Reconsideration Based on Newspaper Opinion," *Journal of Southern History* 26 (Aug. 1960): 322.

20. Adams to George W. Erving, 28 Nov. 1818, in *American State Papers, Foreign Relations,* 4:542.

21. John Quincy Adams to John Adams, 31 Aug. 1811, in Adams, *Writings,* 4:209; *Daily National Intelligencer* (Washington), 11 July 1821.

22. Adams to José María Salazar, 6 Aug. 1824, DNA, RG59, Notes to Foreign Legations, 3:184–86 (M38, R3); Adams, *Memoirs,* 6:197–98.

23. Adams, *Memoirs,* 4:207. The interpretation in this and the following paragraph is drawn from Lipsky, *John Quincy Adams,* pp. 299–311.

24. Pierre de Polética to Count Nesselrode, 12 July 1821, in "Correspondence of Russian Ministers in Washington, 1818–1825," *American Historical Review* 18 (Jan. 1913): 327; Ammon, *James Monroe,* p. 524; Ernest R. May, *The Making of the Monroe Doctrine* (Cambridge: Belknap Press of Harvard University Press, 1975), pp. 182–86.

25. Adams, *Memoirs,* 5:54.

26. Ibid., 12, 205, 208–10.

27. Samuel Flagg Bemis, *John Quincy Adams and the Foundations of American Foreign Policy* (New York: Alfred A. Knopf, 1949), pp. 423–35; Ammon, *James Monroe,* pp. 526–27; U.S. Senate, *Executive Journal,* 3:385.

28. Henry Clay, "Speech on Domestic Manufactures," 26 Mar. 1810, "Speech on the Direct Tax and Public Affairs," 29 Jan. 1816, "Speech on the Bank of the United States," 3 June 1816, Hammond to Clay, 28 July 1824, and Daniel Drake to Clay, 20 Feb. 1825, in Henry Clay, *The Papers of Henry Clay*, ed James F. Hopkins, Mary W. M. Hargreaves, and Robert Seager II, 8 vols. to date (Lexington: University Press of Kentucky, 1959–), 1:463, 2:157, 199–205, 3:801, 4:80.

29. For the negotiations see Clay, *Papers*, 1:972–1007 passim.

30. Clay, "Speech on Bill to Raise an Additional Military Force," 8 and 9 Jan. 1813, "Debate on Revenue Proposals," 20 Jan. 1816, "Speech on the Direct Tax and Public Affairs," 29 Jan. 1816, and "Speech on Bill for Enforcing Neutrality," 24 Jan. 1817, in Clay, *Papers*, 1:758, 2:135, 155, 289–92.

31. Clay, "Motion and Speech on Recognition of the Independent Provinces of the River Plata," 24 Mar. 1818, and "Toast and Response at Public Dinner," 19 May 1821, in Clay, *Papers*, 2:520, 3:80. For extended discussion of the defensive aspects of Clay's projection of liberty as a goal of foreign policy see Larry Dean Klein, "Henry Clay, Nationalist" (Ph.D. diss., University of Kentucky, 1977), chap. 5.

32. Adams to Robert Walsh, Jr., 10 July 1821, in Adams, *Writings*, 7:117; Clay, "Toast and Response at Public Dinner," 19 May 1821, in Clay, *Papers*, 3:80.

33. Clay to Francis Preston Blair, 8 Jan. 1825, Clay to James Brown, 23 Jan. 1825, and Clay to Thomas I. Wharton, 5 Feb. 1825, in Clay, *Papers*, 4:9, 38, 59.

34. William Plumer, Jr., to Clay, 8 Jan. 1828, in Clay, *Papers*, 7:19–20, quoting journal extracts; [Thomas Hart Benton], *Thirty Years' View; or, A History of the Working of the American Government . . . from 1820 to 1850 . . .* , 2 vols. (New York: D. Appleton & Co., 1859–60), 1:48; Adams, *Memoirs*, 6:447.

35. Adams, *Memoirs*, 6:464–65.

36. Ibid., p. 451.

37. Ibid., pp. 483, 484, 492–93, 499–500; Webster to Henry R. Warfield, 5 Feb. 1825, in Daniel Webster, *The Papers of Daniel Webster*, ed. Charles M. Wiltse and Harold D. Moser, 5 vols. of correspondence to date (Hanover, N.H.: Published for Dartmouth College by the University Press of New England, 1974–), *Correspondence*, 2:21–22 (quoted). For a full account of the wooing of the Federalists see Shaw Livermore, Jr., *The Twilight of Federalism: The Disintegration of the Federalist Party, 1815–1830* (Princeton, N.J.: Princeton University Press, 1962), pp. 172–83.

38. Adams, *Memoirs*, 7:98.

CHAPTER 3
ORGANIZING THE ADMINISTRATION

1. *A Compilation of the Messages and Papers of the Presidents, 1789–1897*, comp. James D. Richardson, 10 vols. (1896–99; reprint ed., New York: Bureau of National Literature and Art, 1901–6), 2:299.

2. Ibid., pp. 297–99.

3. John Quincy Adams, *Memoirs of John Quincy Adams, Comprising Portions of His Diary from 1795 to 1848*, ed. Charles Francis Adams, 12 vols. (Philadelphia: J. B. Lippincott & Co., 1874–77), 6:467.

4. Enclosed in Dutee J. Pearce to Peter Paul Francis Degrand, 2 Dec. 1824, in MHi-Adams Family Papers, Letters Recd. (MR466); see also Joseph E. Sprague to Adams, 1 Dec. 1824, Degrand, citing Levi Lincoln, to Adams, 2 Dec. 1824, and John Braser Davis to Adams, 2 Dec. 1824, ibid.

5. Joseph Blunt to Adams, 26 Nov. 1824, ibid.

6. Adams, *Memoirs*, 6:478.

7. Crawford to Clay, 4 Feb. 1828, in Henry Clay, *The Papers of Henry Clay*, ed. James F. Hopkins, Mary W. M. Hargreaves, and Robert Seager II, 8 vols. to date (Lexington: University Press of Kentucky, 1959–), 7:77; Norman K. Risjord, *The Old Republicans: Southern Conservatism in the Age of Jefferson* (New York: Columbia University Press, 1965), pp. 255–63.

8. Cook to Adams, 21 Jan. 1825, in MHi-Adams Family Papers, Letters Recd. (MR467); cf. Adams, *Memoirs*, 6:476–77, which dates the interview as January 22, and 495–96.

9. See above, pp. 27–29; Robert E. Shalhope, "Jacksonian Politics in Missouri: A Comment on the McCormick Thesis," *Civil War History* 15 (1969): 214; [Anon.] to Adams, and Edward Patchell to Adams, both 27 Jan. 1825, in MHi-Adams Family Papers, Letters Recd. (MR467).

10. Clay, *Papers*, 4:48; Adams, *Memoirs*, 6:483.

11. On Kremer's explanation see statement by William L. Brent, certified by Peter Little and William Dudley Digges, *Daily National Journal* (Washington), 1 and 2 Mar. 1825. For Clay's "Address to the People of the Congressional District," 26 Mar. 1825, and his correspondence with John H. Eaton, 28, 30, and 31 Mar., 1 and 2 Apr. 1825, see Clay, *Papers*, 4:143–66, 191–92, 196–202, 207–8.

12. *Daily National Intelligencer* (Washington), 24 Nov. 1827; U.S. Congress, *Register of Debates*, 18th Cong., 2d sess., cols. 440–44, 463–86, 522–25.

13. Sprague to Adams, 5 Dec. 1824, in MHi-Adams Family Papers, Letters Recd. (MR466).

14. Adams, *Memoirs*, 6:447.

15. Johnson to Clay, 9 Sept. 1827, in Clay, *Papers*, 6:1014. Kendall had advised Clay by a letter dated December 22 that the resolutions would be presented to the legislature, and George Robertson had informed Adams in a letter of January 6 that they had been passed. Postal service between Kentucky and Washington then required approximately two weeks. Adams's diary first mentioned the instructions on January 15, and Washington gossip that evening reported that the Kentucky delegation had met, considered the resolutions, and agreed upon their vote for Adams, "notwithstanding." See Clay, *Papers*, 3:902; Adams, *Memoirs*, 6:467; Robertson to Adams, 6 Jan. 1825, and A[lexander] H[ill] E[verett] to Adams, 17 Jan. 1825, in MHi-Adams Family Papers, Letters Recd. (MR467).

16. Blair to Clay, 4 Feb. 1828, Clay, *Papers*, 7:75.

17. Adams, *Memoirs*, 6:506 (quoted), 508.

18. Walsh to Everett, 17 Feb. 1825, in MHi-Adams Family Papers, Letters Recd. (MR467); Clay, *Papers*, 4:73–76.

19. *Compilation of Messages and Papers*, 2:295–97.

20. [Adams] to Crawford (copy), 10 Feb. 1825, Crawford to Adams, 11 Feb. 1825, and James Gallatin to Andrew Stewart, 16 Feb. 1825 (copy sent by young Gallatin to Adams, 24 Feb. 182[5], in MHi-Adams Family Papers, Letters Recd. (MR467); Adams, *Memoirs*, 6:507 (quoted), 510.

21. [Adams] to Barbour (copy), and Barbour to Adams, both 21 Feb. 1825, in MHi-Adams Family Papers, Letters Recd. (MR467); Adams, *Memoirs*, 6:466, 451.

22. James Gallatin to Adams, 24 Feb. 182[5], McCullok to [Adams], 14 Feb. 1825, and Robert Walsh, Jr., to A[lexander Hill] Everett, 17 Feb. 1825, in MHi-Adams Family Papers, Letters Recd. (MR467).

23. [Lucius Q. C. Elmer], "Samuel L. Southard," *Collections of the New Jersey Historical Society* 7 (1872): 213–14, 219; Adams, *Memoirs*, 6:471.

24. [Elmer], "Samuel L. Southard," pp. 219, 221–22.

25. Wirt to William Pope, 24 June 1828, in MdHi-Wirt Papers (MS1011, MR11).

26. Adams, *Memoirs*, 6:532, 539; McLean to Adams, 24 Mar. 1825 (enclosing Lee to McLean, same date), and Lee to McLean, 6 Sept. 1825, in MHi-Adams Family Papers, Letters Recd. (MR468, 472); Allen to Clay, 18 Sept. 1825, in Clay, *Papers*, 4:651–52.

27. Benjamin W. Dudley to Clay, 17 Aug. 1827, and Smith to Clay, 7 Oct. 1827, in Clay, *Papers*, 6:915–16, 1121–22.

28. Bunce to Adams, Nov. 1825, and McLean to [Henry Waggaman Edwards], 11 Dec. 1825 (copy), with McLean to Adams, 13 Dec. 1825, in MHi-Adams Family Papers, Letters Recd. (MR473); see also E. Carey to Adams, 6 Feb. 1826, ibid. (MR474).

29. Adams, *Memoirs*, 7:162, 282, 509, 532, 531; see also Binns to Clay, 21 Apr. 1826, and Clay to Adams, 8 May 1828, in Clay, *Papers*, 5:265; 7:262.

30. Adams, *Memoirs*, 7:275, 534.

31. Houston to Jackson, 4 Feb. 1827, in Andrew Jackson, *Correspondence of Andrew Jackson*, ed. John Spencer Bassett and John Franklin Jameson, 7 vols. (Washington, D.C.: Carnegie Institution of Washington, 1926–35), 6:492; Campbell to McLean, 29 June 1826, quoted in Francis P. Weisenburger, *The Life of John McLean: A Politician on the United States Supreme Court* (1937; reprint ed., New York: Da Capo Press, 1971), p. 53.

32. Adams, *Memoirs*, 7:544; 8:24–25. McLean's mail contracts with the opposition editors Duff Green and Isaac Hill were also politically controversial.

33. Ibid., 8:51; 6:474.

34. Ibid., 6:474–75.

35. Leonard D. White, *The Jeffersonians: A Study in Administrative History, 1801–1829* (1951; reprint ed., New York: Free Press, 1965), pp. 388–89, 396–98; Adams, *Memoirs*, 6:520–21; 7:425.

36. Adams, *Memoirs*, 7:207–8.

37. White, *Jeffersonians*, p. 358; Clay to Francis T. Brooke, 2 Sept. 1825, in Clay, *Papers*, 4:615; Adams, *Memoirs*, 7:346.

38. Clinton to Adams, 20 May 1825, Robert Wright to Clay, 10 May 1825, Lloyd to Adams, 23 May 1825, Goldsborough to Adams, 20 May 1825, Wirt to Adams, 16 May 1825, Niles to Adams, 16 May 1825, Stephen Pleasonton to Adams, 15 May 1825, and Joseph Anderson to Adams, 16 May 1825, in MHi-Adams Family Papers, Letters Recd. (MR469); Gray to Clay, 5 Apr. 1825, and Smith to Clay, 15 May 1827, in Clay, *Papers*, 4:216-17, 376-77.

39. Clay to Brooke, 30 Nov. 1825, in Clay, *Papers*, 4:867.

40. DuVal to Clay, 25 Apr. 1825, Wright to Clay, 25 Oct. 1827, White to Clay, 8 Dec. 1825 (note), and C[ary] Nicholas to Clay, 28 Sept. 1826, in Clay, *Papers*, 4:200n, 765-66, 887, 5:732; James Dell and others to Adams, 6 Dec. 1825, in MHi-Adams Family Papers, Letters Recd. (MR473); U.S. Senate, *Executive Journal*, 3:573, 576; White to Clay, 20 Oct. 1827 (quoted), DNA, RG59, Applications and Recommendations for Office (M531, R1).

41. Clay to Charles Hammond, 2 May 1825, and S[amuel] L. S[outhard] to Clay, 26 Oct. 1825, in Clay, *Papers*, 4:316, 769; Barbour to Andrew Stevenson, 28 Feb. 1828, in *American State Papers, Military Affairs*, 3:794; Southard to Speaker of House of Representatives, 12 Mar. 1828, *American State Papers, Naval Affairs*, 3:159.

42. Rush to Clay, 18 Dec. 1827, Elias K. Kane to Clay, 30 Mar. 1825, Thomas Biddle to Clay, 21 Feb. 1827, and Samuel Allinson to Clay, 24 Dec. 1827, in Clay, *Papers*, 6:1367-68, 4:198, 6:220, 1379; Barnard Bates to Adams, 19 Dec. 1825, John M. Forbes to Adams, 29 June 1825, J. H. to Adams, 1 Dec. 1825, and James G. Davis to Adams, 20 June 1826, in MHi-Adams Family Papers, Letters Recd. (MR473, 470, 473, 476); Carl Russell Fish, "Removal of Officials by the Presidents of the United States," *Annual Report of the American Historical Association for the Year 1899*, 1:73. On the Tea Cases see below, pp. 236-37.

43. Sprague to Adams, 28 July 1825, and Bailey to Adams, 29 July 1825, in MHi-Adams Family Papers, Letters Recd. (MR471); see also Benjamin Ames to Adams, 25 July 1825, Timothy Fuller to Adams, 9 Aug. 1825, Henry Dearborn to Adams, 28 July 1825, Albion K. Parris to Barbour, 28 July 1825, and John Holmes to Adams, 25 July 1825, ibid.

44. Degrand to Adams, 28 May 1826, ibid. (MR475); Joseph Hopkinson to Daniel Webster, 13 Apr. 1827, in Daniel Webster, *The Papers of Daniel Webster*, ed. Charles M. Wiltse and Harold D. Moser, 5 vols. of correspondence to date (Hanover, N.H.: Published for Dartmouth College by the University Press of New England, 1974-), *Correspondence*, 2:189.

45. See Milton Gregg to Clay, 31 Oct. 1826, in Clay, *Papers*, 5:851.

46. Binns to Clay, 21 Apr. and 10 May 1826, ibid., pp. 265, 352-54.

47. Clay to William Jones, 23 Jan. 1827, Jones to Clay, 25 Jan. 1827, and Clay to Thomas I. Wharton, 11 Apr. 1827, in Clay, *Papers*, 6:110, 119-20, 433; Rush to Jones, 18 May 1827, in *House Docs.*, 20th Cong., 1st sess., no. 108; cf. Benjamin W. Crowninshield to Clay, 14 and 18 Mar. 1827, and Peter Paul Francis Degrand to Clay, 1 June 1827, in Clay, *Papers*, 6:304, 320, 634.

48. Clay to N[athanel] G. Maxwell, 2 Nov. 1826, and Rush to Clay, 18 Dec. 1827, in Clay, *Papers*, 5:858, 6:1368; see also Clay to Joseph M. Street, 11 Feb. 1827, ibid., 6:185.

49. Adams, *Memoirs*, 6:539–40, 7:7; Clay to George Thompson, 23 Sept. 1826, in Clay, *Papers*, 5:707.

50. Wirt to William Pope, 23 Mar. 1828, in MdHi-Wirt Papers (MS1011, MR10).

51. Clay to Francis T. Brooke, 6 Apr. 1825, and Clay to James Brown, 9 May 1825, in Clay, *Papers*, 4:221, 335–36.

52. Adams, *Memoirs*, 7:511–12, 517–18, 541–42; Philip Syng Physick and Nathaniel Chapman to Clay, 11 May 1828, in Clay, *Papers*, 7:270–71.

53. *United States Telegraph* (Washington), 16 and 17 May 1828; Adams, *Memoirs*, 7:525; J. W. Alexander to [—] Hall, 11 May 1829, quoted in [Elmer], "Samuel L. Southard," p. 227; Adams to Barbour, 4 Apr. 1829, in MHi-Adams Family Papers, Letterbook (MR149).

54. Adams to Abigail Adams, 16 May 1817, in Adams, *Writings*, 6:182; Adams, *Memoirs*, 4:445.

55. Adams, *Memoirs*, 6:523–24, 7:380; Clay to [Josephus B. Stuart], 7 Apr. 1825, and Clay to Peter B. Porter, 23 Apr. 1825, in Clay, *Papers*, 4:227, 286.

56. Adams, *Memoirs*, 6:546–47.

57. Endorsement on George W. Owen to Clay, 1 Feb. 1826, in Clay, *Papers*, 5:81.

58. Clay to Francis T. Brooke, 6 Apr. 1825, Clay to John Sloane, 7 Apr. 1825, and Clay to F[ielding] L. Turner, 28 Apr. 1825, ibid., 4:221, 227, 301; cf. also Clay's "Toast and Speech at Lexington Public Dinner," 12 July 1827, ibid., 6:765; Clay to Crawford, 19 Feb. 1828, in DLC-HC (DNA, M212, R3); and below, pp. 260, 299.

59. Clay to [Josephus B. Stuart], 7 Apr. 1825 (quoted), Clay to Peter B. Porter, 28 Nov. 1825, Clay to Amos Kendall, 18 Oct. 1825, and Clay to John J. Crittenden, 10 Mar. 1826, in Clay, *Papers*, 4:227, 858, 747–48, 5:159.

60. Adams to Barbour, 4 Apr. 1829, in MHi-Adams Family Papers, Letterbook, 10:181 (MR149); Clay to George W. Featherstonhaugh, 26 Feb. 1825, and Clay to [Josephus B. Stuart], 7 Apr. 1825, in Clay, *Papers*, 4:83, 227. On Adams's conception that the presidential role entailed responsibility to put forward "a national program above partisanship" see Ralph Ketcham, *Presidents above Party: The First American Presidency, 1789–1829* (Chapel Hill: Published for the Institute of Early American History and Culture, Williamsburg, Va., by the University of North Carolina Press, 1984), pp. 130–40.

CHAPTER 4
A FOREIGN POLICY FOR COMMERCE

1. Adams to Robert Walsh, Jr., 16 Apr. 1836, in MHi-Adams Papers, Private Letterbook, 13:359 (MR152).

2. U.S., *Statutes at Large*, 3:224; *American State Papers, Foreign Relations*, 4:7–8; and cf. above, pp. 11, 30, and below, pp. 93–95. For analysis of the divergent programs of Hamilton and Jefferson see Vernon G. Setser, *The Com-*

mercial Reciprocity Policy of the United States, 1774-1829 (1937; reprint ed., New York: Da Capo Press, 1969), pp. 102-10, 115, 131, 149-57, 168; Richard E. Ellis, *The Jeffersonian Crisis: Courts and Politics in the Young Republic* (New York: Oxford University Press, 1971), pp. 272, 280; Drew R. McCoy, *The Elusive Republic: Political Economy in Jeffersonian America* (Chapel Hill: Published for the Institute of Early American History and Culture, Williamsburg, Va., by the University of North Carolina Press, 1980), pp. 137-45.

3. Clay to King, 10 May 1825, and Clay to Gallatin, 21 June 1826, in Henry Clay, *The Papers of Henry Clay*, ed. James F. Hopkins, Mary W. M. Hargreaves, and Robert Seager II, 8 vols. to date (Lexington: University Press of Kentucky, 1959-), 4:352, 353, 5:484-88; Clive Parry, ed., *The Consolidated Treaty Series*, 234 vols. to date (New York: Oceana Publications, 1969-), 76:458-60.

4. Hughes to Clay, 7 Apr., 21 June, 8 and 15 July, 8 Aug., 1 and 30 Dec. 1825, in Clay, *Papers*, 4:231, 450, 517, 537, 571, 872-73, 957.

5. Clay to Hughes, 24 Mar. 1825, Clay to Appleton, 12 May 1825, Connell to Clay, 24 May 1827, and Wheaton to Clay, 22 Dec. 1827 and 4 Mar. 1828, ibid., pp. 139, 367-68, 6:590, 1376, 7:147.

6. Clay to Brown, 28 May 1827, ibid., 6:598. For monographic treatment of the history of these negotiations see Richard Aubrey McLemore, *Franco-American Diplomatic Relations, 1816-1836* (University: Louisiana State University Press, 1941), chaps. 1 and 3.

7. John Quincy Adams, *Memoirs of John Quincy Adams, Comprising Portions of His Diary from 1795 to 1848*, ed. Charles Francis Adams, 12 vols. (Philadelphia: J. B. Lippincott & Co., 1874-77), 7:59-61; *A Compilation of the Messages and Papers of the Presidents, 1789-1897*, comp. James D. Richardson, 10 vols. (1896-99; reprint ed., New York: Bureau of National Literature and Art, 1901-6), 2:302.

8. *American State Papers, Foreign Relations*, 6:384-553, 613-14.

9. Clay to Brown, 28 May 1827, in Clay, *Papers*, 6:598; Adams, *Memoirs*, 7:267.

10. Thorndike to Clay, 13 Mar. 1825, and Aaron Hobart to Clay, 15 Dec. 1825, in Clay, *Papers*, 4:108, 917; Parry, *Consolidated Treaty Series*, 78:171-72.

11. Clay to Tuyll, 25 Mar. 1825, Clay to William Sturgis, 1 Apr. 1825, Sturgis to Clay, 11 Apr. 1825, and Tuyll to Clay, 19 Apr. 1825, in Clay, *Papers*, 4:141, 207, 240, 270.

12. Parry, *Consolidated Treaty Series*, 75:162-63.

13. Raguet to Clay, 25 May, 27 June, 17 July, and 23 Sept. 1826, Clay, *Papers*, 5:395, 506, 556 (quoted), 709 (quoted).

14. Clay to Raguet, 22 Oct. 1826 and 20 Jan. 1827, and Raguet to Clay, 7 Feb., 12 and 17 Mar. 1827, ibid., 5:709, 6:98-99, 170-71, 295, 317-18; *Compilation of Messages and Papers*, 2:363.

15. Rebello to Clay, 26 Nov. 1825, 30 May and 1 June 1827, and Clay to Rebello, 31 May and 2 June 1827, in Clay, *Papers*, 4:853, 6:614-15, 634-35, 627-28, 641; Adams, *Memoirs*, 7:288, 289.

16. Raguet, "To the People of the United States," *Gazette* (Philadelphia), 27 May 1828, reprinted in *United States Telegraph* (Washington), on 2 June 1828; see also *United States Telegraph*, 9 Apr., 2 May, 8 July, and 22 Sept. 1828.

17. H. D. C. Wright to Clay, 27 Oct. 1827, Forbes to Clay, 30 Oct. 1827, 13 Sept. and 5 Nov. 1828, and Tudor to Clay, 13 Dec. 1828, in Clay, *Papers*, 6:1191, 1214, 7:466, 528, 568.

18. On the Escudéro episode see Thomas Hart Benton to Clay, 3 Jan. 1827, and Clay to Joel R. Poinsett, 5 Jan. 1827; and cf. Poinsett to Clay, 13 Apr. 1827, ibid., 6:9, 21, 443.

19. Benton to Clay, 4 May 1825, ibid., 4:325; see also Chouteau and de Mun to Clay, 3 May 1825, and John Scott to Clay, 8 May 1825, ibid., 4:322-23, 335.

20. Parry, *Consolidated Treaty Series*, 74:456-78; Clay to José María Salazar, 21 Mar. 1825, in Clay, *Papers*, 4:127-28; U.S., *Statutes at Large*, 3:224, 4:2-3; cf. Adams to Richard C. Anderson, 27 May 1823, in William R. Manning, comp., *Diplomatic Correspondence of the United States Concerning the Independence of the Latin-American Nations*, 3 vols. (New York: Oxford University Press, 1925), 1:200.

21. Clay to Poinsett, 26 Mar. 1825, in Clay, *Papers*, 4:169-70.

22. Setser, *Commercial Reciprocity Policy*, pp. 152-53, 197-98, 201.

23. *Compilation of Messages and Papers*, 2:302.

24. William Spence Robertson, *France and Latin-American Independence* (Baltimore, Md.: Johns Hopkins Press, 1939), pp. 471, 479-82, 584; cf. Andrew Armstrong to Clay, 22 Feb. 1827, in Clay, *Papers*, 6:224.

25. Clay to Raguet, 14 Apr. 1825, in Clay, *Papers*, 4:252-53.

26. Raguet to Secretary of State, 11 Mar. 1825, ibid., p. 104.

27. Rebello to Clay, 14 Nov. 1827, and Clay to Rebello, 1 May 1828, ibid., 6:1262-63, 7:255-59; Adams, *Memoirs*, 7:354-57.

28. Clay to Tudor, 23 Oct. 1827, in Clay, *Papers*, 6:1180-84; Parry, *Consolidated Treaty Series*, 79:251-52, 454-56; Setser, *Commercial Reciprocity Policy*, pp. 249-50.

29. Clay to Poinsett, 26 Mar. 1825, in Clay, *Papers*, 4:168-70 (quotation, p. 168).

30. Poinsett to Clay, 5 May, 4 June, 5 and 10 Aug. 1825, ibid., pp. 326, 415 (quoted), 567, 573.

31. "An Exposition of the Policy of the United States toward the New Republics of America," in Manning, *Diplomatic Correspondence . . . Latin-American Nations*, 3:1663-68; Poinsett to Adams, 8 June and 18 July 1827, in MHi-Adams Family Papers, Letters Recd. (MR481); Poinsett to Clay, 8 July 1827, and Clay to Adams, 17 and 23 Aug. 1827, in Clay, *Papers*, 6:752-53, 914-15, 950-51 (quoted).

32. Adams to Clay, 23 and 31 Aug. 1827, and Clay to Poinsett, 19 Nov. 1827, in Clay, *Papers*, 6:950, 984-85, 1284-85; Adams, *Memoirs*, 7:341, 351, 353. On Poinsett's Masonic involvement in Mexico cf. Dorothy M. Parton, *The Diplomatic Career of Joel Roberts Poinsett* (Washington, D.C.: Catholic University of America, 1934), pp. 99, 120, 130-38, 149.

33. Poinsett to Clay, 5 May, 13 Sept., and 16 Dec. 1825, 4 Jan. 1826, in Clay, *Papers*, 4:326, 640-41, 921, 5:10; Parry, *Consolidated Treaty Series*, 77:40-55.

34. Poinsett to Clay, 28 Sept. 1825 and 12 July 1826, in Clay, *Papers*, 4:699-700, 5:543-44; *American State Papers, Foreign Relations*, 6:608-13.

35. Clay to Poinsett, 12 Mar. 1827, in Clay, *Papers,* 6:286–87.

36. Clay to Poinsett, 26 Mar. 1825, in Clay, *Papers,* 4:173–74; Poinsett to Clay, 21 May 1828, in U.S. Congress, *House Docs.,* 25th Cong., 2d sess., no. 351, p. 210; *Compilation of Messages and Papers,* 2:411. For the proposed treaty see *American State Papers, Foreign Relations,* 6:952–57.

37. Parry, *Consolidated Treaty Series,* 75:434–58.

38. Clay to Robert J. Walsh, Jr., 25 Apr. 1836, in DLC-HC (DNA, M212, R5).

39. U.S., *Statutes at Large,* 4:2–3; *Compilation of Messages and Papers,* 2:376–77, 404–5; Parry, *Consolidated Treaty Series,* 77:368–69.

40. *Compilation of Messages and Papers,* 2:301; U.S. Congress, *Register of Debates,* 19th Cong., 1st sess., cols. 70, 74–76, 1119; 20th Cong., 1st sess., cols. 237–44; U.S. Congress, *Senate Journal,* 19th Cong., 1st sess., p. 113; U.S. Congress, *House Journal,* 19th Cong., 1st sess., pp. 198, 449; U.S., *Statutes at Large,* 4:308–9 (24 May 1828).

41. Parry, *Consolidated Treaty Series,* 76:192–96, 77:288–304, 478–87, 78:280–92, 80:54–64; *Compilation of Messages and Papers,* 2:409; Adams, *Memoirs,* 8:74; Clay memorandum, Nov. 1828, in OHi.

42. Parry, *Consolidated Treaty Series,* 76:398–401, 77:34–37; Clay to Rodgers, 6 Sept. 1825, in Clay, *Papers,* 4:623–24.

43. Rodgers to Clay, 14 Feb. 1827, and Offley to Clay, 22 Apr. 1828, in Clay, *Papers,* 6:201, 7:236; Adams to Offley, 21 July 1828, Adams to Crane, 22 July 1828, and Adams to Crane and Offley, 24 July 1828, in DNA, RG59, Dip. Instr., Turkey, 1:94–98, 100–101; Adams to Southard, 5 Apr. 1829, in MHi-Adams Papers, Private Letterbook, 10:184–85 (MR149). For a monographic treatment of Adams's efforts to open trade with the Porte see Henry Merritt Wriston, *Executive Agents in American Foreign Relations,* Albert Shaw Lectures in Diplomatic History (Baltimore, Md.: Johns Hopkins Press, 1929), pp. 321–34.

44. McLemore, *Franco-American Diplomatic Relations,* p. 17.

45. Reuben G. Beasley to Clay, 16 Aug. 1826 and 25 Jan. 1827, and Clay to Mareuil, 20 Mar. 1827, in Clay, *Papers,* 5:624, 6:121, 327–28.

46. Brown to Clay, 28 June, 13 and 30 Aug. 1827, 28 July and 13 Nov. 1828, ibid., 6:725–26, 894–95, 977–78, 7:407, 536–37.

47. Brown to Clay, 13 and 29 Sept. and 12 Oct. 1827, ibid., 6:1028–29, 1093–94, 1139–40.

48. U.S., *Statutes at Large,* 4:272, 309 (19 and 24 May 1828); *Register of Debates,* 20th Cong., 1st sess., cols. 2745–46; Setser, *Commercial Reciprocity Policy,* p. 255.

49. Christopher Hughes to Clay, 11 July 1826, 12 June and 28 Nov. 1827, in Clay, *Papers,* 5:541–42, 6:671–72, 1330.

50. *Compilation of Messages and Papers,* 2:352–53.

51. F. Lee Benns, *The American Struggle for the British West India Carrying Trade, 1815–1830,* Indiana University Studies vol. 10 (1923; reprint ed., Clifton, N.J.: Augustus M. Kelley, 1972), p. 162.

CHAPTER 5
THE COLONIAL TRADE CONTROVERSY

1. Vernon G. Setser, *The Commercial Reciprocity Policy of the United States, 1774-1829* (1937; reprint ed., New York: Da Capo Press, 1969), pp. 241-42; Clive Parry, ed., *The Consolidated Treaty Series*, 234 vols. to date (New York: Oceana Publications, 1969-), 76:194, 77:289-93; see also Alexander Hill Everett to Clay, 15 Feb. 1827, in Henry Clay, *The Papers of Henry Clay*, ed. James F. Hopkins, Mary W. M. Hargreaves, and Robert Seager II, 8 vols. to date (Lexington: University Press of Kentucky, 1959-), 6:202.

2. See table 1, below, p. 111.

3. *A Compilation of the Messages and Papers of the Presidents, 1789-1897*, comp. James D. Richardson, 10 vols. (1896-99; reprint ed., New York: Bureau of National Literature and Art, 1901-6), 1:575; F. Lee Benns, *The American Struggle for the British West India Carrying Trade, 1815-1830*, Indiana University Studies vol. 10 (1923; reprint ed., Clifton, N.J.: Augustus M. Kelley, 1972), pp. 42-44; Setser, *Commercial Reciprocity Policy*, pp. 226-27.

4. U.S., *Statutes at Large*, 3:432-33 (18 Apr. 1818), 602-4 (15 May 1820); Clay speeches, 31 Jan. 1817 and 10 Apr. 1818, in Clay, *Papers*, 2:299-300, 564-66; Benns, *American Struggle*, pp. 51, 53, 69-70.

5. Great Britain, *Statutes*, 3 Geo. 4, c. 44, pp. 704-10 (24 June 1822); Benns, *American Struggle*, pp. 83-86.

6. U.S., *Statutes at Large*, 3:740-42; Benns, *American Struggle*, pp. 94-95.

7. John Quincy Adams, *Memoirs of John Quincy Adams, Comprising Portions of His Diary from 1795 to 1848*, ed. Charles Francis Adams, 12 vols. (Philadelphia: J. B. Lippincott & Co., 1874-77), 6:216; Canning to Adams, 10 Apr. and 17 May 1823, Adams to Canning, 8 Apr. and 14 May 1823, Adams to Rush, 23 June 1823, and Rush to Adams, 12 Aug. 1824, in *American State Papers, Foreign Relations*, 6:231-33, 5:511-20, 535; [Thomas Hart Benton], *Thirty Years' View: or, A History of the Working of the American Government for Thirty Years, from 1820 to 1850 . . .* , 2 vols. (New York: D. Appleton & Co., 1859-60), 1:126; *Compilation of Messages and Papers*, 2:208.

8. Protocols of conferences 22 and 28 July 1824, in *American State Papers, Foreign Relations*, 5:565.

9. Charles R. Vaughan to Clay, 22 Mar. 1826, and Clay to Albert Gallatin, 19 June 1826, in Clay, *Papers*, 5:190, 441-42; King to Adams, 20 and 29 Mar. 1826, in MHi-Adams Family Papers, Letters Recd. (MR475).

10. Adams, *Memoirs*, 6:540; Clay to Smith, 7 and 9 May 1825, in Clay, *Papers*, 4:332, 337-38n.

11. Smith to Clay, 25 June 1825, in Clay, *Papers*, 4:468-75.

12. Lloyd to Clay, 27 June 1825, and Holmes to Clay, 8 June 1825, ibid., pp. 477-86, 421-25.

13. Webster to Clay, 28 Sept. 1825, ibid., pp. 695-98.

14. Rush to Secretary of State, 26 Mar. 1825, ibid., p. 180.

15. William Huskisson, *The Speeches of William Huskisson, with a Biographical Memoir Supplied . . . from Authentic Sources*, 3 vols. (London, 1831), 2:304–59.

16. Great Britain, *Statutes*, 6 Geo. 4, c. 73, pp. 170–76 (27 June 1825), c. 104–14 (5 July 1825), pp. 304–507, c. 105, pp. 323–55.

17. Ibid., c. 114, p. 491.

18. Ibid., c. 73, sec. 6, p. 171; *American Annual Register* 2 (1826/27): 57; Benns, *American Struggle*, pp. 109–10.

19. Smith to Clay, 13 Aug. 1825, in DNA, RG59, Dip. Disp., Great Britain, vol. 32 (M30, R28).

20. *Daily National Intelligencer* (Washington), 7 Sept. 1825, reprinting *New York Albion*. For a survey of general newspaper reaction see Benns, *American Struggle*, pp. 111–12.

21. *Register of Debates*, 19th Cong., 1st sess., cols. 74, 1119.

22. Clay to Cambreleng, 25 Dec. 1825, in Clay, *Papers*, 4:941.

23. Vaughan to Clay, 18 Feb. and 22 Mar. 1826, ibid., 5:115, 190; Benns, *American Struggle*, p. 115. On February 9, however, Samuel Smith transmitted to Adams a report from Nassau indicating the same construction upon the trade regulations as had been first applied at Halifax and stating that the surveyor general of British customs had upheld that interpretation. Dawson Brothers to Sam Smith and Smith to the President, both on 9 Feb. 1826, in MHi-Adams Family Papers, Letters Recd. (MR474).

24. Clay to Gallatin, 19 June 1826, in Clay, *Papers*, 5:466.

25. Gallatin to Clay, 19 Aug. and 13 Sept. 1826, ibid., pp. 630, 685.

26. Gallatin to Clay, 13 Sept. 1826, ibid., pp. 685–86.

27. Gallatin to Clay, 19 Aug. 1826, ibid., p. 630.

28. *Register of Debates*, 19th Cong., 1st sess., cols. 576–90 (18 Apr. 1826).

29. Gallatin to Clay, 14 Sept. 1826, Clay to Vaughan, 19 Oct. 1826, and Vaughan to Clay, 20 Oct. 1826, in Clay, *Papers*, 5:687–88, 806, 808.

30. *Register of Debates*, 19th Cong., 1st sess., col. 588.

31. Clay to Gallatin, 11 Apr. 1827, in Clay, *Papers*, 6:426.

32. Canning to Gallatin, 27 Jan. 1827, with Gallatin to Clay, 28 Jan. 1827, in DNA, RG59, Dip. Disp., Great Britain, vol. 33 (M30, R29); [Clay], Editorial, *Daily National Intelligencer* (Washington), 9 May 1827.

33. William Huskisson, *Navigation Laws, Speech in the House of Commons . . . 12th May . . . on the Present State of the Shipping Interest . . .* (London, 1826), transmitted in Lloyd to Clay, 1 Nov. 1826, in Clay, *Papers*, 5:855–56; "A Comparative Statement of the British and Foreign Tonnage Which Have Entered the Several Ports of Great Britain up to 10th October 1826 . . . ," Great Britain, *Sessional Papers*, 1826/27, 18 (no. 52): 367–70, transmitted and discussed in Gallatin to Clay, 22 Feb. 1827, in Clay, *Papers* 6:224–25; Gallatin to Clay, 14 Sept. 1827, in Clay, *Papers*, 6:1037.

34. Gallatin to Clay, 14 Sept. and 3 Oct. 1827, in DNA, RG59, Dip. Disp., Great Britain, vol. 34 (M30, R30).

35. Adams, *Memoirs*, 7:166, 213–14, 215 (quoted).

36. *Register of Debates*, 19th Cong., 2d sess., cols. 397–454, 456–86, 491–98, 1501–7, 1514–31; U.S. Congress, *Senate Journal*, 19th Cong., 2d sess., pp. 109, 211–12, 239–44, 280–83, 298–300; U.S. Congress, *House Journal*, 19th Cong., 2d sess., pp. 366, 384–86.

37. The Tazewell articles appeared between 20 April and 26 June 1827. Benns surveys other expressions of the Jacksonian criticism and the administration's response in *American Struggle*, pp. 126–27, 135–36, 158–63.

38. Adams, *Memoirs*, 7:149–50; James Lloyd, *Remarks on the Report of the Committee of Commerce . . . on the British Colonial Intercourse* (n.p., 1826); Lloyd to Clay, 16 Oct. 1826, Webster to Clay, 13 Oct. 1826, Goldsborough to Clay, 12 Oct. 1826, and Pleasants to Clay, 9 Dec. 1826, in Clay, *Papers*, 5:801, 790–91, 788–89, 984.

39. Clay to Peter Force, 25 Feb. and 25 Mar. 1827, Clay to Gales and Seaton, 9 May 1827, and Clay to Carey and Lea, 29 Dec. 1826, in Clay, *Papers*, 6:239–40, 353–54, 534–36, 5:1048n; "Documents from the Department of State, Relative to the Colonial Trade," *American Quarterly Review* 2 (Sept. 1827): 267–306 (quotation on p. 306).

40. *Register of Debates*, 20th Cong., 1st sess., cols. 553, 566 (31 Mar. 1828); Mareuil to Clay, 13 Mar. 1827, in Clay, *Papers*, 6:301.

41. *Register of Debates*, 20th Cong., 1st sess., cols. 556–58, 565–70 (quotations in cols. 556, 557, 570).

42. Ibid., cols. 560–61, 569 (quoted).

43. *American State Papers, Foreign Relations*, 6:827–28; U.S., *Statutes at Large*, 4:269 (9 May 1828).

44. Quoted in Benns, *American Struggle*, p. 160.

45. See table 1; see also Robert Monroe Harrison to Clay, 27 May, 9 and 16 Aug., and 24 Dec. 1827, 2 Mar. and 27 May 1828, and B. Aymar & Co. to Clay, 23 June 1828, in Clay, *Papers*, 6:595–96, 867–68, 912, 1378, 7:138, 302, 361; *Register of Debates*, 20th Cong., 1st sess., col. 244; *Niles' Weekly Register* 34 (15 Mar. 1828): 41–42. While there was reference to increased trade through Canada, a movement that was supposedly a particular boon to Adams's New England constituents, the export data show only a modest rise in that to British North America in 1827 and 1829 and a sharp decline in 1828.

46. Computed from U.S. Bureau of the Census and Social Science Research Council, *Historical Statistics of the United States, 1789–1945: A Supplement to the Statistical Abstract of the United States* (Washington, D.C.: Government Printing Office, 1949), ser. K94–104, K124–26, pp. 208, 212; Douglass C. North, *The Economic Growth of the United States, 1790–1860* (1961; reprint ed., New York: W. W. Norton & Co., 1966), table B-VIII, p. 234.

47. Computed from *Historical Statistics of the United States*, ser. M42–55, p. 245; Charles H. Evans, comp., "Exports, Domestic, from the United States to All Countries from 1789 to 1883, Inclusive," U.S. Congress, *House Misc. Docs.*, 48th

Cong., 1st sess., vol. 24, no. 49, pt. 2, table 5, pp. 79–95. Cf. Tudor to Clay, 3 Jan. 1828, in Clay, *Papers*, 7:8–9.

48. North, *Economic Growth*, pp. 71, 190–91, 233 (table A-VIII).

Chapter 6
Diplomacy of Mission

1. *Daily National Intelligencer* (Washington), 9 Sept. 1825.

2. J. Orin Oliphant, "The Parvin-Brigham Mission to Spanish America, 1823–1826," *Church History* 14 (June, 1945): 85–103, quoting, on p. 93, the Brigham "Report"; Sullivan to [Adams], 21 Mar. 1826, in MHi-Adams Family Papers, Letters Recd. (MR475).

3. John Quincy Adams, *Memoirs of John Quincy Adams, Comprising Portions of His Diary from 1795 to 1848*, ed. Charles Francis Adams, 12 vols. (Philadelphia: J. B. Lippincott & Co., 1874–77), 7:125; see also Robert P. Hay, "The Glorious Departure of the American Patriarchs: Contemporary Reactions to the Deaths of Jefferson and Adams," *Journal of Southern History* 35 (Nov. 1969): 543–55.

4. George Canning to Edward J. Dawkins, 18 Mar. 1826, in C. K. Webster, ed., *Britain and the Independence of Latin America, 1812–1830: Select Documents from the Foreign Office Archives*, 2 vols. (1938; reprint ed., New York: Octagon Books, 1970), 1:404.

5. Clay to Poinsett, 26 Mar. 1825, in Henry Clay, *The Papers of Henry Clay*, ed. James F. Hopkins, Mary W. M. Hargreaves, and Robert Seager II, 8 vols. to date (Lexington: University Press of Kentucky, 1959–), 4:173.

6. Clay to Pablo Obregón, 19 Feb. 1827, Clay to Poinsett, 15 and 29 Mar. 1827, and Clay to John W. Smith, 27 Mar. 1827, ibid., 6:209, 308–9, 368–69, 376.

7. Clay to Gallatin, 19 June 1826, Clay to Levi Lincoln and to Albion K. Parrish, 15 Dec. 1825, and Clay to Charles R. Vaughan, 17 Nov. 1827, 20 Feb. and 17 Mar. 1828, ibid., 5:448, 4:910–11, 6:1273–74; *American State Papers, Foreign Relations*, 6:1015–16, 1018–19.

8. *A Compilation of the Messages and Papers of the Presidents, 1789–1897*, comp. James D. Richardson, 10 vols. (1896–99; reprint ed., New York: Bureau of National Literature and Art, 1901–6), 2:302–3, Peter B. Porter to Clay, 31 Oct. 1826, and Clay to Gallatin, 19 June 1826, in Clay, *Papers*, 5:850, 457–60.

9. Gallatin to Clay, 19 June and 14 Nov. 1826, 21 and 28 Sept. and 1 Oct. 1827, and Clay to Gallatin, 19 and 23 June and 8 Aug. 1826, in Clay, *Papers*, 5:480n, 926, 6:1059–60, 1086, 1103–4, 5:455, 495, 598.

10. Clive Parry, ed., *The Consolidated Treaty Series*, 234 vols. to date (New York: Oceana Publications, 1969–), 78:36–40, 77:414–18, 366–67; Enoch Lincoln to Clay, 3 Sept. and 16 Nov. 1827, Porter to Clay, 30 Oct. 1827, Joseph Delafield to Clay, 6 Nov. 1827, and Lawrence to Clay, 29 Mar. 1828, in Clay, *Papers*, 6:994–95, 1272, 1208–9, 1239, 7:199.

11. U.S. Congress, *House Journal*, 18th Cong., 1st sess., p. 35; Clay, *Papers*, 3:598, 608. On the importance of the Smyrna trade see James A. Field, Jr.,

America and the Mediterranean World, 1776–1882 (Princeton, N.J.: Princeton University Press, 1969), pp. 114, 123.

12. U.S. Congress, *Annals of Congress*, 18th Cong., 1st sess., cols. 1084–1214 passim (quoted from cols. 1133, 1182).

13. Clay to Somerville, 6 Sept. 1825, in Clay, *Papers*, 4:624–25.

14. Clay to Somerville, 14 Apr. 1825, Edward Ingersoll to Clay, 7 May 1825, Hughes to Clay, 21 June 1825, Somerville to Clay, 16 Aug. 1825, and Clay to John J. Crittenden, 22 Aug. 1825, ibid., pp. 255–56, 334, 452, 577–78, 585; Adams, *Memoirs*, 6:533, 7:47, 49.

15. Clay to Somerville, 6 Sept. 1825, in Clay, *Papers*, 4:624.

16. Lafayette to Clay, 22 Jan. 1826, ibid., 5:51.

17. Clay to James Brown, 22 May 1826, ibid., 5:388; U.S., *Statutes at Large*, 4:168–69 (17 May 1826); Douglas Dakin, *British and American Philhellenes during the War of Greek Independence, 1821–1833* (Thessaloniki, 1955), pp. 119–20; Field, *America and the Mediterranean World*, pp. 123, 128.

18. *Compilation of Messages and Papers*, 2:384, 408.

19. Ibid., p. 407; English to Adams, n.d. (recd. 30 Dec. 1825), in MHi-Adams Family Papers, Letters Recd. (MR473); Offley to Clay, 4 Jan. 1827, in Clay, *Papers*, 6:14.

20. Carey to Clay, 3 Mar. 1827, Clay to Southard, 8 Mar. 1827, Southard to Clay, 9 Mar. 1827, Clay to Carey, 10 Mar. 1827, and David Offley to Clay, 4 Jan. 1827, in Clay, *Papers*, 6:256–57, 270, 277, 278, 14; Field, *America and the Mediterranean World*, pp. 127–28, 146.

21. Clay to Miller, 22 Apr. 1825, in Clay, *Papers*, 4:278. The following account of the formation of the federation is drawn largely from Joseph Byrne Lockey, *Pan-Americanism: Its Beginnings* (New York: Macmillan Co., 1920), pp. 72–79.

22. Clay to Miller, 22 Apr. 1825, and Clay to Cañaz, 18 Apr. 1825, in Clay, *Papers*, 4:280, 264.

23. Clay to Williams, 10 Feb. 1826, ibid., 5:93–94; *Daily National Intelligencer* (Washington), 26 Apr. 1825; *Niles' Weekly Register* 28 (7 May 1825): 152–53; Blunt to Adams, 19 July 1825, in MHi-Adams Family Papers, Letters Recd. (MR471).

24. Josiah Shelden, Henry Kennedy, and J. Hervey to Adams, 20 Dec. 1825, in MHi-Adams Family Papers, Letters Recd. (MR473); Clay to Richard C. Anderson and John Sergeant, 8 May 1826, in Clay, *Papers*, 5:335–36.

25. Charles Hay to Adams, 18 Feb. 1826, enclosing a copy of the decree, in MHi-Adams Family Papers, Letters Recd. (MR474).

26. Blunt to Adams, 19 July 1825 and Williams to Adams, 18 June 1826, ibid. (MR471, 476).

27. Williams to Adams, 18 June 1826, Phillips to Clay, 3 Feb. 1827, and Phillips to Clay, 6 Jan. 1828, in Clay, *Papers*, 6:159–60, 7:15; U.S. Congress, *House Reports*, 30th Cong. 2d sess., no. 145, pp. 362–75.

28. Phillips to Clay, 2 Mar. 1827, in Clay, *Papers*, 6:255.

29. Clay, Speeches of 24, 25, and 28 Mar. 1818, in Clay, *Papers*, 2:517, 546, 551; Arthur Preston Whitaker, *The United States and the Independence of Latin*

America, 1800-1830 (1941; reprint ed., New York: Russell & Russell, 1962), pp. 551, 552.

30. George A. Lipsky, *John Quincy Adams: His Theory and Ideas* (New York: Thomas Y. Crowell Co., 1950), pp. 290-91; Adams to Heman Allen, 23 Nov. 1823, in DNA, RG59, Dip. Instr., All Countries, vol. 10, p. 130 (M77, R5); Adams, *Memoirs*, 6:194; *Compilation of Messages and Papers*, 2:333.

31. Watts to Clay, 14 June 1827, Clay to Adams, 2 July 1827, Bolívar to Clay, 21 Nov. 1827, Clay to James Cooley, 18 Dec. 1827, and Clay to Bolívar, 27 Oct. 1828, in Clay, *Papers*, 6:684-85, 738, 1298-99, 1369, 7:517-18.

32. Tudor to Clay, 3 Feb. 1827, ibid., 6:161.

33. Larned to Clay, 5 Nov. 1825, 16 Mar., 25 Aug., and 10 Nov. 1826, and Forbes to Clay, 1 July (quoted) and 16 Nov. 1825 and 17 June 1826, ibid., 4:792, 5:177, 648, 894, 4:495, 833, 5:438.

34. John Quincy Adams, *Writings of John Quincy Adams*, ed. Worthington Chauncey Ford, 7 vols. (New York: Macmillam Co., 1913-17), 7:372-79; Adams, *Memoirs*, 6:199-213 (quoted from pp. 199-200); Worthington C. Ford, "Some Original Documents on the Genesis of the Monroe Doctrine," *Proceedings of the Massachusetts Historical Society*, 2d ser., 15 (1901-2): 405-8. The written response to Tuyll, misdated as 15 Nov. 1823, is found in DNA, RG59, Notes to Foreign Legations, 3:158 (M38, R3). For development of these concepts see Samuel Flagg Bemis, *John Quincy Adams and the Foundations of American Foreign Policy* (New York: Alfred A. Knopf, 1949), pp. 384-90; John A. Logan, Jr., *No Transfer: An American Security Principle* (New Haven, Conn.: Yale University Press, 1961), p. 172.

35. Clay to Poinsett, 26 Mar. and 9 Nov. 1825, and Clay to Brown, 25 Oct. 1825, in Clay, *Papers*, 5:170-71, 805 (quoted), 762-63. On the significance of this linkage see Dexter Perkins, *The Monroe Doctrine, 1823-1826* (Cambridge: Harvard University Press, 1932), p. 203, and cf. Logan, *No Transfer*, pp. 172, 244-52.

36. Adams to José María Salazar, 6 Aug. 1824, in DNA, RG59, Notes to Foreign Legations, 3:184-86 (M38, R3); Clay to José Silvestre Rebello, 13 Apr. 1825, in Clay, *Papers*, 4:244. For discussion of the "American Aftermath" of the Monroe Doctrine see Perkins, *Monroe Doctrine*, pp. 185-222.

37. Poinsett to Clay, 21 Aug. 1825, and Clay to Brown, 25 Oct. 1825, in Clay, *Papers*, 4:584, 763.

38. Clay to John M. Forbes, 3 Jan. 1828, ibid., 7:6-8.

39. Harold Temperley, *The Foreign Policy of Canning, 1822-1827* . . . (London: G. Bell & Sons, 1925), pp. 147-51; Rush to Adams, 18 Jan. 1825, in DNA, RG59, Dip. Disp., Great Britain, vol. 32 (M30, R28).

40. Nelson to Secretary of State, 8 Mar. 1825, Clay to Middleton, 10 May 1825, Clay to King, 11 May 1825, and Clay to Brown, 13 May 1825, in Clay, *Papers*, 4:93-94, 355-62, 366-67, 372-73. The instructions to Poinsett, dated 26 Mar. 1825 (ibid., pp. 166-77), and to Everett, dated 27 Apr. 1825 (ibid., pp. 292-99), had urged the importance of resolving the war between Spain and its former colonies and had cited the threat that the war posed in relation to Cuba but had not mentioned the administration's intention to seek the czar's intervention.

CHAPTER 7
THE CUBAN PROBLEM AND THE PANAMA CONGRESS
IN THE NEW WORLD SYSTEM

1. Samuel Flagg Bemis, *John Quincy Adams and the Foundations of American Foreign Policy* (New York: Alfred A. Knopf, 1949), p. 381; Clay to Brown, 25 Oct. 1825, in Henry Clay, *The Papers of Henry Clay*, ed. James F. Hopkins, Mary W. M. Hargreaves, and Robert Seager II, 8 vols. to date (Lexington: University Press of Kentucky, 1959–), 4:578–79, 762.

2. Nelson to Clay, 15 June 1825, in Clay, *Papers*, 4:442.

3. Rufus King to Clay, 9 and 11 Aug. 1825, ibid., pp. 572, 574.

4. Clay to King, 17 and 26 Oct. 1825, ibid., pp. 743 (quoted), 766–67.

5. Philip S. Foner, *A History of Cuba and Its Relations with the United States*, 2 vols. (New York: International Publishers, 1962), 1:125–28.

6. Ibid., pp. 139–42; John Quincy Adams, *Memoirs of John Quincy Adams, Comprising Portions of His Diary from 1795 to 1848*, ed. Charles Francis Adams, 12 vols. (Philadelphia: J. B. Lippincott & Co., 1874–77), 6:70–74.

7. Adams, *Memoirs*, 6:138; James Madison to [James] Monroe, 30 Oct. 1823, in James Monroe Papers, Presidential Papers Series, Microfilm (MR8).

8. Clay to Everett, 27 Apr. 1825, in Clay, *Papers*, 4:298.

9. Everett to Adams, 30 Nov. 1825, in MHi-Adams Family Papers, Letters Recd. (MR472).

10. Clay to Everett, 13 Apr. 1826, in Clay, *Papers*, 5:237–38.

11. Gallatin to Clay, 30 Dec. 1826 and 5 Feb. 1827, Brown to Clay, 13 Feb. 1827, Clay to Nicholas Biddle, 13 Mar. 1827, and Everett to Clay, 17 Aug., 19 Oct., and 12 Dec. 1827 and 4 Apr. 1828, ibid., 5:1057, 6:165-66, 193, 302, 920–21, 1169, 1353, 7:214; see also Everett to Clay, 9 June 1827, and Forbes to Clay, 18 July 1827, ibid., 6:664, 801.

12. Harris Gaylord Warren, *The Sword Was Their Passport: A History of American Filibustering in the Mexican Revolution* (Baton Rouge: Louisiana State University Press, 1943), pp. 11–32, 57–66 passim; Foner, *History of Cuba*, 1:129–30; Charles Carroll Griffin, *The United States and the Disruption of the Spanish Empire, 1810–1822* . . . (New York: Columbia University Press, 1937), pp. 53–54.

13. Irvine to Clay, 18, 20, and 29 Jan. 1824, and Clay to Monroe, 12 June 1824, in Clay, *Papers*, 3:594–96, 600, 618–19, 775; Adams, *Memoirs*, 6:430–31.

14. John M. Forsyth to Adams, 20 Nov. 1822, in William R. Manning, comp., *Diplomatic Correspondence of the United States Concerning the Independence of the Latin-American Nations*, 3 vols. (New York: Oxford University Press, 1925), 3:2025; Foner, *History of Cuba*, 1:104, 111, 119–21.

15. Adams to Randall, 29 Apr. 1823, in DNA, RG59, Cons. Instr., 2:283 (M78, R2); Robertson to Clay, 20 Apr. 1825, in Clay, *Papers*, 4:271–74.

16. Clay to Adams, 3 Oct. 1825, in Clay, *Papers*, 4:711–12.

17. Clay to Robertson, 7 Dec. 1825, ibid., pp. 882–84.

18. Robertson to Clay, 19 Jan. 1826, Clay to Cook, 12 Mar. 1827, and Clay to Vives, 14 Mar. 1827, ibid., 5:47–48, 6:295–96, 302–3; Adams, *Memoirs*, 7:238.

19. Vives to Clay, 4 May 1827, and Ninian Edwards to Clay, 1 Nov. 1827, in Clay, *Papers*, 6:519, 1223; Edwards to Clay, 2 Jan. 1828, in MHi-Adams Family Papers, Letters Recd. (MR483); Cook's report, n.d., in DNA, RG59, Dip. Disp., Special Agents (M37, R9).

20. Daniel McLaughlin to Clay, 19 June 1828, in DNA, RG59, Applications and Recommendations for Office (M531, R7).

21. See William W. Freehling, *Prelude to Civil War: The Nullification Controversy in South Carolina, 1816–1836* (New York: Harper & Row, 1965), pp. 16, 50, 55–65; James Brown to Clay, 13 May 1826, and Everett to Clay, 7 Jan. 1827, in Clay, *Papers*, 5:366, 6:27.

22. Translation quoted in Foner, *History of Cuba*, 1:153.

23. Poinsett to Clay, 15 June, 21 Aug., 13 and 21 Sept. and 2 Dec. 1825 and 25 Feb. 1826, in Clay, *Papers*, 4:443, 584, 641, 667, 876, 5:133.

24. Adams, *Memoirs*, 7:10, 88; Clay to José María Salazar and to Pablo Obregón, 20 Dec. 1825, and Clay to Everett, 13 Apr. 1826, ibid., 4:929–31, 5:236–37. On December 8 Clay had received a private letter from Middleton, reporting that Prince Metternich approved the proposed peace effort, that "France no doubt wishes something of the kind . . . and as Prussia assents to every thing which is agreeable to the majority of the allies," he (Middleton) considered "the question as settled." The Russian response, as Middleton reported in his official dispatch, received on the same date, had, however, been cautious. Middleton to Clay, 8 Sept. 1825, dispatch no. 49 and the "Private" letter of the same date, in Clay, *Papers*, 4:630–31.

25. Everett to Clay, 1 Jan. 1826, in Clay, *Papers*, 5:1.

26. Salazar to Clay, 19 Mar. 1826, and Poinsett to Clay, 8 and 18 Mar. 1826, ibid., pp. 180–81, 153–54, 179.

27. Joseph Byrne Lockey, *Pan-Americanism: Its Beginnings* (New York: Macmillan Co., 1920), pp. 286–312, 327; Clay to Richard C. Anderson, 16 Sept. 1825, in Clay, *Papers*, 4:645.

28. Adams, *Memoirs*, 6:531, 536–37, 542; Clay to Pablo Obregón, 30 Nov. 1825, in Clay, *Papers*, 4:868. Wirt discussed his reservations relating to the proposal in a letter to Southard, 1 May 1825, in NjP-Southard Papers.

29. *Daily National Intelligencer* (Washington), 26 Apr. 1825.

30. U.S. Congress, *Register of Debates*, 19th Cong., 1st sess., col. 2363; Adams, *Memoirs*, 6:531 (quoted), 536–37. Platt H. Crosby, a New York lawyer who had long been active in disseminating propaganda for Latin-American independence and was translater of a tract by Bernardo Monteagudo, *The Necessity of a General Federation between the States of Spanish America* (Lima, 1825), appears to have been at least instrumental in the preparation of the Philadelphia article. His translation and notes by the Peruvian editor are located in PHi-John Sergeant Papers. Clay's enthusiasm for the Panama Congress was certainly great; but Adams, too, had already expressed interest in the opportunity that it afforded to develop policies of strong personal concern. See Charles Wilson Hackett, "The Development of John Quincy Adams's Policy with Respect to an American Confederation and the Panama Congress, 1822–1825," *Hispanic American Historical Review* 9 (Nov. 1928): 505–11, 526.

31. José María Salazar to Clay, 2 Nov. 1825, translation in DNA, RG59, Notes from Colombian Legation, vol. 1, pt. 2 (M51, R2).

32. *A Compilation of Messages and Papers of the Presidents, 1789–1897*, comp. James D. Richardson, 10 vols. (1896–99; reprint ed., New York: Bureau of National Literature and Art, 1901–6), 2:318–20.

33. U.S. Congress, *Senate Docs.*, 19th Cong., 1st sess., no. 68, pp. 57–76 (quoted from p. 75).

34. Ibid., p. 100. For the full debate see *Register of Debates*, 19th Cong., 1st sess., cols. 142–343, 384–405. On the organization of the opposition see Robert V. Remini, *Martin Van Buren and the Making of the Democratic Party* (New York: Columbia University Press, 1959), pp. 105–11.

35. On the appropriation bill see *House Journal*, 19th Cong., 1st sess., p. 462; *Senate Journal*, 19th Cong., 1st sess., p. 291; *Register of Debates*, 19th Cong., 1st sess., cols. 1208–19, 1226–32, 1237–46, 1253–1302, 1765, 2009–98, 2135–2514 passim. On the issue of the Poinsett "pledge" see the protocol of the conference with the Mexican negotiators, 28 Sept. 1825, in *American State Papers, Foreign Relations*, 6:589 (quoted); *Register of Debates*, 19th Cong., 1st sess., cols. 1765–68, 1798–1820; *Enquirer* (Richmond, Va.), 31 Mar. 1826.

36. On the effect of the debate see Clay to Brown, 29 May 1826, in Clay, *Papers*, 5:404; Arthur Preston Whitaker, *The United States and the Independence of Latin America, 1800–1830* (1941; reprint ed., New York: Russell & Russell, 1962), pp. 579–80; Foner, *History of Cuba*, 1:166–69.

37. For Adams's message of 15 Mar. 1826, reviewing the issues, see *Compilation of Messages and Papers*, 2:329–40 (quotations from pp. 336, 337, 333, 334, 336, 335, 331). For the instructions, with annotations on the revisions in the drafting process, see Clay, *Papers*, 5:313–44. Clay subsequently delineated this as his most important public paper; see Clay to Robert Walsh, Jr., 25 Apr. 1836, in DLC-HC (DNA, M212, R5).

38. Quotation in Clay, *Papers*, 5:317. Clay had previously supplied a similar statement for the president's response to a House inquiry concerning Poinsett's "pledge"; cf. Clay to Adams, 29 Mar. 1826, ibid., p. 202.

39. Ladd to Adams, 15 Mar. 1826, in MHi-Adams Family Papers, Letters Recd. (MR475). See also J. B. Sutherland to Adams (quoted), 6 Feb. 1826, T. Worthington to [Adams], 11 Feb. 1826, W. Duane to [Adams], 21 Mar. 1826, George Sullivan to [Adams], 21 Mar. 1826, H. Niles to [Adams], 21 Mar. 1826, Robert Oliver to Adams, 26 Mar. 1826, Levi Lincoln to Adams, 30 Mar. 1826, and John A. Dix to Jacob Brown, 1 Apr. 1826, ibid. (MR474, 475); [Thomas Hart Benton], *Thirty Years' View; or, A History of the Working of the American Government for Thirty Years, from 1820 to 1850 . . .* , 2 vols. (New York: D. Appleton & Co., 1859, 1860), 1:65.

40. Canning to Dawkins, 18 Mar. 1826, and Dawkins to Canning, 15 Oct. 1826, in C. K. Webster, ed., *Britain and the Independence of Latin America, 1812–1830: Select Documents . . .* , 2 vols. (1938; reprint ed., New York: Octagon Books, 1970), 1:404, 423.

41. Dawkins to Canning, 7 and 15 July and 15 Oct. 1826, ibid., pp. 413, 416–23 (pp. 422, 423 quoted).

42. Brown to Clay, 13 Jan. 1826, and Everett to Clay, 3 Feb. 1826, in Clay, *Papers*, 5:29, 82.

43. Infantado's remarks are reported in Everett to Clay, 2 June 1826, ibid., p. 414.

44. Everett to Clay, 2 and 25 June and 20 July 1826, and Salazar to Clay, 19 Mar. 1826, ibid., pp. 414 (quoted), 504, 559, 180–81. Spain was not willing to acknowledge the independence of its American colonies until a decade later, and the process of formal recognition was not completed until the early 1890s.

45. Frances L. Reinhold, "New Research on the First Pan-American Congress—Held at Panama in 1826," *Hispanic American Historical Review* 18 (Aug. 1938): [342], 353, 363; *Register of Debates*, 19th Cong., 1st sess., cols. 2079–80.

46. Whitaker, *United States and the Independence of Latin America*, p. 575.

47. *Compilation of Messages and Papers*, 2:339.

48. Ibid., pp. 331–32.

49. Adams to Barbour, 4 Apr. 1829, in MHi-Adams Family Papers, Private Letterbook, 10:181–82 (MR149).

50. Gallatin to Clay, 5 Nov. 1826, and Brown to Clay, 12 June and 12 Oct. 1827, in Clay, *Papers*, 5:864–65, 6:667, 1139–40 (quoted).

CHAPTER 8

THE AMERICAN SYSTEM AT HOME

1. *A Compilation of the Messages and Papers of the Presidents, 1789–1897*, comp. James D. Richardson, 10 vols. (1896–99; reprint ed., New York: Bureau of National Literature and Art, 1901–6), 2:298–99.

2. Ibid., p. 311.

3. Ibid., p. 316.

4. John Quincy Adams, *Memoirs of John Quincy Adams, Comprising Portions of His Diary from 1795 to 1848*, ed. Charles Francis Adams, 12 vols. (Philadelphia: J. B. Lippincott & Co., 1874–77), 7:59–63.

5. *Register of Debates*, 19th Cong., 1st sess., cols. 695–96; 19th Cong., 2d sess., cols. 373–76, 380, 1497–1500 (quotation from col. 1499).

6. *Compilation of Messages and Papers*, 2:313.

7. Ibid., pp. 312–13.

8. *Register of Debates*, 19th Cong., 2d sess., cols. 948–49. For a background account of this project see William Stanton, *The Great United States Exploring Expedition of 1828–1842* (Berkeley: University of California Press, 1975), pp. 8–25.

9. "Annual Report of the Secretary of the Navy . . . 1827," *American State Papers, Naval Affairs*, 3:54.

10. U.S. Congress, *House Journal*, 20th Cong., 1st sess., pp. 774, 796.

11. Adams, *Memoirs*, 8:75, 57–58.

12. "Annual Report of the Secretary of the Navy . . . 1828," *American State Papers, Naval Affairs*, 3:211–12.

13. *House Journal*, 20th Cong., 2d sess., pp. 134–35.

14. *Register of Debates*, 20th Cong., 2d sess., pp. 50–52, 215, app., pp. 33–38.

15. *Senate Journal*, 20th Cong., 2d sess., p. 177.

16. Stanton, *Great United States Exploring Expedition*, pp. 5–6; U.S., *Statutes at Large*, 3:425 (14 Apr. 1818).

17. "Annual Report of the Secretary of the Navy . . . 1825," *American State Papers, Naval Affairs*, 2:99; "Annual Report of the Secretary of the Navy . . . 1827," ibid., 3:53; "Annual Report of the Secretary of the Navy . . . 1828," ibid., p. 212; U.S., *Statutes at Large*, 4:48 (26 May 1824).

18. Ninian Edwards to Clay, 18 July 1825, in Henry Clay, *The Papers of Henry Clay*, ed. James F. Hopkins, Mary W. M. Hargreaves, and Robert Seager II, 8 vols. to date (Lexington: University Press of Kentucky, 1959–), 4:543.

19. Adams, *Memoirs*, 7:64. On Monroe's views see Harry Ammon, *James Monroe: The Quest for National Identity* (New York: McGraw-Hill Book Co., 1971), pp. 387–92.

20. Alexander Macomb to James Barbour, 20 Nov. 1827, attached to Barbour's report of 26 Nov. 1827, in U.S. Congress, *Senate Docs.*, 20th Cong., 1st sess., no. 1, p. 55.

21. Report dated 1 Dec. 1825, "Documents Accompanying the President's Message . . . December 6, 1825," *Senate Docs.*, 19th Cong., 1st sess., no. 2, p. 6.

22. Paul Wallace Gates, *History of Public Land Law Development* (Washington, D.C.: Government Printing Office, 1968), pp. 345–52; Clay, *Papers*, 4:32–33n.

23. Ralph D. Gray, *The National Waterway: A History of the Chesapeake and Delaware Canal, 1769–1965* (Urbana: University of Illinois Press, 1967), pp. 53–64; U.S., *Statutes at Large*, 4:162 (13 May 1826), 352 (2 Mar. 1829); "Report on the Louisville and Portland Canal," *House Misc. Docs.*, 40th Cong., 2d sess., no. 83 (28 Feb. 1868), p. 5; Carter Goodrich, *Government Promotion of American Canals and Railroads, 1800–1890* (New York: Columbia University Press, 1960), pp. 40–41; "Annual Report on the State of the Finances," 6 Dec. 1828, *House Docs.*, 20th Cong., 2d sess., no. 9, p. 5.

24. *United States Telegraph* (Washington), 21 July 1827.

25. Harry N. Scheiber, "State Policy and the Public Domain: The Ohio Canal Lands," *Journal of Economic History* 25 (Mar. 1965): 99; John Bell Rae, "Federal Land Grants in Aid of Canals," *Journal of Economic History* 4 (Nov. 1944): 167, 173–75; Logan Esarey, *A History of Indiana from Its Exploration to 1850* (Indianapolis, Ind.: W. K. Stewart Co., 1915), pp. 356–60, 385–93.

26. For basic accounts of this project see George Washington Ward, *The Early Development of the Chesapeake and Ohio Canal Project*, Johns Hopkins University Studies in Historical and Political Science, ser. 17, nos. 9–11 (Sept.–Nov. 1899); Walter S. Sanderlin, *The Great National Project: A History of the Chesapeake and Ohio Canal* (Baltimore: Johns Hopkins University Press, 1946); Joseph H. Harrison, Jr., "Simon Bernard, the American System, and the Ghost of the French Alliance," in *America, the Middle Period: Essays in Honor of Bernard Mayo*, ed. John B. Boles (Charlottesville: University of Virginia Press, 1973), pp. 156–57.

27. U.S. Congress, *House Docs.*, 19th Cong., 2d sess., no. 10, p. 62.

28. Adams, *Memoirs,* 7:190–91.

29. Ibid., 8:48–49; *Daily National Intelligencer* (Washington), 7 July 1828.

30. Adams, *Memoirs,* 8:50.

31. *Register of Debates,* 20th Cong., 1st sess., cols. 1513–21, 1609–1819 (quotation from col. 1513).

32. Ibid., col. 640.

33. Ibid., cols. 645–46.

34. On these votes see ibid., 19th Cong., 2d sess., cols. 122, 165, 209, 227, 277.

35. Ibid., cols. 288–89. Those who voted inconsistently were Holmes (Me.), Samuel Bell and Woodbury (N.H.), Calvin Willey (Conn.), Dickerson (N.J.), Randolph and Tazewell (Va.), Branch and Nathaniel Macon (N.C.), Smith (S.C.), Thomas W. Cobb (Ga.), Thomas B. Reed (Miss.), White (Tenn.), and Ruggles (Ohio). Only Bell, Willey, and Ruggles were adherents of the administration. On Bell's vote cf. Donald B. Cole, *Jacksonian Democracy in New Hampshire, 1800–1851* (Cambridge: Harvard University Press, 1970), p. 72. On the inconsistency characterizing the voting behavior of Van Buren's "southern friends" cf. his *Autobiography,* ed. John C. Fitzpatrick, *American Historical Association Annual Report for the Year 1918,* vol. 2 (Washington, D.C.: Government Printing Office, 1920), pp. 214–15.

36. U.S., *Statutes at Large,* 3:379–80 (3 Mar. 1817); Rush, "Report," 6 Dec. 1828, *House Docs.,* 20th Cong., 2d sess., no. 9, p. 2.

37. Richard Rush, "Report," 22 Dec. 1825, *Senate Docs.,* 19th Cong., 1st sess., no. 6, pp. 10–13; "Report," 12 Dec. 1826, *American State Papers, Finance,* 5:523–24; "Report," 8 Dec. 1827, ibid., 5:630; *Compilation of Messages and Papers,* 2:358.

38. Rush, "Report," 8 Dec. 1827, *American State Papers, Finance,* 5:632–33.

39. Rush, "Report," 22 Dec. 1825, *Senate Docs.,* 19th Cong., 1st sess., no. 6, p. 12; *House Reports,* 19th Cong., 1st sess., no. 64, p. 26.

40. *Register of Debates,* 19th Cong., 2d sess., col. 851.

41. Ibid., cols. 1120–22.

42. On the discussion in this and the following paragraph see Walter Buckingham Smith, *Economic Aspects of the Second Bank of the United States* (Cambridge: Harvard University Press, 1953), pp. 46, 53, 67, 92, 139–46; Peter Temin, *The Jacksonian Economy* (New York: W. W. Norton & Co., 1969), pp. 44–57; and cf. Fritz Redlich, *The Molding of American Banking, Men and Ideas* (New York: Hafner Publishing Co., 1947; also published as vol. 2, pt. 1, of the *History of American Business Leaders* [Ann Arbor, Mich.: Edwards Bros., 1940–51]), pp. 128–38; Thomas Payne Govan, *Nicholas Biddle: Nationalist and Public Banker, 1786–1844* (Chicago: University of Chicago Press, 1959), pp. 91–98; Ralph C. H. Catterall, *The Second Bank of the United States,* Decennial Publications, 2d ser., vol. 2 (Chicago: University of Chicago Press, 1903), pp. 106–12.

43. For Rush's journal see document filed 26 Oct. 1825, in MHi-Adams Family Papers, Letters Recd. (MR472). See also Rush, "Report," 12 Dec. 1826, *American State Papers, Finance,* 5:522.

44. *Register of Debates,* 20th Cong., 1st sess., cols. 815–16.

45. Ibid., col. 816.

46. Ibid., cols. 857–58.

47. Rush, "Report," 6 Dec. 1828, *House Docs.,* 20th Cong., 2d sess., no. 9, p. 9.

48. *Register of Debates,* 19th Cong., 2d sess., cols. 174–81 (quotation from col. 178); *Senate Journal,* 19th Cong., 2d sess., pp. 99, 133.

49. *House Journal,* 20th Cong., 1st sess., p. 638, 20th Cong., 2d sess., p. 346; *Register of Debates,* 20th Cong., 1st sess., cols. 379–94, 144–47, 20th Cong., 2d sess., pp. 18–28, 60; *Senate Docs.,* 20th Cong., 2d sess., no. 92; *American State Papers, Finance,* 5:1065–66. Calhoun had outlined the strategy during the previous summer; cf. John C. Calhoun to Littleton W. Tazewell, 1 July 1827, in John C. Calhoun, *The Papers of John C. Calhoun,* ed. Clyde N. Wilson and W. Edwin Hemphill, 15 vols. to date (Columbia: Published by the University of South Carolina Press for the South Caroliniana Society, 1959–), 10:293.

50. *Register of Debates,* 20th Cong., 1st sess., col. 390.

51. John Quincy Adams to Charles Francis Adams, 26 Mar. 1833, in MHi-Adams Family Papers, Letters Recd. (MR497).

CHAPTER 9

TARIFF, LAND, AND INDIAN POLICIES:

THE POLITICAL FLASH POINTS

1. John Quincy Adams, *Memoirs of John Quincy Adams, Comprising Portions of His Diary from 1795 to 1848,* ed. Charles Francis Adams, 12 vols. (Philadelphia: J. B. Lippincott & Co., 1874–77), 7:365, 361; *A Compilation of the Messages and Papers of the Presidents, 1789–1897,* comp. James D. Richardson, 10 vols. (1896–99; reprint ed., New York: Bureau of National Literature and Art, 1901–6), 2:413.

2. Adams, *Memoirs,* 7:365; Richard N. Current, *Daniel Webster and the Rise of National Conservatism,* Library of American Biography, ed. Oscar Handlin (Boston: Little, Brown & Co., 1955), p. 20; Henry Shaw to Clay, 22 Nov. 1826, in Henry Clay, *The Papers of Henry Clay,* ed. James F. Hopkins, Mary W. M. Hargreaves, and Robert Seager II, 8 vols. to date (Lexington: University Press of Kentucky, 1959–), 5:944.

3. "Speech on Tariff," 30–31 Mar. 1824, in Clay, *Papers,* 3:708–9; Richard Rush, "Report," 12 Dec. 1826, *American State Papers, Finance,* 5:525–26; Douglass C. North, *The Economic Growth of the United States, 1790–1860* (1961; reprint ed., New York: W. W. Norton & Co., 1966), p. 233, table A-VIII.

4. Rush, "Report," 22 Dec. 1825, *Senate Docs.,* 19th Cong., 1st sess., no. 6, pp. 13–19 (quotations from pp. 16, 18).

5. Rush, "Report," 12 Dec. 1826, *American State Papers, Finance,* 5:526.

6. *Enquirer* (Richmond, Va.), 30 Jan., 3, 15, 17, 22, and 24 Feb. 1827; Virginia House of Delegates, *Journal,* 1826/27, pp. 116, 134–36.

7. *Enquirer* (Richmond, Va.), 24 and 27 Feb., 1 and 3 Mar. 1827; Virginia House of Delegates, *Journal*, 1826/27, pp. 185-92; Virginia Senate, *Journal*, 1826/27, pp. 127-38.

8. U.S. Congress, *Register of Debates*, 19th Cong., 2d sess., cols. 892, 994, 998-99.

9. U.S. Congress, *House Journal*, 19th Cong., 2d sess., pp. 179, 197-99, 249, 253-64, 278-84; *Register of Debates*, 19th Cong., 2d sess., col. 1099.

10. *Register of Debates*, 19th Cong., 2d sess., col. 496.

11. Clay to Crowninshield, 18 Mar. 1827, and Porter to Clay, 1 May 1827, in Clay, *Papers*, 6:320, 503.

12. *Niles' Weekly Register* 32 (16 and 30 June, 7, 14, 21, and 28 July, 11 Aug. 1827): 259, 265, 294-95, 308, 314-15, 331, 349, 363-64, 388-96.

13. "Agricola," in *Franklin Repository*, reprinted in *Lancaster* (Pa.) *Weekly Journal*, 20 July 1827, quoted in Philip S. Klein, *Pennsylvania Politics, 1817-1832: A Game without Rules* (Philadelphia: Historical Society of Pennsylvania, 1940), p. 245; Clay, *Papers*, 6:877.

14. For extended discussion of this legislation and the stratagem involved see F. W. Taussig, *The Tariff History of the United States*, 8th ed., rev. (1892, reprint ed., New York: Capricorn Books, 1964), pp. 88-101; John C. Calhoun, "Speech," 23 Feb. 1827, in John C. Calhoun, *The Papers of John C. Calhoun*, ed. Clyde N. Wilson and W. Edwin Hemphill, 15 vols. to date (Columbia: Published by the University of South Carolina Press for the South Caroliniana Society, 1959-), 13:457-60.

15. *Niles' Weekly Register* 35 (20 Sept. 1828): 52-57; *Register of Debates*, 20th Cong., 1st sess., cols. 2327-29.

16. Clay to Crittenden, 14 Feb. 1828, and Clay to Peter B. Porter, 1 Mar. 1828, in Clay, *Papers*, 7:95, 136.

17. Clay to Porter, 12 Apr. 1828, ibid., p. 225; *Niles' Weekly Register* 35 (20 Sept. 1828): 57.

18. *Niles' Weekly Register* 34 (10 May 1828): 178; *United States Telegraph* (Washington), 12, 24, and 28 May and 4 June 1828; Current, *Daniel Webster*, p. 53; cf. Robert V. Remini, *Martin Van Buren and the Making of the Democratic Party* (New York: Columbia University Press, 1959), pp. 180-85; John Niven, *Martin Van Buren: The Romantic Age of American Politics* (New York: Oxford University Press, 1983), pp. 196-99.

19. Adams, *Memoirs*, 7:355, 365 (quoted); *National Gazette* (Philadelphia), 7 Dec. 1827; *Liberty Hall and Cincinnati Gazette*, 13 Dec. 1827; Peter B. Porter to Clay, 22 Nov. 1827, and Jabez Hammond to Clay, 11 Dec. 1827, in Clay, *Papers*, 6:1303-4, 1350-51.

20. Clay to Allen Trimble, 27 Dec. 1827, in Clay, *Papers*, 6:1384-85; Adams, *Memoirs*, 7:355, 365 (quoted).

21. *Compilation of Messages and Papers*, 2:414.

22. Ibid., pp. 305, 391.

23. Adams, *Memoirs*, 7:362, 194; Ewing to Clay, 6 Aug. 1825, in Clay, *Papers*, 4:568-69.

24. *Compilation of Messages and Papers*, 2:391; Rush, "Report," 8 Dec. 1827, *American State Papers, Finance*, 5:638.

25. *Register of Debates*, 20th Cong., 1st sess., cols. 483–97.

26. Ibid., col. 678; *United States Telegraph* (Washington), 24 and 26 Apr., 12 May 1828; Daniel Webster to Samuel Bell, 29 July 1828, in Daniel Webster, *The Papers of Daniel Webster*, ed. Charles M. Wiltse and Harold D. Moser, 5 vols. of correspondence to date (Hanover, N.H.: Published for Dartmouth College by the University Press of New England, 1974–), *Correspondence*, 2:357; Adams, *Memoirs*, 7:187–88; Sidney Breese to Clay, 21 July 1827, in Clay, *Papers*, 6:808; John Vollmer Mering, *The Whig Party in Missouri*, University of Missouri Studies vol. 41 (Columbia: University of Missouri Press, 1967), pp. 16–17; David Walter Krueger, "Party Development in Indiana, 1800–1832" (Ph.D. diss., University of Kentucky, 1974), p. 212; Theodore Calvin Pease, *The Centennial History of Illinois*, vol. 2: *The Frontier State, 1818–1848* (Springfield: Illinois Centennial Commission, 1918), p. 104.

27. Calhoun to Speaker of the House of Representatives, 5 Dec. 1818, Calhoun, *Papers*, 3:341–55 (quotation, p. 350). For discussion of the "policy of moderation" see Arthur H. DeRosier, Jr., *The Removal of the Choctaw Indians* (1970; reprint ed., New York: Harper & Row, Harper Torchbooks, 1972), pp. 38–99.

28. Barbour to John Cocks, 3 Feb. 1826, and enclosure, in *American State Papers, Indian Affairs*, 2:646–49.

29. Adams, *Memoirs*, 7:89, 90, 113.

30. William P. DuVal to Adams, 27 July 1826 (enclosing a copy of DuVal to Thomas L. McKenney), and Brooke to George Gibson, 20 Dec. 1825 (enclosed in Barbour to Adams, 14 Feb. 1826), in MHi-Adams Family Papers (MR476, 474).

31. Barbour to Adams, 14 Feb. 1826, in MHi-Adams Family Papers (MR474).

32. Francis Paul Prucha, *American Indian Policy in the Formative Years: The Indian Trade and Intercourse Acts, 1790–1834* (1962; reprint ed., Lincoln: University of Nebraska Press, 1971), pp. 231–32; Clark Howell, *History of Georgia*, 4 vols. (Chicago: S. J. Clarke Publishing Co., 1926), 1:477.

33. Angie Debo, *The Road to Disappearance* (Norman: University of Oklahoma Press, 1941), pp. 87, 90; Adams, *Memoirs*, 7:11, 34.

34. Adams, *Memoirs*, 7:92, 109, 110.

35. "Report and Resolutions of the Legislature of Georgia with Accompanying Documents, January 23, 1827," *House Docs.*, 19th Cong., 2d sess., no. 59, pp. 14, 20–21.

36. Howell, *History of Georgia*, 1:473–74; Habersham to Clay, 25 Feb. 1827, and Clay to Habersham, 27 Apr. 1827, in Clay, *Papers*, 6:242 and note.

37. Troup to Barbour, 17 Feb. 1827, *House Docs.*, 19th Cong., 2d sess., no. 127, p. 5.

38. Adams, *Memoirs*, 7:233; *Compilation of Messages and Papers*, 2:375.

39. *Register of Debates*, 19th Cong., 2d sess., cols. 498, 1533; *Senate Docs.*, 19th Cong., 2d sess., no. 69, pp. 5–6, 8–9; Debo, *Road to Disappearance*, p. 94.

40. For contrasting public reaction on the Georgia protest cf. quotations from the *National Advocate* (New York) and the *National Chronicle* (Philadelphia), reprinted in *Niles' Weekly Register* 29 (3 Sept. 1825): 4–5, and editorial comment, ibid. (26 Nov. 1825): 193; Adam Beatty to Clay, 13 Sept. 1825, William Carroll to Clay, 25 Nov. 1825, and Henry R. Warfield to Clay, 23 Jan. 1826, in Clay, *Papers*, 4:638, 846, 5:55.

41. DeRosier, *Removal of the Choctaw*, p. 93; *Register of Debates*, 20th Cong., 1st sess., cols. 820–23; *Niles' Weekly Register* 33 (19 Jan. 1828): 340.

42. For the debate see *Register of Debates*, 20th Cong., 1st sess., cols. 1533–92 (quotations in this and the following paragraph are from cols. 1553, 1562, 1566).

43. U.S., *Statutes at Large*, 4:300–301, 315 (both 24 May 1828).

44. Porter to Adams, 24 Nov. 1828, *Senate Docs.*, 20th Cong., 2d sess., no. 1, pp. 21–23.

45. *Compilation of Messages and Papers*, 2:416.

46. On the Whig view of Indian policy cf. Daniel Walker Howe, *The Political Culture of the American Whigs* (Chicago: University of Chicago Press, 1979), pp. 40–42.

47. Clay to Webster, 7 June 1827, in Clay, *Papers*, 6:654.

CHAPTER 10
PROBLEMS OF GOVERNMENTAL ADMINISTRATION

1. John Quincy Adams, *Memoirs of John Quincy Adams, Comprising Portions of His Diary from 1795 to 1848*, ed. Charles Francis Adams, 12 vols. (Philadelphia: J. B. Lippincott & Co., 1874–77), 7:235.

2. U.S. Congress, *House Reports*, 19th Cong., 1st sess., no. 122, pp. 14, 15; *Register of Debates*, 19th Cong., 1st sess., col. 2655; *United States Telegraph* (Washington), 1 Jan. 1827.

3. Adams, *Memoirs*, 7:508–13.

4. *Register of Debates*, 20th Cong., 1st sess., cols. 2716–23; *United States Telegraph* (Washington), 8 May 1828.

5. Clay to Louis McLane, 14 Jan. 1826, and Clay to Daniel Webster, 10 Feb. 1826, in Henry Clay, *The Papers of Henry Clay*, ed. James F. Hopkins, Mary W. M. Hargreaves, and Robert Seager II, 8 vols. to date (Lexington: University Press of Kentucky, 1959–), 5:34, 109–10.

6. Leonard D. White, *The Jeffersonians: A Study in Administrative History, 1801–1829* (1951; reprint ed., New York: Free Press, 1965), pp. 118, 190, 194–95 (quotations from pp. 190, 194).

7. Clay to Louis McLane, 14 Jan. 1826, in Clay, *Papers*, 5:34.

8. Ibid., p. 35; Clay to House of Representatives, 11 Jan. 1827, and Clay to Senate and House of Representatives, 7 Feb. 1827, ibid., 6:41, 171–72.

9. Clay to Nelson, 14 Apr. 1825, in DNA, RG59, Dip. Instr., 10:255–56 (M77, R5); Clay to Rush and to John Adams Smith, both on 11 Apr. 1825, Raguet to Clay, 21 Sept. 1827, Clay to Raguet, 24 Sept. 1827, Lawrence to Clay, 11 Oct.

1827, and Barbour to Clay, 5 Sept. 1828, in Clay, *Papers*, 4:238–39, 6:1061, 1068, 1137, 7:459.

10. White, *Jeffersonians*, p. 190; Clay to Poinsett, 1 Apr. 1826, in Clay, *Papers*, 5:212; *Enquirer* (Richmond, Va.), 31 Mar. 1826; and above, p. 000.

11. Adams to Abigail Adams, 2 Nov. 1817, in John Quincy Adams, *Writings of John Quincy Adams*, ed. Worthington Chauncey Ford, 7 vols. (New York: Macmillan Co., 1913–17), 6:227–28.

12. White, *Jeffersonians*, p. 188n; Adams, *Memoirs*, 7:84.

13. White, *Jeffersonians*, pp. 171–72, 188; *A Compilation of the Messages and Papers of the Presidents, 1789–1897*, comp. James D. Richardson, 10 vols. (1896–99; reprint ed., New York: Bureau of National Literature and Art, 1901–6), 2:314–15; Clay to Lewis McLane, 14 Jan. 1826, and Clay to Webster, 16 Feb. 1826, in Clay, *Papers*, 5:33–35, 109–12.

14. Adams, *Memoirs*, 7:84; U.S. Congress, *House Journal*, 19th Cong., 1st sess., p. 640; Clay to McLane, 29 Apr. 1826, in Clay, *Papers*, 5:290.

15. *North American Review* 23 (Oct. 1826): 295–303 (quotation from p. 296).

16. White, *Jeffersonians*, pp. 206–10.

17. Browne to Clay, 7 and 29 Mar. and 11 May 1825, Clay to Wirt, 15 Apr. 1825, and Wirt to Clay, 16 Apr. 1825, in Clay, *Papers*, 4:92–93, 195, 367, 258–59, 262.

18. Clay to Browne, 20 Apr., 13 May, and 12 Sept. 1825, ibid., pp. 275, 373, 636; Thornton to Adams, 25 Nov. 1825, in MHi-Adams Family Papers, Letters Recd. (MR472).

19. On this incident see Withers to Clay, 21 Feb. 1827, and notes, in Clay, *Papers*, 6:218–19.

20. Homer Cummings and Carl McFarland, *Federal Justice: Chapters in the History of Justice and the Federal Executive* (New York: Macmillan Co., 1937), pp. 78–92; see also White, *Jeffersonians*, pp. 337–46.

21. Wirt to James Barbour, 18 Feb. 1828, quoted in Cummings and McFarland, *Federal Justice*, pp. 83–84; ''On Retrenching the Expenses of the Government,'' 15 May 1828, *American State Papers, Finance*, 5:1056; Wirt to E[lizabeth] W. Wirt, 20 June 1828, in MdHi-Wirt Papers (MS1011, MR11).

22. Wirt to Clay, 3 Feb. 1820, *American State Papers, Miscellaneous*, 2:575; Wirt to Dabney Carr, 21 Jan. 1818, and Wirt to Hugh Nelson, 27 Mar. 1818, published in John P. Kennedy, *Memoirs of the Life of William Wirt*, 2 vols. (Philadelphia: Lea & Blanchard, 1850), 2:67, 60; italics as written.

23. White, *Jeffersonians*, pp. 234–40, 263.

24. Barbour to James Hamilton, Jr., 10 Jan. 1826, and Barbour to Speaker of the House of Representatives, 8 Apr. 1826, in *American State Papers, Military Affairs*, 3:185–86, 278–79; C. Gratiot to Porter, 19 Nov. 1828, enclosed in Porter's report of 24 Nov. 1828, in U.S. Congress, *Senate Docs.*, 20th Cong., 2d sess., no. 1, p. 48; U.S. Department of State, *Biennial Register . . . 1825*, pp. 71–74, 77–78; ibid., *1829*, pp. 72–74, 93–94.

25. *Register of Debates*, 19th Cong., 1st sess., col. 1683; U.S., *Statutes at Large*, 4:195 (18 May 1826).

26. *Senate Docs.*, 19th Cong., 2d sess., no. 1, p. 270.

27. *Compilation of Messages and Papers,* 2:361.

28. *Niles' Weekly Register* 34 (31 May 1828): 230; *House Reports,* 19th Cong., 2d sess., no. 92, pp. 2–3 (27 Feb. 1827), and 20th Cong., 2d sess., no. 68, p. 1 (4 Feb. 1829); *Senate Journal,* 19th Cong., 2d sess., pp. 133, 252; White, *Jeffersonians,* pp. 529–36.

29. *Register of Debates,* 20th Cong., 1st sess., col. 1139; *Compilation of Messages and Papers,* 2:438.

30. Carlton B. Smith, "John C. Calhoun, Secretary of War, 1817–25: The Cast Iron Man as an Administrator," in *America, the Middle Period: Essays in Honor of Bernard Mayo,* ed. John B. Boles (Charlottesville: University of Virginia Press, 1973), p. 137.

31. Harry Ammon, *James Monroe: The Quest for National Identity* (New York: McGraw-Hill Book Co., 1971), pp. 500–501; Barbour to Adams, 7 Jan. 1826, in MHi-Adams Family Papers, Letters Recd. (MR474); Adams, *Memoirs,* 7:118 (quoted).

32. Wirt to Adams, 26 Mar. 1826, in MHi-Adams Family Papers, Letters Recd. (MR475).

33. U.S. Congress, Senate, *Executive Journal,* 3:529–31, 542; Adams, *Memoirs,* 7:224–25.

34. Adams, *Memoirs,* 6:537, 547–48 (quoted), 7:252–54, 392; Barbour to Adams, 18 July 1825, in MHi-Adams Family Papers, Letters Recd. (MR471).

35. Adams, *Memoirs,* 7:449–50, 506.

36. Ibid., pp. 505–6; George E. Ironside to Adams, 24 July 1826, in MHi-Adams Family Papers, Letters Recd. (MR476); Clay to Gaines, 29 Apr. 1825, in Clay, *Papers,* 4:309–10.

37. Adams, *Memoirs,* 7:506–7.

38. Ibid., p. 507; Arthur Douglas Howden Smith, *Old Fuss and Feathers: The Life and Exploits of Lt.-General Winfield Scott . . .* (New York: Greystone Press, 1937), pp. 167–68; James W. Silver, *Edmund Pendleton Gaines: Frontier General* (Baton Rouge: Louisiana State University Press, 1949), p. 135n. On the same date, Harrison was approved as minister to Colombia.

39. Charles Winslow Elliott, *Winfield Scott: The Soldier and the Man* (New York: Macmillan Co., 1937), pp. 246–47; Adams, *Memoirs,* 8:42–43.

40. Elliott, *Winfield Scott,* p. 251.

41. *American State Papers, Military Affairs,* 4:42–43, 45–46.

42. Adams, *Memoirs,* 8:91–92.

43. Samuel L. Southard, "Annual Report . . . ," 2 Dec. 1825, 1 Dec. 1827, 27 Nov. 1828, in *American State Papers, Naval Affairs,* 2:101, 3:54, 215. On Southard's administrative role see Michael Birkner, *Samuel L. Southard: Jeffersonian Whig* (Rutherford, N.J.: Fairleigh Dickinson University Press, 1984), chap. 5.

44. Southard, "Annual Report . . . ," 1 Dec. 1827, *American State Papers, Naval Affairs,* 3:55; White, *Jeffersonians,* pp. 293–95; U.S., *Statutes at Large,* 4:305, 60.

45. David F. Long, *Nothing Too Daring: A Biography of Commodore David Porter, 1780–1843* (Annapolis, Md.: United States Naval Institute, 1970), pp. 215–23, 225–26 (quoting Porter).

46. Smith Thompson to Porter, 1 Feb. 1823, summarized, with quotations, ibid., p. 208; Vives to Porter, 10 May 1823, quoted ibid., p. 214; see also pp. 206, 211–14, and cf. above, p. 141.

47. Quoted in Long, *Nothing Too Daring*, ibid., p. 228.

48. Adams, *Memoirs*, 6:453–54; Clay to Hilario de Rivas y Salmon, 29 Apr. 1825, and Rivas y Salmon to Clay, 2 May 1825, in Clay, *Papers*, 4:311, 320.

49. Adams, *Memoirs*, 6:434; Southard to Charles Ewing, 9 July 1825, quoted in Birkner, *Samuel L. Southard*, p. 100.

50. Smith to Clay, 14 July 1825, and Hammond to Clay, 31 Aug. 1825, in Clay, *Papers*, 4:533, 610.

51. *Washington Gazette*, 1 July 1825. For further review of contemporary comment see Long, *Nothing Too Daring*, pp. 250–52.

52. Clay to James Brown, 4 Sept. 1825, in Clay, *Papers*, 4:618.

53. Clay to Hilario de Rivas y Salmon, 31 May and 9 June 1827, Clay to Joel R. Poinsett, 31 May 1827, and Poinsett to Clay, 5 Oct. 1827, in Clay, *Papers*, 6:628–29, 656–59, 1114n.

54. Francisco Tacón to Clay, 4 Oct. 1827 and note, and Clay to Tacón, 29 Oct. 1827, in ibid., 1108, 1198–99; Long, *Nothing Too Daring*, pp. 270–71.

55. Charles Hay to Clay, 6 Aug. 1827 and note, in Clay, *Papers*, 6:856.

56. White, *Jeffersonians*, pp. 167, 173–77.

57. *House Docs.*, 19th Cong., 1st sess., no. 137, pp. 14–16; *United States* vs. *350 Chests of Tea* . . . , U.S. Supreme Court, *Reports* 25 (12 Wheaton): 491; *Niles' Weekly Register* 30 (24 June 1826): 311; White, *Jeffersonians*, pp. 158–60.

58. Webster to Clay, 25 Mar. 1827, in Clay, *Papers*, 6:356.

59. *House Docs.*, 19th Cong., 1st sess., no. 137, p. 19; [Anon.] to Adams, Dec. 1825 (recd. 5 Jan. 1826), in MHi-Adams Family Papers, Letters Recd. (MR474); Adams, *Memoirs*, 7:163–64; cf. also R. P. Henry to Adams, 7–10 Mar. 1826, in MHi-Adams Family Papers, Letters Recd. (MR475).

60. Malcolm J. Rohrbough, *The Land Office Business: The Settlement and Administration of American Public Lands, 1789–1837* (New York: Oxford University Press, 1968), pp. 177–78.

61. Ibid., pp. 172–73; Call and Ward to Graham, 23 Jan. 1827, quoted ibid., p. 173. The salaries were below the statutory limit of $3,000.

62. McRee to Graham, 11 Jan. 1826, quoted in Rohrbough, *Land Office Business*, p. 168.

63. McRee to Graham, 29 Nov. 1826, quoted ibid., p. 179.

64. John McLean, "Condition of the Post Office Department . . . ," 17 Nov. 1828, *American State Papers, Post Office*, p. 183; *Compilation of Messages and Papers*, 2:411, 419; Francis P. Weisenburger, *The Life of John McLean: A Politician on the United States Supreme Court* (1937; reprint ed., New York: Da Capo Press, 1971), p. 46.

65. U.S., *Statutes at Large*, 4:102, sec. 36; McLean, "Condition of the Post Office . . . ," 5 Dec. 1826, and 17 Nov. 1828, *American State Papers, Post Office*, pp. 144, 184; Weisenburger, *Life of John McLean*, pp. 39-40.

66. *Niles' Weekly Register* 30 (3 June 1826): 243, reprinting *National Intelligencer* (Washington); Adams, *Memoirs*, 7:364.

67. *Register of Debates*, 20th Cong., 1st sess., cols. 1064-68.

68. Barbour to Clay, 27 Jan. 1828, in DLC-HC (DNA, M212, R3).

69. *Register of Debates*, 20th Cong., 1st sess., cols. 1064-1458 (cited vote from col. 1128).

70. Barbour to Clay, 27 Jan. 1828, in DLC-HC (DNA, M212, R3); "On Retrenching . . . ," *American State Papers, Finance*, 5:1049; "Report of the Minority of the Committee," *House Reports*, 20th Cong., 1st sess., no. 259, pp. 133-36, 139-40, 145, 147.

71. "Report of the Minority . . . ," pp. 161-63.

72. "On Retrenching . . . ," pp. 1061-62; "Report of the Minority . . . ," pp. 181-83, 186-95.

73. "On Retrenching . . . ," pp. 1049-50, 1054, 1058-59, 1061-64.

74. *Register of Debates*, 20th Cong., 1st sess., cols. 615-16, 628, 645, 647, and 20th Cong., 2d sess., pp. 143-44, 164, 169, 194, 196, 215, 249, 258, 346.

CHAPTER 11

THE ART OF POLITICS

1. [John H. Eaton], *The Letters of Wyoming, to the People of the United States, on the Presidential Election, and in Favour of Andrew Jackson* . . . (Philadelphia: S. Simpson & J. Conrad, 1824), pp. 28 (quoted), 51.

2. John Quincy Adams, *Memoirs of John Quincy Adams, Comprising Portions of His Diary from 1795 to 1848*, ed. Charles Francis Adams, 12 vols. (Philadelphia: J. B. Lippincott & Co., 1874-77), 6:506-7; Rufus King to John King, 27 Feb. 1825, quoted in Robert V. Remini, *The Election of Andrew Jackson*, Critical Periods of History (Philadelphia: J. B. Lippincott Co., 1963), p. 26.

3. Tennessee Senate, *Journal* . . . *1825*, pp. 19, 62, 94, 99, 118-20, 135-36; *Washington Gazette*, 29 Oct. 1825.

4. U.S. Congress, *Register of Debates*, 19th Cong., 1st sess., cols. 20-21; Martin Van Buren, *The Autobiography of Martin Van Buren*, ed. John C. Fitzpatrick, *American Historical Association Annual Report for the Year 1918*, vol. 2 (Washington, D.C.: Government Printing Office, 1920), pp. 192-99, 316-19.

5. *Enquirer* (Richmond, Va.), 28 Mar. 1827, cited in Remini, *Election of Andrew Jackson*, pp. 57-58; Oliver P. Chitwood, *John Tyler: Champion of the Old South* (1939; reprint ed., New York: Russell & Russell, 1964), pp. 78-83; Charles Henry Ambler, *Thomas Ritchie: A Study in Virginia Politics* (Richmond, Va.: Bell Book & Stationery Co., 1913), p. 107. Ambler dates Richie's support of Jackson from an editorial in the *Enquirer*, 16 Jan. 1827.

6. Van Buren to Ritchie, 13 Jan. 1827, copy in DLC-Martin Van Buren Papers, Presidential Papers Series, Microfilm Series 2 (MR7). On Jackson's criticism of the Kentucky militia at New Orleans see Zachary F. Smith, *The Battle of New Orleans* . . . , Filson Club Publications no. 19 (Louisville, Ky.: John P. Morton & Co., 1904), pp. 89-121. For an explanation of the instructions of the Kentucky legislature on the presidential election see George Robertson to Adams, 6 Jan. 1825, in MHi-Adams Family Papers, Letters Recd. (MR467); Francis P. Blair to David White, Jr., 19 Jan. 1825, published in *United States Telegraph* (Washington), 21 July 1828.

7. Robert Wickliffe to Clay, 13 Sept. 1826, in Henry Clay, *The Papers of Henry Clay*, ed. James F. Hopkins, Mary W. M. Hargreaves, and Robert Seager II, 8 vols. to date (Lexington: University Press of Kentucky, 1959-), 5:685.

8. Blair to Clay, 14 Nov. 1827, ibid., 6:1261. For the Kendall letters see *Argus of Western America* (Frankfort, Ky.), 26 Sept. and 10 Oct. 1827, 28 May, 9, 16, and 25 July, and 1 Oct. 1828.

9. Cf. Nathan Sargent, *Public Men and Events from the Commencement of Mr. Monroe's Administration, in 1817, to the Close of Mr. Fillmore's Administration in 1853*, 2 vols. (Philadelphia: J. B. Lippincott & Co., 1875), 1:85; Charles M. Wiltse, *John C. Calhoun* . . . , 4 vols. (Indianapolis, Ind.: Bobbs-Merrill Co., 1944-51), 1:327; Paul C. Nagel, *Descent from Glory: Four Generations of the John Adams Family* (New York: Oxford University Press, 1983), p. 144; George Dangerfield, *The Awakening of American Nationalism, 1815-1828* (New York: Harper & Row, 1965), p. 239.

10. Adams, *Memoirs*, 7:130, 311, 273, 265.

11. John Quincy Adams to Abigail Adams, 14 Apr. 1801, in John Quincy Adams, *Writings* . . . , ed. Worthington Chauncey Ford, 7 vols. (New York: Macmillan Co., 1913-17), 2:529; Louisa C. Adams to Charles Francis Adams, quoted in Nagel, *Descent from Glory*, p. 155.

12. Adams, *Memoirs*, 7:347; Clay to Adams, 2 July 1827, in Clay, *Papers*, 6:738; cf. Ralph Ketcham, *Presidents above Party: The First American Presidency, 1789-1829* (Chapel Hill: Published for the Institute of Early American History and Culture, Williamsburg, Va., by the University of North Carolina Press, 1984).

13. Adams, *Memoirs*, 7:338, 8:50, and above, pp. 178-79; cf. Hammond to Clay, 5 Nov. 1827, and Henry Shaw to Clay, 17 Nov. 1827, in Clay, *Papers*, 6:1232-33n, 1280.

14. *A Compilation of the Messages and Papers of the Presidents, 1789-1897*, comp. James D. Richardson, 10 vols. (1896-99; reprint ed., New York: Bureau of National Literature and Art, 1901-6), 2:296-97.

15. Adams, *Memoirs*, 7:207-8.

16. Tallmadge to Weed, 3 Sept. 1825, quoted in Dangerfield, *Awakening of American Nationalism*, p. 240; see also Clay to Porter, 28 Nov. 1825, and Porter to Clay, 4 Mar. 1826, in Clay, *Papers*, 4:858-59n, 5:143-44; Shaw Livermore, Jr., *The Twilight of Federalism: The Disintegration of the Federalist Party, 1815-1830* (Princeton, N.J.: Princeton University Press, 1962), pp. 232-33.

17. King to Adams, 6 July 1825 (quoted) and 26 Jan. 1826, A[lexander] H. E[verett] to Adams, 17 Apr. 1825, and Henry R. Warfield to [Adams], 23 Sept. 1825, in MHi-Adams Family Papers, Letters Recd. (MR471, 474, 469, 472); Warfield to Clay, 5 July 1826 and 5 Jan. 1827, in Clay, *Papers*, 5:523–25, 6:17–20; Hopkinson to Webster, 13 Apr. 1827, in Daniel Webster, *The Papers of Daniel Webster*, ed. Charles M. Wiltse and Harold D. Moser, 5 vols. of correspondence to date (Hanover, N.H.: Published for Dartmouth College by the University Press of New England, 1974–), *Correspondence*, 2:189.

18. Livermore, *Twilight of Federalism*, pp. 211–12; Webster to John Quincy Adams, 26 and 27 Mar. 1827, in Webster, *Papers, Correspondence*, 2:178–80; Clay to Webster, 14 Apr. 1827, in Clay, *Papers*, 6:445.

19. See Kane to Clay, 30 Mar. 1825, in Clay, *Papers*, 4:198; Michael Birkner, *Samuel L. Southard: Jeffersonian Whig* (Rutherford, N.J.: Fairleigh Dickinson University Press, 1984), pp. 76–78; Herbert Ershkowitz, *The Origins of the Whig and Democratic Parties: New Jersey Politics, 1820–1837* (Washington, D.C.: University Press of America, 1982), pp. 66–67; see also Andrew Parsons to Clay, 25 Sept. 1826, Ephraim Bateman to Clay, 30 Oct. 1826, and Clay to William Rossell, 12 Nov. 1826, in Clay, *Papers*, 5:714–15, 841, 919.

20. Samuel Smith to Clay, 8 Mar. 1825, Brooks to Clay, 26 Nov. 1826, Welles to Clay, 12 May 1826, Kendall to Clay, 23 Mar., 28 Apr., and 4 Oct. 1825, and 8 July 1826, and Clay to Kendall, 18 Oct. 1825, in Clay, *Papers*, 4:95, 5:957, 365, 4:135–36, 305–6, 719, 5:534–35, 4:747 (quoted)–48. On Kendall's swing to Jackson see also Florence Weston, *The Presidential Election of 1828* (1938; reprint ed., Philadelphia: Porcupine Press, 1974), p. 122.

21. Wheaton to Richard Rush, 22 Aug. 1825, James Tallmadge to Adams, 24 Dec. 1824 (quoted) and 13 June 1825 (quoted), also "Algernon Sidney" to Adams, 3 Sept. 1825, Joseph Blunt to Adams, 29 Oct. 1825, in MHi-Adams Family Papers, Letters Recd. (MR471, 466, 470, 472; Edward Ingersoll to Clay, 11 Mar. 1827, and Moses Hayden to Clay, 27 Aug. 1825, in Clay, *Papers*, 6:282, 4:597: Weed, *Autobiography*, ed. Harriet A. Weed (Boston: Houghton Mifflin & Co., 1883), pp. 179–81. On Weed's subsequent appointment see below, p. 266.

22. Clay to Tallmadge, 16 Mar. 1826, and Clay to Richard Peters, Jr., 16 Oct. 1826, in Clay, *Papers*, 5:174, 799.

23. Peters to Clay, 24 Oct. 1826, and Degrand to Clay, 8 Feb. 1827 (quoted), ibid., 820, 6:176; D[egrand] to Adams, 8 Aug. 1825, in MHi-Adams Family Papers, Letters Recd. (MR471).

24. Foot to Adams, 9 Apr. 1825, in Adams Family Papers, Letters Recd. (MR469); Kent to Clay, 25 Feb. 1828, in Clay, *Papers*, 7:120, and the enclosure in DLC-HC, DNA, M212, R3; Joseph Blount Hinton to Adams, 13 July 1826, and Nathaniel Greene Cleary to Adams, 12 July 1826, in MHi-Adams Family Papers, Letters Recd. (MR476); Poindexter to Clay, 1 Dec. 1826, Edwards to Clay, 21 Sept. 1826, and Joseph Durham Learned to Clay, 27 Sept. 1827, in Clay, *Papers*, 5:969, 701, 6:1079.

25. Dudley to Clay, 17 Aug. 1827, Worsley to Clay, 17 Apr. 1827, Sidney Breese to Clay, 21 July 1827, and Peter B. Porter to Clay, 1 May 1827, in Clay, *Papers*, 6:916, 452, 808, 503.

26. Clay to James Taylor, 17 Jan. 1827, and Clay to Peter B. Porter, 13 May 1827, ibid., 76–77, 549.

27. Clay to Webster, 14 Apr. 1827, ibid., 444; Adams, *Memoirs*, 7:257, 262, 297, 281.

28. *Register of Debates*, 19th Cong., 2d sess., cols. 498–99.

29. *Daily National Intelligencer* (Washington), 7 and 20 Mar. 1827.

30. Webster to Clay, 25 Mar. 1827, in Clay, *Papers*, 6:354.

31. Adams, *Memoirs*, 7:186; *Maryland Republican* (Annapolis), reprinted in *Daily National Journal* (Washington), 11 June 1827; Charles Douglas Lowery, "James Barbour: A Politician and Planter of Ante-Bellum Virginia" (Ph.D. diss., University of Virginia, 1966), pp. 308–9.

32. Adams, Memoirs, 7:361, 347; J[ohn] H[arvey] Powell, *Richard Rush: Republican Diplomat, 1780–1859* (Philadelphia: University of Pennsylvania Press, 1942), p. 192. On Rush's admiration of Hamilton see *Report*, 6 Dec. 1828, *House Docs.*, 20th Cong., 2d sess., no. 9, p. 8.

33. *Register of Debates*, 19th Cong., 2d sess., cols. 1347–49, 1390; *United States Telegraph* (Washington), 17 Oct. 1827, 1, 2, 3, 5, and 16 July, 5, 6, 13, and 30 Aug., 2 Sept. (quoting *Eastern Argus* [Portland, Me.]), 4 Sept. (quoting *New York Enquirer*), 5 Sept. (quoting *Muskingum Messenger* [Ohio]), and 24 Sept. 1828; Weston, *Presidential Election*, pp. 156–57, citing Ritchie to Van Buren, 11 Mar. 1828.

34. Benton to Clay, 27 Feb. 1826, in Clay, *Papers*, 5:136; *Register of Debates*, 19th Cong., 1st sess., cols. 672, 707.

35. *House Docs.*, 19th Cong., 1st sess., no. 41, pp. 9–16. On further changes cf. manuscript record of public printers, in DNA, RG59. Notably, however, Levi Woodbury's *New Hampshire Gazette* (Portsmouth) and Edwin Croswell's *Albany* (N.Y.) *Argus*, which were major organs of the Jacksonians, retained the patronage throughout the Adams administration.

36. *Register of Debates*, 19th Cong., 2d sess., cols. 898 (quoted), 1103.

37. Ibid., col. 930; the debate, which ran almost daily from February 1 to 26, was broken off, midway in a speech, by the pressure of other business (ibid., col. 1414).

38. Nathaniel F. Williams to Clay, 3 Jan. 1826, George E. Mitchell to Clay, 16 Jan. 1826, Clay to Mitchell, 17 Jan. 1826, and Webster to Clay, 25 Mar. 1827, in Clay, *Papers*, 5:3, 39, 42, 6:355; Webster to Adams, 23 Mar. 1827, and Webster to Nathaniel F. Williams, 24 Mar. and 7 Apr. 1827, and 25 Sept. 1828, in Webster, *Papers, Correspondence*, 2:172, 174–75n, 183, 365.

39. Pleasants to Adams, 27 May 1826, in MHi-Adams Family Papers, Letters Recd. (MR475); Clay to Webster, 25 Oct. 1827, in Clay, *Papers*, 6:1187; Edward Everett to Webster, [18] Nov. 1827, and Webster to Nathaniel Silsbee, 22 Sept. 1828, in Webster, *Papers, Correspondence*, 2:253–54, 363.

40. Webster to Clay, 29 Oct. and 5 Nov. 1827, in Clay, *Papers*, 6:1201, 1233–34; see also Webster to John C. Wright, 30 Apr. 1827, in Webster, *Papers, Correspondence*, 2:195.

41. Ingersoll to Clay, 22 Sept. 1826, and Elisha Whittlesey to Clay, 13 Mar. 1827, in Clay, *Papers*, 5:703–4, 6:300; *Democratic Press* (Philadelphia), 26 Sept. 1827.

42. Peter B. Porter to Clay, 1 May 1827, and James Strong to Clay, 12 Nov. 1827, in Clay, *Papers*, 6:503, 1253.

43. *United States Telegraph* (Washington), 10 Apr. 1828.

44. Ibid., 4 Nov. 1826, 21 Mar. 1827, and 19 Sept. 1828; Clay to Watterston, 5 Apr. 1827, and Joseph Durham Learned to Clay, 27 Sept. 1827, in Clay, *Papers*, 6:402, 1077, 1079–80; Adams, *Memoirs*, 7:523–24.

45. William E. Ames, *A History of the National Intelligencer* (Chapel Hill: University of North Carolina Press, 1972), pp. 132, 141, 155–64 passim (quotations from p. 164); *Daily National Intelligencer* (Washington), 7, 9, and 12 Mar., 15 and 18 Aug. 1827, and 22 Apr. 1828 (quoted).

46. Hammond to Clay, 27 Sept. 1826, in Clay, *Papers*, 5:723.

47. Ninian Edwards to Clay, 21 Sept. 1826, ibid., 700; cf. Theodore Calvin Pease, *The Frontier State, 1818–1848*, vol. 2 of *The Centennial History of Illinois* (Springfield: Illinois Centennial Commission, 1918), pp. 111–13.

48. Porter Clay to Henry Clay, 22 Feb. 1827, in Clay, *Papers*, 6:223.

49. Porter to Clay, 24 Dec. 1826, ibid., 5:1032.

50. Porter to Clay, 8 Oct. and 7 Nov. 1826, Rochester to Clay, 18 Nov. 1826, Clay to Porter, 10 Oct. and 12 Dec. (quoted) 1826, ibid., 5:763–64, 876–77, 936–37, 769, 995.

51. Rochester to Clay, 17 Sept. 1827, Porter to Clay, 26 Oct., 6 and 22, Nov. 1827, and Webster to Clay, 5 Nov. 1827, ibid., 6:1046, 1189–90, 1240, 1303, 1235.

52. Weston, *Presidential Election*, p. 163; Jerome Mushkat, *Tammany: The Evolution of a Political Machine, 1789–1865* (Syracuse, N.Y.: Syracuse University Press, 1971), pp. 105–7; James Thomas to Clay, 13 May 1827, in Clay, *Papers*, 6:550.

53. Degrand to Joseph E. Sprague, 4 July 1826, copy in MHi-Adams Family Papers, Letters Recd. (MR476); Sergeant to Clay, 28 Sept. 1826, in Clay, *Papers*, 5:730.

54. Clay to Richard Peters, Jr., 16 Oct. 1826, and Clay to Webster, 10 Nov. 1826, and Peters to Clay, 24 Oct. 1826, in Clay, *Papers*, 5:798–99, 889, 819.

55. Markley to Clay, 19 May 1827, and Webster to Clay, 25 Mar. 1827, ibid., 6:571, 355.

56. Sergeant to Clay, 23 Aug. 1827, ibid., 955.

57. Degrand to Clay, 1 June 1827, ibid., 634; *Niles' Weekly Register* 32 (7 and 21 July 1827): 313, 315, 349.

58. *New York Evening Post*, 27 June and 3 Aug., reprinting *Farmers Journal* (Harrodsburg, Ky.), 1827; *Pittsburgh Mercury*, 31 July 1827, quoted to Malcolm Rogers Eiselen, *The Rise of Pennsylvania Protectionism* . . . (Philadelphia: University of Pennsylvania, Ph.D. diss., 1932), p. 77.

59. *Democratic Press* (Philadelphia), 31 May 1827; *Niles' Weekly Register* 32 (21 July 1827): 350. The *New York American* applauded the conduct of the convention as "a falsification of the fears of the opposition"; quoted in *New York Evening*

Post, 9 Aug. 1827, which commented that the politics of the convention was a matter of "private meetings and secret understanding."

60. Sergeant to Clay, 11 and 18 Sept. 1827, and Wharton to Clay, 3 Aug. 1827, in Clay, *Papers*, 6:1023, 1050, 846–47; *United States Gazette* (Philadelphia), 27 Sept. and 10 Oct. 1827; *Daily National Journal* (Washington), 25 Sept. 1827.

61. Crowninshield to Clay, 14 Mar. 1827, in Clay, *Papers*, 6:304; see also Sergeant to Clay, 26 Jan. 1827, Abner Lacock to Clay, 27 Mar. 1827, and Philip S. Markley to Clay, 19 May 1827, ibid., 125, 366, 571; Philip S. Klein, *Pennsylvania Politics, 1817–1832: A Game without Rules* (Philadelphia: Historical Society of Pennsylvania, 1940), pp. 150, 220–23.

62. *National Gazette* (Philadelphia), 7 Dec. 1827; *Pennsylvania Archives*, 4th ser., 5:754–55 (quoted).

63. Samuel Mifflin to Clay, 22 Mar. 1827, and Sergeant to Clay, 30 Oct. 1827, in Clay, *Papers*, 6:340, 1213; Joseph Ritner, "To the Public," 22 Aug. 1827, published in *Harrisburg* (Pa.) *Chronicle*, reprinted in *New York Evening Post*, 7 Sept. 1827; Adams, *Memoirs*, 7:441; Klein, *Pennsylvania Politics*, p. 209.

64. *Boston Daily Advertiser*, 23 Apr. 1827; Daniel Webster, *Writings and Speeches*, National Edition, ed. J. W. McIntyre, 18 vols. (Boston: Little, Brown, & Co., 1903), 12:21–34; Shaw to Clay, 22 Aug. 1827, in Clay, *Papers*, 6:947–48.

65. *Niles' Weekly Register* 32 (19 and 26 May 1827): 198–99, 210; *Daily National Journal* (Washington), 17 and 30 May 1827; *Boston Daily Advertiser*, 13, 16, and 23 July 1827.

66. Webster to Clay, 14 Apr. 1827, in Clay, *Papers*, 6:446.

67. Webster to Clay, 22 June 1827, ibid., p. 709.

68. Sylvester S. Southworth to Clay, 24 Mar. 1827, ibid., p. 350; Livermore, *Twilight of Federalism*, pp. 230–31.

69. Goldsborough to Clay, 9 Aug. 1827, in Clay, *Papers*, 6:866–67n; *Daily National Journal* (Washington), 26 July 1827; Mark H. Haller, "The Rise of the Jackson Party in Maryland, 1820–1829," *Journal of Southern History* 28 (Aug. 1962): 307–20 passim.

70. John A. Munroe, *Louis McLane: Federalist and Jacksonian* (New Brunswick, N.J.: Rutgers University Press, 1973), pp. 186–93 passim, 199–200, 205–9, 217–22, 239; Sergeant to Clay, 18 and 23 Sept. 1827, in Clay, *Papers*, 6:1050, 1062.

71. Adams, *Memoirs*, 7:367.

CHAPTER 12
THE CAMPAIGN OF 1828

1. John Quincy Adams, *Memoirs of John Quincy Adams, Comprising Portions of His Diary from 1790 to 1848*, ed. Charles Francis Adams, 12 vols. (Philadelphia: J. B. Lippincott & Co., 1874–77), 7:356, 390, 366, 449, 443, 474.

2. Ibid., pp. 347, 390, 413, 469–70, 8:4.

3. Clay to Henry, 27 Sept. 1827, in Henry Clay, *The Papers of Henry Clay*, ed James F. Hopkins, Mary W. M. Hargreaves, and Robert Seager II, 8 vols. to date (Lexington: University Press of Kentucky, 1959–), 6:1074–75.

4. *Niles' Weekly Register* 34 (8 Mar. 1828): 20 (quoted), 26.

5. Rochester to Clay, 4 Nov. 1827, Clay to Adams, 23 June 1827, John H. Pleasants to Clay, 4 May 1827, Brooke to Clay, 27 Dec. 1827, and Joseph Kent to Clay, 21 Jan. 1828, in Clay, *Papers*, 6:1228, 714, 519, 1385-86, 7:53-54; *Niles' Weekly Register* 33 (12 Jan. 1828, supp.): 316, 332.

6. *Niles' Weekly Register* 35 (13 Sept. 1828): 33; and cf. *United States Telegraph* (Washington), 11 and 23 July 1828. For surveys of the campaign charges and countercharges see Robert V. Remini, *Andrew Jackson and the Course of American Freedom, 1822-1832* (New York: Harper & Row, 1981), pp. 118-25; Donald B. Cole, *Jacksonian Democracy in New Hampsire, 1800-1851* (Cambridge: Harvard University Press, 1970), pp. 69-78; Florence Weston, *The Presidential Election of 1828* (1938; reprint ed., Philadelphia: Porcupine Press, 1974), pp. 101-2, 142-75.

7. Henry Clay, *An Address . . . to the Public, Containing Certain Testimony in Refutation to the Charges against Him, Made by Gen. Andrew Jackson, Touching the Last Presidential Election* (Washington: P. Force, 1827); Henry Clay, *A Supplement to the Address . . . in December 1827 . . .* (Washington: P. Force, 1828)—White's letter is quoted on pp. 19-20.

8. Andrew Jackson, "To the Public," 18 July 1827, reprinted in *Kentucky Gazette* (Lexington), 27 July 1827; Buchanan's statement of 8 Aug. 1827 was reprinted in *United States Gazette* (Philadelphia), 13 Aug. 1827.

9. Charles S. Todd to Clay, 18 Feb. 1828, in Clay, *Papers*, 7:104; for the text of the inquiry see Kentucky Senate, *Journal . . . 1827*, pp. 298-339 passim.

10. *Daily National Intelligencer* (Washington), 18 Aug. 1827.

11. Reprinted in *United States Telegraph* (Washington), 10 Sept. 1828.

12. Ibid., 2 Aug. 1828.

13. Ibid., 15 Apr, 8 May, 12 and 15 June, and 5 Sept. 1828.

14. *Niles' Weekly Register* 34 (15 Mar. 1828): 33-34.

15. Malcolm Rogers Eiselen, *The Rise of Pennsylvania Protectionism . . .* (Philadelphia: University of Pennsylvania, Ph.D. diss., 1932), pp. 88, 89; Lee F. Crippen, *Simon Cameron: Ante-Bellum Years* (Oxford, Ohio: Mississippi Valley Press, 1942), p. 248, 17n; James Veach to William Hawkins, 13 Jan. 1828, quoted in Philip S. Klein, *Pennsylvania Politics, 1817-1832: A Game without Rules* (Philadelphia: Historical Society of Pennsylvania, 1940), p. 248.

16. *Niles' Weekly Register* 33 (23 Feb. 1828): 439, and 34 (3 May 1828): 158.

17. *United States Telegraph* (Washington), 21 July 1827; *Pittsburgh Mercury*, 24 July 1827, quoted in Herman Hailperin, "Pro-Jackson Sentiment in Pennsylvania," *Pennsylvania Magazine of History and Biography*, 50 (July 1926): 217; Porter to Clay, 22 Nov. 1827, and McGiffin to Clay, 29 Jan. 1828, in Clay, *Papers*, 6:1303-4, 7:64.

18. Adams to Clay, 23 Aug. 1827, in Clay, *Papers*, 6:953.

19. *Niles' Weekly Register* 34 (12 and 26 Apr. and 26 July 1828): 106, 140, 349.

20. Ibid. (10 May 1828), pp. 174, 181 (14 June 1828), p. 258 (quoted), 35 (18 and 25 Oct. and 1 Nov. 1828), pp. 116, 129, 131-32, 147; Jerome Mushkat, *Tammany: The Evolution of a Political Machine, 1789-1865* (Syracuse, N.Y.: Syracuse University Press, 1971), pp. 108. 112.

21. Noted in Mushkat, *Tammany*, p. 113.

22. John R. Commons et al., *History of Labour in the United States* . . . , 4 vols. (New York: Macmillan Co., 1921–35), 1:185–99.

23. Timothy Upham, quoted in Cole, *Jacksonian Democracy*, p. 72; Daniel Mallory to Clay, 28 Sept. 1827, and Russell to Clay, 30 Oct. 1827, in Clay, *Papers*, 6:1083–84, 1210; Worsley to Clay, 30 Mar. 1828, in DLC-HC (DNA, M212, R3); see also Weston, *Presidential Election*, pp. 79–80; Cole, *Jacksonian Democracy*, pp. 77–81.

24. Ronald P. Formisano with Kathleen Smith Kutolowski, "Antimasonry and Masonry: The Genesis of Protest, 1826–1827," *American Quarterly* 29 (Summer 1977): 144–45, 153–57; Kathleen Smith Kutolowski, "Antimasonry Reexamined: Social Bases of the Grass-Roots Party," *Journal of American History* 71 (Sept. 1984): 269–93; Adams to Oliver Heartwell, 19 Apr. 1828, published in *Niles' Weekly Register* 35 (30 Aug. 1828): 5.

25. Charles McCarthy, *The Antimasonic Party: A Study of Political Antimasonry in the United States, 1827–1840*, in *Annual Report of the American Historical Association for the Year 1902*, vol. 1 (Washington, D.C.: Government Printing Office, 1903), pp. 382–83.

26. Clay to Francis T. Brooke, 22 Feb. 1828, in Clay, *Papers*, 7:113; Jabez Hammond, *The History of Political Parties in the State of New York, from the Ratification of the Federal Constitution to December, 1842*, 2 vols. (Albany, N.Y.: C. Van Benthuysen, 1842), 2:268, 282–84; Dixon Ryan Fox, *The Decline of Aristocracy in the Politics of New York, 1801–1840*, ed. Robert V. Remini (1919; reprint ed., New York: Harper & Row, Harper Torchbooks, 1965), p. 344; but cf. Shaw Livermore, Jr., *The Twilight of Federalism: The Disintegration of the Federalist Party, 1815–1830* (Princeton, N.J.: Princeton University Press, 1962), pp. 217, 221–22, 235; Richard P. McCormick, *The Second American Party System: Party Formation in the Jacksonian Era* (Chapel Hill: University of North Carolina Press, 1966), p. 119; Alvin Kass, *Politics in New York State, 1800–1830* (Syracuse, N.Y.: Syracuse University Press, 1965), pp. 175–78.

27. Livermore, *Twilight of Federalism*, pp. 242–43; Adams, *Memoirs*, 8:82; Daniel Webster to Ezekiel Webster, 31 Jan. 1829, in Daniel Webster, *The Papers of Daniel Webster*, ed. Charles M. Wiltse and Harold D. Moser, 5 vols. of correspondence to date (Hanover, N.H.: Published for Dartmouth College by the University Press of New England, 1974–), *Correspondence*, 2:395; *United States Telegraph* (Washington), 1 Nov. 1828.

28. Charles O. Paullin, *Atlas of Historical Geography of the United States*, ed. John K. Wright (Washington, D.C.: Published jointly by the Carnegie Institution of Washington and the American Geographical Society of New York, 1932), plate 103; Fox, *Decline of Aristocracy*, pp. 349–50; John A. Munroe, *Louis McLane: Federalist and Jacksonian* (New Brunswick, N.J.: Rutgers University Press, 1973), pp. 236–39.

29. Klein, *Pennsylvania Politics*, pp. 250, 354; Livermore, *Twilight of Federalism*, pp. 238–39.

30. James Ray to H. S. Handy, 15 May 1828, in *United States Telegraph* (Washington), 15 July 1828; John Vollmer Mering, *The Whig Party in Missouri*, University of Missouri Studies vol. 41 (Columbia: University of Missouri Press, 1967), pp. 12–13, 18.

31. David Walter Krueger, "Party Development in Indiana, 1800–1832" (Ph.D. diss., University of Kentucky, 1974), pp. 189, 194; William W. Worsley to Clay, 30 Mar. 1828, in DLC-HC (DNA, M212, R3), Letcher to Clay, 27 Aug. 1828, Daniel Mayes to Clay, 15 Sept. 1828, and Thomas H. Pindell to Clay, 23 Sept. 1828, in Clay, *Papers*, 7:441, 467, 473.

32. Sergeant to Clay, 15 Oct. 1828, Mifflin to Clay, 7 Sept. 1828, Thomas I. Wharton to Clay, 3 Aug. 1827, Adams to Clay, 23 Aug. 1827, and Charles Hammond to Clay, 5 Nov. 1827, in Clay, *Papers*, 7:503, 459, 6:847, 953, 1233; Adams, *Memoirs*, 7:492.

33. Blair to Clay, 14 Nov. 1827, in Clay, *Papers*, 6:1261; see also *Argus of Western America* (Frankfort, Ky.), 9 and 16 July 1828; *United States Telegraph* (Washington), 16, 18, 20, 21, 22, and 24 Oct. 1828.

34. Speech of 30 Aug. 1828, *Kentucky Reporter* (Lexington), 3 Sept. 1828; Brooke to Clay, 16 Nov. 1828, and John J. Crittenden to Clay, 3 Dec. 1828 (quoted), in Clay, *Papers*, 7:540, 554; Louisa C. Adams to Charles Francis Adams, 10 Feb. 1829, and John Quincy Adams to James Barbour, 4 Apr. 1829, in MHi-Adams Family Papers, Letters Recd. (MR490); Private Letterbook, 10:181–82 (MR149).

35. Adams, *Memoirs*, 8:87–88.

36. Blair to Clay, 3 Oct. 1827, in Clay, *Papers*, 6:1107.

37. Van Buren to Thomas Ritchie, 13 Jan. 1827, Presidential Papers Series, Microfilm Series 2 (R7).

38. E. Webster to Daniel Webster, 15 Feb. 1829, in Webster, *Papers, Correspondence*, 2:396.

39. Blair to Clay, 14 Nov. and 31 Dec. 1827, in Clay, *Papers*, 6:1260, 1404–5; [Thomas Hart Benton], *Thirty Years' View: or, A History of the Working of the American Government for Thirty Years, from 1820 to 1850 . . .* , 2 vols. (New York: D. Appleton & Co., 1859–60), 1:48; Martin Van Buren, *The Autobiography of Martin Van Buren*, ed. John C. Fitzpatrick, *American Historical Association Annual Report for the Year 1918*, vol. 2 (Washington, D.C.: Government Printing Office, 1920), pp. 192–94.

CHAPTER 13

AFTERMATH

1. U.S. Congress, *Register of Debates*, 20th Cong., 2d sess., pp. 70, 74, 80, 81, 95, 361, 390; John Quincy Adams, *Memoirs of John Quincy Adams, Comprising Portions of His Diary from 1795 to 1848*, ed. Charles Francis Adams, 12 vols. (Philadelphia: J. B. Lippincott & Co., 1874–77), 8:91, 95–97, 99.

2. Louisa C. Adams to Charles Francis Adams, 18 and 25 Jan. 1829, in MHi-Adams Family Papers, Letters Recd. (MR490).

3. Adams, *Memoirs*, 7:531, 542, 8:14–16, 21–22, 41.

4. Ibid., 7:443, 8:88, 95, 94.

5. John Quincy Adams, *Correspondence between John Quincy Adams . . . and Several Citizens of Massachusetts Concerning the Charge of a Design to Dissolve the Union Alleged to Have Existed in That State* (Boston: Boston Daily Advertiser, 1829), pp. [15], 17.

6. Adams, *Memoirs*, 8:88, 96–97; Samuel Flagg Bemis, *John Quincy Adams and the Union* (New York: Alfred A. Knopf, 1956), pp. 170n, 171, 174, 182, 194n. The second reply was ultimately published in *Documents Relating to New-England Federalism, 1800–1815*, ed. Henry Adams (Boston: Little, Brown, & Co., 1877), pp. 107–329 (quotation from p. 109).

7. Adams, *Memoirs*, 8:79, 88, 95.

8. For Adams's "Fourth Annual Message," see *A Compilation of the Messages and Papers of the Presidents, 1789–1897*, comp. James D. Richardson, 10 vols. (1896–99; reprint ed., New York: Bureau of National Literature and Art, 1901–6), 2:407–21.

9. Adams, *Memoirs*, 8:77; Richard Rush, "Report," 6 Dec. 1828, *House Docs.*, 20th Cong., 2d sess., no. 9, pp. 2–3, 5–6; Adams, "Fourth Annual Message," pp. 411–12.

10. Adams, "Fourth Annual Message," pp. 412–13; U.S. Bureau of the Census, *Historical Statistics of the United States, 1789–1945 . . .* (Washington, D.C.: Government Printing Office, 1949), Tabular Series M42-55, p. 245, P89–98, pp. 297–98. Rush calculated the increase in imports at more than 15 percent annually and that in exports at an average of 21 percent; see "Report," 6 Dec. 1828, p. 6.

11. *National Gazette* (Philadelphia), 6 Nov. 1822, quoted in Shaw Livermore, Jr., *The Twilight of Federalism: The Disintegration of the Federalist Party, 1815–1830* (Princeton, N.J.: Princeton University Press, 1962), p. 96; Daniel Webster to Henry Clay, 2 June 1827, Henry Clay, *The Papers of Henry Clay*, ed. James F. Hopkins, Mary W. M. Hargreaves, Robert Seager II, 8 vols. to date (Lexington: University Press of Kentucky, 1959–), 6:641.

12. Adams to Charles W. Upham, 2 Feb. 1837, in Edward H. Tatum, Jr., "Ten Unpublished Letters of John Quincy Adams, 1796–1837," *Huntington Library Quarterly* 4 (Apr. 1941): 383.

13. *United States Telegraph* (Washington), 3 May and 2 Oct. 1828.

14. Robert F. Martin, *National Income in the United States, 1799–1938* (New York: National Industrial Conference Board, 1939), pp. 60–61; William N. Parker and Franklee Whartenby, "The Growth of Output before 1840," *Trends in the American Economy in the Nineteenth Century*, National Bureau of Economic Research Studies in Income and Wealth vol. 24 (Princeton, N.J.: Princeton University Press, 1960), pp. 199, 210–11; Stanley Lebergott, *Manpower in Economic Growth: The American Record since 1800* (New York: McGraw-Hill Book Co., 1964), table A-1, p. 510; Eric E. Lampard, "The Evolving System of Cities in the United States: Urbanization and Economic Development," in *Issues in Urban*

Economics . . . , ed. Harvey S. Perloff and Lowdon Wingo, Jr. (Baltimore, Md.: Published for Resources for the Future, Inc., by Johns Hopkins Press, 1968), p. 117.

15. Martin, *National Income,* pp. 60–61; Lampard, "Evolving System of Cities," p. 117; U.S. Bureau of the Census, *Historical Statistics,* tab. ser. B13–23, p. 25; K124–26, p. 212.

16. Harry N. Scheiber, *Ohio Canal Era: A Case Study of Government and the Economy, 1820–1861* (Athens: Ohio University Press, 1969), pp. 187–206; Harold E. Davis, "Economic Basis of Ohio Politics, 1820–1840," *Ohio Archaeological and Historical Quarterly* 47 (1938): 296–97, 303, 306, 311; R. Carlyle Buley, *The Old Northwest: Pioneer Period, 1815–1840,* 2 vols. (Bloomington: Indiana University Press, 1951), 1:436, 533–64, 605–7; Victor S. Clark, *History of Manufactures in the United States,* 1929 ed., 3 vols. (1916; reprint ed., New York: Peter Smith, 1949), 1:348, 497, 500–501; *Niles' Weekly Register* 32 (17 Mar. 1827): 37.

17. David Trimble to Clay, 25 Apr. 1828, in Clay, *Papers,* 7:242.

18. Adams, *Memoirs,* 8:89, 86.

19. Ibid., 80–81, 101.

20. U.S. Congress, *House Reports,* 22d Cong., 2d sess., no. 122; John Quincy Adams to Charles Francis Adams, 26 Mar. 1833, in MHi-Adams Family Papers, Letters Recd. (MR497). On the caucus quarrel over tariff policy in 1832 see Adams, *Memoirs,* 8:444–45.

21. Clay to John Quincy Adams, 24 July 1842, in MHi-Adams Family Papers, Letters Recd. (MR523); Adams, *Memoirs,* 11:431; Bemis, *John Quincy Adams and the Union,* p. 520.

22. Russel Blaine Nye, *Society and Culture in America, 1830–1860* (New York: Harper & Row, Harper Torchbooks, 1974), pp. 241n, 248.

23. Paul Wallace Gates, *History of Public Land Law Development* (Washington, D.C.: Government Printing Office, 1968), pp. 352–61.

24. John Quincy Adams to Charles Francis Adams, 26 Mar. 1833, in MHi-Adams Family Papers, Letters Recd. (MR497).

25. Clay, "Toast and Response at Public Dinner," 19 May 1821, in Clay, *Papers,* 3:80, 81–82; Daniel Walker Howe, *The Political Culture of the American Whigs* (Chicago: University of Chicago Press, 1979), p. 124.

26. Rush, "Report," 8 Dec. 1827, *American State Papers, Finance,* 5:638.

BIBLIOGRAPHICAL ESSAY

Primary Materials

Manuscripts, Newspapers, and Government Documents

In the course of some thirty years of research relating to *The Papers of Henry Clay,* I have had access to several hundred private and institutional collections of manuscripts. To list them here would be impractical and in a sense misleading, for they were searched with specific reference to the Clay Papers Project and not for the broader coverage of the Adams administration. Where they are applicable to the present study, they are identified in the Notes. The only collections generally reviewed in connection with this work were the John Quincy Adams Papers—Letters Received and Private Letterbooks—in the microfilm series of the Massachusetts Historical Society; the Henry Clay Papers assembled in photographic reproduction for the Clay Papers Project at the University of Kentucky, including virtually complete files of records of the State Department and related files of the other governmental departments, from 1825 to 1829, from the National Archives; the Martin Van Buren Papers in the Presidential Papers Microfilm Series of holdings in the Library of Congress; and the William Wirt Papers in Microfilm Series 1011 of the Maryland Historical Society.

Similar qualifications apply to the research on newspapers. Extensive search has been conducted for specific references in relation to editing the Clay Papers, and citation has been given in the Notes to numerous organs consulted in this connection. The only journals that were systematically searched for the period 1825 to 1829 were the *Argus of Western America* (Frankfort, Ky.), the *Kentucky Reporter* (Lexington), *Niles' Weekly Register,* the *Enquirer* (Richmond, Va.; broken file), the *Daily National Intelligencer* (Washington, D.C.), the *Daily*

National Journal (Washington, D.C.), and the *Washington Gazette,* continued as the *United States Telegraph* (Washington, D.C.).

Congressional debates, journals, and documents for the Eighteenth through the Twentieth congresses have been consulted extensively, as well as the *Biennial Registers,* published by the State Department, and the *Statutes at Large.* Federal Supreme Court reports; state legislative journals, statutes, and governors' messages; and British statutes, parliamentary debates, and sessional papers have been cited as applicable. Compilations of important groups of such documents are available in *American State Papers: Documents, Legislative and Executive,* 38 vols. (Washington, D.C.: 1832–61); William R. Manning, comp., *Diplomatic Correspondence of the United States Concerning the Independence of the Latin-American Nations,* 3 vols. (New York: Oxford University Press, 1925); Clive Parry, ed., *The Consolidated Treaty Series,* 234 vols. to date (New York: Oceana Publications, 1969–); James D. Richardson, comp., *A Compilation of the Messages and Papers of the Presidents, 1789–1897,* 10 vols. (1896–99; reprint ed., New York: Bureau of National Literature and Art, 1901–6); and C. K. Webster, ed., *Britain and the Independence of Latin America, 1812–1830: Select Documents from the Foreign Office Archives,* 2 vols. (1938; reprint ed., New York: Octagon Books, 1970).

Published Correspondence, Papers, and Speeches

Published collections of personal papers have provided access to the views of many of the leading figures in this account. Most useful have been *The Papers of John C. Calhoun,* edited by Clyde N. Wilson and W. Edwin Hemphill, 15 vols. to date (Columbia: Published by the University of South Carolina Press for the South Caroliniana Society, 1959–); *The Papers of Henry Clay,* edited by James F. Hopkins, Mary W. M. Hargreaves, and Robert Seager II, 8 vols. to date (Lexington: University Press of Kentucky, 1959–); *Correspondence of Andrew Jackson,* edited by John Spencer Bassett and John Franklin Jameson, 7 vols. (Washington, D.C.: Carnegie Institution of Washington, 1926–35); *The Papers of Daniel Webster,* edited by Charles M. Wiltse and Harold D. Moser, 5 vols. of *Correspondence* to date (Hanover, N.H.: Published for Dartmouth College by the University Press of New England, 1974–); and Daniel Webster's *Writings and Speeches,* edited by J. W. McIntyre, 18 vols. (Boston: Little, Brown, & Co., 1903) Less extensive documentary publications have been cited, as relevant, in the notes.

Reporting of events by contemporary participants has also been helpful, particularly the *Memoirs of John Quincy Adams, Comprising Portions of His Diary from 1795 to 1848,* edited by Charles Francis Adams, 12 vols. (Philadelphia: J. B. Lippincott & Co., 1874–77); [Thomas Hart Benton], *Thirty Years View: or, A History of the Working of the American Government for Thirty Years, from 1820 to 1850* . . . , 2 vols. (New York: D. Appleton & Co., 1859–60); [Lucius Q. C. Elmer], ''Samuel L. Southard,'' *Collections of the New Jersey Historical Society* 7 (1872): [201]–34; Jabez Hammond, *The History of Political Parties in the State of New York, from the Ratification of the Federal Constitution to December, 1842,* 2 vols. (Albany, N.Y.: C. Van Benthuysen, 1842); John P. Kennedy's *Memoirs of the Life of William*

Wirt, 2 vols. (Philadelphia: Lea & Blanchard, 1850); Nathan Sargent, *Public Men and Events from the Commencement of Mr. Monroe's Administration, in 1817, to the Close of Mr. Fillmore's Administration in 1853*, 2 vols. (Philadelphia: J. B. Lippincott & Co., 1875); *The Autobiography of Martin Van Buren*, edited by John C. Fitzpatrick, *American Historical Association Annual Report for the Year 1918*, vol. 2 (Washington, D.C.: Government Printing Office, 1920); and the *Autobiography of Thurlow Weed*, edited by Harriet A. Weed (Boston: Houghton Mifflin & Co., 1883).

SECONDARY MATERIALS

Reference to the extensive literature about the period must be here limited to works of significant interpretive analysis or broad utilization in this study. Those of more limited application have been noted in connection with the relevant passages.

Background Accounts

For general history of the period, excellent surveys are provided by George Dangerfield, *The Awakening of American Nationalism, 1815–1828*, New American Nation Series (New York: Harper & Row, Harper Torchbooks, 1965); Russel Blaine Nye, *Society and Culture in America, 1830–1860*, New American Nation Series (New York: Harper & Row, Harper Torchbooks, 1974); and John Mayfield, *The New Nation, 1800–1845*, American Century Series, rev. ed. (New York: Hill & Wang, 1982). The last study stresses the disruptions of modernization, which are more fully discussed in Rowland Berthoff's *An Unsettled People: Social Order and Disorder in American History* (New York: Harper & Row, 1971), and Richard D. Brown's *Modernization: The Transformation of American Life, 1600–1865*, American Century Series (New York: Hill & Wang, 1976). Richard P. McCormick's *The Presidential Game: The Origins of American Presidential Politics* (New York: Oxford University Press, 1982) also focuses on the "instability, tension, and ambiguity" that characterized presidential elections throughout the half-century culminating in 1844, and most notably in the period from 1824 to 1836.

On political ideology Ralph Ketcham's *Presidents above Party: The First American Presidency, 1789–1829* (Chapel Hill: Published for the Institute of Early American History and Culture, Williamsburg, Va., by University of North Carolina Press, 1984), summarizes effectively the conceptual tradition underlying the views of Adams, and of his five presidential predecessors, on the responsibilities of that leadership role. While somewhat idealized, a portrait focused more upon aspirations than upon practice, the account delineates the difference from the partisan commitments of successors in the office and the dilemma that the New Englander confronted in applying perceptions of a moral order to a nation which, in part because of his efforts, was rapidly moving toward a "commercialization of values" and accompanying social alienation that he resisted.

Rush Welter's *The Mind of America, 1820–1860* (New York: Columbia University Press, 1975) analyzes broadly the resulting Democratic and Whig intellectual divergences. Major L. Wilson, in "The Concept of Time and the Political Dialogue in the United States, 1828–48," *American Quarterly* 19 (Winter 1967): 619–44, identifies the Whig position as one stressing national progress in qualitative development, in contrast to Jacksonian concern for spatial expansion of the entity in its existing character, "already fully realized." Daniel Walker Howe's *The Political Culture of the American Whigs* (Chicago: University of Chicago Press, 1979) surveys the ideas of the Whig leaders more comprehensively than any of the preceding works but by its chronological definition is of somewhat limited applicability to the present study. Adams's views, in particular, were matured and systematized considerably in the interval between 1828 and 1833.

George A. Lipsky's *John Quincy Adams: His Theory and Ideas . . .* (New York: Thomas Y. Crowell Co., 1950), reviews the spectrum of the New Englander's thought, but conveys little of its developmental patterns. Emphasizing his nationalism, Lipsky at the same time attributes Adams's aggressive anti-British diplomacy to his strong concern for American commercial development. Larry Dean Klein, in "Henry Clay, Nationalist" (Ph.D. diss., University of Kentucky, 1977), stresses the Kentuckian's ideological conceptualization in its application to both foreign and domestic concerns.

The debate centering on Thomas Jefferson's views concerning support of "domestic industry" is illustrated in the writing of William D. Grampp, "A Reexamination of Jeffersonian Economics," *Southern Economic Journal* 12 (Jan. 1946): 263–82; Richard E. Ellis, *The Jeffersonian Crisis: Courts and Politics in the Young Republic* (New York: Oxford University Press, 1971); Robert E. Shalhope, "Thomas Jefferson's Republicanism and Antebellum Southern Thought," *Journal of Southern History* 42 (Nov. 1976): 529–56; and Drew R. McCoy, *The Elusive Republic: Political Economy in Jeffersonian America* (Chapel Hill: Published for the Institute of Early American History and Culture, Williamsburg, Va., by University of North Carolina Press, 1980).

On the framework of regional attitudes and divisions within the Jeffersonian South see, for Virginia, Norman K. Risjord's *The Old Republicans: Southern Conservatism in the Age of Jefferson* (New York: Columbia University Press, 1965); Charles Henry Ambler, *Sectionalism in Virginia from 1776 to 1861* (1910; reprint ed., New York: Russell & Russell, 1964); Otis K. Rice, *The Allegheny Frontier: West Virginia Beginnings, 1730–1830* (Lexington: University Press of Kentucky, 1970); and, for South Carolina, William S. Schaper, *Sectionalism and Representation in South Carolina . . .* (1901; reprint ed., New York: Da Capo Press, 1968); Alfred Glaze Smith, Jr., *Economic Readjustment of an Old Cotton State: South Carolina, 1820–1860* (Columbia: University of South Carolina Press, 1958); William W. Freehling, *Prelude to Civil War: The Nullification Controversy in South Carolina, 1816–1836* (New York: Harper & Row, 1965).

State legislative reaction to the postwar depression is discussed in Murray N. Rothbard, *The Panic of 1819: Reactions and Policies* (New York: Columbia

University Press, 1962); Malcolm Rogers Eiselen, *The Rise of Pennsylvania Protectionism* . . . (Philadelphia: University of Pennsylvania, Ph.D. diss., 1932); and Arndt M. Stickles, *The Critical Court Struggle in Kentucky, 1819-29* (Bloomington: Indiana University Press, 1929). The political repercussions are elaborated in Dixon Ryan Fox, *The Decline of Aristocracy in the Politics of New York, 1801-1840* (1919; reprint, edited by Robert V. Remini; New York: Harper & Row, 1965); Alvin Kass, *Politics in New York State, 1800-1830* (Syracuse, N.Y.: Syracuse University Press, 1965); James A. Kehl, *Ill Feeling in the Era of Good Feeling: Western Pennsylvania Political Battles, 1815-1825* (Pittsburgh: University of Pittsburgh Press, 1956); Kim T. Phillips, "The Pennsylvania Origins of the Jackson Movement," *Political Science Quarterly* 91 (Fall 1976): 489-508; Donald J. Ratcliffe, "The Role of Voters and Issues in Party Formation: Ohio, 1824," *Journal of American History* 59 (Mar. 1973): 847-70; Harry R. Stevens, *The Early Jackson Party in Ohio* (Durham, N.C.: Duke University Press, 1957); Chilton Williamson, *American Suffrage from Property to Democracy, 1760-1860* (Princeton, N.J.: Princeton University Press, 1960); and the works by Klein, Davis, and Krueger, which are cited below, on the election of 1828. Ernest R. May, in *The Making of the Monroe Doctrine* (Cambridge: Belknap Press of Harvard University Press, 1975), affords an excellent general survey of state and regional voting preferences as of 1823.

Biographical Accounts

Most of the leading figures in the drama have received extended biographical treatment. Harry Ammon's *James Monroe: The Quest for National Identity* (New York: McGraw-Hill Book Co., 1971) set the stage with an interpretation which featured, and to some extent overdrew, that Virginian's commitment to the program of nationalism. Whatever the limitations of Monroe's conceptualization, his administration had fixed the course that Adams pledged to follow, and the Ammon biography effectively develops that groundwork.

Marie B. Hecht's *John Quincy Adams: A Personal History of an Independent Man* (New York: Macmillan Co., 1972) affords useful detail on Adams's early activities, encompassing third-party observation that supplements the strongly personal record of his diary. She gives limited attention to his presidency and finds that the basis of opposition to him rested primarily upon his identification as a nonslaveholder. Arguing that he had "a misplaced but stiff-necked ethical sense" (p. 488), she questions that he was a "naive" politician—a conclusion that is also argued in Daniel Walker Howe's *Political Culture of the American Whigs*. Paul C. Nagel's *Descent from Glory: Four Generations of the John Adams Family* (New York: Oxford University Press, 1983) draws superbly the picture of psychological and emotional pressures related to the family ties. But for narrative style and depth of policy analysis, Samuel Flagg Bemis's two volumes, *John Quincy Adams and the Foundations of American Foreign Policy* (New York: Alfred A. Knopf, 1949) and *John Quincy Adams and the Union* (New York: Alfred A. Knopf, 1956), notwithstanding strong bias and some inaccuracies, remain the basic biographical record. Bemis, however, provides a scant hundred pages on Adams's role as president.

The fullest biographical accounts of the other members of the administration are Glyndon G. Van Deusen's *The Life of Henry Clay* (Boston: Little, Brown, & Co., 1937); J[ohn] H[arvey] Powell's *Richard Rush: Republican Diplomat, 1780-1859* (Philadelphia: University of Pennsylvania Press, 1942); Charles Douglas Lowery's "James Barbour: A Politician and Planter of Ante-Bellum Virginia" (Ph.D. diss., University of Virginia, 1966); Michael Birkner's *Samuel L. Southard: Jeffersonian Whig* (Rutherford, N.J.: Fairleigh Dickinson University Press, 1984); and Francis P. Weisenburger's *The Life of John McLean: A Politician on the United States Supreme Court* (1937; reprint ed., New York: Da Capo Press, 1971). Only the last two give much analysis of the cabinet roles. There are now more than half a dozen biographies of Daniel Webster, three published in the past decade, but the one by Claude Moore Fuess, *Daniel Webster*, 2 vols. (Boston: Little, Brown, & Co., 1930), alone discusses at length the Federalist leader's legislative concerns during the Adams administration. While Fuess notes that Webster's stands on issues generally supported the administration, he, like the other biographers, ignores the former Federalist's role as political leader under the amalgamation effort.

For the opposition, the second volume of Robert V. Remini's extended biography *Andrew Jackson and the Course of American Freedom, 1822-1832* (New York: Harper & Row, 1981) presents an important interpretive contribution. Retreating from his own earlier focus upon Martin Van Buren's political role as the central figure in Jackson's rise to power, Remini now views the general himself, with his Nashville Committee, as the directing force of the new organization. In part, this is rationalized by shifting the date of Van Buren's meeting with Calhoun to some time after Jackson, in March 1826, had expressed opposition to the Panama Mission. Such chronological juggling is, however, less important than the revived identification of the political controversy as the old social struggle of aristocracy against democracy, a renewal of the conflict between the goals of Jefferson and of Hamilton—"It seemed perpetual: liberty versus power, virtue versus corruption; the people versus an elite" (p. 100). Eaton's "Wyoming Letters," brought to scholarly attention by Robert P. Hay in "The Case for Andrew Jackson in 1824 . . . ," *Tennessee Historical Quarterly* 29 (Summer 1970): 139-51, are central to this analysis. Remini has found in them a linkage of the Jacksonian movement to the revived Jeffersonian ideology of much contemporary historiography and poses a confrontation that minimizes both the sectional interpretation, which was emphasized prior to the work of Arthur Schlesinger, Jr., and the personality theme, which has been prominent since the 1950s. Jackson emerges as the leader of a class conflict that was more consolidated ideologically than I have identified so early as the Adams administration but one that presaged a fundamental response to the neo-Federalist challenge on the issue of the American System. On the significance of Eaton's "Wyoming Letters," attention should also be given to the interpretation of their political purpose and that of the Jacksonians' development of the corruption theme, generally, as presented in M. J. Heale's *The Presidential Quest: Candidates and Images in American Political Culture, 1787-1852* (London: Longman, 1982).

On the contributory figures in the Jackson movement, Charles M. Wiltse's *John C. Calhoun . . .* , 4 vols. (Indianapolis, Ind.: Bobbs-Merrill Co., 1944–51), provides excellent detail. Remini's *Martin Van Buren and the Making of the Democratic Party* (New York: Columbia University Press, 1959), remains outstanding, although augmented with more extensive use of personal correspondence by John Niven, in *Martin Van Buren: The Romantic Age of American Politics* (New York: Oxford University Press, 1983), who again emphasizes the New Yorker's role as political manipulator. Charles Henry Ambler's *Thomas Ritchie: A Study in Virginia Politics* (Richmond, Va.: Bell Book & Stationery Co., 1913) is old but still useful in describing the views of the Richmond Junto, and Norma Lois Peterson's *Littleton Waller Tazewell* (Charlottesville: University Press of Virginia, 1983) affords insight on the dilemma of these proponents of strict construction of the Constitution when they were confronted by Jackson's "imperial Presidency." Neither Philip Shriver Klein's *President James Buchanan: A Biography* (University Park: Pennsylvania State University Press, 1962) nor George Ticknor Curtis's *Life of James Buchanan, Fifteenth President of the United States . . .* , 2 vols. (New York: Harper & Bros., 1883), explains that leader's effectiveness in garnering the German vote. John A. Munroe's *Louis McLane: Federalist and Jacksonian* (New Brunswick, N.J.: Rutgers University Press, 1973) is helpful in accounting for the actions of this Delaware advocate of internal improvements, who, before the midterm election, had committed his support to Jackson.

Foreign Policy

Dexter Perkins's analysis "John Quincy Adams," in *The American Secretaries of State and Their Diplomacy,* edited by Samuel Flagg Bemis, 17 vols. (New York: Alfred A. Knopf, 1927–67), 4:3–111, affords an excellent general survey for that period of the statesman's activities. Theodore E. Burton's section on "Henry Clay, Secretary of State . . . ," in the same work, 4:113–58, is most useful for directing attention to the commercial achievements of the Adams administration. Vernon G. Setser's *The Commercial Reciprocity Policy of the United States, 1774–1829* (1937; reprinted, New York: Da Capo Press, 1969), develops the theme of that title as the key to the commercial policy, and Drew R. McCoy's *The Elusive Republic . . .* delineates the political conceptualization that identified it as Jeffersonian. F. Lee Benns's *The American Struggle for the British West India Carrying Trade, 1815–1830,* Indiana University Studies vol. 10 (1923; reprint ed., Clifton, N.J.: Augustus M. Kelley, 1972), stands as the classic account of this bitter conflict in United States commercial relations. Not much effort has been made by Benns's successors to reevaluate his interpretations; more attention should be given in the record of British-American trade relations to the goals of William Huskisson's policy revisions in 1825.

Old scholarship also still affords the basic studies of the administration's policies in relation to Latin America. Joseph Byrne Lockey's *Pan-Americanism: Its Beginnings* (New York: Macmillan Co., 1920) presents the factual record of the development and progress of the Panama Congress. J. Fred Rippy, in *Rivalry of the United States and Great Britain over Latin America (1808–1830),* Albert Shaw

Lectures on Diplomatic History (1928; Baltimore, Md.: Johns Hopkins Press, 1929), recounts the struggle between British and United States diplomats to win influence and favorable economic concessions throughout the region and, with Dorothy M. Parton, in *The Diplomatic Career of Joel Roberts Poinsett* (Washington, D.C.: Catholic University of America, 1934), considerably justifies the meddling in internal affairs that marked the Americans' activities. Arthur Preston Whitaker, in *The United States and the Independence of Latin America, 1800–1830* (1941; reprint ed., New York: Russell & Russell, 1962), noting the same difficulties for the United States diplomats, traces it also to the political dominance by Creole upper classes in the Latin American states, who found stronger affinity with the leaders of Britain and France than with "the increasingly democratic" northern neighbor.

Samuel Flagg Bemis, in *John Quincy Adams and the Foundations of American Foreign Policy*, discusses the permutations in Adams's conceptualization of the Monroe Doctrine, an interpretation which, however, should be qualified by that of Whitaker, adopted also in Harry Ammon's *James Monroe*. Whitaker, in the aforementioned work and in *The Western Hemisphere Idea: Its Rise and Decline* (Ithaca, N.Y.: Cornell University Press, 1954), finds that Adams was basically reluctant to espouse these ideas, emphasizes Clay's early role in formulating them, and, with Dexter Perkins, in *The Monroe Doctrine, 1823–1826* (Cambridge: Harvard University Press, 1932), attributes to the Kentuckian what development marked their assertion during the Adams administration.

More-recent writers have emphasized the domestic influences in the development and operation of the policy. Ernest R. May, in *The Making of the Monroe Doctrine*, interprets Adams's initial role as a political response to regional voting preferences on the presidential election of 1824. Philip S. Foner, in *A History of Cuba and Its Relations with the United States*, 2 vols. (New York: International Publishers, 1962), vol. 1: *1492–1845, From the Conquest of Cuba to La Escalera*, denotes the basic difficulty of the United States in inter-American relations, generally, as racial concern and fear of stimulating slave revolt. He finds that neither Adams nor Clay was prepared to counter such reactions for the cause of New World freedom.

Domestic Program

Marie-Luise Frings, in *Henry Clays American System und die Sektionale Kontroverse in den Vereinigten Staaten von Amerika, 1815–1829*, Europäische Hochschulschriften, 3d ser., Geschichte und ihre Hilfswissenschaften, vol. 117 (Frankfurt am Main: Peter Lang, 1979), provides a well-researched survey, covering much of the material here utilized, on the rationale and legislation that were urged as the administration's domestic program. However, she sees the essence of Clay's conception as a tariff policy to which, she believes, Adams was basically opposed. She regards Clay's advocacy of the American System as primarily a political move to serve Kentucky interests and argues that, through it, he precipitated sectional tensions at a time when the nation was not politically divided. Sectional cleavage, not politics, under her interpretation, produced the conflict over the administration's domestic program. In an appendix she provides useful tabulations indicating the sectional response to the major legislation on banking, internal improvements, and the tariff during the period from 1816 to 1828.

On the internal-improvements effort, Carter Goodrich, in *Government Promotion of American Canals and Railroads, 1800–1890* (New York: Columbia University Press, 1960), presents a basic summary. The importance of that effort in the Northwest is particularly evidenced in Harry N. Scheiber's *Ohio Canal Era: A Case Study of Government and the Economy, 1820–1861* (Athens: Ohio University Press, 1969), and in R. Carlyle Buley's *The Old Northwest: Pioneer Period, 1815–1840*, 2 vols. (Bloomington: Indiana University Press, 1951). E. C. Nelson, in "Presidential Influence on the Policy of Internal Improvements," *Iowa Journal of History and Politics* 4 (1906): 3–69, citing increased expenditures over the extended period of Jacksonian political power, minimized the effect of Jackson's personal opposition to such projects; but Paul Wallace Gates, in *History of Public Land Law Development* (Washington, D.C.: Government Printing Office, 1968), lauds Adams's "forward-looking" thrust in the development and notes Jackson's curtailment of the program until the mounting western political pressure of the mid thirties. William Stanton's *The Great United States Exploring Expedition of 1828–1842* (Berkeley: University of California Press, 1975), is the basic monograph on that scientific effort.

The role of the second Bank of the United States in developing a central banking function has been emphasized by Fritz Redlich, in *The Molding of American Banking, Men and Ideas* (New York: Hafner Publishing Co., 1947; also published as vol. 2, pt. 1, of the *History of American Business Leaders* [Ann Arbor, Mich.: Edwards Bros., 1940–51]); by Bray Hammond, in *Banks and Politics in America, from the Revolution to the Civil War* (Princeton, N.J.: Princeton University Press, 1957); and by Thomas Payne Govan, in *Nicholas Biddle: Nationalist and Public Banker, 1786–1844* (Chicago: University of Chicago Press, 1959); but it is questioned by Walter Buckingham Smith, in *Economic Aspects of the Second Bank of the United States* (Cambridge: Harvard University Press, 1953), and by Peter Temin, in *The Jacksonian Economy* (New York: W. W. Norton & Co., 1969), who argue that the Bank's policy of credit constriction during financial crises failed to reflect the elasticity requisite to central banking operations. Charles G. Sellers, Jr., in "Banking and Politics in Jackson's Tennessee, 1817–1827," *Mississippi Valley Historical Review* 41 (June 1954): 61–84, contends that Jackson's opposition to the Bank of the United States was locally known prior to the election of 1824; but Sellers also notes that several of the general's closest political associates were pressing for a Nashville branch of the bank, which they subsequently attained. Jean Alexander Wilburn, in *Biddle's Bank: The Crucial Years* (New York: Columbia University Press, 1967), argues that the bank issue was essentially a partisan one, shaped by the campaign of 1832, and that support for the bank was, in fact, strong in much of the South and the West.

F. W. Taussig's *The Tariff History of the United States*, 8th ed., rev. (1892; reprint ed., New York: Capricorn Books, 1964), provides basic detail on the legislation for protection of United States industry. Strongly committed to a free-trade philosophy, Taussig's observations on the impact of the movement are somewhat counterbalanced by the record of factory openings and closings as reported in Victor S. Clark, *History of Manufactures in the United States,* 1929 ed., 3 vols. (1916; reprint, New York: Peter Smith, 1949). Stanley Lebergott, in *The Americans: An Economic Record* (New York: W. W. Norton & Co., 1984), notes the effect of the legislation, both geographically and industrially, and finds that it was beneficial to southern planters, as well as to Middle State farmers and New England industrialists; but he questions its importance to national economic growth.

No adequate study has been found on the general problem of Indian-removal policy during this period. Arthur H. DeRosier, Jr., in *The Removal of the Choctaw Indians* (1970; reprint ed., New York: Harper & Row, Harper Torchbooks, 1972), affords the most useful background statement.

Administrative Studies

The standard general work is Leonard D. White's *The Jeffersonians: A Study in Administrative History, 1801-1829* (1951; reprint ed., New York: Free Press, 1965). Matthew A. Crenson's *The Federal Machine: Beginnings of Bureaucracy in Jacksonian America* (Baltimore, Md.: Johns Hopkins University Press, 1975) provides useful comparison, countering the theme of administrative continuity stressed by White. Michael Birkner's *Samuel L. Southard* and Weisenburger's *Life of John McLean* include extended discussion on the administrative efforts of those cabinet members. Birkner emphasizes Southard's concern for the role of civil authority in pressing inquiry proceedings against Commodore David Porter, in contradistinction to the interpretation of David F. Long, in *Nothing Too Daring: A Biography of Commodore David Porter, 1780-1843* (Annapolis, Md.: United States Naval Institute, 1970). Homer Cummings and Carl McFarland, in *Federal Justice: Chapters in the History of Justice and the Federal Executive* (New York: Macmillan Co., 1937), discuss the policy and accomplishments of William Wirt. More study is needed on the operations of the Treasury and War departments, but Malcolm J. Rohrbough's *The Land Office Business: The Settlement and Administration of American Public Lands, 1789-1837* (New York: Oxford University Press, 1968), is helpful on a segment of that activity.

Political Developments: The Election of 1828 and Its Aftermath

Ronald P. Formisano's interpretive essay "Toward a Reorientation of Jacksonian Politics: A Review of the Literature, 1959-1975," *Journal of American History* 63 (June 1976): 42-65, discounts many of the generalizations of past analysis and emphasizes the fragmentation that has evolved from recent attention to social forces. Two more recent studies, however, Remini's *Andrew Jackson* and M. J. Heale's *Presidential Quest*, have returned to the old issues of corruption and competence as central concerns in 1828. Florence Weston's *The Presidential Election of 1828* (1938; reprint ed., Philadelphia: Porcupine Press,

1974) and Robert V. Remini's *The Election of Andrew Jackson*, Critical Periods of History (Philadelphia: J. B. Lippincott Co., 1963), still serve as excellent general accounts. Shaw Livermore, Jr., in *The Twilight of Federalism: The Disintegration of the Federalist Party, 1815-1830* (Princeton, N.J.: Princeton University Press, 1962), and Richard P. McCormick, in *The Second American Party System: Party Formation in the Jacksonian Era* (Chapel Hill: University of North Carolina Press, 1966), describe the shifts in basic party structure that operated throughout this period.

Studies of such developments more specifically focused upon individual states are becoming increasingly numerous and are particularly helpful. Only those most useful for this work can be here cited: Donald B. Cole's *Jacksonian Democracy in New Hampshire, 1800-1851* (Cambridge: Harvard University Press, 1970); Jerome Mushkat's *Tammany: The Evolution of a Political Machine, 1789-1865* (Syracuse, N.Y.: Syracuse University Press, 1971); Charles McCarthy's *The Antimasonic Party: A Study of Political Antimasonry in the United States, 1827-1840*, Annual Report of the American Historical Association for the Year 1902, vol. 1 (Washington, D.C.: Government Printing Office, 1903); William Preston Vaughn's *The Antimasonic Party in the United States, 1826-1843* (Lexington: University Press of Kentucky, 1983); Kathleen Smith Kutolowski's "Antimasonry Reexamined: Social Bases of the Grass-Roots Party," *Journal of American History* 71 (Sept. 1984): 269-93; Philip S. Klein's *Pennsylvania Politics, 1817-1832: A Game without Rules* (Philadelphia: Historical Society of Pennsylvania, 1940); Herbert Ershkowitz's *The Origin of the Whig and Democratic Parties: New Jersey Politics, 1820-1837* (Washington, D.C.: University Press of America, 1982); Mark H. Haller's "The Rise of the Jackson Party in Maryland, 1820-1829," *Journal of Southern History* 28 (Aug. 1962): 307-26; Harold E. Davis's "Economic Basis of Ohio Politics, 1820-1840," *Ohio State Archaeological and Historical Quarterly* 47 (1938): 288-318; David Walter Krueger's "Party Development in Indiana, 1800-1832" (Ph.D. diss., University of Kentucky, 1974); Theodore Calvin Pease's *The Frontier State, 1818-1848*, vol. 2 of *The Centennial History of Illinois* (Springfield: Illinois Centennial Comn., 1918); and John Vollmer Mering's *The Whig Party in Missouri*, University of Missouri Studies no. 41 (Columbia: University of Missouri Press, 1967).

The political roles of Adams and Clay in the postadministration years are discussed at length in the Bemis and Van Deusen biographies. Raynor G. Wellington's *The Political and Sectional Influence of the Public Lands, 1828-1842* (Cambridge, Mass.: Riverside Press, 1914), although old and strongly slanted in support of the effort for liberalization of the public-land laws, provides excellent summary of the congressional controversy over graduation and preemption in land sales and over distribution of the land revenues. William J. Cooper, Jr., in *The South and the Politics of Slavery, 1828-1856* (Baton Rouge: Louisiana State University Press, 1978), develops the record of Clay's concessions for southern support during the late 1830s and his strong influence during the "Great Aberration" of 1842-44, when southern Whigs briefly substituted the "politics of economics" for the "politics of slavery." On the other hand, George Rawlings Poage, in *Henry Clay and the Whig Party* (1936; reprint ed., Gloucester,

Mass.: Peter Smith, 1965), which is limited to the period after 1840, finds little disposition to compromise in Clay's effort to reestablish a national bank during the presidency of the States' rights Whig John Tyler. Both Cooper and Poage agree, however, that Tyler's raising of the issue of Texas annexation initiated the formation of a southern sectional party that marked "the failure of the nationalism which was the basis of . . . [Clay's] leadership and the ruin of the Union, love of which, he truly said, was the key to his whole political career" (Poage, p. 146).

INDEX

Green, Duff, 44, 211, 241, 248, 264, 269, 270, 280, 287, 295, 299, 314, 333 n. 32
Gual, Pedro, 147, 149
Guatemala. *See* Central America, Federation of
Gutiérrez-Magee expedition, 141

Habersham, Richard W., 204
Hagner, Peter, 56
Haiti: compensation to refugees from, 144, 244; U.S. diplomatic relations with, 77, 149, 150, 152, 156–57; slave revolt in, 136, 144, 156; trade policy of, 77, 159; trade with, 112; mentioned, 130
Hall, Thomas H., 179, 185
Hamilton, Alexander, 3, 67, 112, 264
Hamilton, James, 294
Hamilton, James, Jr., 152, 242, 266
Hammond, Charles, 51, 60, 194, 233–34, 267, 271
Hammond, Jabez, 196
Hammond, James, 5
Hanover, trade with, 84, 112
Hanseatic League, trade with, 84, 112
Hanson, John M., 58
Harbor improvements, 172, 175, 229, 309, 315, 316
Harrisburg conventions, 194, 263, 274–76, 362–63 n. 59
Harrison, William Henry: as minister to Colombia, 60, 356 n. 38; as Ohio political leader, 271; as president, 319; proposed as chief of staff, 226; proposed as minister to Mexico, 64; his role on Kremer charges, 45
Hartford Convention, 13, 307
Hassler, Ferdinand Rudolph, 172
Hawaii, trade agreement with, 85
Hayne, Robert Y.: on bankruptcy legislation, 181; supports Calhoun, 151; on executive power, 171; on French West India trade, 109; on Panama Mission, 151; on South Seas exploration, 171; on tariff legislation, 5; mentioned, 265
Hemp, tariff on, 189, 192, 194
Hendricks, William, 171
Henry, John F., 282
Herkimer Convention, 271
"High Minders," 294. *See also* King, Charles
Hill, Isaac, 265, 268, 284–85, 333 n. 32
Hill, Mark L., 59
Hoffman, Josiah, 294
Holmes, John: supports Crawford, 59, 151; on Panama Mission, 151; on South Seas

exploration, 171; on West India trade, 96, 97; his vote on bankruptcy legislation, 350 n. 35
Holy Alliance, 31, 32, 35, 79, 128, 130–31, 135, 137, 139, 146, 147, 149, 154, 156, 232, 312, 346 n. 24
Home Department, proposed, 215–16, 217
Home-market argument: linkages of, 5–6, 12, 27, 33–34, 38, 187, 190–97 passim, 208, 288, 303, 309, 311, 312, 321, 322, 323. *See also* Agricultural interests; American System, as concept of administration's domestic policy; Nationalism
Honduras, 122, 123, 125
Hopkinson, Joseph, 256–57, 274, 298
Houston, Sam, 52
Howland, G. G. and S., shipping firm, 121
Hughes, Christopher, Jr., 54–55, 69, 88
Huskisson, William, 97–98, 101–3, 105, 163

Illinois: in election of 1824/25, 39; Indian lands in, 201; politics in, 271, 295; public land grants to, 175, 309. *See also* West, the
Indemnity claims, 69–72, 162–63
Indiana: politics in, 16, 296, 298; public land grants to, 175, 309. *See also* West, the
Indiana Canal, 177, 309, 316
Indian Affairs, Office of, 201, 205, 220, 244, 245
Indians: education of, 199, 200, 207; nationalism of, 202, 207; policy on, 41, 166, 187, 199–207, 208; removal of, 13, 200–207
Indian Springs, treaty of, 202–3, 225
Industrialization. *see* Manufacturing, development of
Infantado, Pedro Alcantara de Toledo, duke del, 139, 146, 160
Ingersoll, Charles J., 237, 275
Ingersoll, Edward, 268
Ingham, Samuel: supports Calhoun, 44, 152, 248, 276; supports Jackson, 44, 242, 248; opposes Panama Mission, 148–49, 152; on tariff legislation, 193, 194, 274; mentioned, 265
Internal improvements: Adams on, 29, 41–42, 165, 166, 173–79 passim, 187, 197, 208, 250, 289, 309, 311, 313, 318–22 passim, 323; as administration program, 173–80, 182, 186, 229, 246, 250, 287, 305, 309–16 passim, 323; in auction protest, 291; Clay on, 34, 165, 177, 311, 318, 320; Crawford on, 25–26; Jackson on, 27, 289, 296, 313, 315, 321; Jefferson on, 3; Madison on, 3; in Middle States, 6, 177–78, 179, 247, 300, 312; New England views on, 2, 180, 208,

312; southern views on, 3, 4, 5, 179–80, 191–92, 312, 323; in Tyler's presidency, 320; western views on, 6, 166, 172–73, 177, 180, 247, 300, 312, 313, 321
Internal Improvements, Board of, 6, 173, 177, 178
Irish, 301
Iron, tariff on, 3, 189, 194
Ironside, George E., 214
Irvine, Baptis, 141, 231
Isacks, Jacob C., 44, 248
Itúrbide, Augustín de, 123

Jackson, Andrew: Adams administration's criticism of, 285–88 passim, 301; administrative reforms under, 209; in Battle of New Orleans, 12, 21, 251, 283, 286; on federal-state relations, 26–29 passim, 300; as governor of Florida, 20, 21, 286; Indian policy of, 207; on internal improvements, 27, 289, 296, 313, 315, 321; as a Mason, 292; on militia, 223; on national banking, 27, 315, 321; popularity of, 20, 29, 300, 301; as presidential candidate—in 1824/ 25, 16, 19, 20–21, 26–27, 28–29, 36–37, 39, 44–45, 270,—in 1828, 43, 47, 248–49, 251, 252; is proposed as cabinet member, 48, 255; on retrenchment, 289; in Seminole campaign, 21, 30, 232, 234, 286; supporters of, 42–44, 50, 52, 151, 152, 167, 168, 170, 181–87 passim, 192–96 passim, 199, 204, 224, 225, 240, 241, 242, 249, 252, 261, 263, 270–82 passim, 285, 291–302 passim, 305 (see also Jacksonian press); on tariff legislation, 26–27, 288–89, 294, 296–97, 315, 321
Jacksonians' criticism of Adams's administration: Adams's bellicosity, 107, 110, 162, 163; his Federalist ties, 112, 287, 294, 295; his life style, 210, 247, 287; his personal relations, 211, 234, 285, 301; his religious views, 287, 301; his sectional identity, 107, 300, 302, 311; his administration's nationalism, 112, 199, 247; its stand on tariff, 194–95, 196, 289, 294, 300; its entangling alliances, 151, 152, 162; its executive usurpation, 150–51, 152, 205, 214, 234, 247, 287, 300; its indifference on neutral rights, 74, 110, 163; its ineffective government, 59, 163, 214, 244, 248, 265; its patronage, 52, 58, 59, 143–44, 167, 241–48 passim, 265, 266–67; its threat to slavery, 151–52; its loss of West Indies trade, 107, 110, 294. See also Anti-intellectualism, "Bargain-and-corruption" charge; Disestablishmentarianism;

Egalitarianism; Retrenchment, agitation for; States' rights
Jarvis, Russell, 210–11
Jefferson, Thomas: on bankruptcy legislation, 180; on coastal survey, 172; on Cuba, 137, 144–45; death of, 115; on foreign alliances, 151; on internal improvements, 3; on manufacturing, 3, 7; on Monroe Doctrine, 35; patronage policy of, 51, 259; on world trade, 67, 76, 89, 112; mentioned, 212, 287, 312
Jeffersonian party. See Republican party
John VI, of Portugal, 78
Johns, Kensey, Jr., 279
Johnson, Francis, 46
Johnson, Jeromus, 291
Johnson, Richard M., 43, 181, 248
Johnson family, 28
Johnston, Josiah Stoddard, 109, 181, 186, 187
Jones, Roger, 223
Jones, Thomas ap Catesby, 85, 170
Jones, William, 60–61
Jubliee. See Declaration of Independence
Junta Promotora de le Libertad de Cuba, 145

Kane, Elias Kent, 257
Kempt, Sir James, 101
Kendall, Amos, 252, 257, 266, 299
Kent, James, 256
Kent, Joseph, 259, 267, 279
Kentucky: in election of 1824/25, 39, 46–47, 332 n. 15; politics in, 14, 15–16, 251–52, 254, 271, 296–301 passim; views on Jackson in, 20, 251, 298. See also Relief movement; West, the
Kentucky Senate's investigation of bribery charge, 286
Khosref Mehemet, Pasha, 86, 121–22
King, Charles, 256, 272, 294, 295
King, John A., 56, 242, 243–44
King, Rufus: is defeated for presidency in 1816, 15; on discriminating duties, 93; as minister to Great Britain, 55, 56, 68, 95, 100, 132, 136, 144, 242, 243, 244, 255
King, William Rufus de Vane, 181
King family, 268
Knapp, Samuel Lorenzo, 269–70
Kremer, George, 45, 296

Labor: organization of, 291–92, 313; supply of, 2, 10, 198, 314–15, 316
Laborde, Angel, 234
Lacock, Abner, 7
Ladd, William, 158